Elasticsearch 7.0 Cookbook
Fourth Edition

Over 100 recipes for fast, scalable, and reliable search
for your enterprise

Alberto Paro

BIRMINGHAM - MUMBAI

Elasticsearch 7.0 Cookbook
Fourth Edition

Commissioning Editor: Pravin Dhandre
Acquisition Editor: Devika Battike
Content Development Editor: Athikho Sapuni Rishana
Technical Editor: Utkarsha S. Kadam
Copy Editor: Safis Editing
Language Support Editor: Storm Mann
Project Coordinator: Kirti Pisat
Proofreader: Safis Editing
Indexer: Rekha Nair
Graphics: Jisha Chirayil
Production Coordinator: Jyoti Chauhan

First published: December 2013
Second edition: January 2015
Third edition: February 2017
Fourth edition: April 2019

Production reference: 2170919

Published by Packt Publishing Ltd.
Livery Place
35 Livery Street
Birmingham
B3 2PB, UK.

ISBN 978-1-78995-650-4

www.packtpub.com

mapt.io

Mapt is an online digital library that gives you full access to over 5,000 books and videos, as well as industry leading tools to help you plan your personal development and advance your career. For more information, please visit our website.

Why subscribe?

- Spend less time learning and more time coding with practical eBooks and Videos from over 4,000 industry professionals

- Improve your learning with Skill Plans built especially for you

- Get a free eBook or video every month

- Mapt is fully searchable

- Copy and paste, print, and bookmark content

Packt.com

Did you know that Packt offers eBook versions of every book published, with PDF and ePub files available? You can upgrade to the eBook version at www.packt.com and as a print book customer, you are entitled to a discount on the eBook copy. Get in touch with us at customercare@packtpub.com for more details.

At www.packt.com, you can also read a collection of free technical articles, sign up for a range of free newsletters, and receive exclusive discounts and offers on Packt books and eBooks.

Contributors

About the author

Alberto Paro is an engineer, project manager, and software developer. He currently works as Big Data Practice Leader in NTTDATA in Italy on big data technologies, native cloud, and NoSQL solutions. He loves to study emerging solutions and applications mainly related to cloud and big data processing, NoSQL, NLP, and neural networks. In 2000, he graduated in computer science engineering from Politecnico di Milano. Then, he worked with many companies mainly using Scala/Java and Python on knowledge management solutions and advanced data mining products using the state-of-the-art big data software. A lot of his time is spent teaching how to effectively use big data solutions, NoSQL datastores, and related technologies.

It would have been difficult for me to complete this book without the support of a large number of people. First, I would like to thank my wife, my children (Andrea and Giulia) and the rest of my family for their support. A personal thanks to my best friends, Mauro and Michele, colleagues and to all the people that helped me and my family. I'd like to express my gratitude to everyone at Packt Publishing who are involved in the development and production of this book. I'd like to thank Athikho Sapuni Rishana for guiding this book to completion and the reviewers for patiently going through the first draft and providing their valuable feedback. Their professionalism, courtesy, good judgment, and passion for books are much appreciated.

About the reviewer

Craig Brown is an independent consultant, offering services for Elasticsearch, and other big data software. He is a core Java developer of over 25 years' experience, and more than 10 years of Elasticsearch experience. He is also well practiced with machine learning, Hadoop, and Apache Spark, and is a co-founder of Big Mountain Data user group in Utah and a speaker on Elasticsearch and other big data topics. Craig has founded NosqlRevolution LLC, focused on Elasticsearch and big data services; and PicoCluster LLC, a desktop data center designed for learning and prototyping cluster computing and big data frameworks.

Packt is searching for authors like you

If you're interested in becoming an author for Packt, please visit `authors.packtpub.com` and apply today. We have worked with thousands of developers and tech professionals, just like you, to help them share their insight with the global tech community. You can make a general application, apply for a specific hot topic that we are recruiting an author for, or submit your own idea.

Table of Contents

Preface   1

Chapter 1: Getting Started   7
Technical requirements   7
Downloading and installing Elasticsearch   8
  Getting ready   8
  How to do it…   8
  How it works…   10
  There's more…   12
  See also   13
Setting up networking   13
  Getting ready   13
  How to do it…   13
  How it works…   15
  See also   16
Setting up a node   16
  Getting ready   16
  How to do it…   16
  How it works…   17
  See also   18
Setting up Linux systems   18
  Getting ready   18
  How to do it…   19
  How it works…   19
Setting up different node types   20
  Getting ready   20
  How to do it…   20
  How it works…   21
  There's more…   22
Setting up a coordinator node   22
  Getting ready   22
  How to do it…   23
  How it works…   23
Setting up an ingestion node   24
  Getting ready   24
  How to do it…   24
  How it works…   25
  There's more…   26
Installing plugins in Elasticsearch   26
  Getting ready   27

How to do it… 27
How it works… 28
There's more… 29
See also 30
Removing a plugin 30
Getting ready 31
How to do it… 31
How it works… 31
Changing logging settings 32
Getting ready 32
How to do it… 32
How it works… 33
Setting up a node via Docker 33
Getting ready 34
How to do it… 34
How it works… 35
There's more… 36
See also 36
Deploying on Elasticsearch Cloud Enterprise 36
Getting ready 37
How to do it… 37
How it works… 43
See also 44
Chapter 2: Managing Mapping 45
Using explicit mapping creation 46
Getting ready 46
How to do it... 47
How it works... 48
There's more... 49
See also 50
Mapping base types 50
Getting ready 50
How to do it... 51
How it works... 51
There's more... 53
See also 54
Mapping arrays 54
Getting ready 55
How to do it... 55
How it works... 55
Mapping an object 56
Getting ready 56
How to do it... 56
How it works... 57

See also 58
Mapping a document 58
Getting ready 58
How to do it... 58
How it works... 59
See also 59
Using dynamic templates in document mapping 60
Getting ready 60
How to do it... 60
How it works... 61
There's more... 62
See also 62
Managing nested objects 63
Getting ready 63
How to do it... 63
How it works... 64
There's more... 65
See also 65
Managing a child document with a join field 65
Getting ready 66
How to do it... 66
How it works... 68
There's more... 68
See also 69
Adding a field with multiple mappings 69
Getting ready 69
How to do it... 70
How it works... 70
There's more... 71
See also 72
Mapping a GeoPoint field 72
Getting ready 72
How to do it... 72
How it works... 73
There's more... 74
Mapping a GeoShape field 74
Getting ready 74
How to do it... 75
How it works... 75
See also 75
Mapping an IP field 76
Getting ready 76
How to do it... 76
How it works... 76
Mapping an alias field 77

Getting ready | 77
How to do it... | 77
How it works... | 79
Mapping a Percolator field | 79
Getting ready | 80
How to do it... | 80
How it works... | 81
Mapping feature and feature vector fields | 82
Getting ready | 82
How to do it... | 82
How it works... | 84
Adding metadata to a mapping | 85
Getting ready | 85
How to do it... | 85
How it works... | 85
Specifying different analyzers | 86
Getting ready | 86
How to do it... | 86
How it works... | 87
See also | 88
Mapping a completion field | 88
Getting ready | 88
How to do it... | 88
How it works... | 89
See also | 90
Chapter 3: Basic Operations | 91
Creating an index | 92
Getting ready | 92
How to do it... | 93
How it works... | 94
There's more... | 94
See also | 96
Deleting an index | 96
Getting ready | 96
How to do it... | 97
How it works... | 98
See also | 98
Opening or closing an index | 98
Getting ready | 98
How to do it... | 99
How it works... | 99
See also | 100
Putting a mapping in an index | 100
Getting ready | 100

How to do it...   101
How it works...   102
There's more...   102
See also   103
Getting a mapping   103
Getting ready   103
How to do it...   103
How it works...   104
See also   105
Reindexing an index   105
Getting ready   105
How to do it...   106
How it works...   107
See also   108
Refreshing an index   109
Getting ready   109
How to do it...   109
How it works...   110
See also   111
Flushing an index   111
Getting ready   111
How to do it...   111
How it works...   112
See also   113
ForceMerge an index   113
Getting ready   113
How to do it...   113
How it works...   114
There's more...   115
See also   115
Shrinking an index   115
Getting ready   116
How to do it...   116
How it works...   118
There's more...   119
See also   119
Checking if an index exists   119
Getting ready   120
How to do it...   120
How it works...   120
Managing index settings   121
Getting ready   121
How to do it...   122
How it works...   123
There's more...   124

See also   124
Using index aliases   124
Getting ready   125
How to do it...   125
How it works...   126
There's more...   127
Rolling over an index   128
Getting ready   128
How to do it…   128
How it works...   130
See also   130
Indexing a document   130
Getting ready   130
How to do it...   131
How it works...   132
There's more...   133
See also   134
Getting a document   135
Getting ready   135
How to do it...   135
How it works...   136
There's more...   138
See also   138
Deleting a document   138
Getting ready   138
How to do it...   139
How it works...   140
See also   140
Updating a document   141
Getting ready   141
How to do it...   141
How it works...   143
See also   145
Speeding up atomic operations (bulk operations)   145
Getting ready   145
How to do it...   145
How it works...   146
Speeding up GET operations (multi GET)   148
Getting ready   148
How to do it...   149
How it works...   150
See also...   150

Chapter 4: Exploring Search Capabilities   151
Technical requirements   152

Executing a search 152
Getting ready 152
How to do it... 153
How it works... 155
There's more... 160
See also 161
Sorting results 162
Getting ready 162
How to do it... 162
How it works... 163
There's more... 165
See also 167
Highlighting results 168
Getting ready 168
How to do it... 168
How it works... 169
See also 172
Executing a scrolling query 172
Getting ready 173
How to do it... 173
How it works... 175
There's more... 176
See also 177
Using the search_after functionality 177
Getting ready 177
How to do it... 178
How it works... 179
See also 180
Returning inner hits in results 180
Getting ready 180
How to do it... 181
How it works... 182
See also 183
Suggesting a correct query 183
Getting ready 183
How to do it... 183
How it works... 184
See also 185
Counting matched results 185
Getting ready 186
How to do it... 186
How it works... 187
There's more... 187
See also 188
Explaining a query 188

Getting ready   188
How to do it...   189
How it works...   190
Query profiling   190
Getting ready   190
How to do it...   191
How it works...   192
Deleting by query   192
Getting ready   193
How to do it...   193
How it works...   194
There's more...   195
See also   195
Updating by query   196
Getting ready   196
How to do it...   196
How it works...   198
There's more...   199
See also   199
Matching all the documents   199
Getting ready   200
How to do it...   200
How it works...   201
See also   201
Using a Boolean query   201
Getting ready   202
How to do it...   202
How it works...   203
There's more...   203
Using the search template   205
Getting ready   205
How to do it...   205
How it works...   208
See also   209

Chapter 5: Text and Numeric Queries   211
Using a term query   212
Getting ready   212
How to do it...   212
How it works...   215
There's more...   216
Using a terms query   217
Getting ready   217
How to do it...   217
How it works...   218

There's more... 219
See also 220
Using a prefix query 221
Getting ready 221
How to do it... 221
How it works... 222
There's more... 224
See also 225
Using a wildcard query 225
Getting ready 225
How to do it... 226
How it works... 227
See also 227
Using a regexp query 228
Getting ready 228
How to do it... 228
How it works... 229
See also 230
Using span queries 230
Getting ready 231
How to do it... 231
How it works... 236
See also 238
Using a match query 238
Getting ready 238
How to do it... 238
How it works... 240
See also 242
Using a query string query 242
Getting ready 242
How to do it... 242
How it works... 244
There's more... 245
See also 246
Using a simple query string query 246
Getting ready 246
How to do it... 247
How it works... 248
See also 249
Using the range query 249
Getting ready 249
How to do it... 250
How it works... 251
There's more... 252
The common terms query 252

Getting ready 253
How to do it... 253
How it works... 254
See also 255
Using an IDs query 256
Getting ready 256
How to do it... 256
How it works... 257
See also 258
Using the function score query 258
Getting ready 259
How to do it... 259
How it works... 261
See also 263
Using the exists query 264
Getting ready 264
How to do it... 264
How it works... 265
Chapter 6: Relationship and Geo Queries 267
Using the has_child query 268
Getting ready 268
How to do it... 269
How it works... 270
There's more... 271
See also 272
Using the has_parent query 272
Getting ready 272
How to do it... 273
How it works... 274
See also 275
Using nested queries 275
Getting ready 275
How to do it... 275
How it works... 277
See also 277
Using the geo_bounding_box query 278
Getting ready 278
How to do it... 278
How it works... 279
See also 280
Using the geo_polygon query 280
Getting ready 280
How to do it... 281
How it works... 282

See also   282
Using the geo_distance query   283
　Getting ready   283
　How to do it...   283
　How it works...   284
　See also   285
Chapter 7: Aggregations   287
　Executing an aggregation   288
　　Getting ready   288
　　How to do it...   289
　　How it works...   290
　　See also   293
　Executing stats aggregations   294
　　Getting ready   294
　　How to do it...   294
　　How it works...   295
　　See also   297
　Executing terms aggregation   297
　　Getting ready   297
　　How to do it...   297
　　How it works...   299
　　There's more...   300
　　See also   301
　Executing significant terms aggregation   301
　　Getting ready   302
　　How to do it...   302
　　How it works...   304
　Executing range aggregations   305
　　Getting ready   305
　　How to do it...   305
　　How it works...   307
　　There's more...   307
　　See also   310
　Executing histogram aggregations   310
　　Getting ready   310
　　How to do it...   311
　　How it works...   312
　　There's more...   314
　　See also   314
　Executing date histogram aggregations   315
　　Getting ready   315
　　How to do it...   315
　　How it works...   317
　　There's more...   318

See also | 319
Executing filter aggregations | 319
Getting ready | 319
How to do it... | 320
How it works... | 321
There's more... | 321
See also | 322
Executing filters aggregations | 322
Getting ready | 322
How to do it... | 323
How it works... | 325
Executing global aggregations | 325
Getting ready | 325
How to do it... | 326
How it works... | 327
Executing geo distance aggregations | 327
Getting ready | 327
How to do it... | 328
How it works... | 329
See also | 331
Executing children aggregations | 331
Getting ready | 331
How to do it... | 332
How it works... | 334
Executing nested aggregations | 334
Getting ready | 334
How to do it... | 335
How it works... | 336
There's more... | 336
Executing top hit aggregations | 338
Getting ready | 338
How to do it... | 338
How it works... | 340
See also | 341
Executing a matrix stats aggregation | 341
Getting ready | 341
How to do it... | 342
How it works... | 343
Executing geo bounds aggregations | 343
Getting ready | 344
How to do it... | 344
How it works... | 345
See also | 345
Executing geo centroid aggregations | 345
Getting ready | 346

How to do it...   346
How it works...   347
See also   347
Executing pipeline aggregations   347
Getting ready   348
How to do it...   349
How it works...   351
See also   352
Chapter 8: Scripting in Elasticsearch   353
Painless scripting   354
Getting ready   354
How to do it...   354
How it works...   356
There's more...   357
See also   358
Installing additional script plugins   359
Getting ready   359
How to do it...   359
How it works...   361
There's more...   362
Managing scripts   362
Getting ready   362
How to do it...   363
How it works...   364
There's more...   365
See also   366
Sorting data using scripts   366
Getting ready   367
How to do it...   367
How it works...   369
There's more...   370
Computing return fields with scripting   372
Getting ready   372
How to do it...   372
How it works...   374
See also   375
Filtering a search using scripting   375
Getting ready   375
How to do it...   376
How it works...   377
See also   378
Using scripting in aggregations   378
Getting ready   378
How to do it...   379

How it works...   381
Updating a document using scripts   382
Getting ready   382
How to do it...   383
How it works...   384
There's more...   385
Reindexing with a script   387
Getting ready   387
How to do it...   387
How it works...   390

Chapter 9: Managing Clusters   391
Controlling the cluster health using an API   392
Getting ready   392
How to do it...   392
How it works...   393
There's more...   395
See also   396
Controlling the cluster state using an API   396
Getting ready   397
How to do it...   397
How it works...   399
There's more...   402
See also   402
Getting cluster node information using an API   403
Getting ready   403
How to do it...   403
How it works...   406
There's more...   409
See also   409
Getting node statistics via the API   409
Getting ready   410
How to do it...   410
How it works...   414
There's more...   416
Using the task management API   417
Getting ready   417
How to do it...   417
How it works...   418
There's more...   419
See also   420
Using the hot threads API   420
Getting ready   420
How to do it...   420
How it works...   421

Managing the shard allocation   422
   Getting ready   422
   How to do it...   422
   How it works...   423
   There's more...   424
   See also   425
Monitoring segments with the segment API   425
   Getting ready   425
   How to do it...   425
   How it works...   427
   See also   428
Cleaning the cache   428
   Getting ready   428
   How to do it...   429
   How it works...   429

Chapter 10: Backups and Restoring Data   431
   Managing repositories   432
      Getting ready   432
      How to do it...   433
      How it works...   434
      There's more...   435
      See also   435
   Executing a snapshot   436
      Getting ready   436
      How to do it...   436
      How it works...   438
      There's more...   439
   Restoring a snapshot   441
      Getting ready   441
      How to do it...   441
      How it works...   442
   Setting up an NFS share for backups   443
      Getting ready   443
      How to do it...   444
      How it works...   446
   Reindexing from a remote cluster   446
      Getting ready   446
      How to do it...   447
      How it works...   447
      See also   448

Chapter 11: User Interfaces   449
   Installing and using Cerebro   450
      Getting ready   450
      How to do it...   451

How it works...   451
There's more...   458
Installing and using Elasticsearch HQ   459
Getting ready   459
How to do it...   459
How it works...   460
Installing Kibana   468
Getting ready   469
How to do it...   469
How it works...   469
See also   474
Managing Kibana discovery   474
Getting ready   474
How to do it...   475
How it works...   476
Visualizing data with Kibana   479
Getting ready   480
How to do it...   480
How it works...   483
Using Kibana Dev tools   486
Getting ready   486
How to do it...   486
How it works...   487
There's more...   488

Chapter 12: Using the Ingest Module   489
Pipeline definition   490
Getting ready   490
How to do it...   490
How it works...   491
There's more...   491
See also   492
Inserting an ingest pipeline   493
Getting ready   493
How to do it...   493
How it works...   494
Getting an ingest pipeline   495
Getting ready   495
How to do it...   495
How it works...   496
There's more...   496
Deleting an ingest pipeline   496
Getting ready   497
How to do it...   497
How it works...   497

Simulating an ingest pipeline 498
Getting ready 498
How to do it... 498
How it works... 500
There's more... 502
Built-in processors 503
Getting ready 503
How to do it... 503
How it works... 505
See also 506
Grok processor 507
Getting ready 507
How to do it... 507
How it works... 508
See also 511
Using the ingest attachment plugin 511
Getting ready 511
How to do it... 512
How it works... 514
Using the ingest GeoIP plugin 514
Getting ready 514
How to do it... 515
How it works... 516
See also 517

Chapter 13: Java Integration 519
Creating a standard Java HTTP client 520
Getting ready 520
How to do it... 520
How it works... 522
See also 525
Creating an HTTP Elasticsearch client 525
Getting ready 525
How to do it... 526
How it works... 527
See also 530
Creating a high-level REST client 530
Getting ready 530
How to do it... 531
How it works... 532
See also 532
Managing indices 533
Getting ready 533
How to do it... 533
How it works... 535

See also	537
Managing mappings	537
Getting ready	537
How to do it...	537
How it works...	539
There's more...	541
See also	541
Managing documents	541
Getting ready	542
How to do it...	542
How it works...	544
See also	546
Managing bulk actions	547
Getting ready	547
How to do it...	547
How it works...	550
Building a query	551
Getting ready	551
How to do it...	552
How it works...	552
There's more...	554
Executing a standard search	554
Getting ready	554
How to do it...	555
How it works...	556
See also	558
Executing a search with aggregations	558
Getting ready	559
How to do it...	559
How it works...	561
See also	563
Executing a scroll search	563
Getting ready	564
How to do it...	564
How it works...	565
See also	566
Integrating with DeepLearning4j	566
Getting ready	567
How to do it...	567
How it works...	571
See also	572
Chapter 14: Scala Integration	573
Creating a client in Scala	574
Getting ready	574

How to do it...	574
How it works...	576
See also	577
Managing indices	577
Getting ready	577
How to do it...	578
How it works...	579
See also	580
Managing mappings	580
Getting ready	580
How to do it...	580
How it works...	582
See also	583
Managing documents	583
Getting ready	583
How to do it...	583
How it works...	585
There's more...	586
See also	587
Executing a standard search	588
Getting ready	588
How to do it...	588
How it works...	590
See also	590
Executing a search with aggregations	590
Getting ready	590
How to do it...	591
How it works...	592
See also	593
Integrating with DeepLearning.scala	593
Getting ready	593
How to do it...	594
How it works...	596
See also	597
Chapter 15: Python Integration	599
Creating a client	600
Getting ready	600
How to do it...	601
How it works...	602
See also	603
Managing indices	603
Getting ready	603
How to do it...	604
How it works...	605

There's more…   606
See also   607
Managing mappings include the mapping   607
Getting ready   607
How to do it…   607
How it works…   608
See also   609
Managing documents   609
Getting ready   609
How to do it…   610
How it works…   612
See also   614
Executing a standard search   614
Getting ready   614
How to do it…   614
How it works…   616
See also   618
Executing a search with aggregations   618
Getting ready   618
How to do it…   619
How it works…   620
See also   621
Integrating with NumPy and scikit-learn   621
Getting ready   621
How to do it...   622
How it works...   623
See also   624

Chapter 16: Plugin Development   625
Creating a plugin   626
Getting ready   626
How to do it...   626
How it works...   628
There's more...   630
Creating an analyzer plugin   630
Getting ready   631
How to do it...   631
How it works...   633
There's more...   635
Creating a REST plugin   635
Getting ready   636
How to do it...   636
How it works...   638
See also   641
Creating a cluster action   641

Getting ready 641
How to do it... 641
How it works... 645
See also 650
Creating an ingest plugin 650
Getting ready 650
How to do it... 650
How it works... 655
Chapter 17: Big Data Integration 659
Installing Apache Spark 660
Getting ready 660
How to do it... 660
How it works... 661
There's more... 662
Indexing data using Apache Spark 663
Getting ready 663
How to do it... 663
How it works... 664
See also 665
Indexing data with meta using Apache Spark 665
Getting ready 665
How to do it... 666
How it works... 667
There's more... 667
Reading data with Apache Spark 669
Getting ready 669
How to do it... 669
How it works... 670
Reading data using Spark SQL 670
Getting ready 670
How to do it... 671
How it works... 672
Indexing data with Apache Pig 672
Getting ready 673
How to do it... 673
How it works... 675
Using Elasticsearch with Alpakka 676
Getting ready 677
How to do it... 677
How it works... 679
See also 681
Using Elasticsearch with MongoDB 681
Getting ready 682
How to do it... 682

How it works...   684
See also   685

Another Book You May Enjoy   687

Index   689

Preface

Elasticsearch is a Lucene-based distributed search server that allows users to index and search unstructured content with petabytes of data. In this book, you'll be guided through comprehensive recipes on what's new in Elasticsearch 7, and see how you can create and run complex queries and analytics.

Packed with recipes on performing index mapping, aggregation, and scripting using Elasticsearch, this fourth edition of *Elasticsearch Cookbook* will get you acquainted with numerous solutions and quick techniques to perform both every day and uncommon tasks, such as how to deploy Elasticsearch nodes, integrate other tools to Elasticsearch, and create different visualizations. You will install Kibana to monitor a cluster and will also extend it using a variety of plugins. Finally, you will integrate your Java, Scala, Python, and big data applications, such as Apache Spark and Pig, with Elasticsearch, and create efficient data applications powered by enhanced functionalities and custom plugins.

By the end of this book, you will have gained in-depth knowledge of implementing Elasticsearch architecture, and you'll be able to manage, search, and store data efficiently and effectively using Elasticsearch.

Who this book is for

If you're a software engineer, big data infrastructure engineer, or Elasticsearch developer, you'll find this book useful. This Elasticsearch book will also help data professionals working in the e-commerce and FMCG industries who use Elastic for metrics evaluation and search analytics to get deeper insights for better business decisions.

Prior experience with Elasticsearch will help you get the most out of this book.

What this book covers

Chapter 1, *Getting Started*, covers the basic steps to start using Elasticsearch from the simple installation to the cloud. We will also cover several setup cases.

Chapter 2, *Managing Mapping*, covers the correct definition of the data fields to improve both indexing and searching quality.

Chapter 3, *Basic Operations*, teaches the most common actions that are required to ingest data in Elasticsearch and to manage it.

Chapter 4, *Exploring Search Capabilities*, talks about executing search, sorting, and related APIs calls. The API discussed in this chapter are the essential ones.

Chapter 5, *Text and Numeric Queries*, talks about the Search DSL part of text and numeric fields – the core of the search functionalities of Elasticsearch.

Chapter 6, *Relationship and Geo Queries*, talks about queries that work on related documents (child/parent and nested) and geo-located fields.

Chapter 7, *Aggregations*, covers another capability of Elasticsearch, the possibility to execute analytics on search results to improve both the user experience and to drill down the information contained in Elasticsearch.

Chapter 8, *Scripting in Elasticsearch*, shows how to customize Elasticsearch with scripting and how to use the scripting capabilities in different parts of Elasticsearch (search, aggregation, and ingest) using different languages. The chapter is mainly focused on Painless, the new scripting language developed by the Elastic team.

Chapter 9, *Managing Cluster*, shows how to analyze the behavior of a cluster/node to understand common pitfalls.

Chapter 10, *Backup and Restore*, covers one of the most important components in managing data: backup. It shows how to manage a distributed backup and the restoration of snapshots.

Chapter 11, *User Interfaces*, describes two of the most common user interfaces for Elasticsearch 5.x: Cerebro, mainly used for admin activities, and Kibana, with X-Pack as a common UI extension for Elasticsearch.

Chapter 12, *Using the Ingest Module*, talks about the ingest functionality for importing data in Elasticsearch via an ingestion pipeline.

Chapter 13, *Java Integration*, describes how to integrate Elasticsearch in a Java application using both REST and native protocols.

Chapter 14, *Scala Integration*, describes how to integrate Elasticsearch in Scala using elastic4s: an advanced type-safe and feature rich Scala library based on native Java API.

Chapter 15, *Python Integration*, covers the usage of the official Elasticsearch Python client.

Chapter 16, *Plugin Development*, describes how to create native plugins to extend Elasticsearch functionalities. Some examples show the plugin skeletons, the setup process, and the building of them.

Chapter 17, *Big Data Integration*, covers how to integrate Elasticsearch in common big data tools, such as Apache Spark and Apache Pig.

To get the most out of this book

A basic knowledge of Java, Scala, and Python would be beneficial.

Download the example code files

You can download the example code files for this book from your account at www.packt.com. If you purchased this book elsewhere, you can visit www.packt.com/support and register to have the files emailed directly to you.

You can download the code files by following these steps:

1. Log in or register at www.packt.com.
2. Select the **SUPPORT** tab.
3. Click on **Code Downloads & Errata**.
4. Enter the name of the book in the **Search** box and follow the onscreen instructions.

Once the file is downloaded, please make sure that you unzip or extract the folder using the latest version of the following:

- WinRAR/7-Zip for Windows
- Zipeg/iZip/UnRarX for Mac
- 7-Zip/PeaZip for Linux

The code bundle for the book is also hosted on GitHub at https://github.com/PacktPublishing/Elasticsearch-7.0-Cookbook. In case there's an update to the code, it will be updated on the existing GitHub repository.

We also have other code bundles from our rich catalog of books and videos available at https://github.com/PacktPublishing/. Check them out!

Download the color images

We also provide a PDF file that has color images of the screenshots/diagrams used in this book. You can download it here: `https://www.packtpub.com/sites/default/files/downloads/9781789956504_ColorImages.pdf`.

Conventions used

There are a number of text conventions used throughout this book.

`CodeInText`: Indicates code words in text, database table names, folder names, filenames, file extensions, pathnames, dummy URLs, user input, and Twitter handles. Here is an example: "Mount the downloaded `WebStorm-10*.dmg` disk image file as another disk in your system."

A block of code is set as follows:

```
{
  "acknowledged" : true,
  "shards_acknowledged" : true,
  "index" : "myindex"
}
```

Any command-line input or output is written as follows:

```
elasticsearch-plugin.bat remove ingest-attachment
```

Bold: Indicates a new term, an important word, or words that you see onscreen. For example, words in menus or dialog boxes appear in the text like this. Here is an example: "You can now press on **Create Deployment** to fire your first Elasticsearch cluster."

Warnings or important notes appear like this.

Tips and tricks appear like this.

Get in touch

Feedback from our readers is always welcome.

General feedback: If you have questions about any aspect of this book, mention the book title in the subject of your message and email us at customercare@packtpub.com.

Errata: Although we have taken every care to ensure the accuracy of our content, mistakes do happen. If you have found a mistake in this book, we would be grateful if you would report this to us. Please visit www.packt.com/submit-errata, selecting your book, clicking on the Errata Submission Form link, and entering the details.

Piracy: If you come across any illegal copies of our works in any form on the internet, we would be grateful if you would provide us with the location address or website name. Please contact us at copyright@packt.com with a link to the material.

If you are interested in becoming an author: If there is a topic that you have expertise in and you are interested in either writing or contributing to a book, please visit authors.packtpub.com.

Reviews

Please leave a review. Once you have read and used this book, why not leave a review on the site that you purchased it from? Potential readers can then see and use your unbiased opinion to make purchase decisions, we at Packt can understand what you think about our products, and our authors can see your feedback on their book. Thank you!

For more information about Packt, please visit packt.com.

Getting Started 1

In this chapter, we will cover the following recipes:

- Downloading and installing Elasticsearch
- Setting up networking
- Setting up a node
- Setting up Linux systems
- Setting up different node types
- Setting up a coordinator node
- Setting up an ingestion node
- Installing plugins in Elasticsearch
- Removing a plugin
- Changing logging settings
- Setting up a node via Docker
- Deploying on Elasticsearch Cloud Enterprise

Technical requirements

Elasticsearch runs on Linux/macOS X/Windows and its only requirement is to have Java 8.x installed. Usually, I recommend using the Oracle JDK, which is available at `https://github.com/aparo/elasticsearch-7.x-cookbook`.

 If you don't want to go into the details of installing and configuring your Elasticsearch instance, for a quick start, you can skip to the *Setting up a node via Docker* recipe at the end of this chapter and fire up Docker Compose, which will install an Elasticsearch instance with Kibana and other tools quickly.

Downloading and installing Elasticsearch

Elasticsearch has an active community and the release cycles are very fast.

Because Elasticsearch depends on many common Java libraries (Lucene, Guice, and Jackson are the most famous ones), the Elasticsearch community tries to keep them updated and fixes bugs that are discovered in them and in the Elasticsearch core. The large user base is also a source of new ideas and features for improving Elasticsearch use cases.

For these reasons, if possible, it's best to use the latest available release (usually the more stable and bug-free one).

Getting ready

To install Elasticsearch, you need a supported operating system (Linux/macOS X/Windows) with a Java **Java virtual machine** (**JVM**) 1.8 or higher installed (the Sun Oracle JDK is preferred. More information on this can be found at `http://www.oracle.com/technetwork/java/javase/downloads/jdk8-downloads-2133151.html`). A web browser is required to download the Elasticsearch binary release. At least 1 GB of free disk space is required to install Elasticsearch.

How to do it...

We will start by downloading Elasticsearch from the web. The latest version is always downloadable at `https://www.elastic.co/downloads/elasticsearch`. The versions that are available for different operating systems are as follows:

- `elasticsearch-{version-number}.zip` and `elasticsearch-{version-number}.msi` are for the Windows operating systems.
- `elasticsearch-{version-number}.tar.gz` is for Linux/macOS X, while `elasticsearch-{version-number}.deb` is for Debian-based Linux distributions (this also covers the Ubuntu family); this is installable with Debian using the `dpkg -i elasticsearch-*.deb` command.
- `elasticsearch-{version-number}.rpm` is for Red Hat-based Linux distributions (this also covers the Cent OS family). This is installable with the `rpm -i elasticsearch-*.rpm` command.

The preceding packages contain everything to start Elasticsearch. This book targets version 7.x or higher. The latest and most stable version of Elasticsearch was 7.0.0. To check out whether this is the latest version or not, visit `https://www.elastic.co/downloads/elasticsearch`.

Extract the binary content. After downloading the correct release for your platform, the installation involves expanding the archive in a working directory.

Choose a working directory that is safe to charset problems and does not have a long path. This prevents problems when Elasticsearch creates its directories to store index data.

For the Windows platform, a good directory in which to install Elasticsearch could be `c:\es`, on Unix and `/opt/es` on macOS X.

To run Elasticsearch, you need a JVM 1.8 or higher installed. For better performance, I suggest that you use the latest Sun/Oracle version.

If you are a macOS X user and you have installed `Homebrew` (`http://brew.sh/`), the first and the second steps are automatically managed by the `brew install elasticsearch` command.

Let's start Elasticsearch to check if everything is working. To start your Elasticsearch server, just access the directory, and for Linux and macOS X execute the following:

```
# bin/elasticsearch
```

Alternatively, you can type the following command line for Windows:

```
# bin\elasticserch.bat
```

Your server should now start up and show logs similar to the following:

```
[2018-10-28T16:19:41,189][INFO ][o.e.n.Node ] [] initializing ...
  [2018-10-28T16:19:41,245][INFO ][o.e.e.NodeEnvironment ] [fyBySLM]
using [1] data paths, mounts [[/ (/dev/disk1s1)]], net usable_space
[141.9gb], net total_space [465.6gb], types [apfs]
  [2018-10-28T16:19:41,246][INFO ][o.e.e.NodeEnvironment ] [fyBySLM]
heap size [989.8mb], compressed ordinary object pointers [true]
  [2018-10-28T16:19:41,247][INFO ][o.e.n.Node ] [fyBySLM] node name
derived from node ID [fyBySLMcR3uqKiYC32P5Sg]; set [node.name] to
override
  [2018-10-28T16:19:41,247][INFO ][o.e.n.Node ] [fyBySLM]
```

```
version[6.4.2], pid[50238],
build[default/tar/04711c2/2018-09-26T13:34:09.098244Z], OS[Mac OS
X/10.14/x86_64], JVM[Oracle Corporation/Java HotSpot(TM) 64-Bit Server
VM/1.8.0_181/25.181-b13]
 [2018-10-28T16:19:41,247][INFO ][o.e.n.Node ] [fyBySLM] JVM arguments
[-Xms1g, -Xmx1g,
... truncated ...
 [2018-10-28T16:19:42,511][INFO ][o.e.p.PluginsService ] [fyBySLM]
loaded module [aggs-matrix-stats]
 [2018-10-28T16:19:42,511][INFO ][o.e.p.PluginsService ] [fyBySLM]
loaded module [analysis-common]
 ...truncated...
[2018-10-28T16:19:42,513][INFO ][o.e.p.PluginsService ] [fyBySLM] no
plugins loaded
 ...truncated...
[2018-10-28T16:19:46,776][INFO ][o.e.n.Node ] [fyBySLM] initialized
 [2018-10-28T16:19:46,777][INFO ][o.e.n.Node ] [fyBySLM] starting ...
 [2018-10-28T16:19:46,930][INFO ][o.e.t.TransportService ] [fyBySLM]
publish_address {127.0.0.1:9300}, bound_addresses {[::1]:9300},
{127.0.0.1:9300}
 [2018-10-28T16:19:49,983][INFO ][o.e.c.s.MasterService ] [fyBySLM]
zen-disco-elected-as-master ([0] nodes joined)[, ], reason: new_master
{fyBySLM}{fyBySLMcR3uqKiYC32P5Sg}{-
pUWNdRlTwKuhv89iQ6psg}{127.0.0.1}{127.0.0.1:9300}{ml.machine_memory=17
179869184, xpack.installed=true, ml.max_open_jobs=20, ml.enabled=true}
 ...truncated...
[2018-10-28T16:19:50,452][INFO ][o.e.l.LicenseService ] [fyBySLM]
license [b2754b17-a4ec-47e4-9175-4b2e0d714a45] mode [basic] - valid
```

How it works...

The Elasticsearch package generally contains the following directories:

- `bin`: This contains the scripts to start and manage Elasticsearch.
- `elasticsearch.bat`: This is the main executable script to start Elasticsearch.
- `elasticsearch-plugin.bat`: This is a script to manage plugins.
- `config`: This contains the Elasticsearch configs. The most important ones are as follows:
    - `elasticsearch.yml`: This is the main `config` file for Elasticsearch
    - `log4j2.properties`: This is the logging `config` file
- `lib`: This contains all the libraries required to run Elasticsearch.

- `logs`: This directory is empty at installation time, but in the future, it will contain the application logs.
- `modules`: This contains the Elasticsearch default plugin modules.
- `plugins`: This directory is empty at installation time, but it's the place where custom plugins will be installed.

During Elasticsearch startup, the following events happen:

- A node name is generated automatically (that is, `fyBySLM`) if it is not provided in `elasticsearch.yml`. The name is randomly generated, so it's a good idea to set it to a meaningful and memorable name instead.
- A node name `hash` is generated for this node, for example, `fyBySLMcR3uqKiYC32P5Sg`.
- The default installed modules are loaded. The most important ones are as follows:
    - `aggs-matrix-stats`: This provides support for aggregation matrix stats.
    - `analysis-common`: This is a common analyzer for Elasticsearch, which extends the language processing capabilities of Elasticsearch.
    - `ingest-common`: These include common functionalities for the ingest module.
    - `lang-expression/lang-mustache/lang-painless`: These are the default supported scripting languages of Elasticsearch.
    - `mapper-extras`: This provides an extra mapper type to be used, such as `token_count` and `scaled_float`.
    - `parent-join`: This provides an extra query, such as `has_children` and `has_parent`.
    - `percolator`: This provides percolator capabilities.
    - `rank-eval`: This provides support for the experimental rank evaluation APIs. These are used to evaluate hit scoring based on queries.
    - `reindex`: This provides support for `reindex` actions (`reindex`/`update` by query).
    - `x-pack-*`: All the `xpack` modules depend on a subscription for their activation.
- If there are plugins, they are loaded.

- If not configured, Elasticsearch binds the following two ports on the localhost `127.0.0.1` automatically:
    - `9300`: This port is used for internal intranode communication.
    - `9200`: This port is used for the HTTP REST API.
- After starting, if indices are available, they are restored and ready to be used.

If these port numbers are already bound, Elasticsearch automatically increments the port number and tries to bind on them until a port is available (that is, `9201`, `9202`, and so on).

There are more events that are fired during Elasticsearch startup. We'll see them in detail in other recipes.

There's more...

During a node's startup, a lot of required services are automatically started. The most important ones are as follows:

- **Cluster services**: This helps you manage the cluster state and intranode communication and synchronization
- **Indexing service**: This helps you manage all the index operations, initializing all active indices and shards
- **Mapping service**: This helps you manage the document types stored in the cluster (we'll discuss mapping in `Chapter 2`, *Managing Mapping*)
- **Network services**: This includes services such as HTTP REST services (default on port `9200`), and internal Elasticsearch protocol (port `9300`) if the thrift plugin is installed
- **Plugin service**: This manages loading the plugin
- **Aggregation services**: This provides advanced analytics on stored Elasticsearch documents such as statistics, histograms, and document grouping
- **Ingesting services**: This provides support for document preprocessing before ingestion such as field enrichment, NLP processing, types conversion, and automatic field population
- **Language scripting services**: This allows you to add new language scripting support to Elasticsearch

See also

The *Setting up networking* recipe we're going to cover next will help you with the initial network setup. Check the official Elasticsearch download page at `https://www.elastic.co/downloads/elasticsearch` to get the latest version.

Setting up networking

Correctly setting up networking is very important for your nodes and cluster.

There are a lot of different installation scenarios and networking issues. The first step for configuring the nodes to build a cluster is to correctly set the node discovery.

Getting ready

To change configuration files, you will need a working Elasticsearch installation and a simple text editor, as well as your current networking configuration (your IP).

How to do it...

To setup the networking, use the following steps:

1. Using a standard Elasticsearch configuration `config/elasticsearch.yml` file, your node will be configured to bind on the localhost interface (by default) so that it can't be accessed by external machines or nodes.
2. To allow another machine to connect to our node, we need to set `network.host` to our IP (for example, I have `192.168.1.164`).
3. To be able to discover other nodes, we need to list them in the `discovery.zen.ping.unicast.hosts` parameter. This means that it sends signals to the machine in a unicast list and waits for a response. If a node responds to it, they can join in a cluster.

4. In general, from Elasticsearch version 6.x, the node versions are compatible. You must have the same cluster name (the `cluster.name` option in `elasticsearch.yml`) to let nodes join with each other.

> The best practice is to have all the nodes installed with the same Elasticsearch version (major.minor.release). This suggestion is also valid for third-party plugins.

5. To customize the network preferences, you need to change some parameters in the `elasticsearch.yml` file, as follows:

```
cluster.name: ESCookBook
node.name: "Node1"
network.host: 192.168.1.164
discovery.zen.ping.unicast.hosts:
["192.168.1.164","192.168.1.165[9300-9400]"]
```

6. This configuration sets the cluster name to Elasticsearch, the node name, the network address, and it tries to bind the node to the address given in the discovery section by performing the following tasks:

   - We can check the configuration during node loading
   - We can now start the server and check whether the networking is configured, as follows:

```
[2018-10-28T17:42:16,386][INFO ][o.e.c.s.MasterService ]
[Node1] zen-disco-elected-as-master ([0] nodes joined)[, ],
reason: new_master
{Node1}{fyBySLMcR3uqKiYC32P5Sg}{IX1wpA01QSKkruZeSRPlFg}{192.16
8.1.164}{192.168.1.164:9300}{ml.machine_memory=17179869184,
xpack.installed=true, ml.max_open_jobs=20, ml.enabled=true}
  [2018-10-28T17:42:16,390][INFO
][o.e.c.s.ClusterApplierService] [Node1] new_master
{Node1}{fyBySLMcR3uqKiYC32P5Sg}{IX1wpA01QSKkruZeSRPlFg}{192.16
8.1.164}{192.168.1.164:9300}{ml.machine_memory=17179869184,
xpack.installed=true, ml.max_open_jobs=20, ml.enabled=true},
reason: apply cluster state (from master [master
{Node1}{fyBySLMcR3uqKiYC32P5Sg}{IX1wpA01QSKkruZeSRPlFg}{192.16
8.1.164}{192.168.1.164:9300}{ml.machine_memory=17179869184,
xpack.installed=true, ml.max_open_jobs=20, ml.enabled=true}
committed version [1] source [zen-disco-elected-as-master ([0]
nodes joined)[, ]]])
  [2018-10-28T17:42:16,403][INFO
][o.e.x.s.t.n.SecurityNetty4HttpServerTransport] [Node1]
```

```
publish_address {192.168.1.164:9200}, bound_addresses
{192.168.1.164:9200}
  [2018-10-28T17:42:16,403][INFO ][o.e.n.Node ] [Node1] started
  [2018-10-28T17:42:16,600][INFO ][o.e.l.LicenseService ]
[Node1] license [b2754b17-a4ec-47e4-9175-4b2e0d714a45] mode
[basic] - valid
```

As you can see from my screen dump, the transport is bound to 192.168.1.164:9300. The REST HTTP interface is bound to 192.168.1.164:9200.

How it works...

The following are the main important configuration keys for networking management:

- cluster.name: This sets up the name of the cluster. Only nodes with the same name can join together.
- node.name: If not defined, this is automatically assigned by Elasticsearch.

node.name allows defining a name for the node. If you have a lot of nodes on different machines, it is useful to set their names to something meaningful in order to easily locate them. Using a valid name is easier to remember than a generated name such as fyBySLMcR3uqKiYC32P5Sg.

 You must always set up a node.name if you need to monitor your server. Generally, a node name is the same as a host server name for easy maintenance.

network.host defines the IP of your machine to be used to bind the node. If your server is on different LANs, or you want to limit the bind on only one LAN, you must set this value with your server IP.

discovery.zen.ping.unicast.hosts allows you to define a list of hosts (with ports or a port range) to be used to discover other nodes to join the cluster. The preferred port is the transport one, usually 9300.

The addresses of the hosts list can be a mix of the following:

- Hostname, that is, myhost1
- IP address, that is, 192.168.1.12

- IP address or hostname with the port, that is, `myhost1:9300`, `192.168.168.1.2:9300`
- IP address or hostname with a range of ports, that is, `myhost1:[9300-9400]`, `192.168.168.1.2:[9300-9400]`

See also

The *Setting up a node* recipe in this chapter

Setting up a node

Elasticsearch allows the customization of several parameters in an installation. In this recipe, we'll see the most used ones to define where to store our data and improve overall performance.

Getting ready

As described in the *downloading and installing Elasticsearch* recipe, you need a working Elasticsearch installation and a simple text editor to change configuration files.

How to do it...

The steps required for setting up a simple node are as follows:

1. Open the `config/elasticsearch.yml` file with an editor of your choice.
2. Set up the directories that store your server data, as follows:

    - For Linux or macOS X, add the following path entries (using `/opt/data` as the base path):

    ```
    path.conf: /opt/data/es/conf
    path.data: /opt/data/es/data1,/opt2/data/data2
    path.work: /opt/data/work
    path.logs: /opt/data/logs
    path.plugins: /opt/data/plugins
    ```

- For Windows, add the following path entries (using `c:\Elasticsearch` as the base path):

```
path.conf: c:\Elasticsearch\conf
path.data: c:\Elasticsearch\data
path.work: c:\Elasticsearch\work
path.logs: c:\Elasticsearch\logs
path.plugins: c:\Elasticsearch\plugins
```

3. Set up the parameters to control the standard index shard and replication at creation. These parameters are as follows:

```
index.number_of_shards: 1
index.number_of_replicas: 1
```

How it works...

The `path.conf` parameter defines the directory that contains your configurations, mainly `elasticsearch.yml` and `logging.yml`. The default is `$ES_HOME/config`, with `ES_HOME` to install the directory of your Elasticsearch server.

It's useful to set up the `config` directory outside your application directory so that you don't need to copy the configuration files every time you update your Elasticsearch server.

The `path.data` parameter is the most important one. This allows us to define one or more directories (in a different disk) where you can store your index data. When you define more than one directory, they are managed similarly to `RAID 0` (their space is sum up), favoring locations with the most free space.

The `path.work` parameter is a location in which Elasticsearch stores temporary files.

The `path.log` parameter is where log files are put. These control how a log is managed in `logging.yml`.

The `path.plugins` parameter allows you to override the plugins path (the default is `$ES_HOME/plugins`). It's useful to put system-wide plugins in a shared path (usually using NFS) in case you want a single place where you store your plugins for all of the clusters.

The main parameters are used to control index and shards in `index.number_of_shards`, which controls the standard number of shards for a new created index, and `index.number_of_replicas`, which controls the initial number of replicas.

See also

Refer to the following points to learn more about topics related to this recipe:

- The *Setting up for Linux systems* recipe
- You can refer to the official Elasticsearch documentation at `https://www.elastic.co/guide/en/elasticsearch/reference/master/setup.html`.

Setting up Linux systems

If you are using a Linux system (generally in a production environment), you need to manage extra setup to improve performance or to resolve production problems with many indices.

This recipe covers the following two common errors that happen in production:

- Too many open files that can corrupt your indices and your data
- Slow performance in search and indexing due to the garbage collector

 Big problems arise when you run out of disk space. In this scenario, some files can get corrupted. To prevent your indices from corruption and possible data, it is best to monitor the storage spaces. Default settings prevent index writing and block the cluster if your storage is over 80% full.

Getting ready

As we described in the *Downloading and installing Elasticsearch* recipe in this chapter, you need a working Elasticsearch installation and a simple text editor to change configuration files.

How to do it...

To improve the performance on Linux systems, we will perform the following steps:

1. First, you need to change the current limit for the user that runs the Elasticsearch server. In these examples, we will call this `elasticsearch`.

2. To allow Elasticsearch to manage a large number of files, you need to increment the number of file descriptors (number of files) that a user can manage. To do so, you must edit your `/etc/security/limits.conf` file and add the following lines at the end:

   ```
   elasticsearch - nofile 65536
   elasticsearch - memlock unlimited
   ```

3. Then, a machine restart is required to be sure that the changes have been made.

4. The new version of Ubuntu (that is, version 16.04 or later) can skip the `/etc/security/limits.conf` file in the `init.d` scripts. In these cases, you need to edit `/etc/pam.d/` and remove the following comment line:

   ```
   # session required pam_limits.so
   ```

5. To control memory swapping, you need to set up the following parameter in `elasticsearch.yml`:

   ```
   bootstrap.memory_lock
   ```

6. To fix the memory usage size of the Elasticsearch server, we need to set up the same values for `Xms` and `Xmx` in `$ES_HOME/config/jvm.options` (that is, we set 1 GB of memory in this case), as follows:

   ```
   -Xms1g
   -Xmx1g
   ```

How it works...

The standard limit of file descriptors (`https://www.bottomupcs.com/file_descriptors.xhtml`) (maximum number of open files for a user) is typically 1,024 or 8,096. When you store a lot of records in several indices, you run out of file descriptors very quickly, so your Elasticsearch server becomes unresponsive and your indices may become corrupted, causing you to lose your data.

Changing the limit to a very high number means that your Elasticsearch doesn't hit the maximum number of open files.

The other setting for memory prevents Elasticsearch from swapping memory and give a performance boost in a environment. This setting is required because, during indexing and searching, Elasticsearch creates and destroys a lot of objects in memory. This large number of create/destroy actions fragments the memory and reduces performance. The memory then becomes full of holes and, when the system needs to allocate more memory, it suffers an overhead to find compacted memory. If you don't set `bootstrap.memory_lock: true`, Elasticsearch dumps the whole process memory on disk and defragments it back in memory, freezing the system. With this setting, the defragmentation step is done all in memory, with a huge performance boost.

Setting up different node types

Elasticsearch is natively designed for the cloud, so when you need to release a production environment with a huge number of records and you need high availability and good performance, you need to aggregate more nodes in a cluster.

Elasticsearch allows you to define different types of nodes to balance and improve overall performance.

Getting ready

As described in the *Downloading and installing Elasticsearch* recipe, you need a working Elasticsearch installation and a simple text editor to change the configuration files.

How to do it…

For the advanced setup of a cluster, there are some parameters that must be configured to define different node types.

These parameters are in the `config/elasticsearch.yml`, file and they can be set with the following steps:

1. Set up whether the node can be a master or not, as follows:

    ```
    node.master: true
    ```

2. Set up whether a node must contain data or not, as follows:

```
node.data: true
```

3. Set up whether a node can work as an ingest node, as follows:

```
node.ingest: true
```

How it works...

The `node.master` parameter establishes that the node can become a master for the cloud. The default value for this parameter is `true`. A master node is an arbiter for the cloud; it takes decisions about shard management, keeps the cluster status, and is the main controller of every index action. If your master nodes are on overload, all the clusters will have performance penalties. The master node is the node that distributes the search across all data nodes and aggregates/rescores the result to return them to the user. In big data terms, it's a Redux layer in the Map/Redux search in Elasticsearch.

The number of master nodes must always be even.

The `node.data` parameter allows you to store data in the node. The default value for this parameter is true. This node will be a worker that is responsible for indexing and searching data.

By mixing these two parameters, it's possible to have different node types, as shown in the following table:

node.master	node.data	Node description
true	true	This is the default node. It can be the master, which contains data.
false	true	This node never becomes a master node; it only holds data. It can be defined as a workhorse for your cluster.
true	false	This node only serves as a master in order to avoid storing any data and to have free resources. This will be the coordinator of your cluster.
false	false	This node acts as a search load balancer (fetching data from nodes, aggregating results, and so on). This kind of node is also called a coordinator or client node.

The most frequently used node type is the first one, but if you have a very big cluster or special needs, you can change the scopes of your nodes to better serve searches and aggregations.

There's more...

Related to the number of master nodes, there are settings that require at least half of them plus one to be available to ensure that the cluster is in a safe state (no risk of split brain: `https://www.elastic.co/guide/en/elasticsearch/reference/6.4/modules-node.html#split-brain`). This setting is `discovery.zen.minimum_master_nodes`, and it must be set to the following equation:

```
(master_eligible_nodes / 2) + 1
```

To have a **High Availability (HA)** cluster, you need at least three nodes that are masters with the value of `minimum_master_nodes` set to `2`.

Setting up a coordinator node

The master nodes that we have seen previously are the most important for cluster stability. To prevent the queries and aggregations from creating instability in your cluster, coordinator (or client/proxy) nodes can be used to provide safe communication with the cluster.

Getting ready

You need a working Elasticsearch installation, as we described in the *Downloading and installing Elasticsearch* recipe in this chapter, and a simple text editor to change configuration files.

How to do it...

For the advance setup of a cluster, there are some parameters that must be configured to define different node types.

These parameters are in the `config/elasticsearch.yml`, file and they can be setup a coordinator node with the following steps:

1. Set up the node so that it's not a master, as follows:

    ```
    node.master: false
    ```

2. Set up the node to not contain data, as follows:

    ```
    node.data: false
    ```

How it works...

The coordinator node is a special node that works as a proxy/pass thought for the cluster. Its main advantages are as follows:

*   It can easily be killed or removed from the cluster without causing any problems. It's not a master, so it doesn't participate in cluster functionalities and it doesn't contain data, so there are no data relocations/replications due to its failure.
*   It prevents the instability of the cluster due to a developers' /users bad queries. Sometimes, a user executes aggregations that are too large (that is, date histograms with a range of some years and intervals of 10 seconds). Here, the Elasticsearch node could **crash**. (In its newest version, Elasticsearch has a structure called **circuit breaker** to prevent similar issues, but there are always borderline cases that can bring instability using scripting, for example. The coordinator node is not a master and its overload doesn't cause any problems for cluster stability.
*   If the coordinator or client node is embedded in the application, there are less round trips for the data, speeding up the application.
*   You can add them to balance the search and aggregation throughput without generating changes and data relocation in the cluster.

Setting up an ingestion node

The main goals of Elasticsearch are indexing, searching, and analytics, but it's often required to modify or enhance the documents before storing them in Elasticsearch.

The following are the most common scenarios in this case:

- Preprocessing the log string to extract meaningful data
- Enriching the content of textual fields with **Natural Language Processing** (**NLP**) tools
- Enriching the content using **machine learning** (**ML**) computed fields
- Adding data modification or transformation during ingestion, such as the following:
  - Converting IP in geolocalization
  - Adding datetime fields at ingestion time
  - Building custom fields (via scripting) at ingestion time

Getting ready

You need a working Elasticsearch installation, as described in the *Downloading and installing Elasticsearch* recipe, as well as a simple text editor to change configuration files.

How to do it...

To set up an ingest node, you need to edit the `config/elasticsearch.yml` file and set up the `ingest` property to `true`, as follows:

```
node.ingest: true
```

 Every time you change your `elasticsearch.yml` file, a node restart is required.

How it works...

The default configuration for Elasticsearch is to set the node as an ingest node (refer to `Chapter 12`, *Using the Ingest module*, for more information on the ingestion pipeline).

As the coordinator node, using the ingest node is a way to provide functionalities to Elasticsearch without suffering cluster safety.

 If you want to prevent a node from being used for ingestion, you need to disable it with `node.ingest: false`. It's a best practice to disable this in the master and data nodes to prevent ingestion error issues and to protect the cluster. The coordinator node is the best candidate to be an ingest one.

If you are using NLP, attachment extraction (via, attachment ingest plugin), or logs ingestion, the best practice is to have a pool of coordinator nodes (no master, no data) with ingestion active.

The attachment and NLP plugins in the previous version of Elasticsearch were available in the standard data node or master node. These give a lot of problems to Elasticsearch due to the following reasons:

- High CPU usage for NLP algorithms that saturates all CPU on the data node, giving bad indexing and searching performances
- Instability due to the bad format of attachment and/or Apache Tika bugs (the library used for managing document extraction)
- NLP or ML algorithms require a lot of CPU or stress the Java garbage collector, decreasing the performance of the node

The best practice is to have a pool of coordinator nodes with ingestion enabled to provide the best safety for the cluster and ingestion pipeline.

There's more...

Having known about the four kinds of Elasticsearch nodes, you can easily understand that a waterproof architecture designed to work with Elasticsearch should be similar to this one:

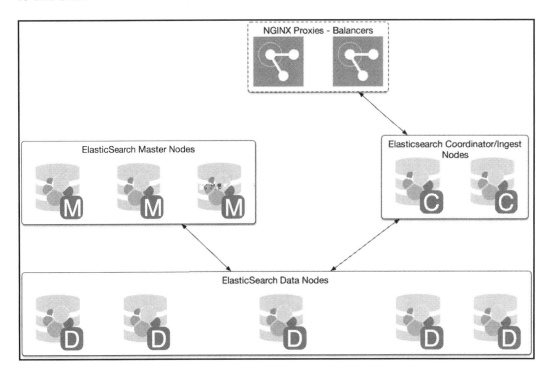

Installing plugins in Elasticsearch

One of the main features of Elasticsearch is the possibility to extend it with plugins. Plugins extend Elasticsearch features and functionalities in several ways.

In Elasticsearch, these plugins are native plugins. These are JAR files that contain application code, and are used for the following reasons:

- Script engines
- Custom analyzers, tokenizers, and scoring
- Custom mapping

- REST entry points
- Ingestion pipeline stages
- Supporting new storages (Hadoop, GCP Cloud Storage)
- Extending X-Pack (that is, with a custom authorization provider)

Getting ready

You need a working Elasticsearch installation, as we described in the *Downloading and installing Elasticsearch* recipe, as well as a prompt/shell to execute commands in the Elasticsearch install directory.

How to do it...

Elasticsearch provides a script for automatic downloads and for the installation of plugins in `bin/directory` called `elasticsearch-plugin`.

The steps that are required to install a plugin are as follows:

1. Calling the plugin and installing the Elasticsearch command with the plugin name reference.

   For installing the ingested attachment plugin used to extract text from files, simply call and type the following command if you're using Linux:

   ```
   bin/elasticsearch-plugin install ingest-attachment
   ```

   And for Windows, type the following command:

   ```
   elasticsearch-plugin.bat install ingest-attachment
   ```

2. If the plugin needs to change security permissions, a warning is prompted and you need to accept this if you want to continue.
3. During the node's startup, check that the plugin is correctly loaded.

In the following screenshot, you can see the installation and the startup of the Elasticsearch server, along with the installed plugin:

```
alberto  iMacParo   16:52   elasticsearch/elasticsearch
       bin/elasticsearch-plugin install ingest-attachment
-> Downloading ingest-attachment from elastic
[=============================================] 100%
@@@@@@@@@@@@@@@@@@@@@@@@@@@@@@@@@@@@@@@@@@@@@@@@@@@@@@@@@@@@@@@@@
@      WARNING: plugin requires additional permissions      @
@@@@@@@@@@@@@@@@@@@@@@@@@@@@@@@@@@@@@@@@@@@@@@@@@@@@@@@@@@@@@@@@@
* java.lang.RuntimePermission accessClassInPackage.sun.java2d.cmm.kcms
* java.lang.RuntimePermission accessDeclaredMembers
* java.lang.RuntimePermission getClassLoader
* java.lang.reflect.ReflectPermission suppressAccessChecks
* java.security.SecurityPermission createAccessControlContext
* java.security.SecurityPermission insertProvider
* java.security.SecurityPermission putProviderProperty.BC
See http://docs.oracle.com/javase/8/docs/technotes/guides/security/permissions.html
for descriptions of what these permissions allow and the associated risks.

Continue with installation? [y/N]y
-> Installed ingest-attachment

alberto  iMacParo   16:52   elasticsearch/elasticsearch
```

Remember that a plugin installation requires an Elasticsearch server restart.

How it works...

The `elasticsearch-plugin.bat` script is a wrapper for the Elasticsearch plugin manager. This can be used to install or remove a plugin (using the remove options).

There are several ways to install the plugin, for example:

- Passing the URL of the plugin (ZIP archive), as follows:

```
bin/elasticsearch-plugin install
http://mywoderfulserve.com/plugins/awesome-plugin.zip
```

- Passing the file path of the plugin (ZIP archive), as follows:

  ```
  bin/elasticsearch-plugin install file:///tmp/awesome-
  plugin.zip
  ```

- Using the `install` parameter with the GitHub repository of the plugin. The `install` parameter, which must be given, is formatted in the following way:

  ```
  <username>/<repo>[/<version>]
  ```

During the installation process, Elasticsearch plugin manager is able to do the following:

- Download the plugin
- Create a plugins directory in `ES_HOME/plugins`, if it's missing
- Optionally, ask if the plugin wants special permission to be executed
- Unzip the `plugin` content in the `plugin` directory
- Remove temporary files

The installation process is completely automatic; no further actions are required. The user must only pay attention to the fact that the process ends with an `Installed` message to be sure that the install process has completed correctly.

Restarting the server is always required to be sure that the plugin is correctly loaded by Elasticsearch.

There's more...

If your current Elasticsearch application depends on one or more plugins, a node can be configured to start up only if these plugins are installed and available. To achieve this behavior, you can provide the `plugin.mandatory` directive in the `elasticsearch.yml` configuration file.

For the previous example (`ingest-attachment`), the config line to be added is as follows:

```
plugin.mandatory:ingest-attachment
```

There are also some hints to remember while installing plugins: updating some plugins in a node environment can cause malfunctions due to different plugin versions in different nodes. If you have a big cluster for safety, it's better to check for updates in a separate environment to prevent problems (and remember to upgrade the plugin in all the nodes).

To prevent the fact updating an Elasticsearch version server which could also break your custom binary plugins due to some internal API changes, in Elasticsearch 5.x or higher, the plugins need to have the same version of Elasticsearch server in their manifest.

 Upgrading an Elasticsearch server version means upgrading all the installed plugins.

See also

On the Elasticsearch site, there is an updated list of available plugins: `https://www.elastic.co/guide/en/elasticsearch/plugins/current/index.html`.

The actual Elasticsearch documentation doesn't cover all available plugins. I suggest going to GitHub (`https://github.com`) and searching for them with these or similar queries: `elasticsearch plugin`, `elasticsearch lang`, and `elasticsearch ingest`.

Removing a plugin

You have installed some plugins, and now you need to remove a plugin because it's not required. Removing an Elasticsearch plugin is easy if everything goes right, otherwise you will need to manually remove it.

This recipe covers both cases.

Getting ready

You need a working Elasticsearch installation, as described in the *Downloading and installing Elasticsearch* recipe, and a prompt or shell to execute commands in the Elasticsearch install directory. Before removing a plugin, it is safer to stop the Elasticsearch server to prevent errors due to the deletion of a plugin JAR.

How to do it...

The steps to remove a plugin are as follows:

1. Stop your running node to prevent exceptions that are caused due to the removal of a file.
2. Use the Elasticsearch plugin manager, which comes with its script wrapper (`bin/elasticsearch-plugin`).

   On Linux and macOS X, type the following command:

   ```
   elasticsearch-plugin remove ingest-attachment
   ```

   On Windows, type the following command:

   ```
   elasticsearch-plugin.bat remove ingest-attachment
   ```

3. Restart the server.

How it works...

The plugin manager's remove command tries to detect the correct name of the plugin and remove the directory of the installed plugin.

If there are undeletable files on your plugin directory (or strange astronomical events that hit your server), the plugin script might fail to manually remove a plugin, so you need to follow these steps:

1. Go into the plugins directory
2. Remove the directory with your plugin name

Changing logging settings

Standard logging settings work very well for general usage.

Changing the log level can be useful for checking for bugs or understanding malfunctions due to bad configuration or strange plugin behavior. A verbose log can be used from the Elasticsearch community to solve such problems.

If you need to debug your Elasticsearch server or change how the logging works (that is, remoting send events), you need to change the `log4j2.properties` file.

Getting ready

You need a working Elasticsearch installation, as we described in the *Downloading and installing Elasticsearch* recipe, and a simple text editor to change configuration files.

How to do it...

In the config directory in your Elasticsearch install directory, there is a `log4j2.properties` file that controls the working settings.

The steps that are required for changing the logging settings are as follows:

1. To emit every kind of logging Elasticsearch could produce, you can change the current root level logging, which is as follows:

   ```
   rootLogger.level = info
   ```

2. This needs to be changed to the following:

   ```
   rootLogger.level = debug
   ```

3. Now, if you start Elasticsearch from the command line (with `bin/elasticsearch -f`), you should see a lot of information, like the following, which is not always useful (except to debug unexpected issues):

How it works...

The Elasticsearch logging system is based on the `log4j` library (`http://logging.apache.org/log4j/`).

Log4j is a powerful library that's used to manage logging. Covering all of its functionalities is outside the scope of this book; if a user needs advanced usage, there are a lot of books and articles on the internet about it.

Setting up a node via Docker

Docker (`https://www.docker.com/`) has become a common way to deploy application servers for testing or production.

Docker is a container system that makes it possible to easily deploy replicable installations of server applications. With Docker, you don't need to set up a host, configure it, download the Elasticsearch server, unzip it, or start the server—everything is done automatically by Docker.

Getting ready

You need a working Docker installation to be able to execute Docker commands (`https://www.docker.com/products/overview`).

How to do it...

1. If you want to start a vanilla server, just execute the following command:

```
docker pull
docker.elastic.co/elasticsearch/elasticsearch:7.0.0
```

2. An output similar to the following will be shown:

```
7.0.0: Pulling from elasticsearch/elasticsearch
 256b176beaff: Already exists
 1af8ca1bb9f4: Pull complete
 f910411dc8e2: Pull complete
 0c0400545052: Pull complete
 6e4d2771ff41: Pull complete
 a14f19907b79: Pull complete
 ea299a414bdf: Pull complete
 a644b305c472: Pull complete
 Digest:
sha256:3da16b2f3b1d4e151c44f1a54f4f29d8be64884a64504b24ebcbdb4
e14c80aa1
 Status: Downloaded newer image for
docker.elastic.co/elasticsearch/elasticsearch:7.0.0
```

3. After downloading the Elasticsearch image, we can start a develop instance that can be accessed outside from Docker:

```
docker run -p 9200:9200 -p 9300:9300 -e "http.host=0.0.0.0" -e
"transport.host=0.0.0.0"
docker.elastic.co/elasticsearch/elasticsearch:7.0.0
```

You'll see the output of the ElasticSearch server starting.

4. In another window/Terminal, to check if the Elasticsearch server is running, execute the following command:

```
docker ps
```

The output will be similar to the following:

```
CONTAINER ID IMAGE COMMAND CREATED STATUS PORTS NAMES
 b99b252732af
docker.elastic.co/elasticsearch/elasticsearch:7.0.0
"/usr/local/bin/dock..." 2 minutes ago Up 2 minutes
0.0.0.0:9200->9200/tcp, 0.0.0.0:9300->9300/tcp gracious_bassi
```

5. The default exported ports are 9200 and 9300.

How it works...

The Docker container provides a Debian Linux installation with Elasticsearch installed.

Elasticsearch Docker installation is easily repeatable and does not require a lot of editing and configuration.

The default installation can be tuned into in several ways, for example:

1. You can pass a parameter to Elasticsearch via the command line using the –e flag, as follows:

```
docker run -d
docker.elastic.co/elasticsearch/elasticsearch:7.0.0
elasticsearch -e "node.name=NodeName"
```

2. You can customize the default settings of the environment that's providing custom Elasticsearch configuration by providing a volume mount point at /usr/share/elasticsearch/config, as follows:

```
docker run -d -v "$PWD/config":/usr/share/elasticsearch/config
docker.elastic.co/elasticsearch/elasticsearch:7.0.0
```

3. You can persist the data between Docker reboots configuring a local data mount point to store index data. The path to be used as a mount point is /usr/share/elasticsearch/config, as follows:

```
docker run -d -v "$PWD/esdata":/usr/share/elasticsearch/data
docker.elastic.co/elasticsearch/elasticsearch:7.0.0
```

There's more...

The official Elasticsearch images are not only provided by Docker. There are also several customized images for custom purposes. Some of these are optimized for large cluster deployments or more complex Elasticsearch cluster topologies than the standard ones.

Docker is very handy for testing several versions of Elasticsearch in a clean way, without installing too much stuff on the host machine.

In the code repository directory `ch01/docker/`, there is a `docker-compose.yaml` file that provides a full environment that will set up the following elements:

- `elasticsearch`, which will be available at `http://localhost:9200`
- `kibana`, which will be available at `http://localhost:5601`
- `cerebro`, which will be available at `http://localhost:9000`

To install all the applications, you can simply execute `docker-compose up -d`. All the required binaries will be downloaded and installed in Docker, and they will then be ready to be used.

See also

- The official Elasticsearch Docker documentation at `https://www.elastic.co/guide/en/elasticsearch/reference/5.1/docker.htm l`
- The **Elasticsearch, Logstash, and Kibana (ELK)** Stack via Docker at `https://hub.docker.com/r/sebp/elk/`
- The Docker documentation at `https://docs.docker.com/`

Deploying on Elasticsearch Cloud Enterprise

The Elasticsearch company provides **Elasticsearch Cloud Enterprise (ECE)**, which is the same tool that's used in the Elasticsearch Cloud (`https://www.elastic.co/cloud`) and is offered for free. This solution, which is available on PAAS on AWS or GCP (Google Cloud Platform), can be installed on-premise to provide an enterprise solution on top of Elasticsearch.

If you need to manage multiple elastic deployments across teams or geographies, you can leverage ECE to centralize deployment management for the following functions:

- Provisioning
- Monitoring
- Scaling
- Replication
- Upgrades
- Backup and restoring

Centralizing the management of deployments with ECE enforces uniform versioning, data governance, backup, and user policies. Increased hardware utilization through better management can also reduce the total cost.

Getting ready

As this solution targets large installations of many servers, the minimum testing requirement is an 8 GB RAM node. The ECE solution lives at the top of Docker and must be installed on the nodes.

ECE supports only some operative systems, such as the following:

- Ubuntu 16.04 with Docker 18.03
- Ubuntu 14.04 with Docker 1.11
- RHEL/CentOS 7+ with Red Hat Docker 1.13

On other configurations, the ECE could work, but it is not supported in case of issues.

How to do it...

Before installing ECE, the following prerequisities are to be checked:

1. Your user must be a Docker enabled one. In the case of an error due to a non-Docker user, add your user with `sudo usermod -aG docker $USER`.
2. In the case of an error when you try to access `/mnt/data`, give your user permission to access this directory.
3. You need to add the following line to your `/etc/sysctl.conf` (a reboot is required): `vm.max_map_count = 262144`.

4. To be able to use the ECE, it must initially be installed on the first host, as follows:

```
bash <(curl -fsSL
https://download.elastic.co/cloud/elastic-cloud-enterprise.sh)
install
```

The installation process should manage these steps automatically, as shown in the following screenshot:

At the end, the installer should provide your credentials so that you can access your cluster in a similar output, as follows:

```
~~~~~~~~~~~~~~~~~~~~~~~~~~~~~~~~~~~~~~~~~~~~~~~~~~~~~~~~~~~~~~~~~~~~~~~~~
~~~~~~~~~~~~~~~~~~~~~~~~~~~~~~~~~~~~~~~~~~~~~~~~~~~~~~~~~~~~~~
  Elastic Cloud Enterprise installation completed successfully
Ready to copy down some important information and keep it safe?
Now you can access the Cloud UI using the following addresses:
http://192.168.1.244:12400
https://192.168.1.244:12443

Admin username: admin
Password: OCqHHqvF0JazwXPm48wfEHTKN0euEtn9YWyWe1gwbs8
Read-only username: readonly
Password: M27hoE3z3v6x5xyHnNleE5nboCDK43X9KoNJ346MEqO

Roles tokens for adding hosts to this installation:
Basic token (Don't forget to assign roles to new runners in the Cloud
UI after installation.)
eyJ0eXAiOiJKV1QiLCJhbGciOiJIUzI1NiJ9.eyJzdWIiOiJiZDI3NjZjZi1iNWExLTQ4Y
TYtYTRlZi1iYzE4NTlkYjQ5ZmEiLCJyb2xlcyI6W10sImlzcyI6ImN1cnJlbnQiLCJwZXJ
zaXN0ZW50Ijp0cnVlfQ.lbh9oYPiJjpy7gI3I-_yFBz9T0blwNbbwtWF_-c_D3M

Allocator token (Simply need more capacity to run Elasticsearch
clusters and Kibana? Use this token.)
eyJ0eXAiOiJKV1QiLCJhbGciOiJIUzI1NiJ9.eyJzdWIiOiJjYTk4ZDgyNi1iMWYwLTRkZ
mYtODBjYS0wYWYwMTM3M2MyOWYiLCJyb2xlcyI6WyJhbGxvY2F0b3IiXSwiaXNzIjoiY3V
ycmVudCIsInBlcnNpc3RlbnQiOnRydWV9.v9uvTKO3zgaE4nr0SDfg6ePrpperIGtvcGVf
ZHtmZmY
Emergency token (Lost all of your coordinators? This token will save
your installation.)
eyJ0eXAiOiJKV1QiLCJhbGciOiJIUzI1NiJ9.eyJzdWIiOiI5N2ExMzg5Yi1jZWE4LTQ2M
GItODM1ZC00MDMzZDllNjAyMmUiLCJyb2xlcyI6WyJjb29yZGluYXRvciIsInByb3h5Iiw
iZGlyZWN0b3IiXSwiaXNzIjoiY3VycmVudCIsInBlcnNpc3RlbnQiOnRydWV9._0IvJrBQ
7RkqzFyeFGhSAQxyjCbpOO15qZqhzH2crZQ

To add hosts to this Elastic Cloud Enterprise installation, include
the following parameters when you install the software
on additional hosts: --coordinator-host 192.168.1.244 --roles-token
'eyJ0eXAiOiJKV1QiLCJhbGciOiJIUzI1NiJ9.eyJzdWIiOiJiZDI3NjZjZi1iNWExLTQ4
YTYtYTRlZi1iYzE4NTlkYjQ5ZmEiLCJyb2xlcyI6W10sImlzcyI6ImN1cnJlbnQiLCJwZX
JzaXN0ZW50Ijp0cnVlfQ.lbh9oYPiJjpy7gI3I-_yFBz9T0blwNbbwtWF_-c_D3M'

These instructions use the basic token, but you can substitute one of
the other tokens provided. You can also generate your own tokens. For
example:
curl -H 'Content-Type: application/json' -u
admin: OCqHHqvF0JazwXPm48wfEHTKN0euEtn9YWyWe1gwbs8
```

```
http://192.168.1.244:12300/api/v1/platform/configuration/security/enro
llment-tokens -d '{ "persistent": true, "roles": [ "allocator"] }'

To learn more about generating tokens, see Generate Role Tokens in the
documentation.

System secrets have been generated and stored in
/mnt/data/elastic/bootstrap-state/bootstrap-secrets.json.
Keep the information in the bootstrap-secrets.json file secure by
removing the file and placing it into secure storage, for example.


~~~~~~~~~~~~~~~~~~~~~~~~~~~~~~~~~~~~~~~~~~~~~~~~~~~~~~~~~~~~~~~~~~~~~~~~~
~~~~~~~~~~~~~~~~~~~~~~~~~~~~~~~~~~~~~~~~~~~~~~~~~~~~~~~~~~~~~
```

5. In my case, I can access the installed interface
   at `http://192.168.1.244:12400`.

   After logging into the admin interface, you will see your actual cloud
   state, as follows:

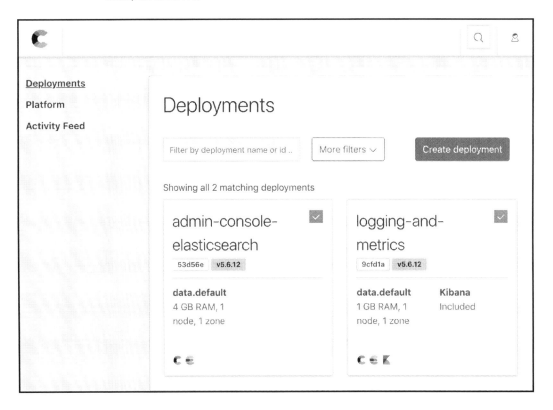

6. You can now press on **Create Deployment** to fire your first Elasticsearch cluster, as follows:

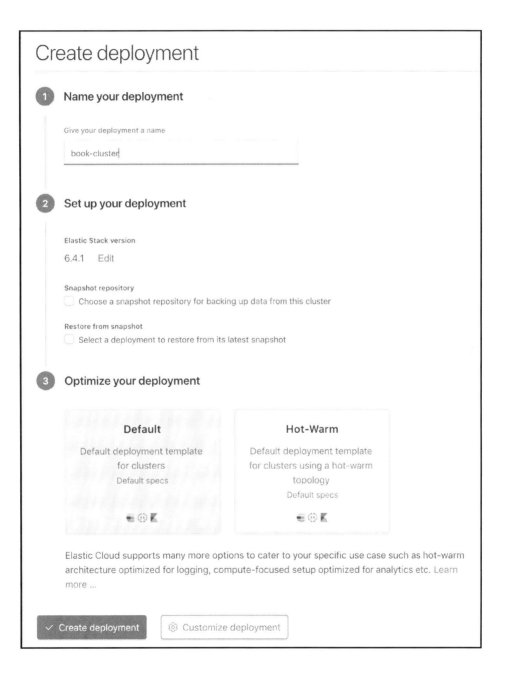

7. You need to define a name (that is, a book-cluster). Using standard options for this is okay. After pressing **Create Deployment**, ECE will start to build your cluster, as follows:

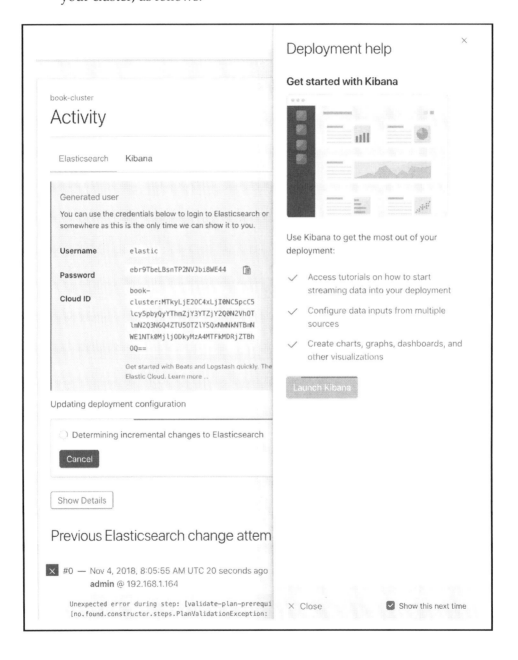

8. After a few minutes, the cluster should be up and running, as follows:

How it works...

Elasticsearch Cloud Enterprise allows you to manage a large Elasticsearch cloud service that can create an instance via deployments. By default, the standard deployment will fire an ElasticSearch node with 4 GB RAM, 32 GB disk, and a Kibana instance.

You can define a lot of parameters during the deployments for ElasticSearch, such as the following:

- The RAM used for instances from 1 GB to 64 GB. The storage is proportional to the memory, so you can go from 1 GB RAM and 128 GB storage to 64 GB RAM and 2 TB storage.
- If the node requires ML.
- Master configurations if you have more than six data nodes.
- The plugins that are required to be installed.

For Kibana, you can only configure the memory (from 1 GB to 8 GB) and pass extra parameters (usually used for custom maps).

ECE does all the provisioning and, if you want a monitoring component and other X-Pack features, it's able to autoconfigure your cluster to manage all the required functionalities.

Elasticsearch Cloud Enterprise is very useful if you need to manage several Elasticsearch/Kibana clusters, because it leverages all the infrastructure problems.

 A benefit of using a deployed Elasticsearch cluster is that, during deployment, a proxy is installed. This is very handy for managing the debugging of Elasticsearch calls.

See also

You can refer to the following links for further information on the topics that were covered in this recipe:

- Visit `https://www.elastic.co/cloud` for a PAAS managed cloud provider for ElasticSearch
- The complete documentation of Elasticsearch Cloud Enterprise at `https://www.elastic.co/guide/en/cloud-enterprise/current/index.html`
- The ECE documentation for monitoring integrating Elastic Beats at `https://www.elastic.co/guide/en/cloud-enterprise/2.0/ece-cloud-id.html`

2
Managing Mapping

Mapping is a very important concept in Elasticsearch, as it defines how the search engine should process a document and its fields.

Search engines perform the following two main operations:

- **Indexing**: This is the action to receive a document and to process it and store it in an index
- **Searching**: This is the action to retrieve the data from the index

These two parts are strictly connected; an error in the indexing step leads to unwanted or missing search results.

Elasticsearch has explicit mapping on an index level. When indexing, if a mapping is not provided, a default one is created, and guesses the structure from the data fields that the document is composed of. This new mapping is then automatically propagated to all cluster nodes.

The default type mapping has sensible default values, but when you want to change their behavior or customize several other aspects of indexing (storing, ignoring, completion, and so on), you need to provide a new mapping definition.

In this chapter, we'll look at all possible mapping field types that document mappings are composed of.

This chapter will cover the following recipes:

- Using explicit mapping creation
- Mapping base types
- Mapping arrays
- Mapping an object
- Mapping a document

- Using dynamic templates in document mapping
- Managing nested objects
- Managing a child document with a join field
- Adding a field with multiple mappings
- Mapping a GeoPoint field
- Mapping a GeoShape field
- Mapping an IP field
- Mapping an alias field
- Mapping a Percolator field
- Mapping feature and feature vector fields
- Adding metadata to a mapping
- Specifying a different analyzers
- Mapping a completion field

Using explicit mapping creation

If we consider the index as a database in the SQL world, mapping is similar to the table definition.

Elasticsearch is able to understand the structure of the document that you are indexing (reflection) and create the mapping definition automatically (explicit mapping creation).

Getting ready

To execute the code in this recipe, you need an up-and-running Elasticsearch installation, as described in the *Downloading and installing Elasticsearch* recipe in `Chapter 1`, *Getting Started*.

To execute these commands, any HTTP client can be used, such as `curl` (`https://curl.haxx.se/`), postman (`https://www.getpostman.com/`), or other similar platforms. I suggest using the Kibana console to provide code completion and better character escaping for Elasticsearch.

To better understand the examples and code in this recipe, a basic knowledge of JSON is required.

How to do it...

You can explicitly create a mapping by adding a new document in Elasticsearch. For this, we will perform the following steps:

1. Create an index like so:

    ```
    PUT test
    ```

    The answer will be as follows:

    ```
    {
     "acknowledged" : true,
     "shards_acknowledged" : true,
     "index" : "test"
     }
    ```

2. Put a document in the index, as shown in the following code:

    ```
    PUT test/_doc/1
    {"name":"Paul", "age":35}
    ```

    The answer will be as follows:

    ```
    {
      "_index" : "test",
      "_type" : "_doc",
      "_id" : "1",
      "_version" : 1,
      "result" : "created",
      "_shards" : {
        "total" : 2,
        "successful" : 1,
        "failed" : 0
      },
      "_seq_no" : 0,
      "_primary_term" : 1
    }
    ```

3. Get the mapping with the following code:

    ```
    GET test/_mapping
    ```

4. The result mapping that's autocreated by Elasticsearch should be as follows:

```
{
  "test" : {
    "mappings" : {
      "properties" : {
        "age" : {
          "type" : "long"
        },
        "name" : {
          "type" : "text",
          "fields" : {
            "keyword" : {
              "type" : "keyword",
              "ignore_above" : 256
            }
          }
        }
      }
    }
  }
}
```

5. To delete the index, you can call the following:

```
DELETE test
```

The answer will be as follows:

```
{
  "acknowledged" : true
}
```

How it works...

The first command line creates an index where we'll configure the type/mapping and insert the documents.

The second command inserts a document in the index (we'll see the index's creation in the *Creating an index* recipe in `Chapter 3`, *Basic Operations*, and record indexing in the *Indexing a document* recipe in `Chapter 3`, *Basic Operations*).

During the document index phase, Elasticsearch internally checks if the _doc type exists, otherwise it creates one dynamically.

Elasticsearch reads all the default properties for the field of the mapping and starts to process them as follows:

- If the field is already present in the mapping and the value of the field is valid (it matches the correct type), Elasticsearch does not need to change the current mappings.
- If the field is already present in the mapping but the value of the field is of a different type, it tries to upgrade the field type (that is, from integer to long). If the types are not compatible, it throws an exception and the index process fails.
- If the field is not present, it tries to auto detect the type of field. It updates the mappings with a new field mapping.

There's more...

In Elasticsearch, the separation of documents in types is logical, not physical. The Elasticsearch core engine transparently manages this. Physically, all the document types go in the same Lucene index, so there is no full separation between them. The concept of types is purely logical and enforced by Elasticsearch. The user is not bothered about this internal management, but in some cases where you have huge amounts of records, this has an impact on the performance of reading and writing records because all the records are stored in the same index files.

Every document has a unique identifier, called UID for index, which is stored in the special _uid field of the document. This is automatically calculated by adding the type of the document to the _id. In our example, the _uid will be _doc#1.

The _id can be provided at index time or it can be assigned automatically by Elasticsearch if it is missing.

When a mapping type is created or changed, Elasticsearch automatically propagates mapping changes to all nodes in the cluster, so that all the shards are aligned to process that particular type.

 Every index can contain only a single type; the name of the type in previous versions of Elasticsearch can vary. Because the type is deprecated in 7.x, it's best practice to call the _doc type.

See also

- Refer to the following sections in `Chapter 3`, *Basic Operations*:
    - The *Creating an index* recipe, which is about putting new mappings in an index during creation
    - The *Putting a mapping* recipe, which is about extending a mapping in an index

Mapping base types

Using explicit mapping makes it possible to be faster in starting to ingest the data using a schema-less approach without being concerned about field types. Thus, to achieve better results and performance in indexing, it's required to manually define a mapping.

Fine-tuning mapping brings some advantages, such as the following:

- Reducing the index size on the disk (disabling functionalities for custom fields)
- Indexing only interesting fields (general speed up)
- Precooking data for fast search or real-time analytics (such as facets)
- Correctly defining whether a field must be analyzed in multiple tokens or considered as a single token

Elasticsearch allows you to use base fields with a wide range of configurations.

Getting ready

You need an up-and-running Elasticsearch installation, as we described in the *Downloading and installing Elasticsearch* recipe in `Chapter 1`, *Getting Started*.

To execute the commands, any HTTP client can be used, such as curl (`https://curl.haxx.se/`), postman (`https://www.getpostman.com/`), or similar. I suggest using Kibana console, which provides code completion and better character escaping for Elasticsearch.

To execute this recipe's examples, you need to create an index with a `test` name, where you can put mappings, as explained in the *Using explicit mapping creation* recipe.

How to do it...

Let's use a semi real-world example of a shop order for our eBay-like shop:

1. First, we define an order:

Name	Type	Description
id	identifier	Order identifier
date	date(time)	Date of order
customer_id	id reference	Customer ID reference
name	string	Name of the item
quantity	integer	How many items?
price	double	The price of the item
vat	double	VAT for item
sent	boolean	The order was sent

2. Our `order` record must be converted into an Elasticsearch mapping definition as follows:

```
PUT test/_mapping
{
    "properties" : {
      "id" : {"type" : "keyword"},
      "date" : {"type" : "date"},
      "customer_id" : {"type" : "keyword"},
      "sent" : {"type" : "boolean"},
      "name" : {"type" : "keyword"},
      "quantity" : {"type" : "integer"},
      "price" : {"type" : "double"},
      "vat" : {"type" : "double", "index":"false"}
    }
}
```

Now, the mapping is ready to be put in the index. We will see how to do this in the *Putting a Mapping in an Index* recipe in `Chapter 4`, *Basic Operations*.

How it works...

Field types must be mapped to one of the Elasticsearch base types, and options about how the field must be indexed need to be added.

The following table is a reference for the mapping types:

Type	ES-Type	Description
`String`, `VarChar`	`keyword`	This is a text field that is not tokenizable: `CODE001`
`String`, `VarChar`, `Text`	`text`	This is a text field to be tokenizated: a nice text
`Integer`	`integer`	This is an Integer (32-bit): 1,2,3, or 4
`long`	`long`	This is a long value (64-bit)
`float`	`float`	This is a floating-point number (32-bit): 1.2, or 4.5
`double`	`double`	This is a floating point number (64 bit)
`boolean`	`boolean`	This is a Boolean value: true or false
`date/datetime`	`date`	This is a date or datetime value: `2013-12-25`, `2013-12-25T22:21:20`
`bytes/binary`	`binary`	This includes some bytes that are used for binary data, such as file or stream of bytes.

Depending on the data type, it's possible to give explicit directives to Elasticsearch when processing the field for better management. The most used options are as follows:

- `store` (default `false`): This marks the field to be stored in a separate index fragment for fast retrieval. Storing a field consumes disk space, but reduces computation if you need to extract it from a document (that is, in scripting and aggregations). The possible values for this option are `false` and `true`.

> The stored fields are faster than others in aggregations.

- `index`: This defines whether or not the field should be indexed. The possible values for this parameter are `true` and `false`. Index fields are not searchable (default `true`).
- `null_value`: This defines a default value if the field is null.
- `boost`: This is used to change the importance of a field (default `1.0`).

> Boost works on a term level only, so it's mainly used in term, terms, and match queries.

- `search_analyzer`: This defines an analyzer to be used during the search. If not defined, the analyzer of the parent object is used (default `null`).
- `analyzer`: This sets the default analyzer to be used (default `null`).
- `include_in_all`: This marks the current field to be indexed in the special `_all` field (a field that contains the concatenated text of all fields) (default `true`).
- `norms`: This controls the Lucene norms. This parameter is used to better score queries. If the field is used only for filtering, it's best practice to disable it to reduce resource usage (default `true` for analyzed fields and `false` for `not_analyzed` ones).
- `copy_to`: This allows you to copy the content of a field to another one to achieve functionalities, similar to the `_all` field.
- `ignore_above`: This allows you to skip the indexing string that's bigger than its value. This is useful for processing fields for exact filtering, aggregations, and sorting. It also prevents a single term token from becoming too big and prevents errors due to the Lucene term byte-length limit of 32766 (default `2147483647`).

There's more...

In the previous version of Elasticsearch, the standard mapping for the string was `string`. In version 5.x, the string mapping is deprecated and migrated to keyword and text mappings.

In Elasticsearch version 6.x, as shown in the *Using explicit mapping creation* recipe, the explicit inferred type for a string is a multifield mapping:

- The default processing is `text`. This mapping allows textual queries (that is, term, match, and span queries). In the example provided in the *Using explicit mapping creation* recipe, this was `name`.
- The `keyword` subfield is used for `keyword` mapping. This field can be used for exact term matching and for aggregation and sorting. In the example provided in the *Using explicit mapping creation* recipe, the referred field was `name.keyword`.

Another important parameter, available only for `text` mapping, is the `term_vector` (the vector of terms that compose a string. Refer to the Lucene documentation for further details at `http://lucene.apache.org/core/6_1_0/core/org/apache/lucene/index/Terms.html`).

The `term_vector` can accept the following values:

- `no`: This is the default value, skip term vector
- `yes`: This is the store term vector
- `with_offsets`: This is the store term vector with token offset (start, end position in a block of characters)
- `with_positions`: This is used to store the position of the token in the term vector
- `with_positions_offsets`: This stores all term vector data

 Term vectors allow fast highlighting, but consume disk space due to storing of additional text information. It's a best practice to only activate in fields that require highlighting, such as title or document content.

See also

- The online documentation on Elasticsearch provides a full description of all properties for the different mapping fields at `https://www.elastic.co/guide/en/elasticsearch/reference/master/mapping-params.html`
- *The Specifying a different Analyzer* recipe at the end of this chapter shows alternative analyzers to the standard one
- For newcomers who want to explore the concepts of tokenization, I would suggest reading the official Elasticsearch documentation at `https://www.elastic.co/guide/en/elasticsearch/reference/current/analysis-tokenizers.html`

Mapping arrays

An array or multi-value fields are very common in data models (such as multiple phone numbers, addresses, names, aliases, and so on), but not natively supported in traditional SQL solutions.

In SQL, multi-value fields require the creation of accessory tables that must be joined to gather all the values, leading to poor performance when the cardinality of records is huge.

Elasticsearch, which works natively in JSON, provides support for multi-value fields transparently.

Getting ready

You need an up-and-running Elasticsearch installation, as we described in the *Downloading and installing Elasticsearch* recipe in `Chapter 1`, *Getting Started.*

To execute these commands, any HTTP client can be used, such as curl (`https://curl.haxx.se/`), postman (`https://www.getpostman.com/`), or similar. I suggest using the Kibana console, which provides code completion and better character escaping for Elasticsearch.

How to do it...

1. Every field is automatically managed as an array. For example, to store tags for a document, the mapping will be as follows:

```
{
    "properties" : {
      "name" : {"type" : "keyword"},
      "tag" : {"type" : "keyword", "store" : "yes"},
      ...
      }
}
```

2. This mapping is valid for indexing both documents. The following is the code for `document1`:

```
{"name": "document1", "tag": "awesome"}
```

3. The following is the code for `document2`:

```
{"name": "document2", "tag": ["cool", "awesome", "amazing"] }
```

How it works...

Elasticsearch transparently manages the array: there is no difference if you declare a single value or a multi-value due to its Lucene core nature.

Multi-values for fields are managed in Lucene, and so you can add them to a document with the same field name. For people with a SQL background, this behavior may be quite strange, but this is a key point in the NoSQL world as it reduces the need for the join query and creates different tables to manage multi-values. An array of embedded objects has the same behavior as simple fields.

Mapping an object

An object is a base structure (analogous to a record in SQL). Elasticsearch extends the traditional use of objects, thus allowing for recursive embedded objects.

Getting ready

You need an up-and-running Elasticsearch installation as we described in the *Downloading and installing Elasticsearch* recipe in `Chapter 1`, *Getting Started*.

To execute the commands, any HTTP client can be used such as curl (`https://curl.haxx.se/`), postman (`https://www.getpostman.com/`), or similar. Again, I suggest using Kibana console, which provides code completion and better character escaping for Elasticsearch.

How to do it...

We can rewrite the mapping code found in the previous example recipe using an array of items:

```
PUT test/_doc/_mapping
{
    "properties" : {
      "id" : {"type" : "keyword"},
      "date" : {"type" : "date"},
      "customer_id" : {"type" : "keyword", "store" : "yes"},
      "sent" : {"type" : "boolean"},
      "item" : {
        "type" : "object",
        "properties" : {
          "name" : {"type" : "text"},
          "quantity" : {"type" : "integer"},
          "price" : {"type" : "double"},
          "vat" : {"type" : "double"}
          }
```

```
            }
        }
    }
```

How it works...

Elasticsearch speaks native JSON, so every complex JSON structure can be mapped into it.

When Elasticsearch is parsing an object type, it tries to extract fields and processes them as its defined mapping. If not, it learns the structure of the object using reflection.

The most important attributes for an object are as follows:

- `properties`: This is a collection of fields or objects (we can consider them as columns in the SQL world).
- `enabled`: This establishes whether or not the object should be processed. If it's set to false, the data contained in the object is not indexed and it cannot be searched (default `true`).
- `dynamic`: This allows Elasticsearch to add new field names to the object using a reflection on the values of the inserted data. If it's set to `false`, when you try to index an object containing a new field type, it'll be rejected silently. If it's set to `strict`, when a new field type is present in the object, an error is raised, skipping the index process. The dynamic parameter allows you to be safe about changes in the document structure (default `true`).
- `include_in_all`: This adds the object values to the special _all field (used to aggregate the text of all document fields) (default `true`).

The most used attribute is `properties`, which allows you to map the fields of the object in Elasticsearch fields.

Disabling the indexing part of the document reduces the index size; however, the data cannot be searched. In other words, you end up with a smaller file on disk, but there is a cost in functionality.

See also

There are special objects that are described in the following recipes:

- The *Mapping a document* recipe
- The *Managing a child document with a join field* recipe
- The *Mapping nested objects* recipe

Mapping a document

The document is also referred to as the root object. This has special parameters that control its behavior, which are mainly used internally to do special processing, such as routing or time-to-live of documents.

In this recipe, we'll take a look at these special fields and learn how to use them.

Getting ready

You need an up-and-running Elasticsearch installation, as we described in the *Downloading and installing Elasticsearch* recipe in Chapter 1, *Getting Started*.

To execute these commands, every HTTP client can be used, such as curl (https://curl.haxx.se/), postman (https://www.getpostman.com/), or similar. I suggest using the Kibana console, which provides code completion and better character escaping for Elasticsearch.

How to do it...

We can extend the preceding order example by adding some of the special fields, for example:

```
PUT test/_mapping
{
    "_source": {        "store": true
    },
    "_routing": {        "required": true
    },
    "_index": {
      "enabled": true
    },     "properties": {
```

```
... truncated ....
    }
}
```

How it works...

Every special field has its own parameters and value options, such as the following:

- `_id`: This allows you to index only the ID part of the document. All the ID queries will speed up using the ID value (default not indexed and not stored).
- `_index`: This controls whether or not the index must be stored as part of the document. It can be enabled by setting the `"enabled"`: `true` parameter (enabled=false default).
- `_source`: This controls the storage of the document source. Storing the source is very useful, but it's a storage overhead, so it is not required. Consequently, it's better to turn it off (enabled=true default).
- `_routing`: This defines the shard that will store the document. It supports additional parameters, such as `required` (true/false). This is used to force the presence of the routing value, raising an exception if not provided.

Controlling how to index and process a document is very important and allows you to resolve issues related to complex data types.

Every special field has parameters to set particular configurations, and some of their behaviors could change in different releases of Elasticsearch.

See also

- You can refer to the *Using dynamic templates in document mapping* recipe in this chapter and the *Putting a Mapping in an Index* in Chapter 3, *Basic Operations, to learn more*

Using dynamic templates in document mapping

In the *Using explicit mapping creation* recipe, we have seen how Elasticsearch is able to guess the field type using reflection. In this recipe, we'll see how we can help it improve its guessing capabilities via dynamic templates.

The dynamic template feature is very useful. For example, it may be useful in situations in which you need to create several indices with similar types because it allows you to move the need to define mappings from coded initial routines to automatic index-document creation. A typical usage is to define types for Logstash log indices.

Getting ready

You need an up-and-running Elasticsearch installation as we described in the *Downloading and installing Elasticsearch* recipe in `Chapter 1`, *Getting Started*.

To execute these commands, any HTTP client can be used, such as curl (`https://curl.haxx.se/`), postman (`https://www.getpostman.com/`), or similar. I suggest using Kibana console, which provides code completion and better character escaping for Elasticsearch.

How to do it...

We can extend the previous mapping by adding document-related settings, as follows:

```
PUT test/_mapping
{
    "dynamic_date_formats":["yyyy-MM-dd", "dd-MM-yyyy"],\
    "date_detection":true,
    "numeric_detection":true,
    "dynamic_templates":[
      {"template1":{
        "match":"*",
        "match_mapping_type":"long",
        "mapping":{"type":" {dynamic_type}", "store":true}
      }}    ],
    "properties" : {...}
}
```

How it works...

The root object (document) controls the behavior of its fields and all its children object fields. In document mapping, we can define the following:

- `date_detection`: This enables the extraction of a date from a string (`true` default).
- `dynamic_date_formats`: This is a list of valid date formats. This is used if `date_detection` is active.
- `numeric_detection`: This enables you to convert strings into numbers, if possible (`false` default).
- `dynamic_templates`: This is a list of templates that's used to change the explicit mapping inference. If one of these templates is matched, the rules defined in it are used to build the final mapping.

A dynamic template is composed of two parts: the matcher and the mapping one.

To match a field to activate the template, several types of matchers are available such as:

- `match`: This allows you to define a match on the field name. The expression is a standard GLOB pattern (`http://en.wikipedia.org/wiki/Glob_ (programming)`).
- `unmatch`: This allows you to define the expression to be used to exclude matches (optional).
- `match_mapping_type`: This controls the types of the matched fields. For example, string, integer, and so on (optional).
- `path_match`: This allows you to match the dynamic template against the full dot notation of the field, for example, `obj1.*.value` (optional).
- `path_unmatch`: This will do the opposite of `path_match`, excluding the matched fields (optional).
- `match_pattern`: This allows you to switch the matchers to `regex` (regular expression); otherwise, the glob pattern match is used (optional).

The dynamic template mapping part is a standard one, but with the ability to use special placeholders, such as the following:

- `{name}`: This will be replaced with the actual dynamic field name
- `{dynamic_type}`: This will be replaced with the type of the matched field

The order of the dynamic templates is very important; only the first one that is matched is executed. It is good practice to order the ones with more strict rules first, and then the others.

There's more...

The dynamic template is very handy when you need to set a mapping configuration to all the fields. This action can be done by adding a dynamic template, similar to this one:

```
"dynamic_templates" : [
  {
    "store_generic" : {
     "match" : "*",
      "mapping" : {
        "store" : "true"
      }
    }
  }
]
```

In this example, all the new fields, which will be added with explicit mapping, will be stored.

See also

- You can see the default Elasticsearch behavior in to create a mapping in the *Using explicit mapping creation* recipe and the base way to define a mapping in the *Mapping a document* recipe.
- The glob pattern is available at `http://en.wikipedia.org/wiki/Glob_pattern`.

Managing nested objects

There is a special type of embedded object: the nested one. This resolves a problem related to Lucene indexing architecture, in which all the fields of embedded objects are viewed as a single object. During search, in Lucene, it is not possible to distinguish between values and different embedded objects in the same multi-valued array.

If we consider the previous order example, it's not possible to distinguish an item name and its quantity with the same query, as Lucene puts them in the same Lucene document object. We need to index them in different documents and then join them. This entire trip is managed by nested objects and nested queries.

Getting ready

You need an up-and-running Elasticsearch installation, as we described in the *Downloading and installing Elasticsearch* recipe in `Chapter 1`, *Getting Started*.

To execute these commands, any HTTP client can be used, such as `curl` (`https://curl.haxx.se/`), postman (`https://www.getpostman.com/`), or similar. I suggest using the Kibana console, which provides code completion and better character escaping for Elasticsearch.

How to do it...

A nested object is defined as the standard object with the nested type.

From the example in the *Mapping an object* recipe, we can change the type from object to `nested` as follows:

```
PUT test/_mapping
{
    "properties" : {
      "id" : {"type" : "keyword"},
      "date" : {"type" : "date"},
      "customer_id" : {"type" : "keyword"},
      "sent" : {"type" : "boolean"},
      "item" : {"type" : "nested",
        "properties" : {
            "name" : {"type" : "keyword"},
            "quantity" : {"type" : "long"},
            "price" : {"type" : "double"},
```

```
            "vat" : {"type" : "double"}
        }
    }
  }
}
```

How it works...

When a document is indexed, if an embedded object is marked as `nested`, it's extracted by the original document, before being and indexed in a new external document, saved in a special index position near the parent document.

In the preceding example, we reused the mapping of the *Mapping an Object* recipe, but we changed the type of the item from `object` to `nested`. No other required action must be taken to convert an embedded object into a nested one.

The nested objects are special Lucene documents that are saved in the same block of data of its parent—this approach allows for fast joining with the parent document.

Nested objects are not searchable with standard queries, only with nested ones. They are not shown in standard query results.

The lives of nested objects are related to their parents: deleting/updating a parent automatically deletes/updates all nested children. Changing the parent means Elasticsearch will do the following:

- Mark old documents as deleted
- Mark all nested documents as deleted
- Index the new document version
- Index all nested documents

There's more...

Sometimes, it is required to propagate information of nested objects to their parent or root objects. This is mainly to build simpler queries about the parents (such as terms queries without using nested ones). To achieve this goal, there are two special properties of nested objects that must be used:

- `include_in_parent`: This makes it possible to automatically add the nested fields to the immediate parent
- `include_in_root`: This adds the nested object fields to the root object

These settings add data redundancy, but they reduce the complexity of some queries, thus improving performance.

See also

- Nested objects require a special query to search for them—these will be discussed in the *Using nested Query* recipe in `Chapter 6`, *Relationships and Geo Queries*
- The *Managing child document with join field* recipe shows another way to manage child/parent relations between documents

Managing a child document with a join field

In the previous recipe, we have seen how it's possible to manage relations between objects with the nested object type. The disadvantage of nested objects is their dependence from their parent. If you need to change a value of a nested object, you need to reindex the parent (this brings a potential performance overhead if the nested objects change too quickly). To solve this problem, Elasticsearch allows you to define child documents.

Getting ready

You need an up-and-running Elasticsearch installation, as we described in the *Downloading and installing Elasticsearch* recipe in `Chapter 1`, *Getting Started*.

To execute these commands, any HTTP client can be used, such as curl (`https://curl.haxx.se/`), postman (`https://www.getpostman.com/`), or similar. I suggest using the Kibana console, which provides code completion and better character escaping for Elasticsearch.

How to do it...

In the following example, we have two related objects: an Order and an Item.

Their UML representation is as follows:

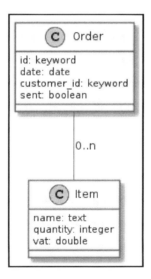

The final mapping should be a merge of the field definitions of both `Order` and `Item`, plus a special field (`join_field`, in this example) that takes the parent/child relationship.

The mapping will be as follows:

```
PUT test1/_mapping
{
  "properties": {
    "join_field": {
```

```
        "type": "join",
        "relations": {
          "order": "item"
        }
      },
      "id": {
        "type": "keyword"
      },
      "date": {
        "type": "date"
      },
      "customer_id": {
        "type": "keyword"
      },
      "sent": {
        "type": "boolean"
      },
      "name": {
        "type": "text"
      },
      "quantity": {
        "type": "integer"
      },
      "vat": {
        "type": "double"
      }
    }
  }
}
```

The preceding mapping is very similar to the one in the previous recipe.

If we want to store the joined records, we will need to save the parent first and then the children in this way:

```
PUT test/_doc/1?refresh
  {
    "id": "1",
    "date": "2018-11-16T20:07:45Z",
    "customer_id": "100",
    "sent": true,
    "join_field": "order"
  }

PUT test/_doc/c1?routing=1&refresh
  {
    "name": "tshirt",
    "quantity": 10,
    "price": 4.3,
```

```
    "vat": 8.5,
    "join_field": {
      "name": "item",
      "parent": "1"
    }
  }
}
```

The child item requires special management because we need to add the `routing` with the parent i. Furthermore, in the object, we need to specify the parent name and its ID.

How it works...

Mapping in the case of multiple item relationships in the same index needs to be computed as the sum of all other mapping fields.

The relationship between objects must be defined in `join_field`.
There must be only a single `join_field` for mapping; if you need to give a lot of relationships, you can provide them in the `relations` object.

The child document must be indexed in the same shard of the parent; so, when indexed, an extra parameter must be passed, which is `routing` (we'll see how to do this in the *Indexing a document* recipe in the next chapter).

A child document doesn't require reindexing the parent document when we want to change its values. Consequently, it's fast in indexing, reindexing (updating), and deleting.

There's more...

In Elasticsearch, we have different ways to manage relations between objects, as follows:

- Embedding with `type=object`: This is implicitly managed by Elasticsearch and it considers the embedding as part of the main document. It's fast, but you need to reindex the main document to change a value of the embedded object.

- Nesting with `type=nested`: This allows for more accurate search and filtering of the parent using nested queries on children. Everything works for the embedded object except for query (you must use a nested query to search for them).
- External children documents: Here, the children are the external document, with a `join_field` property to bind them to the parent. They must be indexed in the same shard as the parent. The join with the parent is a bit slower than the nested one, because the nested objects are in the same data block of the parent in Lucene index and they are loaded with the parent, otherwise, the child document requires more read operations.

Choosing how to model the relation from objects depends on your application scenario.

There is also another approach that can be used, but on big data documents, it brings poor performances—it's decoupling join relation. You do the join query in two steps: first, you collect the ID of the children/other documents and then you search for them in a field of their parent.

See also

- You can refer to the *Using the has_child query*, *Using the top_children query*, and *Using the has_parent query* recipes in `Chapter 7`, *Relationships and Geo Queries*, for more details on child/parent queries

Adding a field with multiple mappings

Often a field must be processed with several core types or in different ways. For example, a string field must be processed as `tokenized` for search and `not-tokenized` for sorting. To do this, we need to define a `fields` multifield special property.

The `fields` property is a very powerful feature of mappings because it allows you to use the same field in different ways.

Getting ready

You need an up-and-running Elasticsearch installation, as we described in the *Downloading and installing Elasticsearch* recipe in Chapter 1, *Getting Started*.

To execute these commands, any HTTP client can be used such as curl (https://curl.haxx.se/), postman (https://www.getpostman.com/), or similar. I suggest using Kibana console, which provides code completion and better character escaping for Elasticsearch.

How to do it...

To define a multifield property, we need to define a dictionary containing the fields subfield. The subfield with the same name as a parent field is the default one.

If we consider the item of our order example, we can index the name in this way:

```
{
  "name": {
    "type": "keyword",
    "fields": {
      "name": {"type": "keyword"},
      "tk": {"type": "text"},
      "code": {"type": "text","analyzer": "code_analyzer"}
    }
  },
```

If we already have a mapping stored in Elasticsearch and we want to migrate the fields in a multi-field property, it's enough to save a new mapping with a different type, and Elasticsearch provides the merge automatically. New subfields in the fields property can be added without problems at any moment, but the new subfields will be available in searching/aggregation only to newly indexed documents.

When you add a new subfield to already indexed data, you need to reindex your record to ensure you have it correctly indexed for all your records.

How it works...

During indexing, when Elasticsearch processes a `fields` property of type multifield, it reprocesses the same field for every subfield defined in the mapping.

To access the subfields of a multifield, we have a new path built on the base field plus the subfield name. If we consider the preceding example, we have the following:

- `name`: This points to the default multifield subfield-field (the keyword one)
- `name.tk`: This points to the standard analyzed (tokenizated) text field
- `name.code`: This points to a field analyzed with a code extractor analyzer

As you may have noticed in the preceding example, we have changed the analyzer to introduce a code extractor analyzer that allows you to extract the item code from a string.

Using the multifield, if we index a string such as `Good Item to buy - ABC1234`, we'll have the following:

- `name` = `Good Item to buy - ABC1234` (useful for sorting)
- `name.tk`= `["good", "item", "to", "buy", "abc1234"]` (useful for searching)
  - `name.code` = `["ABC1234"]` (useful for searching and faceting)

 In the case of the code analyzer, if the code is not found in the string, no tokens are generated. This makes it possible to develop solutions that carry out information retrieval tasks at index time and uses these at search time.

There's more...

The `fields` property is very useful in data processing because it allows you to define several ways to process a field data.

For example, if we are working on documental content (such as articles, word documents, and so on), we can define fields as subfield analyzers to extract names, places, date/time, geo location, and so on.

The subfields of a multifield are standard core type fields—we can do every process we want on them, such as search, filter, aggregation, and scripting.

See also

- The *Specifying a different analyzers* recipe

Mapping a GeoPoint field

Elasticsearch natively supports the use of geolocation types—special types that allow you to localize your document in geographic coordinates (latitude and longitude) around the world.

There are two main types that are used in the geographic world: the point and the shape. In this recipe, we'll look at GeoPoint—the base element of geo location.

Getting ready

You need an up-and-running Elasticsearch installation, as we described in the *Downloading and installing Elasticsearch* recipe in `Chapter 1`, *Getting Started*.

To execute these commands, any HTTP client can be used such as curl (`https://curl.haxx.se/`), postman (`https://www.getpostman.com/`), or similar. I suggest using Kibana console, which provides code completion and better character escaping for Elasticsearch.

How to do it...

The type of the field must be set to `geo_point` to define a GeoPoint.

We can extend the order example by adding a new field that stores the location of a customer. This will be the result as follows:

```
PUT test/_mapping
{
  "properties": {"id": {"type": "keyword",},
    "date": {"type": "date"},
    "customer_id": {"type": "keyword"},
    "customer_ip": {"type": "ip"},
    "customer_location": {"type": "geo_point"},
    "sent": {"type": "boolean"}
```

```
        }
    }
```

How it works...

When Elasticsearch indexes a document with a GeoPoint field (lat,lon), it processes the latitude and longitude coordinates and creates special accessory field data to provide faster query capabilities on these coordinates. This is because a special data structure is created to internally manage latitude and longitude.

Depending on properties, given a latitude and a longitude, it's possible to compute the geohash value (http://en.wikipedia.org/wiki/Geohash), and the index process also optimizes these values for special computation, such as distance, ranges, and in shape match.

GeoPoint has special parameters that allow you to store additional geographic data:

- lat_lon: This allows you to store the latitude and longitude as the .lat and .lon fields. Storing these values improves the performance in many memory algorithms used in distance and in shape calculus (false default).

 It makes sense to set lat_lon to true so that you store them if there is a single point value for a field. This speeds up searches and reduces memory usage during computation.

- geohash: This allows you to store the computed geohash value (false default).
- geohash_precision: This defines the precision to be used in geohash calculus. For example, given a geo point value [45.61752, 9.08363], it will store the following (12 default):
    - customer_location = 45.61752, 9.08363
    - customer_location.lat = 45.61752
    - customer_location.lon = 9.08363
    - customer_location.geohash = u0n7w8qmrfj

There's more...

GeoPoint is a special type and can accept several formats as input:

- `lat` and `lon` as properties, as shown here:

```
{
"customer_location": {
"lat": 45.61752,
"lon": 9.08363
},
```

- `lan` and `lon` as string, as follows:

```
"customer_location": "45.61752,9.08363",
```

- `geohash` string, as shown here:

```
"customer_location": "u0n7w8qmrfj",
```

- As a `GeoJSON` array (note in it `lat` and `lon` are reversed), shown in the following code snippet:

```
"customer_location": [9.08363, 45.61752]
```

Mapping a GeoShape field

An extension to the concept of point is the shape. Elasticsearch provides a type that facilitates the management of arbitrary polygons in GeoShape.

Getting ready

You need an up-and-running Elasticsearch installation, as we described in the *Downloading and installing Elasticsearch* recipe in *Chapter 1*, *Getting Started*.

To be able to use advanced shape management, Elasticsearch requires two JAR libraries in its `classpath` (usually the `lib` directory), as follows:

- Spatial4J (v0.3)
- JTS (v1.13)

How to do it...

To map a geo_shape type, a user must explicitly provide some parameters:

- tree: This is the name of the PrefixTree implementation—geohash for GeohashPrefixTree and quadtree for QuadPrefixTree (geohash default).
- precision: This is used instead of tree_levels to provide a more human value to be used in the tree level. The precision number can be followed by the unit, that is, 10 m, 10 km, 10 miles, and so on.
- tree_levels: This is the maximum number of layers to be used in the prefix tree.
- distance_error_pct: This sets the maximum errors allowed in a prefix tree (0,025% - max 0,5% default).

The customer_location mapping, which we have seen in the previous recipe using geo_shape, will be as follows:

```
"customer_location": {
  "type": "geo_shape",
  "tree": "quadtree",
  "precision": "1m"
},
```

How it works...

When a shape is indexed or searched internally, a path tree is created and used.

A path tree is a list of terms that contain geographic information, and are computed to improve performance in evaluating geo calculus.

The path tree also depends on the shape type: point, linestring, polygon, multipoint, and multipolygon.

See also

To understand the logic behind the GeoShape, some good resources are the Elasticsearch page, which tells you about GeoShape, and the sites of the libraries that are used for geographic calculus (https://github.com/spatial4j/spatial4j and http://central.maven.org/maven2/com/vividsolutions/jts/1.13/).

Mapping an IP field

Elasticsearch is used in a lot of systems to collect and search logs, such as Kibana (`https://www.elastic.co/products/kibana`) and LogStash (`https://www.elastic.co/products/logstash`). To improve search when using IP addresses, Elasticsearch provides the IPv4 and IPv6 type that can be used to store IP addresses in an optimized way.

Getting ready

You need an up-and-running Elasticsearch installation, as we described in the *Downloading and installing Elasticsearch* recipe in `Chapter 1`, *Getting Started*.

How to do it...

You need to define the type of the field that contains an IP address as `ip`.

Using the preceding order example, we can extend it by adding the customer IP with the following:

```
"customer_ip": {
  "type": "ip"
}
```

The IP must be in the standard point notation form, as follows:

```
"customer_ip":"19.18.200.201"
```

How it works...

When Elasticsearch is processing a document, if a field is an IP one, it tries to convert its value to a numerical form and generate tokens for fast value searching.

The IP has special properties:

- `index`: This defines whether the field must be indexed. If not, `false` must be used (`true` default).
- `doc_values`: This defines whether the field values should be stored in a column-stride fashion to speed up sorting and aggregations (`true` default).

The other properties (`store`, `boost`, `null_value`, and `include_in_all`) work as other base types.

The advantage of using IP fields over strings is faster speed in every range and filter and lower resource usage (disk and memory).

Mapping an alias field

It is very common to have a lot of different types in several indices. Because Elasticsearch makes it possible to search in many indices, you should filter for common fields at the same time.

In the real world, these fields are not always called in the same way in all mappings (generally because they are derived from different entities), it's very common to have a mix of `added_date`, `timestamp`, `@timestamp`, and `date_add` fields that are referring to the same date concept.

The `alias` fields allow you to define an alias name to be resolved, as well as a query time to simplify the call of all fields with the same meaning.

Getting ready

You need an up-and-running Elasticsearch installation, as we described in the *Downloading and installing Elasticsearch* recipe in `Chapter 1`, *Getting Started*.

To execute these commands, any HTTP client can be used such as curl (`https://curl.haxx.se/`), postman (`https://www.getpostman.com/`), or similar. I suggest using Kibana console, which provides code completion and better character escaping for Elasticsearch.

How to do it...

If we take the order example that we have seen in the previous recipes, we can add an alias for the price value to cost in the item subfield.

This process can be achieved executing the following actions:

1. To add this alias, we need to have a mapping that's similar to the following:

```
PUT test/_mapping
{
  "properties": {
    "id": {"type": "keyword"},
    "date": {"type": "date"},
    "customer_id": {"type": "keyword"},
    "sent": {"type": "boolean"},
    "item": {
      "type": "object",
      "properties": {
        "name": {"type": "keyword"},
        "quantity": {"type": "long"},
        "cost": {
          "type": "alias",
          "path": "item.price"
        },
        "price": {"type": "double"},
        "vat": {"type": "double"}
      }
    }
  }
}
```

2. We can now index a record as follows:

```
PUT test/_doc/1?refresh
{
  "id": "1",
  "date": "2018-11-16T20:07:45Z",
  "customer_id": "100",
  "sent": true,
  "item": [
    {
      "name": "tshirt",
      "quantity": 10,
      "price": 4.3,
      "vat": 8.5
    }
  ]
}
```

3. We can search it using the `cost` alias like so:

```
GET test/_search
{
  "query": {
    "term": {
      "item.cost": 4.3
    }
  }
}
```

The result will be the saved document.

How it works...

The alias is a convenient way to use the same name for your search field without the need to change the data structure of your fields. An alias field doesn't need to change a document's structure, thus allowing more flexibility for your data models.

The alias is resolved during search indices expansion of the query and has no performance penalties due to its usage.

If you try to index a document with a value in an alias field, an exception will be thrown.

The `path` of the alias field must contain the full resolution of the target field, which must be a concrete field, and must be known when the alias is defined.

In the case of an alias in a nested object, it must be in the same nested scope as the target.

Mapping a Percolator field

The Percolator is a special type field that makes it possible to store an Elasticsearch query inside the field and use it in percolator query.

The Percolator can be used to detect all queries that match a document.

Getting ready

You need an up-and-running Elasticsearch installation, as we described in the *Downloading and installing Elasticsearch* recipe in `Chapter 1`, *Getting Started*.

To execute these commands, any HTTP client can be used such as curl (`https://curl.haxx.se/`), postman (`https://www.getpostman.com/`), or similar. I suggest using Kibana console, which provides code completion and better character escaping for Elasticsearch.

How to do it...

For mapping a percolator field, use the followings steps:

1. We want to create a Percolator that matches some text in a `body` field. We will define mapping in a similar way:

```
PUT test-percolator
{
  "mappings": {
    "properties": {
      "query": {
        "type": "percolator"
      },
      "body": {
        "type": "text"
      }
    }
  }
}
```

2. Now, we can store a document with a query percolator inside it, as follows:

```
PUT test-percolator/_doc/1?refresh
{
  "query": {
    "match": {
      "body": "quick brown fox"
    }
  }
}
```

3. We can now execute a search on it, as shown in the following code:

```
GET test-percolator/_search
{
  "query": {
    "percolate": {
      "field": "query",
      "document": {
        "body": "fox jumps over the lazy dog"
      }
    }
  }
}
```

4. The result will return in the hits of the stored document, as follows:

```
{
    ... truncated...
    "hits" : [
      {
      "_index" : "test-percolator",
      "_type" : "_doc",
      "_id" : "1",
      "_score" : 0.2876821,
      "_source" : {
          "query" : {
              "match" : {
              "body" : "quick brown fox"
              }
          }
      },
      "fields" : {
          "_percolator_document_slot" : [0]
          }
      }
      ]
      }
    }
```

How it works...

The Percolator field stores an Elasticsearch query inside it.

Because all the percolators are cached and always active for performances, all the fields required in the query must be defined in the mapping of the document.

Due to the fact the all the queries in all percolators documents will be executed against every document, for the best performance, the query inside the percolators must be optimized to provide fast execution of them inside the percolator query.

Mapping feature and feature vector fields

It's common to have the requirement to score a document dynamically, depending on the context. For example, scoring more particular documents that are inside a category—the classic scenario is to boost (increase low scored) documents that are based on value such as page rank, hits, or categories.

Elasticsearch 7.x provides two new ways to boost your scores based on values: one is the feature fields and the other is its extension to a vector of values.

Getting ready

You need an up-and-running Elasticsearch installation, as we described in the *Downloading and installing Elasticsearch* recipe in `Chapter 1`, *Getting Started*.

To execute these commands, any HTTP client can be used such as curl (`https://curl.haxx.se/`), postman (`https://www.getpostman.com/`), or similar. I suggest using Kibana console, which provides code completion and better character escaping for Elasticsearch.

How to do it...

We want use the `feature` type to implement a common PageRank scenario where documents are scored base of same characteristics. To achieve this will execute the following steps:

1. To be able to score base on a `pagerank` value and an inverse `url` length, we will use a similar mapping:

```
PUT test-feature
{
  "mappings": {
    "properties": {
      "pagerank": {
        "type": "feature"
```

```
        },
        "url_length": {
          "type": "feature",
          "positive_score_impact": false
        }
      }
    }
  }
}
```

2. Now, we can store a document as shown here:

```
PUT test-feature/_doc/1
{
  "pagerank": 5,
  "url_length": 20
}
```

3. Now, we can execute a feature query on the `pagerank` value to return our record with a similar query, like so:

```
GET test-feature/_search
{
  "query": {
    "feature": {
      "field": "pagerank"
    }
  }
}
```

4. The evolution of the previous feature functionality is to define a vector of values using the `feature_vector` type; usually it cab be use to score by topics, categories, or similar discerning facets. We can implement this functionality using the following steps:

So, the following code defines the mapping for the `categories` field:

```
PUT test-features
{
  "mappings": {
    "properties": {
      "categories": {
        "type": "feature_vector"
      }
    }
  }
}
```

5. We can now store some documents in the index by using the following commands:

```
PUT test-features/_doc/1
{
  "categories": {
    "sport": 14.2,
    "economic": 24.3
  }
}

PUT test-features/_doc/2
{
  "categories": {
    "sport": 19.2,
    "economic": 23.1
  }
}
```

6. Now, we can search based on saved feature values, as shown here:

```
GET test-features/_search
{
  "query": {
    "feature": {
      "field": "categories.sport"
    }
  }
}
```

How it works...

The `feature` and `feature vector` are special type fields that are used for storing values that are used mainly in scoring the results.

The values stored in these fields can only be queried using the `feature` query. This cannot be used in standard query and aggregations.

The value numbers in `feature` and `feature_vector` can only be single positive values (multi-values are not allowed).

In the case of `feature_vector`, the values must be a hash, composed of a string and a positive number value.

There is a flag that changes the behavior of scoring—`positive_score_impact`. This value is `true`by default, but if you want the value of the feature to decrease the score, you can set the `false` parameter. In the `pagerank` example, the length of the `url` reduces the score of the document because the longer the `url`, the less relevant it becomes.

Adding metadata to a mapping

Sometimes, when we are working with our mapping, it is required to store some additional data to be used for display purposes, ORM facilities, permissions, or simply to track them in the mapping.

Elasticsearch allows you to store every kind of JSON data you want in the mapping with the special _meta field.

Getting ready

You need an up-and-running Elasticsearch installation, as we described in the *Downloading and installing Elasticsearch* recipe in `Chapter 1`, *Getting Started*.

How to do it...

The `_meta` mapping field can be populated with any data we want. Consider the following example:

```
{
  "_meta": {
    "attr1": ["value1", "value2"],
    "attr2": {
      "attr3": "value3"
    }
  }
}
```

How it works...

When Elasticsearch processes a new mapping and finds a _meta field, it stores it in the global mapping status and propagates the information to all the cluster nodes.

`_meta` is only used for storing purposes; it's not indexed and searchable.

It can be used for the following reasons:

- Storing type metadata
- Storing **object relational mapping** (**ORM**) related information
- Storing type permission information
- Storing extra type information (that is, icon filename used to display the type)
- Storing template parts for rendering web interfaces

Specifying different analyzers

In the previous recipes, we have looked at how to map different fields and objects in Elasticsearch, and we have described how it's easy to change the standard analyzer with the `analyzer` and `search_analyzer` properties.

In this recipe, we will loot at several analyzers and learn how to use them to improve indexing and searching quality.

Getting ready

You need an up-and-running Elasticsearch installation, as we described in the *Downloading and installing Elasticsearch* recipe in `Chapter 1`, *Getting Started*.

How to do it...

Every core type field allows you to specify custom analyzer for indexing and for searching as field parameters.

For example, if we want the `name` field to use a standard analyzer for indexing and a simple analyzer for searching, the mapping will be as follows:

```
{
  "name": {
    "type": "string",
    "index_analyzer": "standard",
    "search_analyzer": "simple"
  }
}
```

How it works...

The concept of the analyzer comes from Lucene (the core of Elasticsearch). An analyzer is a Lucene element that is composed of a tokenizer that splits a text into tokens, as well as one or more token filter. These filters carry out token manipulation such as lowercasing, normalization, removing stop words, stemming, and so on.

During the indexing phase, when Elasticsearch processes a field that must be indexed, an analyzer is chosen, first checking whether it is defined in the index_analyzer field, then in the document, and finally, in the index.

 Choosing the correct analyzer is essential to getting good results during the query phase.

Elasticsearch provides several analyzers in its standard installation. In the following table, the most common ones are described:

Name	Description
standard	This divides the text using a standard tokenizer: normalize tokens, lowercase tokens, and remove unwanted tokens
simple	This splits text at non-letter and converts them into lowercase
whitespace	This divides text on space separators
stop	This processes the text with the standard analyzer, then applies custom stopwords
keyword	This considers all text as a token
pattern	This divides text using a regular expression
snowball	This works as a standard analyzer, as well as a stemming at the end of processing

For special language purposes, Elasticsearch supports a set of analyzers aimed at analyzing text in a specific language, such as Arabic, Armenian, Basque, Brazilian, Bulgarian, Catalan, Chinese, CJK, Czech, Danish, Dutch, English, Finnish, French, Galician, German, Greek, Hindi, Hungarian, Indonesian, Italian, Norwegian, Persian, Portuguese, Romanian, Russian, Spanish, Swedish, Turkish, and Thai.

See also

There are several Elasticsearch plugins that extend the list of available analyzers. The most famous ones are as follows:

- ICU analysis plugin (`https://www.elastic.co/guide/en/elasticsearch/plugins/master/analysis-icu.html`)
- Phonetic analysis plugin (`https://www.elastic.co/guide/en/elasticsearch/plugins/master/analysis-phonetic.html`)
- Smart chinese analysis plugin (`https://www.elastic.co/guide/en/elasticsearch/plugins/master/analysis-smartcn.html`)
- Japanese (kuromoji) analysis plugin (`https://www.elastic.co/guide/en/elasticsearch/plugins/master/analysis-kuromoji.html`)

Mapping a completion field

To be able to provide search functionalities for our user, one of the most common requirements is to provide a text suggestion for our query.

Elasticsearch provides a helper for archiving this functionality using a special type mapping called **completion**.

Getting ready

You need an up-and-running Elasticsearch installation, as we described in the *Downloading and installing Elasticsearch* recipe in `Chapter 1`, *Getting Started*.

How to do it...

The definition of a completion field is similar to the previous core type fields. For example, to provide a suggestion for a name with an alias, we can write a similar mapping similar to the following:

```
{
  "name": {"type": "string", "copy_to":["suggest"]},
  "alias": {"type": "string", "copy_to":["suggest"]},
  "suggest": {
    "type": "completion",
    "payloads": true,
```

```
        "analyzer": "simple",
        "search_analyzer": "simple"
    }
}
```

In this example, we have defined two string fields: name and alias, as well as a suggest completer for them.

How it works...

There are several ways to provide a suggestion in Elasticsearch. You can obtain a simple term suggestion, or use some queries with wildcards or prefixes, but the completion fields are much faster and powerful due to the use of natively optimized structures.

Internally, Elasticsearch builds a **finite state transducer** (**FST**) structure for suggesting terms. (This topic is described in great detail at the following Wikipedia page: http://en.wikipedia.org/wiki/Finite_state_transducer.)

The most important properties that can be configured to use the completion field are as follows:

- analyzer: This defines the analyzer to be used for indexing within this document. The default is simple to use for keeping stopwords in suggested terms such as at, the, of, and so (simple default).
- search_analyzer: This defines the analyzer to be used for searching (simple default).
- preserve_separators: This controls how tokens are processed. If disabled, the spaces are removed in suggestion; this makes it possible to match fightc as fight club (true default).
- max_input_length: This property reduces the characters in the input string to reduce the suggested terms. Suggesting the longest text is nonsense (no one write long strings of text and want a suggestion on it) (50 default).

- `payloads`: This allows you to store payloads (additional item values to be returned) (`false` default). For example, if you are searching for a book, it will be useful as it not only returns the book title, but also its ISBN. This is shown in the following example:

```
PUT test/_doc/1
{
  "name": "Elasticsearch Cookbook",
  "suggest": {
    "input": ["ES", "Elasticsearch", "Elastic Search",
"ElasticSearch Cookbook"],
    "output": "Elasticsearch Cookbook",
    "payload": {"isbn": "1782166629"},
    "weight": 34
  }
}
```

In the preceding example, we are able to see some functionalities that are available during indexing time for the `completion` field, which are as follows:

- `input`: This manages a list of provided values that are usable for suggesting. If you are able to enrich your data, this can improve the quality of your suggester.
- `output`: This is an optional string to be shown as a result and mainly used for presenting to the user a text representation (optional).
- `payload`: This includes some extra data to be returned (optional).
- `weight`: This is a weight boost to be used to score suggester (optional).

At the start of this recipe, I used a shortcut using the `copy_to` field property to populate the completion field from several fields. The `copy_to` property simply copies the content of one field in one or more other fields.

See also

- In this recipe, we have only discussed the mapping and indexing functionality of completion. The search part will be discussed in the *Suggesting a Correct Query* recipe in `Chapter 4`, *Exploring Search Capabilities*.

3
Basic Operations

Before we start with indexing and searching in Elasticsearch, we need to cover how to manage indices and perform operations on documents. In this chapter, we'll start by discussing different operations on indices, such as `create`, `delete`, `update`, `open`, and `close`. These operations are very important because they allow you to define the container (index) that will store your documents. The index `create`/`delete` actions are similar to the SQL `create`/`delete` database commands.

After the indices management part, we'll learn how to manage mappings to complete the discussion we started in the previous chapter and to lay down the basis for the next chapter, which is mainly centered on searching.

A large portion of this chapter is dedicated to **create-read-update-delete (CRUD)** operations on records that are at the **core** of record storing and management in Elasticsearch.

To improve indexing performance, it's also important to understand bulk operations and avoid their common pitfalls.

This chapter doesn't cover operations involving queries, as this is the main theme of `Chapter 4`, *Exploring Search Capabilities*, `Chapter 5`, *Text and Numeric Queries*, and `Chapter 6`, *Relationships and Geo Queries*, as well as cluster operations, which will be discussed in `Chapter 9`, *Managing Clusters and Nodes*, because they are mainly related to control and monitoring the cluster.

In this chapter, we will cover the following recipes:

- Creating an index
- Deleting an index
- Opening or closing an index
- Putting a mapping in an index
- Getting a mapping

- Reindexing an index
- Refreshing an index
- Flushing an index
- ForceMerge an index
- Shrinking an index
- Checking if an index exists
- Managing index settings
- Using index aliases
- Rolling over an index
- Indexing a document
- Getting a document
- Deleting a document
- Updating a document
- Speeding up atomic operations (bulk operations)
- Speeding up `GET` operations (multi `GET`)

Creating an index

The first operation to undertake before starting indexing data in Elasticsearch is to create an index—the main container of our data.

An index is similar to the concept of a database in SQL; it is a container for types (tables in SQL) and documents (records in SQL).

Getting ready

You need an up-and-running Elasticsearch installation, as we described in the *Downloading and installing Elasticsearch* recipe in `Chapter 1`, *Getting Started*.

To execute the commands, HTTP clients can be used, such as curl (`https://curl.haxx.se/`), postman (`https://www.getpostman.com/`), and others. I suggest using the Kibana console as it provides code completion and better character escaping for Elasticsearch.

How to do it...

The HTTP method to create an index is PUT (but POST also works); the REST URL contains the index name:

```
http://<server>/<index_name>
```

To create an index, we must perform the following steps:

1. From the command line, we can execute a PUT call:

```
PUT /myindex
{
  "settings": {
    "index": {
      "number_of_shards": 2,
      "number_of_replicas": 1
    }
  }
}
```

2. The result returned by Elasticsearch should be like the following:

```
{
  "acknowledged" : true,
  "shards_acknowledged" : true,
  "index" : "myindex"
}
```

3. If the index already exists, a 400 error will be returned:

```
{
  "error": {
    "root_cause": [
      {
        "type": "resource_already_exists_exception",
        "reason": "index [myindex/xaXAnnwcTUiTePcKGWJw3Q]
already exists",
        "index_uuid": "xaXAnnwcTUiTePcKGWJw3Q",
        "index": "myindex"
      }
    ],
    "type": "resource_already_exists_exception",
    "reason": "index [myindex/xaXAnnwcTUiTePcKGWJw3Q] already
exists",
    "index_uuid": "xaXAnnwcTUiTePcKGWJw3Q",
    "index": "myindex"
  },
```

```
        "status": 400
    }
```

How it works...

During index creation, the replication can be set with two parameters in the `settings/index` object:

- The `number_of_shards`, which controls the number of shards that compose the index (every shard can store up to 2^{32} documents)
- The `number_of_replicas`, which controls the number of replications (how many times your data is replicated in the cluster for high availability)
- A good practice is to set this value to at least 1

The API call initializes a new index, which means the following:

- The index is created in a primary node first and then its status is propagated to all the nodes at the cluster level
- A default mapping (empty) is created
- All the shards required by the index are initialized and ready to accept data

The index creation API allows for the definition of mapping during creation time. The parameter that's required to define a mapping is `mapping`, and it accepts multiple mappings. So, in a single call, it is possible to create an index and put the required mappings.

There are also some limitations to the index name; the only accepted characters are as follows:

- ASCII letters `[a-z]`
- Numbers `[0-9]`
- Point ., minus –, &, and _

There's more...

The `create index` command also allows for the passing of the mappings section, which contains the mapping definitions. It is a shortcut for creating an index with mappings without executing an extra `PUT` mapping call.

A common example of this call, using the mapping from the *Putting a mapping in an index* recipe, is as follows:

```
PUT /myindex
{
  "settings": {
    "number_of_shards": 2,
    "number_of_replicas": 1
  },
  "mappings": {
    "properties": {
      "id": {
        "type": "keyword",
        "store": true
      },
      "date": {
        "type": "date",
        "store": false
      },
      "customer_id": {
        "type": "keyword",
        "store": true
      },
      "sent": {
        "type": "boolean"
      },
      "name": {
        "type": "text"
      },
      "quantity": {
        "type": "integer"
      },
      "vat": {
        "type": "double",
        "index": true
      }
    }
  }
}
```

See also

You can view the following recipes for further reference, which are related to this recipe:

- All the main concepts related to indexing are discussed in the *Understanding clusters, replication, and sharding* recipe in `Chapter 1`, *Getting Started*
- After creating an index, you generally need to add a mapping, as described in the *Putting a mapping in an index* recipe in this chapter

Deleting an index

The counterpart of creating an index is deleting one. Deleting an index means deleting its shards, mappings, and data. There are many common scenarios when we need to delete an index, such as the following:

- Removing the index to clean unwanted or obsolete data (for example, old Logstash indices).
- Resetting an index for a scratch restart.
- Deleting an index that has some missing shards, mainly due to some failures, to bring the cluster back in a valid state. (If a node dies and it's storing a single replica shard of an index, this index will be missing a shard, and so the cluster state becomes red. In this case, you'll bring back the cluster to a green status, but you will lose the data contained in the deleted index.)

Getting ready

You need an up-and-running Elasticsearch installation, as we described in the *Downloading and installing Elasticsearch* recipe in `Chapter 1`, *Getting Started*.

To execute the commands, HTTP clients can be used, such as curl (`https://curl.haxx.se/`), postman (`https://www.getpostman.com/`), or others. I suggest using the Kibana console as it provides code completion and better character escaping for Elasticsearch.

The index we created in the previous recipe should be deleted.

How to do it...

The HTTP method that's that's used to delete an index is DELETE. The following URL contains just the index name:

```
http://<server>/<index_name>
```

To delete an index, we will perform the following steps:

1. Execute a DELETE call by writing the following command:

   ```
   DELETE /myindex
   ```

2. We then check the result returned by Elasticsearch. If everything is all right, it should be as follows:

   ```
   {
     "acknowledged" : true
   }
   ```

3. If the index doesn't exist, a 404 error is returned:

   ```
   {
     "error" : {
       "root_cause" : [
         {
           "type" : "index_not_found_exception",
           "reason" : "no such index [myindex]",
           "resource.type" : "index_or_alias",
           "resource.id" : "myindex",
           "index_uuid" : "_na_",
           "index" : "myindex"
         }
       ],
       "type" : "index_not_found_exception",
       "reason" : "no such index [myindex]",
       "resource.type" : "index_or_alias",
       "resource.id" : "myindex",
       "index_uuid" : "_na_",
       "index" : "myindex"
     },
     "status" : 404
   }
   ```

How it works...

When an index is deleted, all the data related to the index is removed from the disk and is lost.

The deleting process is composed of two steps: first, the cluster is updated, and then the shards are deleted from the storage. This operation is very quick; in a traditional filesystem, it is implemented as a recursive delete.

 It's not possible to restore a deleted index if there is no backup.

Also, calling the delete API using the special value `_all` as an index name can be used to remove all the indices. In production, it is good practice to disable the all-indices deletion by adding the following line to `elasticsearch.yml`:

```
action.destructive_requires_name:true
```

See also

The previous recipe, *Creating an index*, is strongly related to this recipe.

Opening or closing an index

If you want to keep your data but save resources (memory or CPU), a good alternative to deleting indexes is to close them.

Elasticsearch allows you to open and close an index, putting it into online or offline mode.

Getting ready

You need an up-and-running Elasticsearch installation, as we described in the *Downloading and installing Elasticsearch* recipe in Chapter 1, *Getting Started*.

To execute these commands, HTTP clients can be used, such as curl (`https://curl.haxx.se/`), postman (`https://www.getpostman.com/`), or others. I suggest using the Kibana console as it provides code completion and better character escaping for Elasticsearch.

To execute the following commands correctly, the index we created in the *Creating an index* recipe is required.

How to do it...

For opening and closing an index, we will perform the following steps:

1. From the command line, we can execute a POST call to close an index using the following command:

```
POST /myindex/_close
```

2. If the call is successful, the result returned by Elasticsearch should be as follows:

```
{
  "acknowledged" : true
}
```

3. To open an index from the command line, type the following command:

```
POST /myindex/_open
```

4. If the call is successful, the result returned by Elasticsearch should be:

```
{
  "acknowledged" : true,
  "shards_acknowledged" : true
}
```

How it works...

When an index is closed, there is no overhead on the cluster (except for metadata state): the index shards are switched off and they don't use file descriptors, memory, or threads.

There are many use cases when closing an index:

- It can disable date-based indices (indices that store their records by date)–for example, when you keep an index for a week, month, or day and you want to keep a fixed number of old indices (that is, 2 months old) online and some offline (that is, from 2 months to 6 months old).
- When you do searches on all the active indices of a cluster and don't want to search in some indices (in this case, using an alias is the best solution, but you can achieve the same concept with an alias with closed indices).

An alias cannot have the same name as an index.
When an index is closed, calling `open` restores its state.

See also

In the *Using index aliases* recipe in this chapter, we will discuss the advanced usage of indices references in a time-based index to simplify management on opened indices.

Putting a mapping in an index

In the previous chapter, we saw how to build mappings by indexing documents. This recipe shows how to put a type mapping in an index. This kind of operation can be considered as the Elasticsearch version of an SQL-created table.

Getting ready

You need an up-and-running Elasticsearch installation, as we described in the *Downloading and installing Elasticsearch* recipe in `Chapter 1`, *Getting Started*.

To execute these commands, HTTP clients can be used, such as curl (`https://curl.haxx.se/`), postman (`https://www.getpostman.com/`), or others. I suggest using the Kibana console as it provides code completion and better character escaping for Elasticsearch.

To execute the following commands correctly, the index we created in the *Creating an index* recipe is required.

How to do it...

The HTTP method to put a mapping is PUT (POST also works). The URL format for putting a mapping is as follows:

```
http://<server>/<index_name>/_mapping
```

To put a mapping in an index, we will perform the following steps:

1. If we consider a possible order data model to be used as a mapping, the call will be as follows:

```
PUT /myindex/_mapping
{
  "properties": {
    "id": {
      "type": "keyword",
      "store": true
    },
    "date": {
      "type": "date",
      "store": false
    },
    "customer_id": {
      "type": "keyword",
      "store": true
    },
    "sent": {
      "type": "boolean"
    },
    "name": {
      "type": "text"
    },
    "quantity": {
      "type": "integer"
    },
    "vat": {
      "type": "double",
      "index": false
    }
  }
}
```

2. In the case of a success, the result returned by Elasticsearch should be like this:

```
{
    "acknowledged" : true
}
```

How it works...

This call checks if the index exists and then it creates one or more types of mapping, as described in the definition. To learn how to define a mapping description, see Chapter 3, *Managing Mapping*.

During mapping insertion, if there is an existing mapping for this type, it is merged with the new one. If there is a field with a different type and the type could not be updated, an exception expanding the fields property is raised. To prevent an exception during the merging mapping phase, it's possible to specify the ignore_conflicts parameter as true (default is false).

The PUT mapping call allows you to set the type for several indices in one go; that is, list the indices separated by commas or, to apply all the indexes, use the _all alias.

There's more...

There is no delete operation for mapping. It's not possible to delete a single mapping from an index. To remove or change a mapping, you need to manage the following steps:

1. Create a new index with the new or modified mapping.
2. Reindex all the records.
3. Delete the old index with an incorrect mapping.

In Elasticsearch 5.x or above, there is also a new operation to speed up this process: the reindex command, which we will see in the *Reindexing an index* recipe in this chapter.

See also

Strongly related to this recipe is the *Getting a mapping* recipe, which allows you to control the exact result of the `put` mapping command

Getting a mapping

After having set our mappings for processing types, we sometimes need to control or analyze the mapping to prevent issues. The action to get the mapping for a type helps us to understand the structure or its evolution due to some merge and implicit type guessing.

Getting ready

You need an up-and-running Elasticsearch installation, as we described in the *Downloading and installing Elasticsearch* recipe in `Chapter 1`, *Getting Started*.

To execute these commands, HTTP clients can be used, such as curl (`https://curl.haxx.se/`), postman (`https://www.getpostman.com/`), or others. I suggest using the Kibana console as it provides code completion and better character escaping for Elasticsearch.

To execute the following commands correctly, the mapping we created in the *Putting a mapping in an index* recipe is required.

How to do it...

The HTTP method to get a mapping is `GET`. The URL formats to get mappings are as follows:

- `http://<server>/_mapping`
- `http://<server>/<index_name>/_mapping`

To get a mapping from an index, we will perform the following steps:

1. If we consider the mapping for the previous recipe, the call will be as follows:

```
GET /myindex/_mapping?pretty
```

The `pretty` argument in the URL is optional, but very handy to print the response output prettily.

2. The result returned by Elasticsearch should be as follows:

```
{
  "myindex" : {
    "mappings" : {
      "properties" : {
        "customer_id" : {
          "type" : "keyword",
          "store" : true
        },
        "date" : {
          "type" : "date"
        },
        ... truncated ...,
        "vat" : {
          "type" : "double",
          "index" : false
        }
      }
    }
  }
}
```

How it works...

The mapping is stored at the cluster level in Elasticsearch. The call checks both the index and type existence, and then it returns the stored mapping.

The returned mapping is in a reduced form, which means that the default values for a field are not returned. To reduce network and memory consumption, Elasticsearch returns non-default values.

Retrieving a mapping is very useful for several purposes:

- Debugging template level mapping
- Checking if implicit mapping was derived correctly by guessing fields
- Retrieving the mapping metadata, which can be used to store type-related information
- Simply checking if the mapping is correct

If you need to fetch several mappings, it is better to do it at the index level or the cluster level to reduce the numbers of API calls.

See also

You can view the following recipes for further reference, which are related to this recipe:

- To insert a mapping in an index, refer to the *Putting a mapping in an index* recipe in this chapter.
- To manage dynamic mapping in an index, refer to the *Using dynamic templates in document mapping* recipe in `Chapter 3`, *Managing Mapping*

Reindexing an index

There are a lot of common scenarios that involve changing your mapping. Due to the limitations of Elasticsearch mapping, it not possible to delete a defined one, so you often need to reindex index data. The most common scenarios are as follows:

- Changing an analyzer for a mapping
- Adding a new subfield to a mapping, whereupon you need to reprocess all the records to search for the new subfield
- Removing an unused mapping
- Changing a record structure that requires a new mapping

Getting ready

You need an up-and-running Elasticsearch installation, as we described in the *Downloading and installing Elasticsearch* recipe in `Chapter 1`, *Getting Started*.

To execute these commands, HTTP clients can be used, such as curl (`https://curl.haxx.se/`), postman (`https://www.getpostman.com/`), or others. I suggest using the Kibana console as it provides code completion and better character escaping for Elasticsearch.

To execute the following commands correctly, the index we created in the *Creating an index* recipe is required.

How to do it...

The HTTP method to reindex an index is `POST`. The URL format to get a mapping is `http://<server>/_reindex`.

To reindex the data between two indices, we will perform the following steps:

1. If we want to reindex data from `myindex` to the `myindex2` index, the call will be as follows:

```
POST /_reindex?pretty=true
{
  "source": {
    "index": "myindex"
  },
  "dest": {
    "index": "myindex2"
  }
}
```

2. The result returned by Elasticsearch should be as follows:

```
{
  "took" : 20,
  "timed_out" : false,
  "total" : 0,
  "updated" : 0,
  "created" : 0,
  "deleted" : 0,
  "batches" : 0,
  "version_conflicts" : 0,
  "noops" : 0,
```

```
      "retries" : {
        "bulk" : 0,
        "search" : 0
      },
      "throttled_millis" : 0,
      "requests_per_second" : -1.0,
      "throttled_until_millis" : 0,
      "failures" : [ ]
    }
```

How it works...

The `reindex` functionality introduced in Elasticsearch 5.x provides an efficient way to reindex a document.

In the previous Elasticsearch version, this functionality had to be implemented at a client level. The advantages of the new Elasticsearch implementations are as follows:

- Fast copying of data because it is completely managed on the server side.
- Better management of the operation due to the new task API.
- Better error-handling support as it is done at the server level. This allows us to manage failovers better during reindex operations.

At the server level, this action is composed of the following steps:

1. Initialization of an Elasticsearch task to manage the operation
2. Creation of the target index and copying the source mappings, if required
3. Executing a query to collect the documents to be reindexed
4. Reindexing all the documents using bulk operations until all documents are reindexed

The main parameters that can be provided for this action are as follows:

- The `source` section manages how to select source documents. The most important subsections are as follows:
    - `index`, which is the source index to be used. It can also be a list of indices.
    - `query` (optional), which is an Elasticsearch query to be used to select parts of the document.
    - `sort` (optional), which can be used to provide a way of sorting the documents.

- The `dest` section manages how to control target written documents. The most important parameters in this section are as follows:
    - `index`, which is the target index to be used. If it is not available, it is to be created.
    - `version_type` (optional), if it is set to external, the external version is preserved.
    - `routing` (optional), which controls the routing in the destination index. It can be any of the following:
        - `keep` (the default), which preserves the original routing
        - `discard`, which discards the original routing
        - `=<text>`, which uses the text value for the routing
    - `pipeline` (optional), which allows you to define a custom pipeline for ingestion. We will see more about the ingestion pipeline in `Chapter 12`, *Using the Ingest Module*.
    - `size` (optional), the number of documents to be reindexed.
    - `script` (optional), which allows you to define a scripting for document manipulation. This case will be discussed in the *Reindex with a custom script* recipe in `Chapter 8`, *Scripting in Elasticsearch*.

See also

You can see view the following recipes for further reference, which are related to this recipe:

- In this chapter, check out the *Speeding up atomic operation* recipe, which will talk about using the bulk operation to ingest data quickly. The bulk actions are used under the hood by the `reindex` functionality.
- To manage task execution, please refer to the *Using the task management API* recipe in `Chapter 9`, *Managing Clusters*.
- The *Reindex with a custom script* recipe in `Chapter 8`, *Scripting in Elasticsearch*, will show several common scenarios for reindexing documents with a custom script.
- `Chapter 12`, *Using the Ingest module*, will discuss how to use the ingestion pipeline.

Refreshing an index

Elasticsearch allows the user to control the state of the searcher using a forced refresh on an index. If not forced, the newly indexed document will only be searchable after a fixed time interval (usually 1 second).

Getting ready

You need an up-and-running Elasticsearch installation, as we described in the *Downloading and installing Elasticsearch* recipe in `Chapter 1`, *Getting Started*.

To execute these commands, HTTP clients can be used, such as curl (`https://curl.haxx.se/`), postman (`https://www.getpostman.com/`), or others. I suggest using the Kibana console as it provides code completion and better character escaping for Elasticsearch.

To execute the following commands correctly, use the index we created in the *Creating an index* recipe.

How to do it...

The HTTP method that's used for both operations is POST. The URL formats for refreshing an index are as follows:

```
http://<server>/<index_name(s)>/_refresh
```

The URL formats for refreshing all the indices in a cluster are as follows:

```
http://<server>/_refresh
```

To refresh an index, we will perform the following steps:

1. If we consider the type order of the previous chapter, the call will be as follows:

   ```
   POST /myindex/_refresh
   ```

2. The result returned by Elasticsearch should be as follows:

   ```
   {
     "_shards" : {
       "total" : 2,
       "successful" : 1,
   ```

```
            "failed" : 0
        }
    }
```

How it works...

Near real-time (NRT) capabilities are automatically managed by Elasticsearch, which automatically refreshes the indices every second if data is changed in them.

To force a refresh before the internal Elasticsearch interval, you can call the refresh API on one or more indices (more indices are comma-separated), or on all the indices.

Elasticsearch doesn't refresh the state of an index at every inserted document to prevent poor performance due to the excessive I/O required in closing and reopening file descriptors.

You must force the refresh to have your last index data available for searching.

Generally, the best time to call the refresh is after indexing a lot of data, to be sure that your records are searchable instantly. It's also possible to force a refresh during a document indexing by adding refresh=true as a query parameter. For example:

```
POST
/myindex/_doc/2qLrAfPVQvCRMe7Ku8r0Tw?refresh=true
{
"id": "1234",
"date": "2013-06-07T12:14:54",
"customer_id": "customer1",
"sent": true,
"in_stock_items": 0,
"items": [
{
"name": "item1",
"quantity": 3,
"vat": 20
},
{
"name": "item2",
"quantity": 2,
"vat": 20
},
{
```

```
"name": "item3",
"quantity": 1,
"vat": 10
}
]
}
```

See also

Refer to the *Flushing an index* recipe in this chapter to force indexed data writing on disk and the *ForceMerge an index* recipe to optimize an index for searching

Flushing an index

For performance reasons, Elasticsearch stores some data in memory and on a transaction log. If we want to free memory, we need to empty the transaction log, and to be sure that our data is safely written on disk, we need to flush an index.

Elasticsearch automatically provides periodic flushing on disk, but forcing flushing can be useful, for example:

- When we need to shut down a node to prevent stale data
- To have all the data in a safe state (for example, after a big indexing operation to have all the data flushed and refreshed)

Getting ready

You need an up-and-running Elasticsearch installation, as we described in the *Downloading and installing Elasticsearch* recipe in `Chapter 1`, *Getting Started*.

To execute these commands, HTTP clients can be used, such as curl (`https://curl.haxx.se/`), postman (`https://www.getpostman.com/`), or others. I suggest using the Kibana console as it provides code completion and better character escaping for Elasticsearch.

To execute the following commands correctly, use the index we created in the *Creating an index* recipe.

How to do it...

The HTTP method that's used for both operations is POST. The URL format for flushing an index is as follows:

```
http://<server>/<index_name(s)>/_flush[?refresh=True]
```

The URL format for flushing all the indices in a cluster is as follows:

```
http:///_flush[?refresh=True]
```

1. For flushing an index, we will perform the following steps: if we consider the type order of the previous chapter, the call will be as follows:

   ```
   POST /myindex/_flush
   ```

2. If everything is fine, the result returned by Elasticsearch should be as follows:

   ```
   {
     "_shards" : {
       "total" : 2,
       "successful" : 1,
       "failed" : 0
     }
   }
   ```

The result contains the shard operation status.

How it works...

To reduce writing, Elasticsearch tries not to put overheads in I/O operations and it caches some data in memory until refreshing occurs, enabling the execution of a multi-documents single write to improve performance.

To clean up memory and force this data on disk, the flush operation is required.

In the flush call, it is possible to give an extra request parameter, refresh, which is also used to force the index to refresh.

 Flushing too often affects index performance. Use it wisely!

See also

In this chapter, refer to the *Refreshing an index* recipe to search for more recently indexed data and the *ForceMerge an index* recipe to optimize an index for searching.

ForceMerge an index

The Elasticsearch core is based on Lucene, which stores the data in segments on disk. During the life of an index, a lot of segments are created and changed. With the increase of segment numbers, the speed of searching is decreased due to the time required to read all of them. The ForceMerge operation allows us to consolidate the index for faster searching performance and reducing segments.

Getting ready

You need an up-and-running Elasticsearch installation, as we described in the *Downloading and installing Elasticsearch* recipe in `Chapter 1`, *Getting Started*.

To execute these commands, HTTP clients can be used, such as curl (`https://curl.haxx.se/`), postman (`https://www.getpostman.com/`), or others. I suggest using the Kibana console as it provides code completion and better character escaping for Elasticsearch.

To execute the following commands correctly, use the index we created in the *Creating an index* recipe.

How to do it...

The HTTP method that's used is `POST`. The URL format for optimizing one or more indices is as follows:

```
http://<server>/<index_name(s)>/_flush[?refresh=True]
```

The URL format for optimizing all the indices in a cluster is:

```
http://<server>/_flush[?refresh=True]
```

For optimizing, or to ForceMerge an index, we will perform the following steps:

1. If we consider the index we created in the *Creating an index* recipe, the call will be as follows:

   ```
   POST /myindex/_forcemerge
   ```

2. The result returned by Elasticsearch should be as follows:

   ```
   {
     "_shards" : {
       "total" : 2,
       "successful" : 1,
       "failed" : 0
     }
   }
   ```

The result contains the shard operation status.

How it works...

Lucene stores your data in several segments on disk. These segments are created when you index a new document or record, or when you delete a document.

In Elasticsearch, the deleted document is not removed from disk, but is marked as deleted (and referred to as a tombstone). To free up space, you need to `forcemerge` to purge deleted documents.

Due to all these factors, the segment numbers can be large. (For this reason, in the setup, we have increased the file description number for Elasticsearch processes.)

Internally, Elasticsearch has a merger, which tries to reduce the number of segments, but it's designed to improve the index performances rather than search performances. The `forcemerge` operation in Lucene tries to reduce the segments in an IO-heavy way by removing unused ones, purging deleted documents, and rebuilding the index with a minimal number of segments.

The main advantages of this are as follows:

- Reducing both file descriptors
- Freeing memory used by the segment readers
- Improving performance during searches due to less segment management

ForceMerge is a very IO-heavy operation. The index can be unresponsive during this optimization. It is generally executed on indices that are rarely modified, such as the logstash for previous days.

There's more...

You can pass several additional parameters to the ForceMerge call, such as the following:

- `max_num_segments`: The default value is `autodetect`. For full optimization, set this value to `1`.
- `only_expunge_deletes`: The default value is `false`. Lucene does not delete documents from segments, but it marks them as deleted. This flag only merges segments that have been deleted.
- `flush`: The default value is `true`. Elasticsearch performs a flush after a ForceMerge.
- `wait_for_merge`: The default value is `true`. If the request needs to wait, then the merge ends.

See also

In this chapter, refer to the *Refreshing an index* recipe to search for more recent indexed data and the *Flushing an index* recipe to force indexed data writing on disk.

Shrinking an index

The latest version of Elasticsearch provides a new way to optimize the index. Using the shrink API, it's possible to reduce the number of shards of an index.

This feature targets several common scenarios:

- There will be the wrong number of shards during the initial design sizing. Often, sizing the shards without knowing the correct data or text distribution tends to oversize the number of shards.
- Reducing the number of shards to reduce memory and resource usage.
- Reducing the number of shards to speed up searching.

Getting ready

You need an up-and-running Elasticsearch installation, as we described in the *Downloading and installing Elasticsearch* recipe in `Chapter 1`, *Getting Started*.

To execute these commands, HTTP clients can be used, such as curl (`https://curl.haxx.se/`), postman (`https://www.getpostman.com/`), or others. I suggest using the Kibana console as it provides code completion and better character escaping for Elasticsearch.

To execute the following commands correctly, use the index we created in the *Creating an index* recipe.

How to do it...

The HTTP method that's used is `POST`. The URL format for optimizing one or more indices is as follows:

```
http://<server>/<source_index_name>/_shrink/<target_index_name>
```

To shrink an index, we will perform the following steps:

1. We need all the primary shards of the index to be shrinking in the same node. We need the name of the node that will contain the shrink index. We can retrieve it using the _nodes API:

    ```
    GET /_nodes?pretty
    ```

Within the result, there will be a similar section:

```
....
"cluster_name" : "elastic-cookbook",
  "nodes" : {
    "9TiCStQuTDaTyMb4LgWDsg" : {
      "name" : "1e9840cf42df",
      "transport_address" : "172.18.0.2:9300",
      "host" : "172.18.0.2",
      "ip" : "172.18.0.2",
      "version" : "7.0.0",
      "build_flavor" : "default",
      "build_type" : "docker",
      "build_hash" : "f076a79",
      "total_indexing_buffer" : 103795916,

    ....
```

The name of my node is `1e9840cf42df`.

2. Now, we can change the index settings, forcing allocation to a single node for our index, and disabling the writing for the index. This can be done using the following code:

```
PUT /myindex/_settings
{
  "settings": {
    "index.routing.allocation.require._name": "1e9840cf42df",
    "index.blocks.write": true
  }
}
```

3. We need to check if all the shards are relocated. We can check for their green status:

```
GET /_cluster/health?pretty
```

The result will be as follows:

```
{
  "cluster_name" : "elastic-cookbook",
  "status" : "yellow",
  "timed_out" : false,
  "number_of_nodes" : 1,
  "number_of_data_nodes" : 1,
  "active_primary_shards" : 2,
  "active_shards" : 2,
  "relocating_shards" : 0,
  "initializing_shards" : 0,
  "unassigned_shards" : 1,
  "delayed_unassigned_shards" : 0,
  "number_of_pending_tasks" : 0,
  "number_of_in_flight_fetch" : 0,
  "task_max_waiting_in_queue_millis" : 0,
  "active_shards_percent_as_number" : 66.66666666666666
}
```

4. The index should be in a read-only state to shrink. We need to disable the writing for the index using this code snippet:

```
PUT /myindex/_settings?
{"index.blocks.write":true}
```

5. If we consider the index we created in the *Creating an index* recipe, the shrink call for creating the `reduced_index` will be as follows:

```
POST /myindex/_shrink/reduced_index
{
  "settings": {
    "index.number_of_replicas": 1,
    "index.number_of_shards": 1,
    "index.codec": "best_compression"
  },
  "aliases": {
    "my_search_indices": {}
  }
}
```

6. The result returned by Elasticsearch should be as follows:

```
{"acknowledged":true}
```

7. We can also wait for a `yellow` status, if the index is ready to work:

```
GET /_cluster/health?wait_for_status=yellow
```

8. Now, we can remove the read-only setting by changing the index settings:

```
PUT /myindex/_settings
{"index.blocks.write":false}
```

How it works...

The shrink API reduces the number of shards by executing the following steps:

1. Elasticsearch creates a new target index with the same definition as the source index, but with a smaller number of primary shards.
2. Elasticsearch hard-links (or copies) segments from the source index into the target index.

If the filesystem doesn't support hard-linking, then all segments are copied into the new index, which is a much more time-consuming process. Elasticsearch recovers the target index as though it were a closed index that has just been reopened. On a Linux system, the process is very fast due to hard links.

The prerequisites for executing a shrink are as follows:

- All the primary shards must be on the same node
- The target index must not exist
- The target number of shards must be a factor of the number of shards in the source index

There's more...

This Elasticsearch functionality provides support for new scenarios in Elasticsearch usage.

The first scenario is when you overestimate the number of shards. If you don't know your data, it's difficult to choose the correct number of shards to be used. So, often, an Elasticsearch user tends to oversize the number of shards.

Another interesting scenario is to use shrinking to provide a boost at indexing time. The main way to speed up Elasticsearch writing capabilities to a high number of documents is to create indices with a lot of shards (in general, the ingestion speed is about equal to the number of shards multiplied for documents per second, as ingested by a single shard). The standard allocation moves the shards on different nodes, so generally the more shards you have, the faster the writing speed will be: so, to achieve fast writing speeds, you should create 15 or 30 shards for an index. After the indexing phase, the index doesn't receive new records (such as time-based indices): the index is only searched, so to speed up the search, you can shrink your shards.

See also

In this chapter, refer to the *ForceMerge an index* recipe to optimize your indices for searching.

Checking if an index exists

A common pitfall error is to query for indices that don't exist. To prevent this issue, Elasticsearch gives the user the ability to check for an index's existence.

This check is often used during an application startup to create indices that are required for correct working.

Getting ready

You need an up-and-running Elasticsearch installation, as we described in the *Downloading and installing Elasticsearch* recipe in Chapter 1, *Getting Started*.

To execute these commands, HTTP clients can be used, such as curl (https://curl.haxx.se/), postman (https://www.getpostman.com/), or others. I suggest using the Kibana console as it provides code completion and better character escaping for Elasticsearch.

To execute the following commands correctly, use the index we created in the *Creating an index* recipe.

How to do it...

The HTTP method for checking an index's existence is HEAD. The URL format for checking an index is as follows:

```
http://<server>/<index_name>/
```

To check if an index exists, we will perform the following steps:

1. If we consider the index we created in the *Creating an index* recipe, the call will be as follows:

   ```
   HEAD /myindex/
   ```

2. If the index exists, an HTTP status code 200 is returned; if it is missing, a 404 code will be returned.

How it works...

This is a typical HEAD REST call to check for something's existence. It doesn't return a body response, only the status code, which is the result status of the operation.

The most common status codes are:

- 20X family, if everything is okay
- 404, if the resource is not available
- 50X family, if there are server errors

 Before every action involved in indexing, generally on an application's startup, it's good practice to check if an index exists to prevent future failures.

Managing index settings

Index settings are more important because they allow you to control several important Elasticsearch functionalities, such as sharding or replication, caching, term management, routing, and analysis.

Getting ready

You need an up-and-running Elasticsearch installation, as we described in the *Downloading and installing Elasticsearch* recipe in Chapter 1, *Getting Started*.

To execute these commands, HTTP clients can be used, such as curl (https://curl.haxx.se/), postman (https://www.getpostman.com/), or others. I suggest using the Kibana console as it provides code completion and better character escaping for Elasticsearch.

To execute the following commands correctly, use the index we created in the *Creating an index* recipe.

How to do it...

For managing the index settings, we will perform the following steps:

1. To retrieve the settings of your current index, use the following URL format: `http://<server>/<index_name>/_settings`

2. We are reading information using the REST API, so the method will be GET. An example of a call, using the index we created in the *Creating an index* recipe, is as follows:

```
GET /myindex/_settings?pretty=true
```

3. The response will be something similar to this:

```
{
  "myindex" : {
    "settings" : {
      "index" : {
        "routing" : {
          "allocation" : {
            "require" : {
              "_name" : "1e9840cf42df"
            }
          }
        },
        "number_of_shards" : "1",
        "blocks" : {
          "write" : "true"
        },
        "provided_name" : "myindex",
        "creation_date" : "1554578317870",
        "number_of_replicas" : "1",
        "uuid" : "sDzB7n80SFi8Of99IgLYtA",
        "version" : {
          "created" : "7000099"
        }
      }
    }
  }
}
```

4. The response attributes depend on the index settings. In this case, the response will be the number of replicas (1), shards (2), and the index creation version (7000099). The UUID represents the unique ID of the index.

5. To modify the index settings, we need to use the `PUT` method. A typical settings change is to increase the replica number:

```
PUT /myindex/_settings
{"index":{ "number_of_replicas": "2"}}
```

How it works...

Elasticsearch provides a lot of options to tune index behaviors, such as the following:

- **Replica management**:
  - `index.number_of_replicas`: This is the number of replicas each shard has
  - `index.auto_expand_replicas`: This allows you to define a dynamic number of replicas related to the number of shards

Using set `index.auto_expand_replicas` to 0-all allows the creation of an index that is replicated in every node. (This is very useful for settings or cluster-propagated data, such as language options or stopwords).

- **Refresh interval (default 1s)**: In the *Refreshing an index* recipe, we saw how to refresh an index manually. The index settings `index.refresh_interval` control the rate of automatic refreshing.
- **Write management**: Elasticsearch provides several settings to block read or write operations in the index and to change metadata. They live in the `index.blocks` settings.
- **Shard allocation management**: These settings control how the shards must be allocated. They live in the `index.routing.allocation.*` namespace.

There are other index settings that can be configured for very specific needs. In every new version of Elasticsearch, the community extends these settings to cover new scenarios and requirements.

There's more...

The `refresh_interval` parameter allows several tricks to optimize the indexing speed. It controls the rate of refresh and refreshing itself, and reduces the indices' performance due to the opening and closing of files. A good practice is to disable the refresh interval (set-1) during a big bulk indexing and to restore the default behavior after it. This can be done by following these steps:

1. Disable the refresh:

```
PUT /myindex/_settings
{"index":{"refresh_interval": "-1"}}
```

2. Bulk-index millions of documents.
3. Restore the refresh:

```
PUT /myindex/_settings
{"index":{"refresh_interval": "1s"}}
```

4. Optionally, you can optimize an index for search performance:

```
POST /myindex/_forcemerge
```

See also

In this chapter, refer to the *Refreshing an index* recipe to search for more recent indexed data and the *ForceMerge an index* recipe to optimize an index for searching.

Using index aliases

Real-world applications have a lot of indices and queries that span more indices. This scenario requires defining all the indices' names on which queries are based; aliases allow grouping of them under a common name.

Some common scenarios for this usage are as follows:

- Log indices divided by date (that is, `log_YYMMDD`) for which we want to create an alias for the last week, the last month, today, yesterday, and so on. This pattern is commonly used in log applications such as Logstash (`https://www.elastic.co/products/logstash`).
- Collecting website contents in several indices (*New York Times*, *The Guardian*, ...) for those we want to be referred to by the index alias sites.

Getting ready

You need an up-and-running Elasticsearch installation, as we described in the *Downloading and installing Elasticsearch* recipe in `Chapter 1`, *Getting Started*.

To execute these commands, HTTP clients can be used, such as curl (`https://curl.haxx.se/`), postman (`https://www.getpostman.com/`), or others. I suggest using the Kibana console as it provides code completion and better character escaping for Elasticsearch.

How to do it...

The URL format for control aliases is as follows:

```
http://<server>/_aliases
http://<server>/<index>/_alias/<alias_name>
```

For managing the index aliases, we will perform the following steps:

1. We are reading the aliases and statuses for all indices using the REST API, so the method will be `GET`. An example of a call is as follows:

   ```
   GET /_aliases
   ```

2. This gives a response similar to this one:

   ```
   {
     ".monitoring-es-7-2019.04.06" : {
       "aliases" : { }
     },
     "myindex" : {
       "aliases" : { }
     }
   }
   ```

3. Aliases can be changed with add and delete commands.

4. To read an alias for a single index, we use the `_alias` endpoint:

```
GET /myindex/_alias
```

The result should be as follows:

```
{
  "myindex" : {
    "aliases" : { }
  }
}
```

5. To add an alias, type the following command:

```
PUT /myindex/_alias/myalias1
```

The result should be as follows:

```
{
  "acknowledged" : true
}
```

This action adds the `myindex` index to the `myalias1` alias.

6. To delete an alias, type the following command:

```
DELETE /myindex/_alias/myalias1
```

The result should be as follows:

```
{
  "acknowledged" : true
}
```

The delete action removed `myindex` from the `myalias1` alias.

How it works...

Elasticsearch, during search operations, automatically expands the alias, so the required indices are selected.

The alias metadata is kept in the cluster state. When an alias is added or deleted, all the changes are propagated to all the cluster nodes.

Aliases are mainly functional structures that simply manage indices when data is stored in multiple indices.

There's more...

Aliases can also be used to define a filter and routing parameter.

Filters are automatically added to the query to filter out data. Routing by using an alias allows us to control which shards to hit during searching and indexing.

An example of this call is as follows:

```
POST /myindex/_aliases/user1alias
{
  "filter": {
    "term": {
      "user": "user_1"
    }
  },
  "search_routing": "1,2",
  "index_routing": "2"
}
```

In this case, we are adding a new alias, user1alias, to a myindex index, and are also adding the following:

- A filter to select only documents that match a field user with a user_1 term.
- A list and a routing key to select the shards to be used during a search.
- A routing key to be used during indexing. The routing value is used to modify the destination shard of the document.

The search_routing parameter allows multi-value routing keys. The index_routing parameter is single-value only.

Rolling over an index

When using a system that manages logs, it is very common to use rolling files for your log entries. By using this idea, we can have indices that are similar to rolling files.

We can define some conditions to be checked and leave it to Elasticsearch to roll new indices automatically and refer the use of an alias just to a **virtual** index.

Getting ready

You need an up-and-running Elasticsearch installation, as we described in *Downloading and installing Elasticsearch* recipe in `Chapter 1`, *Getting Started*.

To execute these commands, HTTP clients can be used, such as curl (`https://curl.haxx.se/`), postman (`https://www.getpostman.com/`), or others. I suggest using the Kibana console as it provides code completion and better character escaping for Elasticsearch.

How to do it...

To enable a rolling index, we need an index with an alias that points to it alone. For example, to set a log rolling index, we would follow these steps:

1. We need an index with a `logs_write` alias that points to it alone:

```
PUT /mylogs-000001
{
  "aliases": {
    "logs_write": {}
  }
}
```

The result will be an acknowledgement, as follows:

```
{
  "acknowledged" : true,
  "shards_acknowledged" : true,
  "index" : "mylogs-000001"
}
```

2. We can add the rolling to the `logs_write` alias in this way:

```
POST /logs_write/_rollover
{
  "conditions": {
    "max_age": "7d",
    "max_docs": 100000
  },
  "settings": {
    "index.number_of_shards": 3
  }
}
```

The result will be as follows:

```
{
  "acknowledged" : false,
  "shards_acknowledged" : false,
  "old_index" : "mylogs-000001",
  "new_index" : "mylogs-000002",
  "rolled_over" : false,
  "dry_run" : false,
  "conditions" : {
    "[max_docs: 100000]" : false,
    "[max_age: 7d]" : false
  }
}
```

3. In case your alias doesn't point to a single index, a similar error is returned:

```
{
"error" : {
"root_cause" : [
{
"type" : "illegal_argument_exception",
"reason" : "source alias maps to multiple indices
}
],
"type" : "illegal_argument_exception",
"reason" : "source alias maps to multiple indices"
},
"status" : 400
}
```

How it works...

The rolling index is a special alias that manages the auto-creation of new indices when one of the conditions is matched.

This is a very convenient functionality because it is completely managed by Elasticsearch, reducing the need for a lot of custom backend user code.

The information for creating the new index is taken from the source, but you can also apply custom settings at the creation of the index.

The naming convention is managed by Elasticsearch, which automatically increments the numeric part of the index name (by default, it uses six ending digits).

See also

Refer to the *Using index aliases* recipe in this chapter to manage aliases for indices.

Indexing a document

In Elasticsearch, there are two vital operations: **index** and **search**.

Indexing means storing one or more documents in an index: a similar concept to inserting records in a relational database.

In Lucene, the core engine of Elasticsearch, inserting or updating a document has the same cost: in Lucene and Elasticsearch, to update means to replace.

Getting ready

You need an up-and-running Elasticsearch installation, as we described in the *Downloading and installing Elasticsearch* recipe in Chapter 1, *Getting Started*.

To execute these commands, HTTP clients can be used, such as curl (https://curl.haxx.se/), postman (https://www.getpostman.com/), or others. I suggest using the Kibana console as it provides code completion and better character escaping for Elasticsearch.

To execute the following commands correctly, use the index and mapping we created in the *Putting a mapping in an index* recipe.

How to do it...

To index a document, several REST entry points can be used:

Method	URL
POST	`http://<server>/<index_name>/_doc`
PUT/POST	`http://<server>/<index_name>/_doc /<id>`
PUT/POST	`http://<server>/<index_name>/_doc/<id>/_create`

To index a document, we need to perform the following steps:

1. If we consider the `order` type of the previous chapter, the call to index a document will be as follows:

```
POST /myindex/_doc/2qLrAfPVQvCRMe7Ku8r0Tw
{
  "id": "1234",
  "date": "2013-06-07T12:14:54",
  "customer_id": "customer1",
  "sent": true,
  "in_stock_items": 0,
  "items": [
    {
      "name": "item1",
      "quantity": 3,
      "vat": 20
    },
    {
      "name": "item2",
      "quantity": 2,
      "vat": 20
    },
    {
      "name": "item3",
      "quantity": 1,
      "vat": 10
    }
  ]
}
```

2. If the index operation was successful, the result returned by Elasticsearch should be as follows:

```
{
  "_index" : "myindex",
  "_type" : "_doc",
```

```
    "_id" : "2qLrAfPVQvCRMe7Ku8r0Tw",
    "_version" : 1,
    "result" : "created",
    "_shards" : {
      "total" : 2,
      "successful" : 1,
      "failed" : 0
    },
    "_seq_no" : 0,
    "_primary_term" : 1
}
```

Some additional information is returned from the index operation, such as the following:

- An auto-generated ID if it's not specified (in this example: 2qLrAfPVQvCRMe7Ku8r0Tw)
- The version of the indexed document as per the optimistic concurrency control (the version is 1 because it was the document's first time of saving or updating)
- Whether the record has been created ("result": "create" in this example)

How it works...

One of the most used APIs in Elasticsearch is the index. Basically, indexing a JSON document consists internally of the following steps:

1. Routing the call to the correct shard based on the ID, or routing, or parent metadata. If the ID is not supplied by the client, a new one is created (see the *Managing your data* recipe in Chapter 1, *Getting Started*, for details).
2. Validating the sent JSON.
3. Processing the JSON according to the mapping. If new fields are present in the document (and the mapping can be updated), new fields are added in the mapping.
4. Indexing the document in the shard. If the ID already exists, it is updated.
5. If it contains nested documents, it extracts them, and it processes them separately.
6. Returning information about the saved document (ID and versioning).

It's important to choose the correct ID for indexing your data. If you don't provide an ID, during the indexing phase, Elasticsearch will automatically associate a new one to your document. To improve performance, the ID should generally be of the same character length to improve the balancing of the data tree that stores them.

Due to the REST call nature, it's better to pay attention when not using ASCII characters due to URL encoding and decoding (or be sure that the client framework you use correctly escapes them).

Depending on the mappings, other actions take place during the indexing phase: propagation on replica, nested processing, and percolator.

The document will be available for standard search calls after a refresh (forced with an API call or after the time slice of 1 second, near real-time): not every GET API on the document requires a refresh, and these can be instantly available.

The refresh can also be forced by specifying the `refresh` parameter during indexing.

There's more...

Elasticsearch allows you to pass the index API URL to several query parameters to control how the document is indexed. The most used ones are as follows:

- `routing`: This controls the shard to be used for indexing, that is:

    ```
    POST /myindex/_doc?routing=1
    ```

- `consistency(one/quorum/all)`: By default, an index operation succeeds if a quorum (`>replica/2+1`) of active shards is available. The right consistency value can be changed for index action:

    ```
    POST /myindex/_doc?consistency=one
    ```

- `replication (sync/async)`: Elasticsearch returns from an index operation when all the shards of the current replication group have executed the index operation. Setting the `async` replication allows us to execute the index action synchronously only on the primary shard and asynchronously on secondary shards. In this way, the API call returns the response action faster:

    ```
    POST /myindex/_doc?replication=async
    ```

- `version`: The version allows us to use the **optimistic concurrency control** (`http://en.wikipedia.org/wiki/Optimistic_concurrency_control`). The first time index of a document, its version 1, is set on the document. At every update, this value is incremented. Optimistic concurrency control is a way to manage concurrency in every insert or update operation. The passed version value is the last seen version (usually returned by a get or a search). The index happens only if the current index version value is equal to the passed one:

```
POST /myindex/_doc?version=2
```

- `op_type`: This can be used to force a `create` on a document. If a document with the same ID exists, the index fails:

```
POST /myindex/_doc?op_type=create
```

- `refresh`: This forces a refresh after having indexed the document. It allows documents to be ready for searching after their indexing:

```
POST /myindex/_doc?refresh=true
```

- `timeout`: This defines a time to wait for the primary shard to be available. Sometimes, the primary shard is not in a writable status (if it's relocating or recovering from a gateway) and a timeout for the write operation is raised after 1 minute:

```
POST /myindex/_doc?timeout=5m
```

See also

You can view the following recipes for further reference, which are related to this recipe:

- The *Getting a document* recipe in this chapter to learn how to retrieve a stored document
- The *Deleting a document* recipe in this chapter to learn how to delete a document
- The *Updating a document* recipe in this chapter to learn how to update fields in a document
- For *optimistic concurrency control*, that is, the Elasticsearch way to manage concurrency on a document, a good reference place can be found at `http://en.wikipedia.org/wiki/Optimistic_concurrency_control`.

Getting a document

After having indexed a document, during your application's life, it will probably need to be retrieved.

The GET REST call allows us to get a document in real time without the need for a refresh.

Getting ready

You need an up-and-running Elasticsearch installation, as we described in the *Downloading and installing Elasticsearch* recipe in `Chapter 1`, *Getting Started*.

To execute these commands, HTTP clients can be used, such as curl (`https://curl.haxx.se/`), postman (`https://www.getpostman.com/`), or others. I suggest using the Kibana console as it provides code completion and better character escaping for Elasticsearch.

To execute the following commands correctly, use the indexed document in the *Indexing a document* recipe.

How to do it...

The `GET` method allows us to return a document given its index, type, and ID.

The REST API URL is as follows:

```
http://<server>/<index_name>/_doc/<id>
```

To get a document, we will perform the following steps:

1. If we consider the document that we indexed in the previous recipe, the call will be as follows:

   ```
   GET /myindex/_doc/2qLrAfPVQvCRMe7Ku8r0Tw
   ```

2. The result returned by Elasticsearch should be the indexed document:

   ```
   {
     "_index" : "myindex",
     "_type" : "_doc",
     "_id" : "2qLrAfPVQvCRMe7Ku8r0Tw",
     "_version" : 1,
   ```

```
      "_seq_no" : 0,
      "_primary_term" : 1,
      "found" : true,
      "_source" : {
        "id" : "1234",
        "date" : "2013-06-07T12:14:54",
        "customer_id" : "customer1",
        ... truncated ...
      }
    }
```

3. Our indexed data is contained in the _source parameter, but other information is returned:

   - _index: The index that stores the document
   - _type: The type of the document
   - _id: The ID of the document
   - _version: The version of the document
   - found: Whether the document has been found

If the record is missing, a 404 error is returned as the status code, and the return JSON will be as follows:

```
{
  "_index" : "myindex",
  "_type" : "_doc",
  "_id" : "2qLrAfPVQvCRMe7Kud8r0Tw",
  "found" : false
}
```

How it works...

The Elasticsearch GET API on the document doesn't require a refresh: all the GET calls are in real time.

This call is very fast because Elasticsearch redirects the search only on the shard that contains the document without another overhead, and the document IDs are often cached in memory for fast lookup.

The source of the document is only available if the _source field is stored (as per the default settings in Elasticsearch).

There are several additional parameters that can be used to control the get call:

- `_source` allows us to retrieve only a subset of fields. This is very useful for reducing bandwidth or for retrieving calculated fields such as the attachment-mapping ones:

      GET /myindex/_doc/2qLrAfPVQvCRMe7Ku8r0Tw?_source=date,sent

- `stored_fields`, similar to source, allows us to retrieve only a subset of fields that are marked as `stored` in the mapping. Stored fields are kept in a separated memory portion of the index, and they can be retrieved without parsing the JSON source:

      GET
      /myindex/_doc/2qLrAfPVQvCRMe7Ku8r0Tw?stored_fields=date,sent

- `routing` allows us to specify the shard to be used for the get operation. To retrieve a document, the routing used in indexing time must be the same as the search time:

      GET /myindex/_doc/2qLrAfPVQvCRMe7Ku8r0Tw?routing=customer_id

- `refresh` allows us to refresh the current shard before performing the get operation (it must be used with care because it slows down indexing and introduces some overhead):

      GET /myindex/_doc/2qLrAfPVQvCRMe7Ku8r0Tw?refresh=true

- `preference` allows us to control which shard replica is chosen to execute the GET method. Generally, Elasticsearch chooses a random shard for the GET call. The possible values are as follows:
    - `_primary` for the primary shard.
    - `_local`, first trying the local shard and then falling back to a random choice. Using the local shard reduces the bandwidth usage and should generally be used with auto-replicating shards (replica set to 0-all).
    - `custom value` for selecting a shard-related value, such as `customer_id` and `username`.

There's more...

The GET API is very fast, so a good practice when developing applications is to try and use it as much as possible. Choosing the correct ID form during application development can bring a big boost in performance.

If the shard, which contains the document, is not bound to an ID, a query with an ID filter (we will see them in Chapter 6, *Text and Numeric Queries*, in the *Using an IDS query* recipe) is required to fetch the document.

If you don't need to fetch the record, and only want to check for its existence, you can replace GET with HEAD, and the response will be status code 200 if it exists, or 404 if it is missing.

The GET call also has a special endpoint, _source, that allows for the fetching of only the source of the document.

The GET source REST API URL is as follows:

```
http://<server>/<index_name>/_doc/<id>/_source
```

To fetch the source of the previous order, we will call the following:

```
GET /myindex/_doc/2qLrAfPVQvCRMe7Ku8r0Tw/_source
```

See also

Refer to the *Speeding up the GET operation* recipe in this chapter to learn how to execute multiple GET operations in one go to reduce fetching time.

Deleting a document

Deleting documents in Elasticsearch is possible in two ways: using the DELETE call or the delete_by_query call, which we'll look at in the next chapter.

Getting ready

You need an up-and-running Elasticsearch installation, as we described in the *Downloading and installing Elasticsearch* recipe in Chapter 1, *Getting Started*.

To execute these commands, HTTP clients can be used such as curl (`https://curl.haxx.se/`), postman (`https://www.getpostman.com/`), or others. I suggest using the Kibana console as it provides code completion and better character escaping for Elasticsearch.

To execute the following commands correctly, use the indexed document in the *Indexing a document* recipe.

How to do it...

The REST API URL is the same as the GET calls, but the HTTP method is DELETE:

```
http://<server>/<index_name>/_doc/<id>
```

To delete a document, we will perform the following steps:

1. If we consider the `order` indexed in the *Indexing a document* recipe, the call to delete a document will be as follows:

```
DELETE /myindex/_doc/2qLrAfPVQvCRMe7Ku8r0Tw
```

2. The result returned by Elasticsearch should be as follows:

```
{
  "_index" : "myindex",
  "_type" : "_doc",
  "_id" : "2qLrAfPVQvCRMe7Ku8r0Tw",
  "_version" : 2,
  "result" : "deleted",
  "_shards" : {
    "total" : 2,
    "successful" : 1,
    "failed" : 0
  },
  "_seq_no" : 3,
  "_primary_term" : 1
}
```

3. If the record is missing, a `404` is returned as the status code, and the return JSON will be as follows:

```
{
  "_index" : "myindex",
  "_type" : "_doc",
  "_id" : "2qLrAfPVQvCRMe7Ku8r0Tw",
```

```
      "_version" : 3,
      "result" : "not_found",
      "_shards" : {
        "total" : 2,
        "successful" : 1,
        "failed" : 0
      },
      "_seq_no" : 4,
      "_primary_term" : 1
    }
```

How it works...

Deleting records only hits shards that contain documents, so there is no overhead. If the document is a child, the parent must be set to look for the correct shard.

There are several additional parameters that can be used to control the delete call. The most important ones are as follows:

- `routing`, which allows you to specify the shard to be used for the delete operation
- `version`, which allows you to define a version of the document to be deleted to prevent modification of that document

The `DELETE` operation has to restore functionality. Every document that is deleted is lost forever.

Deleting a record is a fast operation and very easy to use if the IDs of the documents to delete are available. Otherwise, we must use the `delete_by_query` call, which we will look at in the next chapter.

See also

Refer to the *Deleting by query* recipe in Chapter 4, *Exploring Search Capabilities,* to delete a bunch of documents that match a query.

Updating a document

Documents stored in Elasticsearch can be updated during their lives. There are two available solutions for performing this operation in Elasticsearch: adding a new document, or using the update call.

The update call can work in two ways:

- By providing a script that uses the update strategy
- By providing a document that must be merged with the original one

The main advantage of an update versus an index is the networking reduction.

Getting ready

You need an up-and-running Elasticsearch installation, as we described in the *Downloading and installing Elasticsearch* recipe in `Chapter 1`, *Getting Started*.

To execute these commands, HTTP clients can be used, such as curl (`https://curl.haxx.se/`), postman (`https://www.getpostman.com/`), or others. I suggest using the Kibana console as it provides code completion and better character escaping for Elasticsearch.

To execute the following commands correctly, use the indexed document in the *Indexing a document* recipe.

To use dynamic scripting languages, they must be enabled. See `Chapter 9`, *Managing Cluster*, for more information.

How to do it...

Since we are changing the state of the data, the HTTP method is `POST` and the REST URL is as follows:

```
http://<server>/<index_name>/_update/<id>
```

 The REST format is changed by the previous version of Elasticsearch.

To update a document, we will perform the following steps:

1. If we consider the type order of the previous recipe, the call to update a document will be as follows:

```
POST /myindex/_update/2qLrAfPVQvCRMe7Ku8r0Tw
{
  "script": {
    "source": "ctx._source.in_stock_items += params.count",
    "params": {
      "count": 4
    }
  }
}
```

2. If the request is successful, the result returned by Elasticsearch should be as follows:

```
{
  "_index" : "myindex",
  "_type" : "_doc",
  "_id" : "2qLrAfPVQvCRMe7Ku8r0Tw",
  "_version" : 4,
  "result" : "updated",
  "_shards" : {
    "total" : 2,
    "successful" : 1,
    "failed" : 0
  },
  "_seq_no" : 8,
  "_primary_term" : 1
}
```

3. The record will be as follows:

```
{
  "_index" : "myindex",
  "_type" : "_doc",
  "_id" : "2qLrAfPVQvCRMe7Ku8r0Tw",
  "_version" : 8,
  "_seq_no" : 12,
  "_primary_term" : 1,
  "found" : true,
  "_source" : {
    "id" : "1234",
    "date" : "2013-06-07T12:14:54",
    "customer_id" : "customer1",
    "sent" : true,
```

```
        "in_stock_items" : 4,
    ... truncated ...
      }
}
```

The visible changes are as follows:

- The scripted field has been changed
- The version has been incremented

How it works...

The update operation takes a document, applies the changes required in the script or in the update document to this document, and then reindexes the changed document. In Chapter 8, *Scripting in Elasticsearch*, we will explore the scripting capabilities of Elasticsearch.

The standard language for scripting in Elasticsearch is **Painless**, and it's used in these examples.

The script can operate on ctx._source: the source of the document (it must be stored to work), and it can change the document in situ. It's possible to pass parameters to a script by passing a JSON object. These parameters are available in the execution context.

A script can control Elasticsearch behavior after the script's execution by setting ctx.op value of the context. The available values are as follows:

- ctx.op="delete" by which the document will be deleted after the script's execution.
- ctx.op="none" by which the document will skip the indexing process. A good practice to improve performance is to set ctx.op="none" so that the script doesn't update the document, thus preventing a reindexing overhead.

ctx also manages the timestamp of the record in ctx._timestamp. It's possible to pass an additional object in the upsert property, which will be used if the document is not available in the index:

```
POST /myindex/_update/2qLrAfPVQvCRMe7Ku8r0Tw
{
  "script": {
    "source": "ctx._source.in_stock_items += params.count",
```

```
      "params": {
        "count": 4
      }
    },
    "upsert": {
      "in_stock_items": 4
    }
  }
```

If you need to replace some field values, a good solution is not to write a complex update script, but to use the special property doc, which allows us to overwrite the values of an object. The document provided in the doc parameter will be merged with the original one. This approach is easier to use, but it cannot set ctx.op, so if the update doesn't change the value of the original document, the next successive phase will always be executed:

```
POST /myindex/_update/2qLrAfPVQvCRMe7Ku8r0Tw
{
  "doc": {
    "in_stock_items": 10
  }
}
```

If the original document is missing, it is possible to provide a doc value (the document to be created) for an upsert as a doc_as_upsert parameter:

```
POST /myindex/_update/2qLrAfPVQvCRMe7Ku8r0Tw
{
  "doc": {
    "in_stock_items": 10
  },
  "doc_as_upsert": true
}
```

Using Painless scripting, it is possible to apply advanced operations on fields, such as the following:

- Remove a field, that is:

```
"script" : {"inline": "ctx._source.remove("myfield"}}
```

- Add a new field, that is:

```
"script" : {"inline": "ctx._source.myfield=myvalue"}}
```

The update REST call is very useful because it has some advantages:

- It reduces bandwidth usage because the update operation doesn't need a round trip to the client of the data
- It's safer, because it automatically manages the optimistic concurrent control: if a change happens during script execution, the script that it's re-executed with updates the data
- It can be bulk-executed

See also

Refer to the following recipe, *Speeding up atomic operations*, to learn how to use bulk operations to reduce the networking load and speed up ingestion.

Speeding up atomic operations (bulk operations)

When we are inserting, deleting, or updating a large number of documents, the HTTP overhead is significant. To speed up this process, Elasticsearch allows the execution of the bulk of CRUD calls.

Getting ready

You need an up-and-running Elasticsearch installation, as we described in the *Downloading and installing Elasticsearch* recipe in `Chapter 1`, *Getting Started*.

To execute these commands, HTTP clients can be used, such as curl (`https://curl.haxx.se/`), postman (`https://www.getpostman.com/`), or others. I suggest using the Kibana console as it provides code completion and better character escaping for Elasticsearch.

How to do it...

As we are changing the state of the data, the HTTP method is `POST` and the REST URL is as follows:

```
http://<server>/<index_name/_bulk
```

To execute a bulk action, we will perform the following steps via curl (because it's very common to prepare your data on files and send them to Elasticsearch via the command line):

1. We need to collect the `create`/`index`/`delete`/`update` commands in a structure made of bulk JSON lines, composed of a line of action with metadata, and another optional line of data related to the action. Every line must end with a new line \n. A bulk data file should be presented like this:

    ```
    { "index":{ "_index":"myindex", "_id":"1" } }
    { "field1" : "value1", "field2" : "value2" }
    { "delete":{ "_index":"myindex", "_id":"2" } }
    { "create":{ "_index":"myindex", "_id":"3" } }
    { "field1" : "value1", "field2" : "value2" }
    { "update":{ "_index":"myindex", "_id":"3" } }
    { "doc":{"field1" : "value1", "field2" : "value2" }}
    ```

2. This file can be sent with the following POST:

    ```
    curl -s -XPOST localhost:9200/_bulk --data-binary @bulkdata;
    ```

3. The result returned by Elasticsearch should collect all the responses of the actions.

    You can execute the previous commands in Kibana with the following call:

    ```
    POST /_bulk
    { "index":{ "_index":"myindex", "_id":"1" } }
    { "field1" : "value1", "field2" : "value2" }
    { "delete":{ "_index":"myindex", "_id":"2" } }
    { "create":{ "_index":"myindex", "_id":"3" } }
    { "field1" : "value1", "field2" : "value2" }
    { "update":{ "_index":"myindex", "_id":"3" } }
    { "doc":{"field1" : "value1", "field2" : "value2" }}
    ```

How it works...

The bulk operation allows for the aggregation of different calls as a single one: a header part with the action to be performed, and a body for other operations such as `index`, `create`, and `update`.

The header is composed of the action name and the object of its parameters. Looking at the previous index example, we have the following:

```
{ "index":{ "_index":"myindex", "_id":"1" } }
```

For indexing and creating, an extra body is required with the data:

```
{ "field1" : "value1", "field2" : "value2" }
```

The `delete` action doesn't require optional data, so only the header composes it:

```
{ "delete":{ "_index":"myindex", "_id":"1" } }
```

At least, it is possible use an update action in a bulk with a format similar to the `index` one:

```
{ "update":{ "_index":"myindex", "_id":"3" } }
```

The header accepts all the common parameters of the update action, such as `doc`, `upsert`, `doc_as_upsert`, `lang`, `script`, and `params`. For controlling the number of retries in the case of concurrency, the bulk update defines the `_retry_on_conflict` parameter, set to the number of retries to be performed, before raising an exception.

So, a possible body for the update would be as follows:

```
{ "doc":{"field1" : "value1", "field2" : "value2" }}
```

The bulk item can accept several parameters, such as the following:

- `routing`, to control the routing shard.
- `parent`, to select a parent item shard. This is required if you are indexing some child documents. Global bulk parameters that can be passed using query arguments are as follows:
    - `consistency` (`one`, `quorum`, `all`) (default `quorum`), which controls the number of active shards before executing write operations.
    - `refresh` (default `false`), which forces a refresh in the shards involved in bulk operations. The newly indexed document will be available immediately, without having to wait for the standard refresh interval (1s).
    - `pipeline`, which forces an index using the ingest pipeline provided.

 Previous versions of Elasticsearch required users to pass the `_type` value, but this was removed in version 7.x due to `type removal`.

Usually, Elasticsearch client libraries that use the Elasticsearch REST API automatically implement a serialization of bulk commands.

The correct number of commands to serialize in a bulk execution is a user choice, but there are some things to consider:

- In standard configuration, Elasticsearch limits the HTTP call to 100 MB in size. If the size is over that limit, the call is rejected.
- Multiple complex commands take a lot of time to be processed, so pay attention to client timeout.
- The small size of commands in a bulk doesn't improve performance.

If the documents aren't big, 500 commands in a bulk can be a good number to start with, and it can be tuned depending on data structures (number of fields, number of nested objects, complexity of fields, and so on).

Speeding up GET operations (multi GET)

The standard GET operation is very fast, but if you need to fetch a lot of documents by ID, Elasticsearch provides the multi GET operation.

Getting ready

You need an up-and-running Elasticsearch installation, as we described in the *Downloading and installing Elasticsearch* recipe in Chapter 1, *Getting Started*.

To execute these commands, HTTP clients can be used, such as curl (https://curl.haxx.se/), postman (https://www.getpostman.com/), or others similar. I suggest using the Kibana console as it provides code completion and better character escaping for Elasticsearch.

To execute the following commands correctly, use the indexed document we created in the *Indexing a document* recipe.

How to do it...

The multi GET REST URLs are as follows:

```
http://<server</_mget
http://<server>/<index_name>/_mget
```

To execute a multi GET action, we will perform the following steps:

1. The method is POST with a body that contains a list of document IDs and the index or type if they are missing. As an example, using the first URL, we need to provide the index, type, and ID:

```
POST /_mget
{
  "docs": [
    {
      "_index": "myindex",
      "_id": "2qLrAfPVQvCRMe7Ku8r0Tw"
    },
    {
      "_index": "myindex",
      "_id": "2"
    }
  ]
}
```

This kind of call allows us to fetch documents in several different indices and types.

2. If the index and the type are fixed, a call should also be in the following form:

```
GET /myindex/_mget
{
"ids" : ["1", "2"]
}
```

The multi GET result is an array of documents.

How it works...

Multi GET calling is a shortcut for executing many get commands in one shot.

Internally, Elasticsearch spreads the get in parallel on several shards and collects the results to return to the user.

The get object can contain the following parameters:

- _index: The index that contains the document. It can be omitted if passed in the URL.
- _id: The document ID.
- stored_fields: (optional) A list of fields to retrieve.
- _source: (optional) Source filter object.
- routing: (optional) The shard routing parameter.

The advantages of a multi GET are as follows:

- Reduced networking traffic, both internally and externally for Elasticsearch
- Increased speed if used in an application: the time for processing a multi GET is quite similar to a standard get

See also...

Refer to the *Getting a document* recipe in this chapter to learn how to execute a simple get and for the general parameters of a GET call.

Exploring Search Capabilities

4

Now that we have set the mappings and put the data in the indices, we can start exploring the search capabilities in Elasticsearch. In this chapter, we will cover searching using different factors: sorting, highlighting, scrolling, suggesting, counting, and deleting. These actions are the core part of Elasticsearch; ultimately, everything in Elasticsearch is about serving the query and returning good-quality results.

This chapter is divided into two parts: the first part shows how to perform an API call-related search, and the second part will look at two special query operators that are the basis for building complex queries in the following chapters.

In this chapter, we will cover the following recipes:

- Executing a search
- Sorting results
- Highlighting results
- Executing a scrolling query
- Using the search_after functionality
- Returning inner hits in results
- Suggesting a correct query
- Counting matched results
- Explaining a query
- Query profiling
- Deleting by query
- Updating by query
- Matching all the documents
- Using a Boolean query
- Using the search template

Technical requirements

All the recipes in this chapter require us to prepare and populate the required indices—the online code is available on the PacktPub website or via GitHub (`https:/ /github.com/aparo/elasticsearch-7.x-cookbook`). Here, you can find scripts to initialize all the required data.

Executing a search

Elasticsearch was born as a search engine; its main purpose is to process queries and give results as fast as possible. In this recipe, we'll see that a search in Elasticsearch is not only limited to matching documents - it can also calculate additional information that's required to improve the search quality.

Getting ready

You need an up-and-running Elasticsearch installation, as we described in the *Downloading and installing Elasticsearch* recipe in Chapter 1, *Getting Started*.

To execute these commands any, HTTP client can be used such, as curl (`https:// curl.haxx.se/`), postman (`https://www.getpostman.com/`), or something similar. I suggest using the Kibana console as it provides code completion and better character escaping for Elasticsearch.

 To correctly execute the following commands, you will need an index populated with the `ch04/populate_kibana.txt` commands, which is available in the online code.

The mapping that's used in all the queries in this chapter and searches is similar to the following book representation:

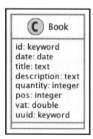

The command to create the schema is as follows:

```
PUT /mybooks
{
  "mappings": {
    "properties": {
      "join_field": {
        "type": "join",
        "relations": {
          "order": "item"
...
...

      "title": {
        "term_vector": "with_positions_offsets",
        "store": true,
        "type": "text",
        "fielddata": true,
        "fields": {
          "keyword": {
            "type": "keyword",
            "ignore_above": 256
          }
        }
      }
    }
  }
}
```

How to do it...

To execute the search and view the results, we will perform the following steps:

1. From the command line, we can execute a search as follows:

```
GET /mybooks/_search
{
  "query": {
    "match_all": {}
  }
}
```

In this case, we have used a match_all query that returns all the documents. We'll discuss this kind of query in the *Matching all the documents* recipe in this chapter.

2. If everything works, the command will return the following:

```
{
    "took" : 0,
    "timed_out" : false,
    "_shards" : {
      "total" : 1,
      "successful" : 1,
      "skipped" : 0,
      "failed" : 0
    },
    "hits" : {
      "total" : 3,
      "max_score" : 1.0,
      "hits" : [
...
...

          "_index" : "mybooks",
          "_type" : "_doc",
          "_id" : "3",
          "_score" : 1.0,
          "_source" : {...truncated...}
        }
      ]
    }
}
```

These results contain the following information:

- took is the milliseconds of time required to execute the query.
- time_out indicates whether a timeout occurred during the search. This is related to the timeout parameter of the search. If a timeout occurs, you will get partial or no results.
- _shards is the status of shards divided into the following sections:
  - total, which is the number of shards
  - successful, which is the number of shards in which the query was successful
  - skipped, which is the number of shards that are skipped during the search (for example, if you are searching more than 720 shards simultaneously)
  - failed, which is the number of shards in which the query failed, because some error or exception occurred during the query

- `hits` are the results, and are composed of the following:
    - `total` is the number of documents that match the query.
    - `max_score` is the match score of first document. It is usually one if no match scoring was computed, for example, in sorting or filtering.
    - `hits`, which is a list of result documents.

The resulting document has a lot of fields that are always available and others that depend on search parameters. The most important fields are as follows:

- `_index`: The index that contains the document.
- `_type`: The type of the document (that is, `_doc`). It will disappear in future ES versions.
- `_id`: The ID of the document.
- `_source`: The document source—the original `json` sent to Elasticsearch.
- `_score`: Query score of the document (if the query doesn't require a score, it's 1.0).
- `sort`: If the document is sorted, values that are used for sorting.
- `highlight`: Highlighted segments if highlighting was requested.
- `stored_fields`: Some fields can be retrieved without needing to fetch the source object.
- `script_fields`: Some fields that can be computed using scripting.

How it works...

The search in Elasticsearch is a distributed computation composed of many steps, and the main ones are as follows:

1. In the master or coordinator nodes, validation of the query body is needed
2. A selection of indices to be used in the query are needed; the shards are randomly chosen
3. Execution of the query part in data nodes that collects the top hits or the query
4. Aggregation of results in the master and coordinator nodes, as well as scoring
5. Return the results to the user

The following diagram shows how the query is distributed in the cluster:

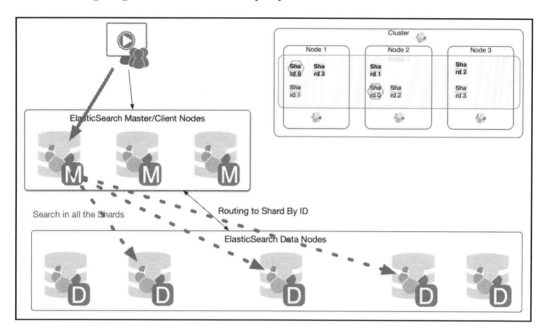

The HTTP method to execute a search is GET (although POST also works); the REST endpoints are as follows:

```
http://<server>/_search
http://<server>/<index_name(s)>/_search
```

 Not all HTTP clients allow you to send data through a GET call, so the best practice, if you need to send body data, is to use the POST call.

Multi-indices and types are comma-separated. If an index or a type is defined, the search is limited only to them. One or more aliases can be used as index names.

The core query is usually contained in the body of the GET/POST call, but a lot of options can also be expressed as URI **query parameters**, such as the following:

- q: This is the query string to perform simple string queries, which can be done as follows:

  ```
  GET /mybooks/_search?q=uuid:11111
  ```

- `df`: This is the default field to be used within the query and can be done as follows:

```
GET /mybooks/_search?df=uuid&q=11111
```

- `from` (the default value is 0): The start index of the hits.
- `size` (the default value is 10): The number of hits to be returned.
- `analyzer`: The default analyzer to be used.
- `default_operator` (the default value is OR): This can be set to AND or OR.
- `explain`: This allows the user to return information about how the score is calculated. It is calculated as follows:

```
GET /mybooks/_search?q=title:joe&explain=true
```

- `stored_fields`: These allow the user to define fields that must be returned, and can be done as follows:

```
GET /mybooks/_search?q=title:joe&stored_fields=title
```

- `sort` (the default value is score): This allows the user to change the documents in order. Sort is ascendant by default; if you need to change the order, add desc to the field, as follows:

```
GET /mybooks/_search?sort=title.keyword:desc
```

- `timeout` (not active by default): This defines the timeout for the search. Elasticsearch tries to collect results until a timeout. If a timeout is fired, all the hits that have been accumulated are returned.
- `search_type`: This defines the search strategy. A reference is available in the online Elasticsearch documentation at https://www.elastic.co/guide/en/elasticsearch/reference/current/search-request-search-type.html.
- `track_scores` (the default value is false): If true, this tracks the score and allows it to be returned with the hits. It's used in conjunction with sort because sorting by default prevents the return of a match score.
- `pretty` (the default value is false): If true, the results will be pretty-printed.

Generally, the query contained in the body of the search is a JSON object. The body of the search is the core of Elasticsearch's search functionalities; the list of search capabilities extends in every release. For the current version (7.x) of Elasticsearch, the available parameters are as follows:

- `query`: This contains the query to be executed. Later in this chapter, we will see how to create different kinds of queries to cover several scenarios.
- `from`: This allows the user to control pagination. The `from` parameter defines the start position of the hits to be returned (default 0) and `size` (default 10).

> The pagination is applied to the currently returned search results. Firing the same query can bring different results if a lot of records have the same score, or a new document is ingested. If you need to process all the result documents without repetition, you need to execute `scan` or `scroll` queries.

- `sort`: This allows the user to change the order of the matched documents. This option is fully covered in the *Sorting results* recipe.
- `post_filter`: This allows the user to filter out the query results without affecting the aggregation count. It's usually used for filtering by facet values.
- `_source`: This allows the user to control the returned source. It can be disabled (`false`), partially returned (`obj.*`), or use multiple exclude/include rules. This functionality can be used instead of fields to return values (for complete coverage of this, take a look at the online Elasticsearch reference at `http://www.elasticsearch.org/guide/en/elasticsearch/reference/current/search-request-source-filtering.html`).
- `filedata_fields`: This allows the user to return a field data representation of the field.
- `stored_fields`: This controls the fields to be returned.

Returning only the required fields reduces the network and memory usage, thus improving performance. The suggested way to retrieve custom fields is to use the _source filtering function because it doesn't need to use Elasticsearch's extra resources.

- aggregations/aggs: These control the aggregation layer analytics. These will be discussed in the next chapter.
- index_boost: This allows the user to define the per-index boost value. It is used to increase/decrease the score of results in boosted indices.
- highlighting: This allows the user to define fields and settings to be used for calculating a query abstract (see the *Highlighting results* recipe in this chapter).
- version (the default value false) This adds the version of a document in the results.
- rescore: This allows the user to define an extra query to be used in the score to improve the quality of the results. The rescore query is executed on the hits that match the first query and filter.
- min_score: If this is given, all the result documents that have a score lower than this value are rejected.
- explain: This returns information on how the TD/IF score is calculated for a particular document.
- script_fields: This defines a script that computes extra fields via scripting to be returned with a hit. We'll look at Elasticsearch scripting in Chapter 8, *Scripting in Elasticsearch*.
- suggest: If given a query and a field, this returns the most significant terms related to this query. This parameter allows the user to implement the Google-like *do you mean* functionality similar to Google one (see the *Suggesting a correct query* recipe).
- search_type: This defines how Elasticsearch should process a query. We'll see the scrolling query in the *Executing a scrolling query* recipe in this chapter.
- scroll: This controls the scrolling in scroll/scan queries. scroll allows the user to have an Elasticsearch equivalent of a DBMS cursor.
- _name: This allows returns for every hit that matches the named queries. It's very useful if you have a Boolean and you want the name of the matched query.

- `search_after`: This allows the user to skip results using the most efficient way of scrolling. We'll see this functionality in the *Using search_after functionality* recipe in this chapter.
- `preference`: This allows the user to select which shard/s to use for executing the query.

There's more...

To improve the quality of the results score, Elasticsearch provides the `rescore` functionality. This capability allows the user to reorder a top number of documents with another query that's generally much more expensive (CPU or time-consuming), for example, if the query contains a lot of match queries or scripting. This approach allows the user to execute the `rescore` query on just a small subset of results, reducing overall computation time and resources.

The `rescore` query, as for every query, is executed at shard level, so it's automatically distributed.

> The best candidates to be executed in the `rescore` query are complex queries with a lot of nested options, and everything that is used is scripting (due to the massive overhead of scripting languages).

The following example will show you how to execute a fast query (a Boolean one) in the first phase and then `rescore` query it with a `match` query in the `rescore` section:

```
POST /mybook/_search
{
  "query": {
    "match": {
      "description": {
        "operator": "or",
        "query": "nice guy joe"
      }
    }
  },
  "rescore": {
    "window_size": 100,
    "query": {
      "rescore_query": {
        "match_phrase": {
          "description": {
            "query": "joe nice guy",
```

```
                "slop": 2
              }
          }
      },
      "query_weight": 0.8,
      "rescore_query_weight": 1.5
    }
  }
}
```

The `rescore` parameters are as follows:

- `window_size`: The example is `100`. This controls how many results per shard must be considered in the `rescore` functionality.
- `query_weight`: The default value is `1.0`, and the `rescore_query_weight` default value is `1.0`. These are used to compute the final score using the following formula:

$$final\_score = query\_score * query\_weight + rescore\_score * rescore\_query\_weight$$

If a user wants to only keep the `rescore` score, they can set the `query_weight` to 0.

See also

You can view the following recipes for further reference, which are related to this recipe:

- *Executing an aggregation* recipe in Chapter 7, *Aggregations*, explains how to use the aggregation framework during queries
- *Highlighting results* recipe in this chapter explains how to use the highlighting functionality for improving the user experience in results
- *Executing a scrolling query* recipe in this chapter covers how to efficiently paginate results
- *Suggesting terms for a query* recipe in this chapter helps to correct text queries

Sorting results

When searching for results, the standard criterion for sorting in Elasticsearch is the relevance to a text query. Real-world applications often need to control the sorting criteria in scenarios, such as the following:

- Sorting a user by last name and first name
- Sorting items by stock symbols, price (ascending and descending)
- Sorting documents by size, file type, source, and so on
- Sorting item related maximum or minimum or average of some children fields

Getting ready

You need an up-and-running Elasticsearch installation, as we described in the *Downloading and installing Elasticsearch* recipe in `Chapter 1`, *Getting Started*.

To execute these commands, any HTTP client can be used, such as curl (`https://curl.haxx.se/`), postman (`https://www.getpostman.com/`), or similar. I suggest using the Kibana console as it provides the code completion and better character escaping for Elasticsearch.

To correctly execute the following commands, you will need an index populated with the `ch04/populate_kibana.txt` commands, which is available in the online code.

How to do it...

In order to sort the results, we will perform the following steps:

1. Add a sort section to your query, as follows:

```
GET /mybooks/_search
{
    "query": {
      "match_all": {}
    },
    "sort": [
      {
        "price": {
          "order": "asc",
          "mode": "avg",
```

```
            "unmapped_type": "double",
            "missing": "_last"
          }
        },
      "_score"
      ]
    }
```

2. The returned result should be similar to the following:

```
...truncated...
  "hits" : {
  "total" : 3,
  "max_score" : null,
  "hits" : [
    {
      "_index" : "mybooks",
      "_type" : "_doc",
      "_id" : "1",
      "_score" : 1.0,
      "_source" : {
        ...truncated...
        "price" : 4.3,
        "quantity" : 50
      },
      "sort" : [
        4.3,
        1.0
      ]

...truncated...
```

The sort result is very special—an extra `sort` field is created to collect the value that's used for sorting.

How it works...

The `sort` parameter can be defined as a list that can contain both simple strings and JSON objects. The sort strings are the names of the fields (such as `field1`, `field2`, `field3`, `field4`, and so on) that are used for sorting and are similar to the `order by` SQL function.

The JSON object allows users extra parameters, as follows:

- order (asc or desc): This defines whether the order must be considered ascendant (default) or descendent.
- unmapped_type (long or int or double or string, and so on): This defines the type of the sort parameter if the value is missing. It's a best practice to define it to prevent sorting errors due to missing values.
- missing (_last or _first): This defines how to manage missing values—whether to put them at the end (_last) of the results or at the start (_first).
- mode: This defines how to manage multi-value fields. The possible values are as follows:
    - min: The minimum value is chosen (that is to say that in the case of multi-price on an item, it chooses the lowest for comparison).
    - max: The maximum value is chosen.
    - sum: The sort value will be computed as the sum of all the values. This mode is only available on numeric array fields.
    - avg: The sort value will be the average of all the values. This mode is only available on numeric array fields.
    - median: The sort value will be the median of all the values. This mode is only available on numeric array fields.

If we want to add the relevance score value to the sort list, we must use the special _score sort field.

In case you are sorting for a nested object, there are two extra parameters that can be used, as follows:

- nested_path: This defines the nested object to be used for sorting. The field defined for sorting will be relative to the nested_path. If not defined, then the sorting field is related to the document root.
- nested_filter: This defines a filter that is used to remove nested documents that don't match from the sorting value extraction. This filter allows for a better selection of values to be used in sorting.

For example, if we have an `address` object nested in a `person` document and we can sort for the `city.name`, we can use the following:

- `address.city.name` without defining the `nested_path`
- `city.name` if we define a `nested_path` address

The sorting process requires that the sorting fields of all the matched query documents are fetched to be compared. To prevent high memory usage, its better to sort numeric fields, and in the case of string sorting, choose short text fields processed with an analyzer that doesn't tokenize the text.

There's more...

If you are using `sort`, pay attention to the tokenized fields, because the sort order depends on the lower order token if ascendant and the higher order token if descendent. In the case of tokenized fields, this behavior is not similar to a common sort because we execute it at term level.

For example, if we sort by the descending `title` field, we use the following:

```
GET /mybooks/_search?sort=title:desc
```

In the preceding example, the results are as follows:

```
{
  ...truncated...
    "hits" : {
      "total" : 3,
      "max_score" : null,
      "hits" : [
        {
          "_index" : "mybooks",
          "_type" : "_doc",
          "_id" : "1",
          "_score" : null,
          "_source" : {
            ...truncated...
              "title" : "Joe Tester",
            ...truncated...
  ...
  ...
            "sort" : [
              "bill"
```

```
          ]
        }
      ]
    }
  }
```

The expected SQL results can be obtained using a not-tokenized keyword field, in this case, `title.keyword`, as follows:

```
GET /mybooks/_search?sort=title.keyword:desc
```

The results are as follows:

```
{
   ...truncated...
    "hits" : {
      "total" : 3,
      "max_score" : null,
      "hits" : [
...
...
          "_index" : "mybooks",
          "_type" : "_doc",
          "_id" : "2",
          ...truncated...
          "sort" : [
            "Bill Baloney"
          ]
        }
      ]
    }
}
```

There are two special sorting types: **geo distance** and **scripting**.

Geo distance sorting uses the distance from a GeoPoint (location) as the metric to compute the ordering. A sorting example could be as follows:

```
...truncated...
  "sort" : [
    {
      "_geo_distance" : {
        "pin.location" : [-70, 40],
        "order" : "asc",
        "unit" : "km"
      }
    }
  ],
...truncated...
```

It accepts special parameters, such as the following:

- `unit`: This defines the metric to be used to compute the distance.
- `distance_type` (`sloppy_arc` or `arc` or `plane`): This defines the type of distance to be computed. The `_geo_distance` name for the field is mandatory.

The point of reference for the sorting can be defined in several ways, as we have already discussed in the *Mapping a GeoPoint field* recipe in Chapter 2, *Managing Mapping*.

Using the scripting for sorting will be discussed in the *Sorting data using scripts* recipe in Chapter 8, *Scripting in Elasticsearch*, after we introduce the scripting capabilities of Elasticsearch.

See also

You can view the following recipes for further reference which are related to this recipe:

- The *Mapping a GeoPoint field* recipe in Chapter 2, *Managing Mapping*, explains how to correctly create a mapping for a GeoPoint field
- The *Sorting with scripts* recipe in Chapter 8, *Scripting in Elasticsearch*, will explain the use of custom script for computing values to sort on

Highlighting results

Elasticsearch performs a good job of finding matching results in big text documents. It's useful for searching text in very large blocks, but to improve user experience, you need to show users the abstract—a small portion of the text part of the document that has matched the query. The abstract is a common way to help users understand how the matched document is relevant to them.

The highlight functionality in Elasticsearch is designed to do this job.

Getting ready

You need an up-and-running Elasticsearch installation, as we described in the *Downloading and installing Elasticsearch* recipe in `Chapter 1`, *Getting Started*.

To execute these commands, any HTTP client can be used, such as curl (`https://curl.haxx.se/`), postman (`https://www.getpostman.com/`), or similar. I suggest using the Kibana console as it provides code completion and better character escaping for Elasticsearch.

To correctly execute the following commands, you will need an index populated with the `ch04/populate_kibana.txt` commands, which is available in the online code.

How to do it...

To search and highlight the results, we will need to perform the following steps:

1. From the command line, we can execute a search with a highlight parameter, as follows:

```
GET /mybooks/_search?from=0&size=10
  {
    "query": {
      "query_string": {
        "query": "joe"
      }
    },
    "highlight": {
      "pre_tags": [
        ""
      ],
      "fields": {
```

```
          "description": {
            "order": "score"
          },
          "title": {
            "order": "score"
          }
        },
        "post_tags": [
          ""
        ]
      }
  }
```

2. If everything works, the command will return the following result:

```
{
  ...truncated...
  "hits" : {
    "total" : 1,
    "max_score" : 1.0126973,
    "hits" : [
      {
        "_index" : "mybooks",
        "_type" : "_doc",
        "_id" : "1",
        "_score" : 1.0126973,
        ...truncated...
        "highlight" : {
          "description" : [
            "<b>Joe</b> Testere nice guy"
          ],
          "title" : [
            "<b>Joe</b> Tester"
          ]
        }
      }
    ]
  }
}
```

As you can see, in the standard results, there is a new highlight field, which contains the highlighted fields within an array of fragments.

How it works...

When the `highlight` parameter is passed to the search object, Elasticsearch tries to execute the highlight on the document results.

The highlighting phase, which is after the document fetch one, tries to extract the highlight using the following steps:

1. It collects the terms that are available in the query
2. It initializes the highlighter with the parameters given during the query
3. It extracts the interested fields and tries to load them if they are stored, otherwise they are taken from the source
4. It executes the query on single fields to detect the more relevant parts
5. It adds the found highlighted fragments to the hit

Using the highlighting functionality is very easy, but there are some important factors to pay attention to:

- The field that must be used for highlighting must be available in one of these forms: stored, in source, or in stored term vector

> The Elasticsearch highlighter checks the presence of the data field first as the term vector (this is a faster way to execute the highlighting). If the field does not use the term vector (a special indexing parameter that allows you to store an index additional positional text data), it tries to load the field value from the stored fields. If the field is not stored, it finally loads the JSON source, interprets it, and extracts the data value, if available. Obviously, the last approach is the slowest and most resource-intensive.

- If a special analyzer is used in the search, it should also be passed to the highlighter (this is often automatically managed)

When executing highlighting on a large number of fields, you can use the wildcard to multi-select them (that is to say `title*`).

The common properties for controlling highlighting field usage are as follows:

- `order`: This defines the matched fragments selection order.
- `force_source`: This skips the term vector or stored field and takes the field from the source (`false` default).
- `type` (optional, valid values are `plain`, `postings`, and `fvh`): This is used to force a specific highlight type.
- `number_of_fragment`: The default value is 5. This parameter controls how many fragments return. It can be configured globally or for a field.
- `fragment_size`: The default value is `100`. This is the number of characters that the fragments must contain. It can be configured globally or for a field.

There are several optional parameters that can be passed in the highlight object to control the highlighting markup, and these are as follows:

- `pre_tags`/`post_tags`: A list of tags to be used for marking the highlighted text.
- `tags_schema="styled"`: This allows the user to define a tag schema that marks highlighting with different tags with ordered importance. This is a helper to reduce the definition of a lot of `pre_tags`/`post_tags` tags.
- `encoder`: The default value is `html`. If this is set to `html`, it will escape HTML tags in the fragments.
- `require_field_match`: The default value is `true`. If this is set to false, it also allow highlighting on fields that don't match the query.
- `boundary_chars`: This is a list of characters that are used for phrase boundaries (that is,; : /).
- `boundary_max_scan`: The default value is `20`. This controls how many characters the highlighting must scan for boundaries in a match. It's used to provide better fragment extraction.
- `matched_fields`: This allows the user to combine multi-fields to execute the highlighting. This is very useful if the field that you use for highlighting is a multi-field that's been analyzed with different analyzers (such as standard, linguistic, and so on). It can only be used when the highlighter is a **Fast Vector Highlighter** (**FVH**). An example of this usage could be as follows:

```
{
  "query": {
    "query_string": {
      "query": "content.plain:some text",
```

```
            "fields": [
              "content"
            ]
          }
        },
        "highlight": {
          "order": "score",
          "fields": {
            "content": {
              "matched_fields": [
                "content",
                "content.plain"
              ],
              "type": "fvh"
            }
          }
        }
      }
    }
```

See also

You can refer to the following points for further reference, which are related to this recipe:

- Refer to the *Executing a search* recipe in this chapter to understand how to structure a search
- The official documentation of Elasticsearch about highlighting for more examples on border cases, at `https://www.elastic.co/guide/en/elasticsearch/reference/master/search-request-highlighting.html`

Executing a scrolling query

Every time a query is executed, the results are calculated and returned to the user in real time. In Elasticsearch, there is no deterministic order for records—pagination on a big block of values can bring inconsistency between results due to added and deleted documents, and also documents with the same score.

The scrolling query tries to resolve this kind of problem, giving a special cursor that allows the user to uniquely iterate all the documents.

Getting ready

You need an up-and-running Elasticsearch installation, as we described in the *Downloading and installing Elasticsearch* recipe in *Chapter 1, Getting Started*.

To execute these commands, any HTTP client can be used, such as curl (https://curl.haxx.se/), postman (https://www.getpostman.com/) or, similar. I suggest using the Kibana console as it provides code completion and better character escaping for Elasticsearch.

To correctly execute the following commands, you will need an index populated with the ch04/populate_kibana.txt commands, which is available in the online code.

How to do it...

In order to execute a scrolling query, we will perform the following steps:

1. From the command line, we can execute a search of type scan, as follows:

    ```
    GET /mybooks/_search?scroll=10m&size=1
    {
      "query": {
        "match_all": {}
      }
    }
    ```

2. If everything works, the command will return the following result:

    ```
    {
      "_scroll_id" :
    "DXF1ZXJ5QW5kRmV0Y2gBAAAAAAAHdMUWNHBwdFp4NGpTTS14Y3BpVlRfZDdSd
    w==",
      ...truncated...
      "hits" : {
        "total" : 3,
        "max_score" : 1.0,
        "hits" : [
          {
            "_index" : "mybooks",
            "_type" : "_doc",
            "_id" : "1",
            "_score" : 1.0,
            ...truncated...
          }
        ]
    ```

```
        }
    }
```

3. The result is composed of the following:

- `scroll_id`: The value to be used for scrolling records
- `took`: The time required to execute the query
- `timed_out`: Whether the query was timed out
- `_shards`: This query status is the information about the status of shards during the query
- `hits`: An object that contains the total count and the result hits

4. With a `scroll_id`, you can use scroll to get the results, as follows:

```
POST /_search/scroll
  {
      "scroll" : "10m",
      "scroll_id" :
"DXF1ZXJ5QW5kRmV0Y2gBAAAAAAAHdMUWNHBwdFp4NGpTTS14Y3BpVlRfZDdSd
w=="
  }
```

5. The result should be something similar to the following:

```
{
    "_scroll_id" :
"DXF1ZXJ5QW5kRmV0Y2gBAAAAAAAHdMUWNHBwdFp4NGpTTS14Y3BpVlRfZDdSd
w==",
    ...truncated...
    "hits" : {
      "total" : 3,
      "max_score" : 1.0,
      "hits" : [
        {
          "_index" : "mybooks",
          "_type" : "_doc",
          "_id" : "2",
          "_score" : 1.0,
          ...truncated...
        }
      ]
    }
}
```

For the most curious readers, the `scroll_id` is a base64 that contains information about the query type and an internal ID. In our case, `DXF1ZXJ5QW5kRmV0Y2gBAAAAAAAHdMUWNHBwdFp4NGpTTS14Y3BpV lRfZDdSdw==` **corresponds to** `queryAndFetcht4pptZx4jSM-xcpiVT_d7Rw.`

How it works...

The scrolling query is interpreted as a standard search. This kind of search is designed to iterate on a large set of results, so the score and the order are not computed.

During the query phase, every shard stores the state of the IDs in memory until timeout. Processing a scrolling query is done in the following ways:

1. The first part executes a query and returns a `scroll_id` used to fetch the results.
2. The second part executes the document scrolling. You iterate the second step, getting the new `scroll_id`, and fetch other documents.

If you need to iterate on a big set of records, the scrolling query must be used, otherwise you could have duplicated results.

The scrolling query is similar to every executed standard query, but there is a special parameter that must be passed in the query string.

The `scroll=(your timeout)` parameter allows the user to define how long the hits should live. The time can be expressed in seconds using the `s` postfix (that is to say, 5s, 10s, 15s, and so on) or in minutes using the `m` postfix (that is to say, 5m, 10m, and so on). If you are using a long timeout, you must be sure that your nodes have a lot of RAM to keep the resulting ID live. This parameter is mandatory and must be always provided.

There's more...

Scrolling is very useful for executing re-indexing actions or iterating on very large result sets, and the best approach for this kind of action is to use the sort by the special _doc field to obtain all the matched documents, and to be more efficient.

So, if you need to iterate on a large bucket of documents for re-indexing, you should execute a query similar to the following:

```
GET /mybooks/_search?scroll=10m&size=1
  {
    "query": {
      "match_all": {}
    },
    "sort": [
      "_doc"
    ]
  }
```

The scroll result values are kept in memory until the scroll timeout. It's good practice to clean this memory if you don't use the scroller any more; to delete a scroll from the Elasticsearch memory, the commands are as follows:

- If you know your scroll ID or IDs, you can provide them to the DELETE scroll API call, as follows:

```
DELETE /_search/scroll
  {
    "scroll_id": [
      "DnF1ZXJ5VGhlbkZldGNoBQAA..."
    ]
  }
```

- If you want to clean all the scrolls, you can use the special _all keyword, as follows:

```
DELETE /_search/scroll/_all
```

See also

You can refer to the following points for further reference, which are related to this recipe:

- The *Executing a search* recipe in this chapter for structuring a search
- The official documentation about scrolling that gives examples on using slice for mapping scrolling on multiple slices, at `https://www.elastic.co/guide/en/elasticsearch/reference/master/search-request-scroll.html`

Using the search_after functionality

Elasticsearch standard pagination using `from` and `size` perform very poorly on large datasets because, for every query, you need to compute and discard all the results before the `from` value. Scrolling doesn't have this problem, but it consumes a lot due to memory search contexts, so it cannot be used for frequent user queries.

To bypass these problems, Elasticsearch 5.x and above provides the `search_after` functionality, which provides a fast skipping for scrolling results.

Getting ready

You need an up-and-running Elasticsearch installation, as we described in the *Downloading and installing Elasticsearch* recipe in *Chapter 1, Getting Started*.

To execute these commands, any HTTP client can be used, such as curl (`https://curl.haxx.se/`), postman (`https://www.getpostman.com/`), or similar. I suggest using the Kibana console as it provides code completion and better character escaping for Elasticsearch.

To correctly execute the following commands, you will need an index populated with the `ch04/populate_kibana.txt` commands, which is available in the online code.

How to do it...

In order to execute a scrolling query, we will perform the following steps:

1. From the command line, we can execute a search, which will provide a sort for your value, and use the _doc or _id of the document as the last sort parameter, as follows:

```
GET /mybooks/_search
{
    "size": 1,
    "query": {
      "mlatch_all": {}
    },
    "sort": [
      {
        "price": "asc"
      },
      {
        "_doc": "desc"
      }
    ]
}
```

2. If everything works, the command will return the following result:

```
{
  ...truncated...
  "hits" : {
    "total" : 3,
    "max_score" : null,
    "hits" : [
      {
        "_index" : "mybooks",
        "_type" : "_doc",
        "_id" : "1",
        "_score" : null,
        "_source" : {
          "uuid" : "11111",
          "position" : 1,
          "title" : "Joe Tester",
          "description" : "Joe Testere nice guy",
          "date" : "2015-10-22",
          "price" : 4.3,
          "quantity" : 50
        },
        "sort" : [
```

```
                            4.3,
                             0
                        ]
                    }
                ]
            }
        }
```

3. To use the `search_after` functionality, you need to keep track of your last sort result, which in this case is [4.3, 0].

4. To fetch the next result, you must provide the `search_after` functionality with the last sort value of your last record, as follows:

```
GET /mybooks/_search
{
    "size": 1,
    "query": {
        "match_all": {}
    },
    "search_after": [
        4.3,
        0
    ],
    "sort": [
        {
            "price": "asc"
        },
        {
            "_doc": "desc"
        }
    ]
}
```

How it works...

Elasticsearch uses Lucene for indexing data. In Lucene indices, all the terms are sorted and stored in an ordered way, so it's natural for Lucene to be extremely fast in skipping to a term value. This operation is managed in the Lucene core with the `skipTo` method. This operation doesn't consume memory and in the case of `search_after`, a query is built using `search_after` values to fast skip in Lucene search and to speed up the result pagination.

The `search_after` functionality was introduced in Elasticsearch 5.x, but it must be kept as an important focal point to improve the user experience in search scrolling/pagination results.

See also

- Refer to the *Executing a search* recipe in this chapter to learn how to structure a search for size pagination and the *Executing a scrolling query* recipe for scrolling values in a query.

Returning inner hits in results

In Elasticsearch, when using nested and child documents, we can have complex data models. Elasticsearch, by default, returns only documents that match the searched type and not the nested or children one that matches the query.

The `inner_hits` function was introduced in Elasticsearch 5.x to provide this functionality.

Getting ready

You need an up-and-running Elasticsearch installation, as we described in the *Downloading and installing Elasticsearch* recipe in `Chapter 1`, *Getting Started*.

To execute these commands, any HTTP client can be used, such as curl (`https://curl.haxx.se/`), postman (`https://www.getpostman.com/`), or similar. I suggest using the Kibana console as it provides code completion and better character escaping for Elasticsearch.

To correctly execute the following commands, you will need an index populated with the `ch04/populate_kibana.txt` commands, which is available in the online code.

How to do it...

To return inner hits during a query, we will perform the following steps:

1. From the command line, we can execute a call by adding `inner_hits`, as follows:

```
POST /mybooks-join/_search
{
  "query": {
    "has_child": {
      "type": "author",
      "query": {
        "term": {
          "name": "peter"
        }
      },
      "inner_hits": {}
    }
  }
}
```

2. The result returned by Elasticsearch, if everything works, should be as follows:

```
{
  ...truncated...
  "hits" : {
    "total" : 1,
    "max_score" : 1.0,
    "hits" : [
      {
        "_index" : "mybooks-join",
        "_type" : "_doc",
        "_id" : "1",
        "_score" : 1.0,
        "_source" : ...truncated...,
        "inner_hits" : {
          "author" : {
            "hits" : {
              "total" : 1,
              "max_score" : 1.2039728,
              "hits" : [
                {
                  "_index" : "mybooks-join",
                  "_type" : "_doc",
                  "_id" : "a1",
```

```
                    "_score" : 1.2039728,
                    "_routing" : "1",
                    "_source" : {
                      "name" : "Peter",
                      "surname" : "Doyle",
                      "join" : {
                        "name" : "author",
                        "parent" : "1"
                      }
                    }
                  }
                ]
              }
            }
          }
        }
      ]
    }
  }
}
```

How it works...

When executing nested or children queries, Elasticsearch executes a two-step query, as follows:

1. It executes the nested or children query and returns the IDs of the referred values
2. It executes the other part of the query filtering by the returned IDs of *Step 1*

Generally, the results of the nested or children query are not taken, because they require memory. Using the `inner_hits`, the nested or children query intermediate hits are kept and returned to the user.

To control the `inner_hits` returned documents, standard parameters for the search are available, such as `from`, `size`, `sort`, `highlight`, `_source`, `explain`, `scripted_fields`, `docvalues_fields`, and `version`.

There is also a special property name used to name `inner_hits`, which allows the user to easily determine it in case of multiple `inner_hits` returning sections.

See also

You can refer to the following points for further reference, which are related to this recipe:

- The *Executing a search* recipe in this chapter for all the standard parameters in searches for controlling returned hits
- The *Using a has_child query, Using a top_children query, Using a has_parent query*, and *Using a nested query* recipes in `Chapter 6`, *Relationships and Geo Queries*, are useful when using queries that can be used for inner hits

Suggesting a correct query

It's very common for users to commit typing errors or to require suggestions for words that they are writing. These issues are solved by Elasticsearch with the suggested functionality.

Getting ready

You need an up-and-running Elasticsearch installation, as we described in the *Downloading and installing Elasticsearch* recipe in `Chapter 1`, *Getting Started*.

To execute these commands, any HTTP client can be used, such as curl (`https://curl.haxx.se/`), postman (`https://www.getpostman.com/`), or similar. I suggest using the Kibana console as it provides code completion and better character escaping for Elasticsearch.

To correctly execute the following commands, you will need an index populated with the `ch04/populate_kibana.txt` commands, which is available in the online code.

How to do it...

To suggest relevant terms by query, we will perform the following steps:

1. From the command line, we can execute a `suggest` call, as follows:

```
GET /mybooks/_search
{
  "suggest": {
    "suggest1": {
```

```
            "text": "we find tester",
            "term": {
              "field": "description"
            }
          }
        }
      }
    }
```

2. The result returned by Elasticsearch, if everything works, should be as follows:

```
{
    ...truncated...
    "suggest" : {
      "suggest1" : [
        {
          "text" : "we",
          "offset" : 0,
          "length" : 2,
          "options" : [ ]
        },
    ...
    ...            {
                "text" : "testere",
                "score" : 0.8333333,
                "freq" : 2
            }
          ]
        }
      ]
    }
}
```

The result is composed of the following:

- The shards' status at the time of the query
- The list of tokens with their available candidates

How it works...

The suggest section works by collecting terms stats on all the index shards. Using Lucene field statistics, it is possible to detect the correct term or complete term. It's a statistic approach!

There are two types of suggester term and phrase, and they are as follows:

- The simpler suggester to use is the term suggester. It requires only the text and the field to work. It also allows the user to set a lot of parameters, such as the minimum size for a word, learn how to sort results, and the suggester strategy. A complete reference is available on the Elasticsearch website at `https://www.elastic.co/guide/en/elasticsearch/reference/master/search-suggesters-term.html`.

- The phrase suggester is able to keep relations between terms that it needs to suggest. The phrase suggester is less efficient than the term, but it provides better results.

The suggest API features, parameters, and options often change between releases.

New suggesters can be added using plugins.

See also

You can refer to the following points for further reference, which are related to this recipe:

- The *Executing a search* recipe in this chapter for how to structure a search
- The phrase suggester online documentation is available at `https://www.elastic.co/guide/en/elasticsearch/reference/current/search-suggesters-phrase.html`
- The completion suggester online documentation is available at `https://www.elastic.co/guide/en/elasticsearch/reference/current/search-suggesters-completion.html`
- The context suggester online documentation is available at `https://www.elastic.co/guide/en/elasticsearch/reference/current/suggester-context.html`

Counting matched results

It is often required to return only the count of the matched results and not the results themselves.

There are a lot of scenarios involving counting, such as the following:

- To return the number of something (how many posts for a blog, how many comments for a post).
- Validating whether some items are available. Are there posts? Are there comments?

Getting ready

You need an up-and-running Elasticsearch installation, as we described in the *Downloading and installing Elasticsearch* recipe in `Chapter 1`, *Getting Started*.

To execute these commands, any HTTP client can be used, such as curl (`https://curl.haxx.se/`), postman (`https://www.getpostman.com/`), or similar. I suggest using the Kibana console as it provides code completion and better character escaping for Elasticsearch.

To correctly execute the following commands, you will need an index populated with the `ch04/populate_kibana.txt` commands, which is available in the online code.

How to do it...

In order to execute a counting query, we will perform the following steps:

1. From the command line, we will execute a count query, as follows:

```
GET /mybooks/_count
{
  "query": {
    "match_all": {}
  }
}
```

2. The result returned by ElasticSearch, if everything works, should be as follows:

```
{
  "count" : 3,
  "_shards" : {
    "total" : 1,
    "successful" : 1,
    "skipped" : 0,
    "failed" : 0
```

```
            }
        }
```

The result is composed of the count result (a long type) and the shard status at the time of the query.

How it works...

The query is interpreted in the same way as it is for searching. The count action is processed and distributed in all the shards, which is executed as a low-level Lucene count call. Every hit shard returns a count that is aggregated and returned to the user.

 In Elasticsearch, counting is faster than searching. In the case that the result source hits are not required, it's good practice to use the count API because it's faster and requires fewer resources.

The HTTP method to execute a count is GET (but also POST works), and the REST endpoints are as follows:

```
http://<server>/_count
http://<server>/<index_name(s)>/_count
```

Multi-indices and types are comma-separated. If an index or a type is defined, the search is limited only to them. An alias can be used as an index name.

Typically, a body is used to express a query, but for simple queries, the q (query argument) can be used. For example, look at the following code:

```
GET /mybooks/_count?q=uuid:11111
```

There's more...

In a previous version of Elasticsearch, the count API call (_count REST entry point) was implemented as a custom action, but in Elasticsearch version 5.x and above, this has been removed. Internally, the previous count API is implemented as a standard search with the size set to 0.

Using this trick, it not only speeds up the searching, but reduces networking. You can use this approach to execute aggregations (we will see them in Chapter 7, *Aggregations*) without returning hits.

The previous query can be also executed as follows:

```
GET /mybooks/_count?q=uuid:11111
```

The result returned by Elasticsearch, if everything works, should be as follows:

```
{
  "count" : 1,
  "_shards" : {
    "total" : 1,
    "successful" : 1,
    "skipped" : 0,
    "failed" : 0
  }
}
```

The count result (a long type) is also available in the standard `_search` result in `hits.total`.

See also

You can refer to the following points for further reference, which are related to this recipe:

- The *Executing a search* recipe in this chapter on using size to paginate
- `Chapter 7`, *Aggregations*, on how to use the aggregations

Explaining a query

When executing searches, it's very common to have documents that don't match the query as expected. To easily debug these scenarios, Elasticsearch provides the explain query call, which allows you to check how the scores are computed against a document.

Getting ready

You need an up-and-running Elasticsearch installation, as we described in the *Downloading and installing Elasticsearch* recipe in `Chapter 1`, *Getting Started*.

To execute these commands, any HTTP client can be used, such as curl (https://curl.haxx.se/), postman (https://www.getpostman.com/), or similar. I suggest using the Kibana console as it provides code completion and better character escaping for Elasticsearch.

To correctly execute the following commands, you will need an index populated with the ch04/populate_kibana.txt commands, which is available in the online code.

How to do it...

The steps that are required to execute the explain query call are as follows:

1. From the command line, we will execute an explain query against a document, as follows:

```
GET /mybooks/_doc/1/_explain?pretty
{
  "query": {
    "term": {
      "uuid": "11111"
    }
  }
}
```

2. The result returned by Elasticsearch, if everything works, should be as follows:

```
{
  "_index" : "mybooks",
  "_type" : "_doc",
  "_id" : "1",
  "matched" : true,
  "explanation" : {
    "value" : 0.9808292,
    "description" : "weight(uuid:11111 in 0)
[PerFieldSimilarity], result of:",
    "details" : [
...
...
              {
                "value" : 3,
                "description" : "N, total number of documents
with field",
                "details" : [ ]
              }
```

```
                    ]
                },
            ...truncated...
        }
```

The important parts of the result are the following:

- `matched`: Whether the documents match or not in the query
- `explanation`: This section is composed of objects made of the following:
    - `value`: A double score of that query section
    - `description`: A string representation of the matching token (in case of wildcards or multi-terms, it can give information about the matched token)
    - `details`: An optional list of explanation objects

How it works...

The explain call is a view of how Lucene computes the results. In the description section of the explain object, there are the Lucene representations of that part of the query.

A user doesn't need to be a Lucene expert to understand the explain descriptions, but they provide a highlight of how the query is executed and the terms are matched.

More complex queries with many subqueries are very hard to debug, mainly if you need to boost some special fields to obtain the desiderata sequence of documents. In these cases, using the explain API helps you manage field boosting because it allows you to easily debug how they interact in your query or document.

Query profiling

This feature is available from Elasticsearch 5.x or above via the profile API. This allows the user to track the time spent by Elasticsearch in executing a search or an aggregation.

Getting ready

You need an up-and-running Elasticsearch installation, as we described in the *Downloading and installing Elasticsearch* recipe in `Chapter 1`, *Getting Started*.

To execute these commands, any HTTP client can be used, such as curl (`https://curl.haxx.se/`), postman (`https://www.getpostman.com/`), or similar. I suggest using the Kibana console as it provides code completion and better character escaping for Elasticsearch.

To correctly execute the following commands, you will need an index populated with the `ch04/populate_kibana.txt` commands, which is available in the online code.

How to do it...

The steps to profile a query are as follows:

1. From the command line, we will execute a search with the `true` profile set as follows:

```
GET /mybooks/_search
{
  "profile": true,
  "query": {
    "term": {
      "uuid": "11111"
    }
  }
}
```

2. The result returned by Elasticsearch, if everything works, should be as follows:

```
{
  ...truncated...
  "profile" : {
    "shards" : [
      {
        "id" : "[4pptZx4jSM-xcpiVT_d7Rw][mybooks][0]",
        "searches" : [
...
...


          ],
          "rewrite_time" : 5954,
          "collector" : [
            {
              "name" : "CancellableCollector",
              "reason" : "search_cancelled",
              "time_in_nanos" : 204857,
```

```
                    "children" : [
                      {
                        "name" : "SimpleTopScoreDocCollector",
                        "reason" : "search_top_hits",
                        "time_in_nanos" : 12288
                      }
                    ]
                  }
                ]
              }
            ],
            "aggregations" : [ ]
          }
        ]
      }
    }
```

The output is very verbose. It's divided for shard and for single hit.

The result exposes the type of query (for example, `TermQuery`) with details on internal Lucene parameters. For every step, the time is tracked in a way that a user can easily detect the bottleneck in their query time.

How it works...

The profile APIs were introduced in Elasticsearch 5.x for tracking times in executing queries and aggregations. When a query is executed, if profiling is activated, all the internal calls are tracked using the internal instrumental API. For this reason, the profile API adds an overhead to the computation.

The output is also very verbose and depends on the internal components of both Elasticsearch and Lucene, so the format of the result can change in the future. The typical usage for this feature is to reduce the execution time tracking, which are the slowest steps in the query, and try to optimize them.

Deleting by query

We saw how to delete a document in the *Deleting a document* in recipe `Chapter 3,` *Basic Operations*. Deleting a document is very fast, but it requires knowing the document ID for direct access, and in some cases, the routing value too.

Elasticsearch provides a call to delete all the documents that match a query using an additional module called **re-index,** which is installed by default.

Getting ready

You need an up-and-running Elasticsearch installation, as we described in the *Downloading and installing Elasticsearch* recipe in `Chapter 1`, *Getting Started*.

To execute these commands, any HTTP client can be used, such as curl (`https://curl.haxx.se/`), postman (`https://www.getpostman.com/`), or similar. I suggest using the Kibana console as it provides code completion and better character escaping for Elasticsearch.

To correctly execute the following commands, you will need an index populated with the `ch04/populate_kibana.txt` commands, which is available in the online code.

How to do it...

In order to delete by query, we will perform the following steps:

1. From the command line, we will execute a query, as follows:

```
POST /mybooks/_delete_by_query?pretty
{
  "query": {
    "match_all": {}
  }
}
```

2. The result returned by Elasticsearch, if everything works, should be as follows:

```
{
  "took" : 10,
  "timed_out" : false,
  "total" : 3,
  "deleted" : 3,
  "batches" : 1,
  "version_conflicts" : 0,
  "noops" : 0,
  "retries" : {
    "bulk" : 0,
    "search" : 0
```

```
    },
    "throttled_millis" : 0,
    "requests_per_second" : -1.0,
    "throttled_until_millis" : 0,
    "failures" : [ ]
}
```

The main components of the result are as follows:

- `total`: The number of documents that match the query
- `deleted`: The number of documents deleted
- `batches`: The number of bulk actions executed to delete the documents
- `version_conflicts`: The number of documents not deleted due to a version conflict during the bulk action
- `noops`: The number of documents not executed to a noop event
- `retries.bulk`: The number of bulk actions that are retried
- `retries.search`: The number of searches that are retried
- `requests_per_second`: The number of requests for seconds executed (-1.0 if this value is not set)
- `throttled_millis`: The time of sleep to conform to `request_per_second` value
- `throttled_until_millis`: This is generally 0, and it indicates the time for the next request if the `request_per_second` value is set
- `failures`: An array of failures

How it works...

The `delete_by_query` function is executed automatically using the following steps:

1. In a master node, the query is executed and the results are scrolled.
2. For every bulk size element (default 1,000), a bulk is executed.
3. The bulk results are checked for conflicts. If no conflicts exist, a new bulk is executed, until all the matched documents are deleted.

The `delete_by_query` call automatically manages back pressure (it reduces the delete command rate if the server has a high load).

When you want to remove all the documents without re-indexing a new index, a `delete_by_query` with a `match_all` query allows you to clean your mapping of all the documents. This call is analogous to the `truncate_table` of the SQL language.

The HTTP method to execute a `delete_by_query` command is `POST`; the REST endpoints are as follows:

```
http://<server>/_delete_by_query
http://<server>/<index_name(s)>/_delete_by_query
```

Multi indices are defined as a unique comma-separated string. If an index or a type is defined, the search is limited only to them. An alias can be used as the index name.

Typically, a body is used to express a query, but for simple queries, the q (query argument) can be used. For example, look at the following code:

```
DELETE /mybooks/_delete_by_query?q=uuid:11111
```

There's more...

Further query arguments are as follows:

- `conflicts`: If it is set to `proceed`, when there is a version conflict, the call doesn't exit; it skips the error and it finishes execution.
- `routing`: This is used to target only some shards.
- `scroll_size`: This controls the size of the scrolling and the bulk (default `1000`).
- `request_per_seconds` (default `-1.0`): This controls how may requests can be executed in a second. The default value is unlimited.

See also

You can refer to the following points for further reference, which are related to this recipe:

- The *Deleting a document* recipe in *Chapter 3, Basic Operations*, is useful for executing a delete for a single document
- The *Delete by query task* recipe in *Chapter 9, Managing Clusters*, is useful for monitoring asynchronous delete by query actions

Updating by query

In the previous chapter, we saw how to update a document in the *Update a document* recipe.

The `update_by_query` API call allows the user to execute the update on all the documents that match a query. It is very useful if you need to do the following:

- Reindex a subset of your records that match a query. It's common if you change your document mapping and need the documents to be reprocessed.
- Update values of your records that match a query.

It's the Elasticsearch version of the SQL update command.

This functionality is provided by an additional module called reindex that is installed by default.

Getting ready

You need an up-and-running Elasticsearch installation, as we described in the *Downloading and installing Elasticsearch* recipe in *Chapter 1, Getting Started*.

To execute these commands, any HTTP client can be used, such as curl (`https://curl.haxx.se/`), postman (`https://www.getpostman.com/`), or similar. I suggest using the Kibana console as it provides code completion and better character escaping for Elasticsearch.

To correctly execute the following commands, you will need an index populated with the `ch04/populate_kibana.txt` commands, which is available in the online code.

How to do it...

In order to execute an update from a query that simply reindexes your documents, we will perform the following steps:

1. From the command line, we will execute a query, as follows:

```
POST /mybooks/_update_by_query
{
  "query": {
    "match_all": {}
```

```
    },
    "script": {
      "source": "ctx._source.quantity=50"
    }
  }
```

2. The result returned by Elasticsearch, if everything works, should be as follows:

```
{
  "took" : 7,
  "timed_out" : false,
  "total" : 3,
  "updated" : 3,
  "deleted" : 0,
  "batches" : 1,
  "version_conflicts" : 0,
  "noops" : 0,
  "retries" : {
    "bulk" : 0,
    "search" : 0
  },
  "throttled_millis" : 0,
  "requests_per_second" : -1.0,
  "throttled_until_millis" : 0,
  "failures" : [ ]
}
```

The most important components of the result are as follows:

- `total`: The number of documents that match the query
- `updated`: The number of documents updated
- `batches`: The number of bulk actions executed to update the documents
- `version_conflicts`: The number of documents not deleted due to a version conflict during bulk action
- `noops`: The number of documents not changed due to a noop event
- `retries.bulk`: The number of bulk actions that are retried
- `retries.search`: The number of searches that are retried
- `requests_per_second`: The number of requests for seconds executed (-1.0 if this value is not set)
- `throttled_millis`: The time of sleep to conform to `request_per_second` value

- `throttled_until_millis`: This is generally 0, and it indicates the time for the next request if `request_per_second` value is set
- `failures`: An array of failures

How it works...

The `update_by_query` function works in a very similar way to the `delete_by_query` API, and is executed automatically using the following steps:

1. In a master node, the query is executed and the results are scrolled.
2. For every bulk size element (default 1,000), a bulk with the update commands is executed.
3. The bulk results are checked for conflicts. If there are no conflicts, a new bulk is executed and the action search or bulk are executed until all the matched documents are deleted.

The HTTP method to execute an `update_by_query` is `POST`, and the REST endpoints are as follows:

```
http://<server>/_update_by_query
http://<server>/<index_name(s)>/<type_name(s)>/_update_by_query
```

Multi indices are defined via a comma-separated string. If an index or a type is defined, the search is limited only to them. An alias can be used as an index name.

The additional query arguments are as follows:

- `conflicts`: If it is set to `proceed`, when there is a version conflict, the call doesn't exit; it skips the error and it finishes execution.
- `routing`: This is used to target only some shards.
- `scroll_size`: This controls the size of the scrolling and the bulk (the default size is `1000`).
- `request_per_seconds` (default `-1.0`): This controls how many requests can be executed in a second. The default value is unlimited.

There's more...

The `update_by_query` API can accept a script section in its body. In this way, it can become a powerful tool for executing custom updates on a subset of documents. (We will see scripting in detail in *Chapter 8, Scripting in Elasticsearch*). It can be considered similar to the SQL `update` command.

With this facility, we can add a new field and initialize its value with a script as follows:

```
POST /mybooks/_update_by_query
{
  "script": {
    "source": "ctx._source.hit=4"
  },
  "query": {
    "match_all": {}
  }
}
```

With the preceding example, we add a `hit` field set to `4` for every document that matches the query. This is similar to the SQL command, which is as follows:

```
update mybooks set hit=4
```

 The `update_by_query` API is one of the more powerful tools that Elasticsearch provides.

See also

The *Update a document* recipe in *Chapter 3, Basic Operations*, is useful for executing an update for a single document.

Matching all the documents

One of the most common queries in the `match_all` query. This kind of query allows the user to return all the documents that are available in an index. The `match_all` and other query operators are part of the Elasticsearch query DSL.

Getting ready

You need an up-and-running Elasticsearch installation, as we described in the *Downloading and installing Elasticsearch* recipe in `Chapter 1`, *Getting Started*.

To execute these commands, any HTTP client can be used, such as curl (`https://curl.haxx.se/`), postman (`https://www.getpostman.com/`), or similar. I suggest using the Kibana console as it provides code completion and better character escaping for Elasticsearch.

To correctly execute the following commands, you will need an index populated with the `ch04/populate_kibana.txt` commands, which is available in the online code.

How to do it...

In order to execute a `match_all` query, we will perform the following steps:

1. From the command line, we execute the query as follows:

```
POST /mybooks/_search
{
  "query": {
    "match_all": {}
  }
}
```

2. The result returned by Elasticsearch, if everything works, should be as follows:

```
{
  "took" : 0,
  "timed_out" : false,
  "_shards" : {
    "total" : 1,
    "successful" : 1,
    "skipped" : 0,
    "failed" : 0
  },
  "hits" : {
    "total" : 3,
    "max_score" : 1.0,
    "hits" : [
      {
        "_index" : "mybooks",
        "_type" : "_doc",
```

```
        "_id" : "1",
        "_score" : 1.0,
        "_source" : {
          "date" : "2015-10-22",
          "hit" : 4,
          "quantity" : 50,
          "price" : 4.3,
          "description" : "Joe Testere nice guy",
          "position" : 1,
          "title" : "Joe Tester",
          "uuid" : "11111"
        }
      },
      ...truncated...
    ]
  }
}
```

The result is a standard query result, as we have seen in *Executing a search* recipe in this chapter.

How it works...

The `match_all` query is one of the most common ones. It's faster because it doesn't require the score calculus (it's wrapped in a Lucene, `ConstantScoreQuery`).

 If no query is defined in the search object, `match_all` will be the default query.

See also

Refer to the *Executing a search* recipe in this chapter for further reference.

Using a Boolean query

Most people using a search engine have, at some time or another, used the syntax with minus (–) and plus (+) to include or exclude query terms. The Boolean query allows the user to programmatically define queries to include, exclude, optionally include (`should`), or filter in the query.

This kind of query is one of the most important ones because it allows the user to aggregate a lot of simple queries or filters that we will see in this chapter to build a big complex one.

Two main concepts are important in searches: **query** and **filter**. The query means that the matched results are scored using an internal Lucene scoring algorithm; for the filter, the results are matched without scoring. Because the filter doesn't need to compute the score, it is generally faster and can be cached.

Getting ready

You need an up-and-running Elasticsearch installation, as we described in the *Downloading and installing Elasticsearch* recipe in `Chapter 1`, *Getting Started*.

To execute these commands, any HTTP client can be used, such as curl (`https://curl.haxx.se/`), postman (`https://www.getpostman.com/`), or similar. I suggest using the Kibana console as it provides code completion and better character escaping for Elasticsearch.

To correctly execute the following commands, you will need an index populated with the `ch04/populate_kibana.txt` commands, which is available in the online code.

How to do it...

For executing a Boolean query, we will perform the following steps:

1. We can execute a Boolean query from the command line as follows:

```
POST /mybooks/_search
{
  "query": {
    "bool": {
      "must": [
        {
          "term": {
            "description": "joe"
          }
        }
      ],
...
...
      "filter": [
        {
```

```
            "term": {
              "description": "joe"
            }
          }
        ],
        "minimum_should_match": 1,
        "boost": 1
      }
    }
  }
```

2. The result returned by Elasticsearch is similar to the previous recipes, but in this case, it should return one record (`id:1`).

How it works...

The `bool` query is often one of the most used because it allows the user to compose a large query using a lot of simpler ones. One of the following four parts is mandatory:

- `must`: A list of queries that must be satisfied. All the `must` queries must be verified to return the hits. It can be seen as an AND filter with all its sub queries.
- `must_not`: A list of queries that must not be matched. It can be seen as not filter of an AND query.
- `should`: A list of queries that can be verified. The minimum number of these queries that must be verified and this value is controlled by `minimum_should_match` (default 1).
- `filter`: A list of queries to be used as the filter. They allow the user to filter out results without changing the score and relevance. The filter queries are faster than standard ones because they don't need to compute the score.

There's more...

If you define multiple subqueries in a Boolean one, understand that whatever query is hit by your result could be very important at the application level; generally, it is better to narrow your results. To obtain this result, you could use the special _name attribute, which can be defined in query components.

The previous query can be changed in this way:

```
POST /mybooks/_search
{
  "query": {
    "bool": {
        "should": [
          {
            "term": {
              "uuid": {
                "value": "11111",
                "_name": "uuid:11111:matched"
              }
            }
          },
          {
            "term": {
              "uuid": {
                "value": "22222",
                "_name": "uuid:22222:matched"
              }
            }
          }
        ],
        "filter": [
          {
            "term": {
              "description": {
                "value": "joe",
                "_name": "fiter:term:joe"
              }
            }
          }
        ],
        "minimum_should_match": 1,
        "boost": 1
    }
  }
}
```

For every matched document, the result will contain the matched queries:

```
{
  ...truncated...
  "hits" : {
    "total" : 1,
    "max_score" : 0.9808292,
    "hits" : [
```

```
{
  "_index" : "mybooks",
  "_type" : "_doc",
  "_id" : "1",
  "_score" : 0.9808292,
  ...truncated...
  "matched_queries" : [
    "uuid:11111:matched",
    "fiter:term:joe"
  ]
}
]
}
}
```

Using the search template

Elasticsearch provides the capability of providing a template and some parameters to fill it. This functionality is very useful because it allows you to manage query templates stored in the `.scripts` index and allows you to change them without changing the application code.

Getting ready

You need an up-and-running Elasticsearch installation, as we described in the *Downloading and installing Elasticsearch* recipe in `Chapter 1`, *Getting Started*.

To execute these commands, any HTTP client can be used, such as curl (`https://curl.haxx.se/`), postman (`https://www.getpostman.com/`), or similar. I suggest using the Kibana console as it provides code completion and better character escaping for Elasticsearch.

To correctly execute the following commands, you will need an index populated with the `ch04/populate_kibana.txt` commands which is available in the online code.

How to do it...

The template query is composed of two components: the query and the parameters that must be filled in. We can execute a template query in several ways; in this recipe, we will look at some query types that we will explore in the next chapters.

Using the new REST entrypoint _search/template is the best way to use the templates. To use it, perform the following steps:

1. We execute the query as follows:

```
POST /_search/template
{
  "source": {
    "query": {
      "term": {
        "uuid": "{{value}}"
      }
    }
  },
  "params": {
    "value": "22222"
  }
}
```

2. The result returned by Elasticsearch, if everything is alright, should be as follows:

```
{
  "took" : 3,
  "timed_out" : false,
  "_shards" : {
    "total" : 3,
    "successful" : 3,
    "skipped" : 0,
    "failed" : 0
  },
  "hits" : {
    "total" : 1,
    "max_score" : 0.9808292,
    "hits" : [
      {
        "_index" : "mybooks",
        "_type" : "_doc",
        "_id" : "2",
        "_score" : 0.9808292,
        "_source" : {
          "uuid" : "22222",
          "position" : 2,
          "title" : "Bill Baloney",
          "description" : "Bill Testere nice guy",
          "date" : "2016-06-12",
          "price" : 5,
          "quantity" : 34
```

```
                        }
                      }
                  ]
              }
          }
```

If we want to use an indexed stored template, the steps are as follows:

1. We store the template in the `.scripts` index:

```
POST _scripts/myTemplate
{
  "script": {
    "lang": "mustache",
    "source": {
      "query": {
        "term": {
          "uuid": "{{value}}"
        }
      }
    }
  }
}
```

2. Now, we can call the template with the following code:

```
POST /mybooks/_search/template
{
  "id": "myTemplate",
  "params": {
    "value": "22222"
  }
}
```

If you have a stored template and you want to validate it, you can use the REST `render` entrypoint.

> The indexed templates and scripts are stored in the `.script` index. This is a normal index, and it can be managed as a standard data index.

If you want to render the query template, mainly for debugging purpose, follow these steps:

1. We render the template using the `_render/template` REST:

    ```
    POST /_render/template
    {
      "id": "myTemplate",
      "params": {
        "value": "22222"
      }
    }
    ```

    The result will be as follows:

    ```
    {
      "template_output" : {
        "query" : {
          "term" : {
            "uuid" : "22222"
          }
        }
      }
    }
    ```

How it works...

A template query is composed of the following two components:

*   A template is a query object that is supported by Elasticsearch. The template uses the `mustache` (`http://mustache.github.io/`) syntax, a very common syntax to express templates.
*   An optional dictionary of parameters that is used to fill the template.

When the search query is called, the template is loaded, populated with the parameter's data, and executed as a normal query. The template query is a shortcut so that you can use the same query with different values.

Typically, the template is generated by executing the query in the standard way and then by adding parameters if required in the process of templating it; the mustache syntax is very rich and provides default values, JSON escaping, conditional parts, and many more (the official documentation at `https://www.elastic.co/guide/en/ elasticsearch/reference/master/search-template.html` covers all these aspects).

It allows you to remove the query execution from application code and put it on the filesystem or indices.

See also

You can refer to the following points for further reference, which are related to this recipe:

- Check the official mustache documentation at `http://mustache.github. io/` to learn about the template syntax
- Check the official Elasticsearch documentation about search template at `https://www.elastic.co/guide/en/elasticsearch/reference/master/ search-template.html` for more samples using the template syntax
- Check the official Elasticsearch documentation about query template at `https://www.elastic.co/guide/en/elasticsearch/reference/master/ query-dsl-template-query.html` with some samples of query usage

Text and Numeric Queries

5

In this chapter, we will see queries that are used for searching text and numeric values. They are simpler and the most common ones that are used in Elasticsearch. The first part of the chapter covers the text queries from the simple term and terms query to the complex query string query. We'll understand how the queries are strongly related to mapping for choosing the correct query based on mapping.

In the last part of this chapter, we will see many special query that covers fields, helpers for building complex queries from strings, and query templates.

In this chapter, we will cover the following recipes:

- Using a term query
- Using a terms query
- Using a prefix query
- Using a wildcard query
- Using a regexp query
- Using span queries
- Using a match query
- Using a query string query
- Using a simple query string query
- Using the range query
- The common terms query
- Using an IDs query
- Using the function score query
- Using the exists query

Using a term query

Searching or filtering for a particular term is done frequently. Term queries work with exact value matches and are generally very fast.

The term queries can be compared to the `equal` (=) query in the SQL world.

Getting ready

You need an up-and-running Elasticsearch installation, as we described in the *Downloading and installing Elasticsearch* recipe in `Chapter 1`, *Getting Started*.

To execute these commands, any HTTP client can be used, such as `curl` (`https://curl.haxx.se/`), postman (`https://www.getpostman.com/`), or similar. I suggest you use the Kibana console, as it provides code completion and better character escaping for Elasticsearch.

To correctly execute the following commands you will need an index populated with the `ch05/kibana_commands_005.txt` commands, which is available in the online code.

How to do it...

To execute a term query, we will perform the following steps:

1. We will execute a term `query` from the command line, as follows:

```
POST /mybooks/_search
{
  "query": {
    "term": {
      "uuid": "33333"
    }
  }
}
```

2. The result returned by Elasticsearch, if everything is alright, should be as follows:

```
{
  "took" : 0,
  "timed_out" : false,
  "_shards" : {
    "total" : 1,
    "successful" : 1,
    "skipped" : 0,
    "failed" : 0
  },
  "hits" : {
    "total" : 1,
    "max_score" : 0.9808292,
    "hits" : [
      {
        "_index" : "mybooks",
        "_type" : "_doc",
        "_id" : "3",
        "_score" : 0.9808292,
        "_source" : {
          "uuid" : "33333",
          "position" : 3,
          "title" : "Bill Klingon",
          "description" : "Bill is not\n nice guy",
          "date" : "2017-09-21",
          "price" : 6,
          "quantity" : 33
        }
      }
    ]
  }
}
```

3. For executing a term query as a filter, we need to use it wrapped in a Boolean `query`. The preceding term `query` will be executed in the following way:

```
POST /mybooks/_search
{
  "query": {
    "bool": {
      "filter": {
        "term": {
          "uuid": "33333"
        }
      }
```

```
            }
          }
        }
```

4. The result returned by Elasticsearch, if everything is alright, should be as follows:

```
{
  "took" : 0,
  "timed_out" : false,
  "_shards" : {
    "total" : 1,
    "successful" : 1,
    "skipped" : 0,
    "failed" : 0
  },
  "hits" : {
    "total" : 1,
    "max_score" : 0.0,
    "hits" : [
      {
        "_index" : "mybooks",
        "_type" : "_doc",
        "_id" : "3",
        "_score" : 0.0,
        "_source" : {
          "uuid" : "33333",
          "position" : 3,
          "title" : "Bill Klingon",
          "description" : "Bill is not\n nice guy",
          "date" : "2017-09-21",
          "price" : 6,
          "quantity" : 33
        }
      }
    ]
  }
}
```

The result is a standard query result, as we have seen in the *Executing a search* recipe in Chapter 4, *Exploring Search Capabilities*.

How it works...

Lucene, due to its inverted index, is one of the fastest engines at searching for a term or value in a field. Every field that is indexed in Lucene is converted into a fast search structure for its particular type:

- The text is split into tokens, if analyzed or saved as a single token
- The numeric fields are converted into their fastest binary representation
- The date and datetime fields are converted into binary forms

In Elasticsearch, all these conversion steps are automatically managed. Search for a term, independent from the value, and you will find it is archived by Elasticsearch using the correct format for the field.

Internally, during a term query execution, all the documents matching the term are collected, and then they are sorted by score (the scoring depends on the Lucene, similarity algorithm chosen by default BM25).

For more details about Elasticsearch similarity algorithms, see `https://www.elastic.co/guide/en/elasticsearch/` `reference/master/index-modules-similarity.html`.

If we look for the results of the previous searches, for the term query of the hit has `0.30685282` as the score, while the filter has `1.0`. The time required for scoring if the sample is very small is not so relevant, but if you have thousands or millions of documents, it takes much more time.

If the score is not important, opt to use the term filter.

The filter is preferred to the query when the score is not important. The typical scenarios are as follows:

- Filtering permissions
- Filtering numerical values
- Filtering ranges

In a filtered query, the filter applies first, narrowing the number of documents to be matched against the query, and then the query is applied.

There's more...

Matching a term is the basis of Lucene and Elasticsearch. To correctly use these queries, you need to pay attention to how the field is indexed.

As we saw in `Chapter 2`, *Managing Mapping*, the terms of an indexed field depend on the analyzer used to index it. To better understand this concept, a representation of a phrase depending on several analyzers in the following table. For standard string analyzers, if we have a similar phrase, for example, `Phrase: Peter's house is big`, the results will be similar to the following table:

Mapping index	Analyzer	Tokens
`"index": false`	(No index)	(No tokens)
`"type": "keyword"`	KeywordAnalyzer	`["Peter's house is big"]`
`"type": "text"`	StandardAnalyzer	`["peter", "s", "house", "is", "big"]`

The common pitfalls in searching are related to misunderstanding the analyzer or mapping configuration. `KeywordAnalyzer`, which is used as the default for the `not tokenized` field, saves the string unchanged as a single token.

`StandardAnalyzer`, the default for the `type="text"` field, tokenizes on whitespaces and punctuation; every token is converted into lowercase. You should use the same analyzer for indexing to analyze the query (the default settings).

In the preceding example, if the phrase is analyzed with `StandardAnalyzer`, you cannot search for the term Peter, but rather for peter because the `StandardAnalyzer` executes lowercase on terms.

When the same field requires one or more search strategies, you need to use the `fields` property using the different analyzers that you need.

Using a terms query

The previous type of search works very well for a single term search. If you want to search for multiple terms, you can process it in two ways: using a Boolean query or using a multi-term query.

Getting ready

You need an up-and-running Elasticsearch installation, as we described in the *Downloading and installing Elasticsearch* recipe in `Chapter 1`, *Getting Started*.

To execute these commands, any HTTP client can be used, such as curl (`https://curl.haxx.se/`), postman (`https://www.getpostman.com/`), or similar. I suggest you use the Kibana console, as it provides code completion and better character escaping for Elasticsearch.

To correctly execute the following commands you will need an index populated with the `ch04/populate_kibana.txt` commands, which is available in the online code.

How to do it...

To execute a terms query, we will perform the following steps:

1. We execute a terms `query` from the command line, as follows:

```
POST /mybooks/_search
{
  "query": {
    "terms": {
      "uuid": [
        "33333",
        "32222"
      ]
    }
  }
}
```

2. The result returned by Elasticsearch, if everything is alright, should be as follows:

```
{
  "took" : 0,
  "timed_out" : false,
  "_shards" : {
    "total" : 1,
    "successful" : 1,
    "skipped" : 0,
    "failed" : 0
  },
  "hits" : {
    "total" : 1,
    "max_score" : 1.0,
    "hits" : [
      {
        "_index" : "mybooks",
        "_type" : "_doc",
        "_id" : "3",
        "_score" : 1.0,
        "_source" : {
          "uuid" : "33333",
          "position" : 3,
          "title" : "Bill Klingon",
          "description" : "Bill is not\n nice guy",
          "date" : "2017-09-21",
          "price" : 6,
          "quantity" : 33
        }
      }
    ]
  }
}
```

How it works...

The terms query is related to the previous kind of query; it extends the term query to support multivalues. This call is very useful because it is very common to the concept of filtering on multivalues. In traditional SQL, this operation is achieved with the in keyword in the where clause, that is, Select * from *** where color in ("red", "green").

In the preceding samples, the query searches for `uuid` with value `33333` or `22222`. The `terms` query is not merely a helper for the term matching function. The `terms` query allows you to define extra parameters to control the query behavior, such as the following:

- `minimum_match/minimum_should_match`: This controls how many matched terms are required to validate the query, as follows:

```
"terms": {
  "color": ["red", "blue", "white"],
  "minimum_should_match":2
}
```

- The preceding query matches all the documents where the `color` field has at least two values among `red`, `blue`, and `white`.
- `boost`: This is the standard query boost value used to modify the query weight. This can be very useful if you want to give more relevance to the terms that have been matched to increase the final document score.

There's more...

Because terms filtering is very powerful, to give some speedup in searching, the terms can be fetched by other documents during the query.

This is a very common scenario. Think, for example, that a user contains the list of groups in which they are associated and you want to filter documents that can be seen only by some groups. The pseudocode should be as follows:

```
GET /my-index/document/_search
{
  "query": {
    "terms": {
      "can_see_groups": {
        "index": "my-index",
        "type": "user",
        "id": "1bw71LaxSzSp_zV6NB_YGg",
        "path": "groups"
      }
    }
  }
}
```

In the preceding example, the list of groups is fetched at runtime from a document (which is always identified by an index, type, and ID) and the path (`field`) that contains the values to put in it. The `routing` parameter is also supported.

 Using a terms query with a lot of terms will be very slow. To prevent this, there is a limit to 65536 terms. This value can be lifted, if required, by setting the index settings `index.max_terms_count`.

This is a similar pattern to SQL, as shown in the following example:

```
select * from xxx where can_see_group in (select groups from user
where user_id='1bw71LaxSzSp_zV6NB_YGg')
```

Generally, NoSQL datastores do not support join, so the data must be optimized to searching using denormalization or other techniques.

Elasticsearch does not provide anything similar to the SQL joins, but it provides similar alternatives, such as the following:

- Child/parent queries via join field
- Nested queries
- Terms filtered with external document term fetching

See also

You can refer to the following points for further reference, all of which are related to this recipe:

- The *Executing a search* recipe in Chapter 4, *Exploring Search Capabilities*
- The *Using a term query* in this chapter
- The *Using a boolean query* recipe in Chapter 4, *Exploring Search Capabilities*
- The *Using the nested query*, *Using the* has_child *query* and *Using the* has_parent *query* recipes in Chapter 6, *Relationships and Geo Queries*

Using a prefix query

The prefix query is used when only the starting part of a term is known. It allows for the completion of truncated or partial terms.

Getting ready

You need an up-and-running Elasticsearch installation, as we described in the *Downloading and installing Elasticsearch* recipe in `Chapter 1`, *Getting Started*.

To execute these commands, any HTTP client can be used, such as curl (`https://curl.haxx.se/`), postman (`https://www.getpostman.com/`) or similar. I suggest you use the Kibana console as it provides code completion and better character escaping for Elasticsearch.

To correctly execute the following commands you will need an index populated with the `ch04/populate_kibana.txt` commands which is, available in the online code.

How to do it...

To execute a prefix query, we will perform the following steps:

1. We execute a prefix `query` from the command line, as follows:

```
POST /mybooks/_search
{
  "query": {
    "prefix": {
      "uuid": "222"
    }
  }
}
```

2. The result returned by Elasticsearch, if everything is alright, should be as follows:

```
{
  "took" : 13,
  "timed_out" : false,
  "_shards" : {
    "total" : 1,
    "successful" : 1,
    "skipped" : 0,
```

```
        "failed" : 0
      },
      "hits" : {
        "total" : 1,
        "max_score" : 1.0,
        "hits" : [
          {
            "_index" : "mybooks",
            "_type" : "_doc",
            "_id" : "2",
            "_score" : 1.0,
            "_source" : {
              "uuid" : "22222",
              "position" : 2,
              "title" : "Bill Baloney",
              "description" : "Bill Testere nice guy",
              "date" : "2016-06-12",
              "price" : 5,
              "quantity" : 34
            }
          }
        ]
      }
    }
```

How it works...

When a prefix query is executed, Lucene has a special method to skip to terms that start with a common prefix: so the execution of a prefix query is very fast.

The prefix query is used, in general, in scenarios where term completion is required, as follows:

- Name completion
- Code completion
- On type completion

When you design a tree structure in Elasticsearch, if the ID of the item contains the hierarchic relation (this approach is called *Materialized Path*), it can speed up the application filtering greatly. The following example shows how it's possible to model fruit and vegetable categories using a materialized path on the id:

Id	Element
001	Fruit
00102	Apple
0010201	Green Apple
0010202	Red Apple
00103	Melon
0010301	White Melon
002	Vegetables

In the preceding example, we have structured the ID that contains information about the tree structure, which allows us to create such queries:

- Filter by all the fruits, as follows:

    ```
    "prefix": {"fruit_id": "001" }
    ```

- Filter by all apple types, as follows:

    ```
    "prefix": {"fruit_id": "001002" }
    ```

- Filter by all the vegetables, as follows:

    ```
    "prefix": {"fruit_id": "002" }
    ```

If it's compared to a standard SQL `parent_id` table on a very large dataset, the reduction in join and the fast search performance of Lucene can filter the results in milliseconds compared to some seconds or minutes.

> Structuring the data in the correct way can give impressive performance boost!

There's more...

The prefix query can be very handy when you are searching for ending text. For example, a user must match a document with a field `filename` with the ending extension `png`. Usually, users tend to execute a poor performance regex query similar to `.*png`. The regex needs to check every term of the fields, so the computation time is very long.

The best practice is to index the filename field with a reverse analyzer to convert a suffix query to a prefix one!

To achieve this, perform the following steps:

1. We define `reverse_analyzer` to index level, putting this in the settings, as follows:

```
{
  "settings": {
    "analysis": {
      "analyzer": {
        "reverse_analyzer": {
          "type": "custom",
          "tokenizer": "keyword",
          "filter": [
            "lowercase",
            "reverse"
          ]
        }
      }
    }
  }
}
```

2. When we define the `filename` field, we use `reverse_analyzer` for its subfield, as follows:

```
"filename": {
  "type": "keyword",
  "fields": {
    "rev": {
      "type": "text",
      "analyzer": "reverse_analyzer"
    }
  }
}
```

3. Now we can search using a prefix `query`, using a similar `query`, as follows:

```
"query": {
    "prefix": {
      "filename.rev": ".jpg"
    }
}
```

Using this approach, for example, when you index a file named `myTest.png`, the internal Elasticsearch data will be similar to the following ones:

```
filename:"myTest.jpg"
filename.rev:"gnp.tsetym"
```

Because the text analyzer is used both for indexing and searching the prefix text, `.png` will be automatically processed in `gnp` when the query is executed.

Moving from regex to prefix for ending match can bring down your execution time from several seconds to several milliseconds!!

See also

- The *Using a term query* recipe, which is about full term search in Elasticsearch

Using a wildcard query

The wildcard query is used when a part of a term is known. It allows completion of truncated or partial terms. They are very famous because they are often used for commands on files within system shells (that is, `ls *.jpg`).

Getting ready

You need an up-and-running Elasticsearch installation as we described in the *Downloading and installing Elasticsearch* recipe in `Chapter 1`, *Getting Started*.

To execute the commands, any HTTP client can be used, such as curl (`https://curl.haxx.se/`), postman (`https://www.getpostman.com/`), or similar. I suggest you use the Kibana console as it provides code completion and better character escaping for Elasticsearch.

To correctly execute the following commands you will need an index populated with the `ch04/populate_kibana.txt` commands, available in the online code.

How to do it...

To execute a wildcard query, we will perform the following steps:

1. We will execute a `wildcard` query from the command line, as follows:

```
POST /mybooks/_search
{
  "query": {
    "wildcard": {
      "uuid": "22?2*"
    }
  }
}
```

2. The result returned by Elasticsearch, if everything is alright, should be as follows:

```
{
  "took" : 2,
  "timed_out" : false,
  "_shards" : {
    "total" : 1,
    "successful" : 1,
    "skipped" : 0,
    "failed" : 0
  },
  "hits" : {
    "total" : 1,
    "max_score" : 1.0,
    "hits" : [
      {
        "_index" : "mybooks",
        "_type" : "_doc",
        "_id" : "2",
        "_score" : 1.0,
        "_source" : {
          "uuid" : "22222",
          "position" : 2,
          "title" : "Bill Baloney",
          "description" : "Bill Testere nice guy",
          "date" : "2016-06-12",
          "price" : 5,
```

```
            "quantity" : 34
        }
      }
    ]
  }
}
```

How it works...

The wildcard is very similar to a regular expression, but it has only two special characters:

- *: This means match zero or more characters
- ?: This means match one character

During the query execution, all the terms of the searched field are matched against the wildcard query. So, the performance of the wildcard query depends on the cardinality of your terms.

To improve performance, it's suggested to not execute the wildcard query that starts with * or ?.

To speed up a search, it's good practice to have some starting characters to use the `skipTo` Lucene method in order to reduce the processed terms.

See also

You can refer to the following points for further reference, all of which are related to this recipe:

- The *Using a regexp query* recipe for more complex rules than wildcard ones
- The *Using a prefix query* recipe for creating a query with terms that start with a prefix

Using a regexp query

In the previous recipes, we have seen different term queries (terms, prefix, and wildcard); another powerful term query is the regexp (regular expression) one.

Getting ready

You need an up-and-running Elasticsearch installation, as we described in the *Downloading and installing Elasticsearch* recipe in `Chapter 1`, *Getting Started*.

To execute the commands, any HTTP client can be used, such as curl (`https://curl.haxx.se/`), postman (`https://www.getpostman.com/`), or similar. I suggest you use a Kibana console as it provides code completion and better character escaping for Elasticsearch.

To correctly execute the following commands you will need an index populated with the `ch04/populate_kibana.txt` commands, available in the online code.

How to do it...

To execute a regexp query, we will perform the following steps:

1. We can execute a `regexp` term query from the command line, as follows:

```
POST /mybooks/_search
{
  "query": {
    "regexp": {
      "description": {
        "value": "j.*",
        "flags": "INTERSECTION|COMPLEMENT|EMPTY"
      }
    }
  }
}
```

2. The query result will be as follows:

```
{
  "took" : 0,
  "timed_out" : false,
  "_shards" : {
    "total" : 1,
```

```
            "successful" : 1,
            "skipped" : 0,
            "failed" : 0
        },
        "hits" : {
          "total" : 1,
          "max_score" : 1.0,
          "hits" : [
            {
              "_index" : "mybooks",
              "_type" : "_doc",
              "_id" : "1",
              "_score" : 1.0,
              "_source" : {
                "uuid" : "11111",
                "position" : 1,
                "title" : "Joe Tester",
                "description" : "Joe Testere nice guy",
                "date" : "2015-10-22",
                "price" : 4.3,
                "quantity" : 50
              }
            }
          ]
        }
      }
```

The score for a matched regex result is always 1.0.

How it works...

The regexp query executes the regular expression against all terms of the documents. Internally, Lucene compiles the regular expression in an automaton to improve performances. Thus, generally, the performance of this query is not fast, as the performance depends on the regular expression used.

To speed up a regexp query, a good approach is to have a regular expression that doesn't start with a wildcard. The parameters that are used to control this process are as follows:

- boost (default 1.0): This includes the values used for boosting the score for this query.

- `flags`: This is a list of one or more flags pipe | delimited. The available flags are:
    - `ALL`: This enables all the optional regexp syntax
    - `ANYSTRING`: This enables any string (`@`)
    - `AUTOMATON`: This enables named automated (`<identifier>`)
    - `COMPLEMENT`: This enables complement (`~`)
    - `EMPTY`: This enables empty language (`#`)
    - `INTERSECTION`: This enables intersection (`&`)
    - `INTERVAL`: This enables numerical intervals (`<n-m>`)
    - `NONE`: This enables no optional regexp syntax

> To avoid poor performance in a search, don't execute regex starting with `.*`. Instead, use a prefix query on a string processed with a reverse analyzer.

See also

You can see the following points for further reference which are related to this recipe:

- The official documentation for regexp query at `https://www.elastic.co/guide/en/elasticsearch/reference/master/query-dsl-regexp-query.html for the regular expression syntax used by Lucene`
- The *Using a prefix query* recipe for a subset of a regex query that is starting for a part of the term
- The *Using a wildcard query* recipe if your regex can be rewritten in a wildcard query

Using span queries

The big difference between standard databases (SQL, and also many NoSQL databases, such as MongoDB, Riak, or CouchDB) and Elasticsearch is the number of facilities to express text queries. The span query family is a group of queries that control a sequence of text tokens using their positions: the standard queries don't take care of the positional presence of text tokens.

Span queries allow the defining of several kinds of queries:

- The exact phrase query
- The exact fragment query (that is, take off and give up)
- Partial exact phrase with a slop (other tokens between the searched terms, that is, the man with slop 2 can also match the strong man, the old wise man, and so on).

Getting ready

You need an up-and-running Elasticsearch installation as we described in the *Downloading and installing Elasticsearch* recipe in `Chapter 1`, *Getting Started*.

To execute the commands, any HTTP client can be used, such as curl (`https://curl.haxx.se/`), postman (`https://www.getpostman.com/`), or similar. I suggest you use the Kibana console as it provides the code completion and better character escaping for Elasticsearch.

To correctly execute the following commands you will need an index populated with the `ch04/populate_kibana.txt` commands, available in the online code.

How to do it...

To execute span queries, we will perform the following steps:

1. The main element in span queries is `span_term` whose usage is similar to the term of the standard query. It is possible to aggregate more than one `span_term` to formulate a span query.

2. The `span_first` query defines a query in which the `span_term` must match in the first token, or near it. The following code is an example of this:

```
POST /mybooks/_search
{
  "query": {
    "span_first": {
      "match": {
        "span_term": {
          "description": "joe"
        }
      },
      "end": 5
```

```
      }
    }
  }
}
```

3. The `span_or` query is used to define multivalues in a span query. This is very handy for simple synonym search, as shown in the following example:

```
POST /mybooks/_search
{
  "query": {
    "span_or": {
      "clauses": [
        {
          "span_term": {
            "description": "nice"
          }
        },
        {
          "span_term": {
            "description": "cool"
          }
        },
        {
          "span_term": {
            "description": "wonderful"
          }
        }
      ]
    }
  }
}
```

The list of clauses is the core of `span_or` query, because it contains the span terms that should match.

1. Similar to `span_or`, there is a `span_multi` query, which wraps multi-term queries such as prefix, wildcard, and so on. Consider the following code, for example:

```
POST /mybooks/_search
{
  "query": {
    "span_multi": {
      "match": {
        "prefix": {
          "description": {
            "value": "jo"
```

```
                              }
                            }
                          }
                        }
                      }
                    }
```

2. Queries can be used to create the span_near query, which allows you to control the token sequence of the query, as follows:

```
POST /mybooks/_search
{
  "query": {
    "span_near": {
      "clauses": [
        {
          "span_term": {
            "description": "nice"
          }
        },
        {
          "span_term": {
            "description": "joe"
          }
        },
        {
          "span_term": {
            "description": "guy"
          }
        }
      ],
      "slop": 3,
      "in_order": false
    }
  }
}
```

3. For complex queries, skipping matching given positional tokens is very important. This can be achieved with the span_not query, as shown in the following example:

```
POST /mybooks/_search
{
  "query": {
    "span_not": {
      "include": {
        "span_term": {
          "description": "nice"
```

```
          }
        },
        "exclude": {
          "span_near": {
            "clauses": [
              {
                "span_term": {
                  "description": "not"
                }
              },
              {
                "span_term": {
                  "description": "nice"
                }
              }
            ],
            "slop": 1,
            "in_order": true
          }
        }
      }
    }
  }
}
```

The `include` section contains the span that must be matched; `exclude` contains the span that must not be matched. It matches documents with the term `nice`, but not `not nice`. This can be very useful for excluding negative phrases!!!

1. For searching with a span query that is surrounded by other terms, we can use the `span_containing` variable, as follows:

```
POST /mybooks/_search
{
  "query": {
    "span_containing": {
      "little": {
        "span_term": {
          "description": "nice"
        }
      },
      "big": {
        "span_near": {
          "clauses": [
            {
              "span_term": {
                "description": "not"
              }
```

```
        },
        {
          "span_term": {
            "description": "guy"
          }
        }
      ],
      "slop": 5,
      "in_order": true
    }
   }
  }
 }
}
```

The little section contains the span that must be matched. The big section contains the span that contains the little matches. In the preceding case, the matched expression will be something similar to not * nice * guy.

1. For searching with a span query that is enclosed by other span terms, we can use the span_within variable, as follows:

```
POST /mybooks/_search
{
  "query": {
    "span_within": {
      "little": {
        "span_term": {
          "description": "nice"
        }
      },
      "big": {
        "span_near": {
          "clauses": [
            {
              "span_term": {
                "description": "not"
              }
            },
            {
              "span_term": {
                "description": "guy"
              }
            }
          ],
          "slop": 5,
          "in_order": true
```

```
                          }
                      }
                  }
              }
          }
```

The `little` section contains the span that must be matched. The `big` section contains the span that contains the `little` matches.

How it works...

Lucene provides the span queries available in Elasticsearch. The base span query is the `span_term` that works exactly as the term query. The goal of this span query is to match an exact term (field plus text). It can be composed to formulate other kinds of span queries.

 The main usage of span query is a proximity search: terms that are close to each other.

Using `span_term` in `span_first` means to match a term, which must be in the first position. If the end parameter (integer) is defined, it extends the first token matching to the passed value.

One of the most powerful span queries is `span_or` that allows defining multiple terms in the same position. It covers several scenarios, such as:

- Multinames
- Synonyms
- Several verbal forms

The `span_or` query does not have the counterpart `span_and`, which should have no meaning, because span queries are positional.

If the number of terms that must be passed to a `span_or` is huge, it can be reduced with a `span_multi` query with a prefix or a wildcard. This approach allows matching of, for example, all the terms play, playing, plays, player, players, and so on, using a prefix query with `play`.

Otherwise, the most powerful span query is span_near, which allows defining a list of span queries (clauses) to be matched in sequence or not. The parameters that can be passed to this span query are:

- in_order: This defines that the term matched in the clauses must be executed in order. If you define two span near queries with two span terms to match joe and black, and in_order is true, you will not be able to match black joe text (default true).
- slop: This defines the distance between terms that must be matched from the clauses (default 0).

> If you set the values of slop to 0 and in_order to true, you are creating an exact phrase match query that we will see in the next recipe.

The span_near query and slop can be used to create a phrase matching that is able to have some terms that are unknown. For example, consider matching an expression such as the house. If you need to execute an exact match, you need to write a similar query, as shown in the following example:

```
{
  "query": {
    "span_near": {
      "clauses": [
        {
          "span_term": {
            "description": "the"
          }
        },
        {
          "span_term": {
            "description": "house"
          }
        }
      ],
      "slop": 0,
      "in_order": true
    }
  }
}
```

Now, if you have, for example, an adjective between the `the` article and `house` (that is, the wonderful house, the big house, and so on), the previous query never matches them. To achieve this goal, it is required to set the slop to 1.

Usually, slop is set to 1, 2, or 3 as values: high values (`> 10`) have no meaning.

See also

The *Using a match query* recipe for a simplified way to create simple span queries.

Using a match query

Elasticsearch provides a helper to build complex span queries that depend on simple preconfigured settings. This helper is called **match query**.

Getting ready

You need an up-and-running Elasticsearch installation, as we described in the *Downloading and installing Elasticsearch* recipe in `Chapter 1`, *Getting Started*.

To execute these commands, any HTTP client can be used, such as curl (`https://curl.haxx.se/`), postman (`https://www.getpostman.com/`), or similar. I suggest you use the Kibana console as it provides code completion and better character escaping for Elasticsearch.

To correctly execute the following commands you will need an index populated with the `ch04/populate_kibana.txt` commands, which is available in the online code.

How to do it...

To execute match queries, we will perform the following steps:

1. The standard usage of a match query simply requires the field name and the query text. Consider the following example:

```
POST /mybooks/_search
{
  "query": {
    "match": {
```

```
      "description": {
        "query": "nice guy",
        "operator": "and"
      }
    }
  }
}
```

2. If you need to execute the same query as a phrase query, the type from match changes in `match_phrase`, as shown in the following example:

```
POST /mybooks/_search
{
  "query": {
    "match_phrase": {
      "description": "nice guy"
    }
  }
}
```

3. An extension of the previous query used in text completion or in `search as you type` functionality is `match_phrase_prefix`, as follows:

```
POST /mybooks/_search
{
  "query": {
    "match_phrase_prefix": {
      "description": "nice gu"
    }
  }
}
```

4. A common requirement is the possibility to search for several fields with the same `query`. The `multi_match` parameter provides this capability, as shown in the following example:

```
POST /mybooks/_search
{
  "query": {
    "multi_match": {
      "fields": [
        "description",
        "name"
      ],
      "query": "Bill",
      "operator": "and"
    }
```

```
        }
    }
```

How it works...

The match query aggregates several frequently used query types that cover standard query scenarios.

The standard match query creates a Boolean query that can be controlled by these parameters:

- operator: This defines how to store and process the terms. If it's set to OR, all the terms are converted in a boolean query with all the terms in should clauses. If it's set to AND, the terms build a list of must clauses (default OR).
- analyzer: This allows overriding of the default analyzer of the field (default based on mapping or set in searcher).
- fuzziness: This allows defining of a fuzzy term. Related to this parameter, prefix_length and max_expansion are available.
- zero_terms_query (none/all): This allows you to define a tokenizer filter that removes all terms from the query. The default behavior is to return nothing or all the documents. This is the case when you build an English query searching for the or a that means it could match all the documents (default none).
- cutoff_frequency: This allows the handling of dynamic stopwords (very common terms in text) at runtime. During query execution, terms over the cutoff_frequency are considered stopwords. This approach is very useful as it allows you to convert a general query to a domain-specific query, because terms to skip depend on text statistics. The correct value must be defined empirically.
- auto_generate_synonyms_phrase_query: (default true), if the match query should use the multi-terms synonym expansion with the synonym_graph token filter (For more references look at https://www.elastic.co/guide/en/elasticsearch/reference/current/analysis-synonym-graph-tokenfilter.html).

The Boolean query created from the match query is very handy, but it suffers from some common problems related to Boolean query, such as term position. If the term position matters, you need to use another family of match queries, the phrase one.

The `match_phrase` type in match query builds long span queries from the query text. The parameters that can be used to improve the quality of phrase query are the analyzer, for text processing, and the `slop`, which controls the distance between terms (refer to the *Using span queries* recipe).

If the last term is partially complete, and you want to provide your users query while writing functionality, the phrase type can be set to `match_phrase_prefix`. This type builds a span near query in which the last clause is a span prefix term. This functionality is often used for `typehead` widgets such as the one shown in the following screenshot:

The match query is a very useful query type, or, as I previously defined, it is a helper to build several common queries internally.

The `multi_match` parameter is similar to a `match` query that allows you to define multiple fields to search on. For defining these fields, there are several helpers that can be used, such as:

- **Wildcards field definition**: Using wildcards is a simple way to define multiple fields in one shot. For example, if you have fields for languages such as `name_en`, `name_es`, and `name_it`, you can define the search field as `name_*` to automatically search all the name fields.
- **Boosting some fields**: Not all the fields have the same importance. You can boost your fields using the ^ operator. For example, if you have title and content fields, and title is more important than content, you can define the fields in this way:

```
"fields":["title^3", "content"]
```

See also

You can see the following points for further reference which are related to this recipe:

- The *Using span queries* recipe to build more complex text queries
- The *Using prefix query* recipe for simple initial typehead

Using a query string query

In the previous recipes, we have seen several type of queries that use text to match the results. The query string query is a special type of query that allows us to define complex queries by mixing the field rules.

It uses the Lucene query parser to parse text to complex queries.

Getting ready

You need an up-and-running Elasticsearch installation, as we described in the *Downloading and installing Elasticsearch* recipe in `Chapter 1`, *Getting Started*.

To execute the commands, any HTTP client can be used, such as curl (`https://curl.haxx.se/`), postman (`https://www.getpostman.com/`), or similar. I suggest you use the Kibana console as it provides code completion and better character escaping for Elasticsearch.

To correctly execute the following commands you will need an index populated with the `ch04/populate_kibana.txt` commands, which is available in the online code.

How to do it...

To execute a `query_string` query, we will perform the following steps:

1. We want to search for the text `nice guy`, but with a condition of discarding the term `not` and displaying a price less than `5`. The query will be as follows:

```
POST /mybooks/_search
{
  "query": {
    "query_string": {
```

```
          "query": """"nice guy" -description:not price:{ * TO 5 }
""",
          "fields": [
            "description^5"
          ],
          "default_operator": "and"
        }
      }
    }
```

2. The result returned by Elasticsearch, if everything is alright, should be as follows:

```
{
  "took" : 17,
  "timed_out" : false,
  "_shards" : {
    "total" : 1,
    "successful" : 1,
    "skipped" : 0,
    "failed" : 0
  },
  "hits" : {
    "total" : 1,
    "max_score" : 2.3786995,
    "hits" : [
      {
        "_index" : "mybooks",
        "_type" : "_doc",
        "_id" : "1",
        "_score" : 2.3786995,
        "_source" : {
          "uuid" : "11111",
          "position" : 1,
          "title" : "Joe Tester",
          "description" : "Joe Testere nice guy",
          "date" : "2015-10-22",
          "price" : 4.3,
          "quantity" : 50
        }
      }
    ]
  }
}
```

How it works...

The `query_string` query is one of the most powerful types of queries. The only required field is `query`, which contains the query that must be parsed with the Lucene query parser. For more information, refer to the following link: `http://lucene.apache.org/core/7_0_0/queryparser/org/apache/lucene/queryparser/classic/package-summary.html`.

The Lucene query parser is able to analyze complex query syntax and convert it into many of the query types that we have seen in the previous recipes.

The optional parameters that can be passed to the query string query are as follows:

- `default_field`: This defines the default field to be used to the query. It can also be set at an index level defining the `index` property `index.query.default_field` (default `_all`).
- `fields`: This defines a list of fields to be used. It replaces the `default_field`. The `fields` parameter also allows us to use wildcards as values (that is, `city.*`).
- `default_operator`: This is the default operator to be used for text in the `query` parameter (the default `OR`; the available values are `AND` and `OR`).
- `analyzer`: This is the analyzer that must be used for a query string.
- `allow_leading_wildcard`: Here, the `*` and `?` wildcards are allowed as first characters. Using similar wildcards gives performance penalties (default `true`).
- `lowercase_expanded_terms`: This controls whether all expansion terms (generated by fuzzy, range, wildcard, and prefix) must be lowercase (default `true`).
- `enable_position_increments`: This enables the position increment in queries. For every query token, the positional value is incremented by `1` (default `true`).
- `fuzzy_max_expansions`: This controls the number of terms to be used in fuzzy term expansion (default `50`).
- `fuzziness`: This sets the fuzziness value for fuzzy queries (default `AUTO`).
- `fuzzy_prefix_length`: This sets the prefix length for fuzzy queries (default `0`).
- `phrase_slop`: This sets the default slop (number of optional terms that can be present in the middle of the given terms) for phrases. If it sets to zero, the query is an exact phrase match (default `0`).

- `boost`: This defines the boost value of the query (default `1.0`).
- `analyze_wildcard`: This enables the processing of wildcard terms in the query (default `false`).
- `auto_generate_phrase_queries`: This enables the auto-generation of phrase queries from the query string (default `false`).
- `minimum_should_match`: This controls how many `should` clauses should be verified to match the result. The value could be an integer value (that is, 3) or a percentage (that is, 40%) or a combination of both (default 1).
- `lenient`: If it's set to true, the parser will ignore all format-based failures (such as text to number of date conversion) (default `false`).
- `locale`: This is the locale used for string conversion (default `ROOT`).

There's more...

The query parser is a very powerful tool to support a wide range of complex queries. The most common cases are the following:

- `field:text`: This is used to match a field that contains some text. It's mapped on a term query.
- `field:(term1 OR term2)`: This is used to match some terms in `OR`. It's mapped on a terms query.
- `field:"text"`: This is used to match the exact text. It's mapped on a match query.
- `_exists_:field`: This is used to match documents that have a field. It's mapped on an exists filter.
- `_missing_:field`: This is used to match documents that don't have a field. It's mapped on a missing filter.
- `field:[start TO end]`: This is used to match a range from the `start` value to the `end` value. The `start` and `end` values could be terms, numbers, or a valid date-time value. The `start` and `end` values are included in the range; if you want to exclude a range, you must replace the `[]` delimiters with `{}`.
- `field:/regex/`: This is used to match a regular express.

The query parser also supports the text modifier, and is used to manipulate the text functionalities. The most used ones are as follows:

- Fuzziness using the form `text~`. The default fuzziness value is `2`, which allows a Damerau-Levenshtein edit-distance algorithm (`http://en.wikipedia.org/wiki/Damerau%E2%80%93Levenshtein_distance`) of 2.
- Wildcards with `?` which replace a single character, or `*` to replace zero or more characters. (That is, `b?ll` or `bi*` to match bill.)
- Proximity search `"term1 term2"~3`, allows matching phrase terms with a defined slop. (That is, `"my umbrella"~3` matches `"my green umbrella"`, `"my new umbrella"`, and so on.)

See also

You can see the following points for further reference which are related to this recipe:

- Refer to the Lucene official query parser syntax at `http://lucene.apache.org/core/8_0_0/queryparser/org/apache/lucene/queryparser/classic/package-summary.html` which provides a complete description of all the syntax.
- The official Elasticsearch documentation about query string query at `https://www.elastic.co/guide/en/elasticsearch/reference/master/query-dsl-query-string-query.html`.

Using a simple query string query

Typically, the programmer has the control to build complex query using Boolean query and the other query types. Thus, Elasticsearch provides two kinds of queries that give the user the ability to create string queries with several operators in it.

These kinds of queries are very common on advanced search engine usage, such as Google, which allow us to use the + and – operators on terms.

Getting ready

You need an up-and-running Elasticsearch installation as we described in the *Downloading and installing Elasticsearch* recipe in `Chapter 1`, *Getting Started*.

To execute the commands, any HTTP client can be used, such as curl (`https://curl.haxx.se/`), postman (`https://www.getpostman.com/`), or similar. I suggest you use a Kibana console as it provides the code completion and better character escaping for Elasticsearch.

To correctly execute the following commands you will need an index populated with the `ch04/populate_kibana.txt` commands, available in the online code.

How to do it...

To execute a simple query string query, we will perform the following steps:

1. We want to search for text `nice guy`, but not excluding the term `not`. The query will be as follows:

```
POST /mybooks/_search
{
  "query": {
    "simple_query_string": {
      "query": """"nice guy" -not""",
      "fields": [
        "description^5",
        "_all"
      ],
      "default_operator": "and"
    }
  }
}
```

2. The result returned by Elasticsearch, if everything is alright, should be as follows:

```
{
  ...truncated...
  "hits" : {
    "total" : 2,
    "max_score" : 2.3786995,
    "hits" : [
      {
        "_index" : "mybooks",
        "_type" : "_doc",
        "_id" : "1",
        "_score" : 2.3786995,
        "_source" : {
          "uuid" : "11111",
```

```
                "position" : 1,
                "title" : "Joe Tester",
                "description" : "Joe Testere nice guy",
                "date" : "2015-10-22",
                "price" : 4.3,
                "quantity" : 50
            }
        },
        {
          "_index" : "mybooks",
          "_type" : "_doc",
          "_id" : "2",
          "_score" : 2.3786995,
          "_source" : {
            "uuid" : "22222",
            "position" : 2,
            "title" : "Bill Baloney",
            "description" : "Bill Testere nice guy",
            "date" : "2016-06-12",
            "price" : 5,
            "quantity" : 34
          }
        }
      ]
    }
}
```

How it works...

The simple query string query takes the query text, tokenizes it, and builds a Boolean query applying the rules provided in your text query.

It's a good tool, if given to the final user, to express simple advanced queries. Its parser is very complex, so it's able to extract fragments for exact match to be interpreted as span queries.

 The advantage of simple query string query is that the parser always gives you a valid query.

If you are use the previous query, *query string query*, in case the user gives you, as input, a malformed query, it will throw an error. If you use the simple query string, also, if malformed, it will be will "fixed" and executed without errors.

See also

For a complete reference of these query type syntaxes, the official documentation is available at `https://www.elastic.co/guide/en/elasticsearch/reference/master/query-dsl-simple-query-string-query.html` for simple query string query.

Using the range query

All the previous queries work with defined or partially defined values, but it's very common in real world application to work for a range of values. The most common standard scenarios are:

- Filtering by numeric value range (that is, price, size, and age)
- Filtering by date (that is, events of `03/07/12` can be a range query from `03/07/12 00:00:00` to `03/07/12 24:59:59`)
- Filtering by term range (that is, from A to D).

Getting ready

You need an up-and-running Elasticsearch installation as we described in the *Downloading and installing Elasticsearch* recipe in `Chapter 1`, *Getting Started*.

To execute the commands, any HTTP client can be used, such as curl (`https://curl.haxx.se/`), postman (`https://www.getpostman.com/`), or similar. I suggest you use the Kibana console as it provides the code completion and better character escaping for Elasticsearch.

To correctly execute the following commands you will need an index populated with the `ch04/populate_kibana.txt` commands, available in the online code.

How to do it...

To execute a range query, we will perform the following steps:

1. Consider the sample data of the previous examples, which contains an integer field `position`. Using it to execute a query for filtering positions between 3 and 5, we will have the following output:

```
POST /mybooks/_search
{
  "query": {
    "range": {
      "position": {
        "from": 3,
        "to": 4,
        "include_lower": true,
        "include_upper": false
      }
    }
  }
}
```

2. The result returned by Elasticsearch, if everything is alright, should be as follows:

```
{
  "took" : 0,
  "timed_out" : false,
  "_shards" : {
"total" : 1,
    "successful" : 1,
    "skipped" : 0,
    "failed" : 0
  },
  "hits" : {
    "total" : 1,
    "max_score" : 1.0,
    "hits" : [
      {
        "_index" : "mybooks",
        "_type" : "_doc",
        "_id" : "3",
        "_score" : 1.0,
        "_source" : {
          "uuid" : "33333",
          "position" : 3,
          "title" : "Bill Klingon",
```

```
                    "description" : "Bill is not\n nice guy",
                    "date" : "2017-09-21",
                    "price" : 6,
                    "quantity" : 33
                }
            }
        ]
    }
}
```

How it works...

The range query is used because scoring results can cover several interesting scenarios, such as:

- Items with high availability in stocks should be presented first
- New items should be boosted
- Most bought items should be boosted

The range query is very handy with numeric values, as the preceding example shows. The parameters that a range query accepts are:

- `from`: This is the starting value for the range (optional)
- `to`: This is the ending value for the range (optional)
- `include_in_lower`: This includes the starting value in the range (optional, default `true`)
- `include_in_upper`: This includes the ending value in the range (optional, default `true`)

In range query, other helper parameters are available to simplify search, which are listed as follows:

- `gt`: (greater than), this has the same functionality to set the `from` parameter and `include_in_lower` to `false`
- `gte`: (greater than or equal), this has the same functionality to set the `from` parameter and `include_in_lower` to `true`
- `lt`: (less than), this has the same functionality to set the `to` parameter and the `include_in_upper` to `false`
- `lte`: (less than or equal to), this has the same functionality to set the `to` parameter and the `include_in_upper` to `true`

There's more...

In Elasticsearch, which kind of query covers several types of SQL range queries, such as <, <=, >, >= on numeric values. Because, in Elasticsearch, date or time fields are managed internally as numeric fields, it's possible to use the range queries or filters with date values. If the field is a `date` field, every value in the range query is automatically converted in a numeric value. For example, if you need to filter the documents of this year, the range fragment will be ass follows:

```
"range": {
  "timestamp": {
    "from": "2014-01-01",
    "to": "2015-01-01",
    "include_lower": true,
    "include_upper": false
  }
}
```

For `date` fields, it is also possible to specify a `time_zone` value to be used in order to correctly compute the matches.

If you are using a date value you can use a date math (https://www.elastic.co/guide/en/elasticsearch/reference/master/common-options.html#date-math) to round the values.

The common terms query

When the user is searching some text with a query, not all the terms that the user uses have the same importance. The more common terms are generally removed for query execution, to reduce the noise generated by them. These terms are called stop words and they are generally articles, conjunctions, and common language words (that is, `the`, `a`, `so`, `and`, `or`, and so on).

The list of stop words depends on the language, and is independent from your documents. Lucene provides ways to dynamically compute the stop words list based on your indexed document a `query` time using the **common terms query**.

Getting ready

You need an up-and-running Elasticsearch installation, as we described in the *Downloading and installing Elasticsearch* recipe in `Chapter 1`, *Getting Started*.

To execute the commands, any HTTP client can be used, such as curl (`https://curl.haxx.se/`), postman (`https://www.getpostman.com/`), or similar. I suggest you use the Kibana console as provide the code completion and better character escaping for Elasticsearch.

To correctly execute the following commands you will need an index populated with the `ch04/populate_kibana.txt` commands, available in the online code.

How to do it...

To execute a common term query, we will perform the following steps:

1. We want to search for `a nice guy`, so we will use the following code:

```
POST /mybooks/_search
{
  "query": {
    "common": {
      "description": {
        "query": "nice guy",
        "cutoff_frequency": 0.001
      }
    }
  }
}
```

2. The result returned by Elasticsearch, if everything is alright, should be as follows:

```
{
  ...truncated...
  "hits" : {
    "total" : 3,
    "max_score" : 0.2757399,
    "hits" : [
      {
        "_index" : "mybooks",
        "_type" : "_doc",
        "_id" : "1",
        "_score" : 0.2757399,
```

```
              "_source" :...truncated...,
           {
              "_index" : "mybooks",
              "_type" : "_doc",
              "_id" : "2",
              "_score" : 0.2757399,
              "_source" :...truncated...,,
           {
              "_index" : "mybooks",
              "_type" : "_doc",
              "_id" : "3",
              "_score" : 0.25124985,
              "_source" :...truncated...,
           }
        ]
     }
  }
```

How it works...

Lucene, the core engine of Elasticsearch, provides a lot of statistics on your indexed terms that are required to compute the algorithms for the different score types.

These statistics use a query time, in common terms, a query to differentiate the query terms in two categories:

- **Low frequency terms**: These are the less common terms in your index. They are generally the most important ones for your current query. For the preceding query, the terms could be ["nice", "guy"].
- **High frequency terms**: They are the most common ones and mainly defined as stop words. For the preceding query, the term could be ["a"].

The preceding query, based on term statistics, is internally converted in Elasticsearch into a similar query, as follows:

```
{
  "query": {
    "bool": {
      "must": [ # low frequency terms
        {
          "term": {
            "description": "nice"
          }
        },
        {
```

```
        "term": {
          "description": "guy"
        }
      }
    ],
    "should": [ # high frequency terms
      {
        "term": {
          "description": "a"
        }
      }
    ]
  }
}
}
```

To control the common term query, the following options are available:

- `cutoff_frequency`: This value defines the cut frequency that allows to us to partition the low and high frequency term lists. Its better value depends on your data. Some empirical tests are needed to evaluate the correct value
- `minimum_should_match`. This can be defined in two ways:
  - As a single value. This defines the minimum terms that must be matched for low frequency terms, that is, `"minimum_should_match" : 2`
  - As an object containing the low and high values, that is as follows:

```
"minimum_should_match": {
  "low_freq": 1,
  "high_freq": 2
}
```

Pay attention that the term's statistics depend on the data in your Lucene indices, so they are in Elasticsearch as shard level.

See also

You can see the following points for further reference which are related to this recipe:

- The *Using a term query* recipe for a simple term match.
- The *Using a boolean query* recipe in `Chapter 4`, *Exploring Search Capabilities*

Using an IDs query

The IDs query allows matching documents by their IDs, spreading the query in all the searched shards.

Getting ready

You need an up-and-running Elasticsearch installation as we described in the *Downloading and installing Elasticsearch* recipe in `Chapter 1`, *Getting Started*.

To execute the commands, any HTTP client can be used, such as curl (`https://curl.haxx.se/`), postman (`https://www.getpostman.com/`), or similar. I suggest you use the Kibana console as it provides the code completion and better character escaping for Elasticsearch.

To correctly execute the following commands you will need an index populated with the `ch04/populate_kibana.txt` commands, available in the online code.

How to do it...

To execute the IDs queries or filters, we will perform the steps given, as follows:

1. The IDs query for fetching IDs "1", "2", "3" of type `test-type` is in the following form:

```
POST /mybooks/_search
{
  "query": {
    "ids": {
      "type": "test-type",
      "values": [
        "1",
        "2",
        "3"
      ]
    }
  }
}
```

2. The result returned by Elasticsearch, if everything is alright, should be as follows:

```
{
  ...truncated...
  "hits" : {
    "total" : 3,
    "max_score" : 0.2757399,
    "hits" : [
      {
        "_index" : "mybooks",
        "_type" : "_doc",
        "_id" : "1",
        "_score" : 0.2757399,
        "_source" :...truncated...,
      {
        "_index" : "mybooks",
        "_type" : "_doc",
        "_id" : "2",
        "_score" : 0.2757399,
        "_source" :...truncated...,,
      {
        "_index" : "mybooks",
        "_type" : "_doc",
        "_id" : "3",
        "_score" : 0.25124985,
        "_source" :...truncated...,
      }
    ]
  }
}
```

In the results, the request ID order is not respected. So, in case you ask multitypes, you need to use the document metadata (_index, _type, _id) to better manage your results.

How it works...

Query by ID is a very fast operation because IDs are often cached in memory for fast lookup.

The parameters used in this query are:

- `ids`: This includes a list of IDs that must be matched (required)
- `type`: This is a string, or a list of strings, which defines the types in which we need to search. If not defined, they are taken from the URL of the call (optional).

 Elasticsearch internally stores the ID of a document in a special field called `_id`. An `_id` is unique in an index.

Usually, the standard way of using IDs query is to select documents; this query allows fetching documents without knowing the shard that contains the documents. The documents are stored in shards, which are chosen based on a modulo operation computed on the document ID. If a parent ID, or a routing, is defined, they are used to choose the shard: in this case, the only way to fetch the document knowing its ID is to use the IDs query.

If you need to fetch multi-IDs and there are no routing changes (due to `routing` parameter at index time), it's better not to use this kind of query, but to use get or multi-get API calls to get documents as they are much faster and also work in real-time.

See also

You can see the following points for further reference which are related to this recipe:

- The *Getting a document* recipe in `Chapter 3`, *Basic Operations.*
- The *Speeding up GET operations (Multi GET)* recipe in `Chapter 3`, *Basic Operations.*

Using the function score query

This kind of query is one of the most powerful queries available, because it allows extensive customization of a scoring algorithm. The function score query allows us to define a function that controls the score of the documents which are returned by a query.

Generally, these functions are CPU intensive and executing them on a large dataset requires a lot of memory, but computing them on a small subset can significantly improve the search quality.

The common scenarios used for this query are:

- Creating a custom score function (with decay function, for example)
- Creating a custom boost factor, for example, based on another field (that is, boosting a document by distance from a point)
- Creating a custom filter score function, for example, based on scripting Elasticsearch capabilities
- Ordering the documents randomly.

Getting ready

You need an up-and-running Elasticsearch installation as we described in the *Downloading and installing Elasticsearch* recipe in `Chapter 1`, *Getting Started*.

To execute the commands, any HTTP client can be used, such as curl (`https://curl. haxx.se/`), postman (`https://www.getpostman.com/`), or similar. I suggest you use the Kibana console as it provides the code completion and better character escaping for Elasticsearch.

To correctly execute the following commands you will need an index populated with the `ch04/populate_kibana.txt` commands, available in the online code.

How to do it...

To execute a function score query, we will perform the following steps:

1. We can execute a `function_score` query from the command line, as follows:

```
POST /mybooks/_search
{
  "query": {
    "function_score": {
      "query": {
        "query_string": {
          "query": "bill"
        }
```

```
        },
        "functions": [
          {
            "linear": {
              "position": {
                "origin": "0",
                "scale": "20"
              }
            }
          }
        ],
        "score_mode": "multiply"
      }
    }
  }
}
```

We execute a query searching for `bill` and we score the result with the `linear` function on the `position` field.

1. The result should be as follows:

```
{
  "took" : 32,
  "timed_out" : false,
  "_shards" : {
    "total" : 1,
    "successful" : 1,
    "skipped" : 0,
    "failed" : 0
  },
  "hits" : {
    "total" : 2,
    "max_score" : 0.46101078,
    "hits" : [
      {
        "_index" : "mybooks",
        "_type" : "_doc",
        "_id" : "2",
        "_score" : 0.46101078,
        "_source" : ...truncated...
      },
      {
        "_index" : "mybooks",
        "_type" : "_doc",
        "_id" : "3",
        "_score" : 0.43475336,
        "_source" : ...truncated...
      }
```

```
            ]
        }
    }
```

How it works...

The function score query is probably the most complex query type to master due to the natural complexity of mathematical algorithms involved in the scoring.

The generic full form of the function score query is as follows:

```
"function_score": {
  "(query|filter)": {},
  "boost": "boost for the whole query",
  "functions": [
    {
      "filter": {},
      "FUNCTION": {}
    },
    {
      "FUNCTION": {}
    }
  ],
  "max_boost": number,
  "boost_mode": "(multiply|replace|...)",
  "score_mode": "(multiply|max|...)",
  "script_score": {},
  "random_score": {
    "seed ": number
  }
}
```

The parameters that are used are as follows:

- query or filter: This is the query used to match the required documents (optional, default a match all query).
- boost: This is the boost to apply to the whole query (default 1.0).
- functions: This is a list of functions used to score the queries. In a simple case, use only one function. In the function object, a filter can be provided to apply the function only to a subset of documents, because the filter is applied first.
- max_boost: This sets the maximum allowed value for the boost score (default java FLT_MAX).

- `boost_mode`: This parameter defines how the function score is combined with the query score (default `"multiply"`). The possible values are:

  - `multiply` (default): Here, the query score and function score are multiplied

  - `replace`: Here, only the function score is used; the query score is ignored

  - `sum`: Here, the query score and function score are added

  - `avg`: Here, the average between query score and function score is taken

  - `max`: This is the maximum of query score and function score

  - `min`: This is the minimum of query score and function score

  - `score_mode` (default `multiply`): This parameter defines how the resulting function scores (when multiple functions are defined) are combined. The possible values are:

    - `multiply`: The scores are multiplied

    - `sum`: The scores are summed

    - `avg`: The scores are averaged

    - `first`: The first function that has a matching filter is applied

    - `max`: The maximum score is used

    - `min`: The minimum score is used

- `script_score`: This allows you to define a script score function to be used to compute the score (optional). (Elasticsearch scripting will be discussed in `Chapter 8`, *Scripting in Elasticsearch*.) This parameter is very useful in implementing simple script algorithms. The original score value is in the `_score` function scope. This allows the defining of similar algorithms, as follows:

```
"script_score": {
    "script": {
      "params": {
        "param1": 2,
        "param2": 3.1
      },
      "source": "_score * doc['my_numeric_field'].value
/pow(param1, param2)"
    }
  }
```

In Elasticsearch 7.x, the `script_score` can be used as a **Script Score Query** as experimental functionality (https://www.elastic.co/guide/en/elasticsearch/reference/7.0/query-dsl-script-score-query.html).

- `random_score`: This allows us to randomly score the documents. It is very useful for retrieving records randomly (optional).

Elasticsearch provides native support for the most common scoring decay distribution algorithms, such as:

- **Linear**: This is used to linearly distribute the scores based on a distance from a value
- **Exponential (exp)**: This is used for an exponential decay function
- **Gaussian (gauss)**: This is used for the Gaussian decay function

 Choosing the correct function distribution depends on the context and data distribution.

See also

You can refer to the following points for further reference, all of which are related to this recipe:

- Refer to the official Elasticsearch documentation at https://www.elastic.co/guide/en/elasticsearch/reference/current/query-dsl-function-score-query.html for a complete reference on all the function Score Query parameters.
- Refer to the blog post at https://www.elastic.co/blog/found-function-scoring for several scenarios of using this kind of query.
- Refer to the Experimental Script Score Query provided by Elasticsearch 7.x at https://www.elastic.co/guide/en/elasticsearch/reference/7.0/query-dsl-script-score-query.html .

Using the exists query

One of the main characteristics of Elasticsearch is its schema-less indexing capability. Records in Elasticsearch can have missing values. Due to its schema-less nature, two kinds of queries are required:

- **Exists field**: This is used to check if a field exists in a document.
- **Missing field**: This is used to check if a field is missing in a document.

Getting ready

You need an up-and-running Elasticsearch installation as we described in the *Downloading and installing Elasticsearch* recipe in `Chapter 1`, *Getting Started*.

To execute the commands, any HTTP client can be used, such as curl (`https://curl.haxx.se/`), postman (`https://www.getpostman.com/`), or similar. I suggest you use the Kibana console as it provides code completion and better character escaping for Elasticsearch.

To correctly execute the following commands you will need an index populated with the `ch04/populate_kibana.txt` commands, which is available in the online code.

How to do it...

To execute existing and missing filters, we will perform the following steps:

1. To search all the test-type documents that have a field called `description`, the query will be as follows:

   ```
   POST /mybooks/_search
   {
     "query": {
       "exists": {
         "field": "description"
       }
     }
   }
   ```

2. To search all the test-type documents that do not have a field called `description` because there is not a missing query, and we can obtain it using the boolean or not query; the query will be as follows:

```
POST /mybooks/_search
{
  "query": {
    "bool": {
      "must_not": {
        "exists": {
          "field": "description"
        }
      }
    }
  }
}
```

How it works...

The exists and missing filters take only a `field` parameter, which contains the name of the field to be checked. Using simple fields, there are no pitfalls; however, if you are using a single embedded object, or a list of them, you need to use a sub-object field because of the way Elasticsearch and Lucene work.

The following example helps you to understand how Elasticsearch maps JSON objects to Lucene documents internally if you are trying to index a JSON document:

```
{
  "name": "Paul",
  "address": {
    "city": "Sydney",
    "street": "Opera House Road",
    "number": "44"
  }
}
```

Elasticsearch will internally index it, as follows:

```
name:paul
address.city:Sydney
address.street:Opera House Road
address.number:44
```

As we can see, there is no field `address` indexed, so an exists filter on `address` fails. To match documents with an address, you must search for a subfield (that is, `address.city`).

6
Relationship and Geo Queries

In this chapter, we will explore special queries that can be used to search for relationships between Elasticsearch and geo location documents.

When we have a parent-child relationship (based on `join` field mapping), we can use special queries to query for a similar relationship. Elasticsearch doesn't provide SQL join, but it lets you search child/parent related documents; it makes it possible to retrieve child documents via parent selection or by matching parent documents and filtering it by its children. The way to create a parent-child relationship in to create a relationship in Elasticsearch is very powerful and can help resolve many common data relationship issues that are used to easily solve issues in traditional relational databases in Elasticsearch. These features, in my experience, aren't popular among young Elasticsearch users, but are valuable if you manage intelligence data sources.

In this chapter, we will also look at how to query nested objects using a nested query. The last part of this chapter is related to geo localization queries that provide queries based on the distance, box, and polygon for matching documents that meet this criteria.

In this chapter, we will cover the following recipes:

- Using the has_child query
- Using the has_parent query
- Using the nested query
- Using the geo_bounding_box query
- Using the geo_polygon query
- Using the geo_distance query

Using the has_child query

Elasticsearch does not only support simple unrelated documents, it also lets you define a hierarchy based on parents and children. The `has_child` query allows you to query for parent documents of children by matching other queries.

Getting ready

As we described in the *Downloading and installing Elasticsearch* recipe in `Chapter 1`, *Getting Started*, you need an up and running Elasticsearch installation to execute the current recipe code.

To execute the code in the following section, any HTTP client can be used. This includes curl (`https://curl.haxx.se/`), Postman (`https://www.getpostman.com/`), or other similar versions. I suggest using Kibana console, as this provides the code completion and better character escaping for Elasticsearch.

To correctly execute the following commands, you will need an index populated with the `ch04/populate_kibana.txt` commands available in the online code.

The index used in this recipe is `mybooks-join`, and the **Unified Modeling Language** (**UML**) of the data model is as follows:

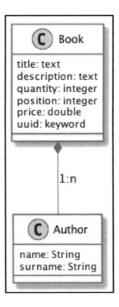

How to do it...

To execute the `has_child` queries, we will perform the following steps:

1. We want to search the parent `book` of the children `author`, which has a term in the `name` field called `martin`. We can create this kind of query using the following code:

```
POST /mybooks-join/_search
{
  "query": {
    "has_child": {
      "type": "author",
      "query": {
        "term": {
          "name": "martin"
        }
      },
      "inner_hits" : {}
    }
  }
}
```

2. If everything is working well, the result returned by Elasticsearch should be as follows:

```
{
  ...truncated...,
  "hits" : {
    "total" : 1,
    "max_score" : 1.0,
    "hits" : [
      {
        "_index" : "mybooks-join",
        "_type" : "_doc",
        "_id" : "3",
        "_score" : 1.0,
        "_source" : ...truncated...,
        "inner_hits" : {
          "author" : {
            "hits" : {
              "total" : 1,
              "max_score" : 1.2039728,
              "hits" : [
                {
                  "_index" : "mybooks-join",
                  "_type" : "_doc",
```

```
              "_id" : "a3",
              "_score" : 1.2039728,
              "_routing" : "3",
              "_source" : {
                "name" : "Martin",
                "surname" : "Twisted",
                "join" : {
                  "name" : "author",
                  "parent" : "3"
                }
              }
            }
          ]
        }
      }
    }
  }
]
}
}
```

For this example, we have used `inner_hits` to return matched children.

How it works...

This kind of query works by returning parent documents whose children match the query. The query can be of any type. The prerequisite of this kind of query is that the children must be correctly indexed in the shard of their parent. Internally, this kind of query is executed on the children, and all the IDs of the children are used to filter the parent. A system must have enough memory to store the children IDs.

The parameters that are used to control this process are as follows:

- The `type` parameter describes the type of children. This type is part of the same index of the parent: it's the name provided in the join field parameter at index time.
- The `query` parameter can be executed for selection of the children. Any kind of query can be used.
- If defined, the `score_mode` parameter (the default is `none`; available values are `max`, `sum`, `avg`, and `none`) allows you the aggreagate the children scores with the parent ones.

- `min_children` and `max_children` are optional parameters. This is the minimum/maximum number of children that are required to match the parent document.
- `ignore_unmapped` (default `false`), when set to `true`, will ignore unmapped types. This is very useful when executing a query on multiple indices and some types are missing. The default behavior is to throw an exception if there is a mapping error.

 In Elasticsearch, a document must have only one parent because the parent ID is used to choose the shard to put the children in. When working with child documents, it is important to remember that they must be stored in the same shard as their parents. Special precautions must be taken when fetching, modifying, and deleting them if the routing is unknown.

As the parent-child relation can be considered to be similar to a foreign key in standard SQL, there are some limitations due to the distributed nature of Elasticsearch. This includes the following:

- There must be only one parent for each type
- The join part of child or parent is done in a shard and not distributed on all the clusters to reduce networking and increase performance

There's more...

Sometimes, you need to sort the parents according to their child field. In order to do this, you need to sort the parents by looking at the max score of the child field. To execute this kind of query, you can use the `function_score` query in the following way:

```
POST /mybooks-join/_search
{
  "query": {
    "has_child": {
      "type": "author",
      "score_mode": "max",
      "query": {
        "function_score": {
          "script_score": {
            "script": """doc["rating"].value"""
          }
        }
```

```
        },
        "inner_hits": {}
      }
    }
  }
```

By executing this query for every child of a parent, the maximum score is taken (using the `function_score`), which is the value of the field that we want to sort.

In the preceding example, we have used scripting, which will be discussed in `Chapter 9`, *Managing Cluster*. This needs to be active so that it can be used.

See also

You can refer to the following recipes for further information related to this recipe:

- *The Indexing a document* recipe in `Chapter 3`, *Basic Operations*
- *The Mapping a child document with a join field* recipe in `Chapter 2`, *Managing Mapping*
- *Using a function score query* recipe in `Chapter 6`, *Text and Numeric Queries*

Using the has_parent query

In the previous recipe, we saw the `has_child` query. Elasticsearch provides a query to search child documents based on the parent query, `has_parent`.

Getting ready

You need an up and running Elasticsearch installation, as we described in the *Downloading and installing Elasticsearch* recipe in `Chapter 1`, *Getting Started*.

To execute these commands, I suggest using the Kibana console, as this provides code completion and better character escaping for Elasticsearch.

To correctly execute the following commands, you will need an index populated with the `ch04/populate_kibana.txt` commands, which is available in the online code. The index that's used in this recipe is `mybooks-join`.

How to do it...

To execute the `has_parent` query, we will perform the following steps:

1. We want to search for the children `author` of the parents `book` that has the term `joe` in the `description` field. We can create this kind of query using the following code:

```
POST /mybooks-join/_search
{
  "query": {
    "has_parent": {
      "parent_type": "book",
      "query": {
        "term": {
          "description": "bill"
        }
      }
    }
  }
}
```

2. If everything is fine here, the result returned by Elasticsearch should be as follows:

```
{
  ...truncated...
  "hits" : {
    "total" : 2,
    "max_score" : 1.0,
    "hits" : [
      {
        "_index" : "mybooks-join",
        "_type" : "_doc",
        "_id" : "a2",
        "_score" : 1.0,
        "_routing" : "2",
        "_source" : {
          "name" : "Agatha",
          "surname" : "Princeton",
          "rating" : 2.1,
          "join" : {
            "name" : "author",
            "parent" : "2"
          }
        }
      },
```

```
{
  "_index" : "mybooks-join",
  "_type" : "_doc",
  "_id" : "a3",
  "_score" : 1.0,
  "_routing" : "3",
  "_source" : {
    "name" : "Martin",
    "surname" : "Twisted",
    "rating" : 3.2,
    "join" : {
      "name" : "author",
      "parent" : "3"
    }
  }
}
          ]
        }
      }
```

How it works...

This kind of query works by returning child documents whose parent ones match a subquery. Internally, this subquery is executed on the parents, and all the IDs of the matching parents are used to filter the children. The system must have enough memory to store all the parent IDs.

The parameters that are used to control this process are as follows:

- `parent_type`: This is the type of the parent.
- `query`: This is the query that can be executed to select the parents. Every kind of query can be used.
- `score`: The default value is `false`. Using the default configuration of `false`, Elasticsearch ignores the scores for parent documents, thus reducing memory and increasing performance. If it's set to `true`, the parent query score is aggregated into the children's.

Using the computed score, you can sort the resulting hits based on a parent with the same approach that was shown in the previous recipe using `function_score`.

See also

You can refer to the following recipes for further information related to this recipe:

- *The Indexing a document* recipe in `Chapter 4`, *Exploring Search Capabilities*
- *The Mapping a child document with a join field* recipe in `Chapter 3`, *Basic Operations*

Using nested queries

For queries based on nested objects, as we saw in `Chapter 2`, *Managing Mapping*, there is a special nested query. This kind of query is required because nested objects are indexed in a special way in Elasticsearch.

Getting ready

You need an up and running Elasticsearch installation, as we described in the *Downloading and installing Elasticsearch* recipe in `Chapter 1`, *Getting Started*.

To execute these commands, any HTTP client can be used, such as curl (`https://curl.haxx.se/`), Postman (`https://www.getpostman.com/`), or similar. I suggest using the Kibana console, as it provides code completion and better character escaping for querying text.

To correctly execute the following commands, you will need an index populated with the `ch04/populate_kibana.txt` commands, which is available in the online code.

The index that's used in this recipe is `mybooks-join`.

How to do it...

To execute the nested query, we will perform the following steps:

1. We want to search the document for nested objects that are `blue` and whose size is greater than `10`. The `nested` query will be as follows:

   ```
   POST /mybooks-join/_search
   {
     "query": {
       "nested": {
   ```

```
                  "path": "versions",
                  "score_mode": "avg",
                  "query": {
                    "bool": {
                      "must": [
                        {
                          "term": {
                            "versions.color": "blue"
                          }
                        },
                        {
                          "range": {
                            "versions.size": {
                              "gt": 10
                            }
                          }
                        }
                      ]
                    }
                  }
                }
              }
            }
          }
        }
      }
```

2. The result returned by Elasticsearch, if everything is alright, should be as follows:

```
{
  ...truncated...
  "hits" : {
    "total" : 1,
    "max_score" : 1.8754687,
    "hits" : [
      {
        "_index" : "mybooks-join",
        "_type" : "_doc",
        "_id" : "1",
        "_score" : 1.8754687,
        "_source" : {
          ...truncated...
          "versions" : [
            {
              "color" : "yellow",
              "size" : 5
            },
            {
              "color" : "blue",
              "size" : 15
```

```
                    }
                ]
            }
        }
    ]
}
}
```

How it works...

Elasticsearch manages nested objects in a special way. During indexing, they are extracted from the main document and indexed as a separate document, which is saved in the same Lucene chunk of the main document.

The nested query executes the first query on the nested documents and after gathering the result IDs, they are used to filter the main document. The parameters that are used to control this process are as follows:

- `path`: This is the path of the parent document that contains the nested objects.
- `query`: This is the query that can be executed to select the nested objects. Every kind of query can be used.
- `score_mode`: The default value is `avg`. The valid values are `avg`, `sum`, `min`, `max`, and `none`, which control how to use the score of the nested document matches to better improve the query.

Using `score_mode`, you can sort the result documents based on a nested object using the `function_score` query.

See also

You can refer to the following recipes for further information related to this recipe:

- *The Managing nested objects* recipe in `Chapter 3`, *Managing Mappings*
- *The Using the has_child* query recipe in this chapter

Using the geo_bounding_box query

One of most common operations in geo localization is searching for a box (square). The square is usually an approximation of the shape of a shop, a building, or a city.

This kind of query can be used in a percolator for real-time monitoring if users, documents, or events are entering a special place.

Getting ready

You need an up and running Elasticsearch installation, as we described in the *Downloading and installing Elasticsearch* recipe in Chapter 1, *Getting Started*.

To execute these commands, any HTTP client can be used, such as curl (https://curl.haxx.se/), Postman (https://www.getpostman.com/), or similar. I prefer using the Kibana console, as it provides code completion, formatting, and better character escaping for Elasticsearch.

To correctly execute the following commands, you will need an index populated with the ch04/populate_kibana.txt commands, which is available in the online code.

The index that's used in this section is mygeo-index.

How to do it...

To execute a geo bounding box query, we will perform the following steps:

1. A search to filter documents related to a with the coordinates 40.03, 72.0 and 40.717, 70.99 can be achieved with the following query:

```
POST /mygeo-index/_search?pretty
{
  "query": {
    "geo_bounding_box": {
      "pin.location": {
        "bottom_right": {
          "lat": 40.03,
          "lon": 72
        },
        "top_left": {
          "lat": 40.717,
          "lon": 70.99
```

```
                    }
                  }
                }
              }
            }
```

2. The result returned by Elasticsearch, if everything is alright, should be as follows:

```
{
  "took" : 2,
  "timed_out" : false,
  "_shards" : {
    "total" : 1,
    "successful" : 1,
    "skipped" : 0,
    "failed" : 0
  },
  "hits" : {
    "total" : 1,
    "max_score" : 1.0,
    "hits" : [
      {
        "_index" : "mygeo-index",
        "_type" : "_doc",
        "_id" : "2",
        "_score" : 1.0,
        "_source" : {
          "pin" : {
            "location" : {
              "lat" : 40.12,
              "lon" : 71.34
            }
          }
        }
      }
    ]
  }
}
```

How it works...

Elasticsearch has a lot of optimizations to facilitate searching for a box shape. Latitude and longitude are indexed for fast range checks, so this kind of filter is executed very quickly. In Elasticsearch 5.x or above, geo queries are faster than previous versions due to massive improvements on geo data indexing in Lucene 6.2.x.

The parameters that are required to execute a geo bounding box filter are the `top_left` (the top and left coordinates of the box) and `bottom_right` (the bottom and right coordinates of the box) geo points.

It's possible to use several representations of geo points, as described in the *Mapping a GeoPoint field* recipe in `Chapter 2`, *Managing Mapping*.

See also

You can refer to the following recipe for further information related to this recipe:

- *The Mapping a GeoPoint* field recipe in `Chapter 2`, *Managing Mapping*

Using the geo_polygon query

The *Using the geo_bounding_box query* recipe shows how to filter the square section, which is the most common case; Elasticsearch provides a way to filter user-defined polygonal shapes using the `geo_polygon` filter. This query is useful if the polygon represents a country or region, or a district shape.

Getting ready

You need an up and running Elasticsearch installation, as we described in the *Downloading and installing Elasticsearch* recipe in `Chapter 1`, *Getting Started*.

To execute these commands, I suggest using the Kibana console, as this provides code completion, code formatting, and better character escaping for Elasticsearch.

To correctly execute the following commands, you will need an index populated with the `ch04/populate_kibana.txt` commands, which is available in the online code.

The index that's used in this section is `mygeo-index`.

How to do it...

To execute a `geo_polygon` query, we will perform the following steps:

1. Searching documents in which `pin.location` is part of a triangle (its shape is made up of three geo points) is done with a query similar to the following:

```
POST /mygeo-index/_search
{
  "query": {
    "geo_polygon": {
      "pin.location": {
        "points": [
          {
            "lat": 50,
            "lon": -30
          },
          {
            "lat": 30,
            "lon": -80
          },
          {
            "lat": 80,
            "lon": -90
          }
        ]
      }
    }
  }
}
```

2. The result returned by Elasticsearch, if everything is alright, should be as follows:

```
{
  "took" : 2,
  "timed_out" : false,
  "_shards" : {
    "total" : 1,
    "successful" : 1,
    "skipped" : 0,
    "failed" : 0
  },
  "hits" : {
    "total" : 1,
    "max_score" : 1.0,
```

```
      "hits" : [
        {
          "_index" : "mygeo-index",
          "_type" : "_doc",
          "_id" : "1",
          "_score" : 1.0,
          "_source" : {
            "pin" : {
              "location" : {
                "lat" : 40.12,
                "lon" : -71.34
              }
            }
          }
        }
      ]
    }
  }
```

How it works...

The `geo_polygon` query allows you to define your own shape with a list of geo points so that Elasticsearch can filter documents that are used in the polygon. This can be considered as an extension of a geo bounding box for generic polygonal forms.

The `geo_polygon` query allows the usage of the `ignore_unmapped` parameter, which helps to safely execute a search in the case of multi-indices or types where the field is not defined (the GeoPoint field is not defined for some indices or shards, and thus fails silently without giving errors).

See also

You can refer to the following recipes for further information related to this recipe:

- *The Mapping a GeoPoint field* recipe in Chapter 2, *Managing Mapping*
- *The Using the geo_bounding_box query* recipe in this chapter

Using the geo_distance query

When you are working with geo locations, one common task is to filter results based on the distance from a location. This scenario covers very common site requirements, such as the following:

- Finding the nearest restaurant within a distance of 20 km
- Finding my nearest friends within a range of 10 km

The `geo_distance` query is used to achieve this goal.

Getting ready

You need an up and running Elasticsearch installation, as we described in the *Downloading and installing Elasticsearch* recipe in `Chapter 1`, *Getting Started*.

To execute these commands, any HTTP client can be used, such as curl (`https://curl.haxx.se/`), Postman (`https://www.getpostman.com/`), or similar. I suggest using the Kibana console, as it provides code completion and better character escaping for Elasticsearch.

To correctly execute the following commands, you will need an index populated with the `ch04/populate_kibana.txt` commands, which is available in the online code.

The index that's used in this recipe is `mygeo-index`.

How to do it...

To execute a `geo_distance` query, we will perform the following steps:

1. Searching documents in which `pin.location` is `200km` away from `lat` as `40` and `lon` as `70` is done with a query similar to the following:

```
GET /mygeo-index/_search
{
  "query": {
    "geo_distance": {
      "pin.location": {
        "lat": 40,
        "lon": 70
      },
      "distance": "200km"
```

```
          }
        }
      }
```

2. The result returned by Elasticsearch, if everything is alright, should be as
   follows:

```
{
  "took" : 1,
  "timed_out" : false,
  "_shards" : {
    "total" : 1,
    "successful" : 1,
    "skipped" : 0,
    "failed" : 0
  },
  "hits" : {
    "total" : 1,
    "max_score" : 1.0,
    "hits" : [
      {
        "_index" : "mygeo-index",
        "_type" : "_doc",
        "_id" : "2",
        "_score" : 1.0,
        "_source" : {
          "pin" : {
            "location" : {
              "lat" : 40.12,
              "lon" : 71.34
            }
          }
        }
      }
    ]
  }
}
```

How it works...

As we discussed in the *Mapping a GeoPoint field* recipe, there are several ways to
define a geo point to internally save searched items in an optimized way. The
distance query executes a distance calculation between a given geo point and the
points in the documents, returning hits that satisfy the distance requirement.

The parameters that control the distance query are as follows:

- The field and the point of reference to be used to calculate the distance. In the preceding example, we have `pin.location` and `(40,70)`.
- `distance` defines the distance to be considered. It is usually expressed as a string by a number plus a unit.
- `unit` (optional) can be the unit of the distance value, if distance is defined as a number. The valid values are as follows:
  - `in` or `inch`
  - `yd` or `yards`
  - `m` or `miles`
  - `km` or `kilometers`
  - `m` or `meters`
  - `mm` or `millimeters`
  - `cm` or `centimeters`
- `distance_type` (default: `sloppy_arc`; valid choices are `arc`, `sloppy_arc`, or `plane`) defines the type of algorithm to calculate the distance.
- `validation_method` (default `STRICT`) is used for validating the geo point. The valid values are as follows:
  - `IGNORE_MALFORMED` is used to accept invalid values for latitude and longitude
  - `COERCE` is used to try to correct wrong values
  - `STRICT` is used to reject invalid values
- `ignore_unmapped` is used to safely execute the query in the case of multi-indices that can have a missing definition of *GeoPoint*.

See also

You can refer to the following recipes for further information related to this recipe:

- *The Mapping a GeoPoint field* recipe in `Chapter 2`, *Managing Mapping*
- *The Using the range query* recipe in `Chapter 5`, *Text and Numeric Queries*

7
Aggregations

In developing search solutions, not only are the results important, but they also help us to improve the quality and the search focus. Elasticsearch provides a powerful tool to achieve these goals: the **aggregations**. The main usage of aggregations is to provide additional data to the search results to improve their quality or to augment them with additional information.

For example, in a search for news articles, some facets that could be interesting to calculate could be the authors who wrote the articles and the date histogram of the publishing date. Thus, aggregations are used, not only to improve the results focus, but also to provide insight on stored data (analytics): this is the way that a lot of tools such as **Kibana** (`https://www.elastic.co/products/kibana`) are born.

Generally, aggregations are displayed to the end user with graphs or a group of filtering options (for example, a list of categories for the search results). Because the Elasticsearch aggregation framework provides scripting functionalities, it is able to cover a wide spectrum of scenarios. In this chapter, some simple scripting functionalities are shown relating to aggregations, but we will cover in-depth scripting in the next chapter.

The aggregation framework is also the base for advanced analytics, as shown in such software as Kibana. It's very important to understand how the various types of aggregations work and when to choose them.

In this chapter, we will cover the following recipes:

- Executing an aggregation
- Executing stats aggregations
- Executing terms aggregations
- Executing significant terms aggregations
- Executing range aggregations
- Executing histogram aggregations
- Executing date histogram aggregations
- Executing filter aggregations
- Executing filters aggregations
- Executing global aggregations
- Executing geo distance aggregations
- Executing children aggregations
- Executing nested aggregations
- Executing top hit aggregations
- Executing a matrix stats aggregation
- Executing geo bounds aggregations
- Executing geo centroid aggregations
- Executing pipeline aggregations

Executing an aggregation

Elasticsearch provides several functionalities other than search; this allows you to execute statistics and real-time analytics on searches using the aggregations.

Getting ready

You need an up and running Elasticsearch installation, as we described in the *Downloading and installing Elasticsearch* recipe in `Chapter 1`, *Getting Started*.

To execute these commands, any HTTP client can be used, such as curl (`https://curl.haxx.se/`), postman (`https://www.getpostman.com/`), or similar. Using the Kibana console is recommended, as it provides code completion and better character escaping for Elasticsearch.

To correctly execute the following commands, you will need an index populated with the `ch07/populate_aggregation.txt` commands, which is available in the online code.

The index that's used in this recipe is `index-agg`.

How to do it...

To execute an aggregation, we will perform the following steps:

1. Compute the top 10 tags by name using the command line, executing a similar query with aggregations, as follows:

```
POST /index-agg/_search?size=0
{
  "aggregations": {
    "tag": {
      "terms": {
        "field": "tag",
        "size": 10
      }
    }
  }
}
```

In this case, we have used a term aggregation to count the terms.

2. The result returned by Elasticsearch, if everything is okay, should be:

```
{
  "took" : 0,
  "timed_out" : false,
  "_shards" : {
    "total" : 1,
    "successful" : 1,
    "skipped" : 0,
    "failed" : 0
  },
  "hits" : {
    "total" : 1000,
    "max_score" : null,
    "hits" : [ ]
  },
  "aggregations" : {
    "tag" : {
      "doc_count_error_upper_bound" : 0,
```

```
            "sum_other_doc_count" : 2640,
            "buckets" : [
              {
                "key" : "laborum",
                "doc_count" : 31
              },
              {
                "key" : "facilis",
                "doc_count" : 25
              },
              {
                "key" : "maiores",
                "doc_count" : 25
              },
              {
                "key" : "ipsam",
                "doc_count" : 24
              },
              ... truncated ...
            ]
          }
        }
      }
    }
```

The results are not returned because we have fixed the result size to 0. The aggregation result is contained in the `aggregations` field. Each type of aggregation has its own result format (the explanation of this kind of result is given in the *Executing term aggregation* recipe in this chapter).

It's possible to execute only an aggregation calculation without returning search results to reduce the bandwidth. This is done by passing the search `size` parameter set to 0.

How it works...

Every search can return an aggregation calculation, computed on the query results: the aggregation phase is an additional step in query post-processing, as for example, the highlighting. To activate the aggregation phase, an aggregation must be defined using the `aggs` or `aggregations` keyword.

There are several types of aggregation that can be used in Elasticsearch. In this chapter, we'll cover all the standard aggregations that are available; additional aggregation types can be provided with plugins and scripting.

Aggregations are the basis for real-time analytics. They allow us to execute the following:

- Counting
- Histogram
- Range aggregation
- Statistics
- Geo distance aggregation

The following are examples of the graphs that are generated by histogram aggregations:

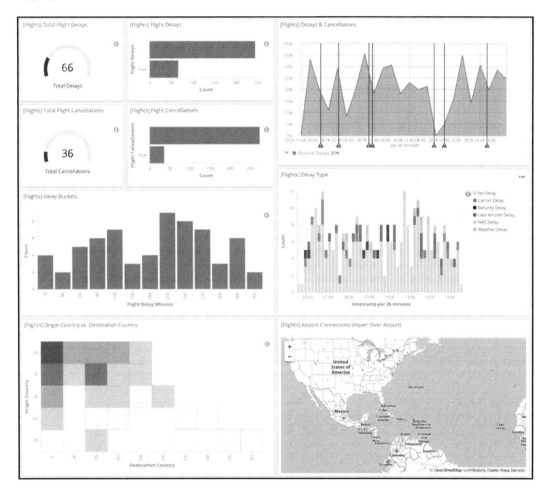

The aggregations are always executed on search hits; they are computed in a map or reduce way. The map step is distributed in shards, while the reduce step is done in the called node. During aggregation computation, a lot of data should be kept in memory and it can, therefore, be very memory-intensive.

For example, when executing a term aggregation, it requires that all the unique terms in the field that are used for aggregating are kept in memory. Executing this operation on millions of documents requires storing a large number of values in memory.

The aggregation framework was introduced in Elasticsearch 1.x as an evolution of the facets feature. Its main difference from the old facet framework is the possibility to execute the analytics with several nesting levels of sub-aggregations. Aggregations keep information of which documents go into an aggregation bucket and an aggregation output can be the input of the next aggregation.

Aggregations can be composed in a complex tree of sub-aggregations without depth limits.

The generic form for an aggregation is as follows:

```
"aggregations" : {
  "<aggregation_name>" : {
    "<aggregation_type>" : {
      <aggregation_body>
    }
    [,"aggregations" : { [<sub_aggregation>]+ } ]?
  }
  [,"<aggregation_name_2>" : { ... } ]*
}
```

Aggregation nesting allows for covering very advanced scenarios in executing analytics, such as aggregating data by country, by region, and by persons' ages, where age groups are ordered in descending order. There are no more limits in mastering analytics.

The following four kinds of aggregators can be used in Elasticsearch 7.x:

- **Bucketing aggregators**: These produce buckets, where a bucket has an associated value and a set of documents (that is, the terms aggregator produces a bucket per term for the field it's aggregating on). A document can end up in multiple buckets if the document has multiple values for the field being aggregated on (in our example, the document with **id=3**). If a bucket aggregator has one or more downstream (child) aggregators, they are run on each generated bucket.
- **Metric aggregators**: These receive a set of documents as input and produce statistical results that have been computed for the specified field. The output of metric aggregators does not include any information that's linked to individual documents, just the statistical data.
- **Matrix aggregators**: These operate on multiple fields and produce a matrix result based on the values extracted from the requested document fields.
- **Pipeline aggregators**: These aggregate the output of other aggregations and their associated metrics. (This is an experimental feature and can change and be removed in the future).

Generally, the order of buckets depends on the bucket aggregator that's used.

For example, using the terms aggregator, the buckets are, by default, ordered by count. The aggregation framework allows ordering by sub-aggregation metrics (that is, the preceding example can be ordered by the `stats.avg` value).

It's easy to create complex nested sub-aggregations that return huge numbers of results. Developers need to pay attention to the cardinality of returned aggregation results: it's very easy to return thousands of values!

See also

Refer to the *Executing a terms aggregation* recipe in this chapter for a more detailed explanation of aggregations that are used in this example. For pipeline aggregations, the official documentation can be found at `https://www.elastic.co/guide/en/elasticsearch/reference/master/search-aggregations-pipeline.html`. Because, as the official Elasticsearch documentation says, it's not safe to use, this feature could be removed in the future, and it is therefore not described in detail in the book.

Executing stats aggregations

The most commonly used metric aggregations are stats aggregations. They are generally used as a terminal aggregation step to compute values that will be used directly or for further sorting.

Getting ready

You need an up and running Elasticsearch installation, as we described in the *Downloading and installing Elasticsearch* recipe in `Chapter 1`, *Getting Started*.

To execute these commands, any HTTP client can be used, such as curl (`https://curl.haxx.se/`), Postman (`https://www.getpostman.com/`), or similar. Using the Kibana Console is recommended, as it provides code completion and better character escaping for Elasticsearch.

To correctly execute the following commands, you will need an index populated with the `ch07/populate_aggregation.txt` commands available in the online code.

The index that's used in this recipe is `index-agg`.

How to do it...

For executing a stat aggregation, we will perform the following steps:

1. We want to calculate all statistics values of a matched query on the `age` field. The REST call should be as follows:

```
POST index-agg/_search?size=0
{
  "aggs": {
    "age_stats": {
      "extended_stats": {
        "field": "age"
      }
    }
  }
}
```

2. The result, if everything is okay, should be as follows:

```
{
  ...truncated...
    "aggregations" : {
      "age_stats" : {
        "count" : 1000,
        "min" : 1.0,
        "max" : 100.0,
        "avg" : 53.243,
        "sum" : 53243.0,
        "sum_of_squares" : 3653701.0,
        "variance" : 818.8839509999999,
        "std_deviation" : 28.616148430562767,
        "std_deviation_bounds" : {
          "upper" : 110.47529686112554,
          "lower" : -3.9892968611255313
        }
      }
    }
}
```

In the answer, under the `aggregations` field, we have the statistical results of our aggregation under the defined field, `age_stats`.

How it works...

After the search phase, if any aggregations are defined, they are computed. In this case, we have requested an `extended_stats` aggregation labeled `age_stats`, which computes a lot of statistical indicators.

The available metric aggregators are as follows:

- `min`: Computes the minimum value for a group of buckets.
- `max`: Computes the maximum value for a group of buckets.
- `avg`: Computes the average value for a group of buckets.
- `sum`: Computes the sum of all the buckets.
- `value_count`: Computes the count of values in the bucket.
- `stats`: Computes all the base metrics such as the `min`, `max`, `avg`, `count`, and `sum`.

- extended_stats: Computes the stats metric plus variance, standard deviation (std_deviation), bounds of standard deviation (std_deviation_bounds), and sum of squares (sum_of_squares).

- percentiles: Computes the percentiles (the point at which a certain percentage of observed values occur) of some values (see Wikipedia at http://en.wikipedia.org/wiki/Percentile for more information about percentiles).

- percentile_ranks: Computes the rank of values that hit a percentile range.

- cardinality: Computes an approximate count of distinct values in a field.

- geo_bounds: Computes the maximum geobounds in the document where the GeoPoints are.

- geo_centroid: Computes the centroid in the document where GeoPoints are.

Every metric requires different computational needs, so it is good practice to limit the indicators only to the required one, so as not to waste CPU, memory, and performance.

In the preceding listing, I cited the most used metric aggregation available natively in

Elasticsearch. Other metrics can be provided using custom plugins.

The syntax of all the metric aggregations has the same pattern, independent of the level of nesting, as in the aggregation **Domain Specific Language** (**DSL**): they follow these patterns:

```
"aggs" : {
  "<name_of_aggregation>" : {
    "<metric_name>" : {
      "field" : "<field_name>"
    }
  }
}
```

See also

Refer to the official Elasticsearch documentation about stats aggregation at `https://www.elastic.co/guide/en/elasticsearch/reference/current/search-aggregations-metrics-stats-aggregation.html` and extended stats aggregation at: `https://www.elastic.co/guide/en/elasticsearch/reference/current/search-aggregations-metrics-extendedstats-aggregation.html`

Executing terms aggregation

The most used bucket aggregation is the terms one. It groups the documents in buckets based on a single term value. This aggregation is often used to narrow down the search using the computed values as filters for the queries.

Getting ready

You need an up and running Elasticsearch installation, as we described in the *Downloading and installing Elasticsearch* recipe in `Chapter 1`, *Getting Started*.

To execute the commands, any HTTP client can be used, such as curl (`https://curl.haxx.se/`), Postman (`https://www.getpostman.com/`), or similar. Using the Kibana Console is recommended, as it provides code completion and better character escaping for Elasticsearch.

To correctly execute the following commands, you will need an index populated with the `ch07/populate_aggregation.txt` commands available in the online code.

The index that's used in this recipe is `index-agg`.

How to do it...

For executing a term aggregation, we will perform the following steps:

1. Calculate the top 10 tags of all the documents: the REST call should be as follows:

```
POST /index-agg/_search?size=0
{
  "aggs": {
    "tag": {
```

```
                    "terms": {
                      "field": "tag",
                      "size": 3
                    }
                  }
                }
              }
            }
```

In this example, we need to match all the items, so the `match_all` query is used.

2. The result returned by Elasticsearch, if everything is okay, should be as follows:

```
{
  ...truncated...
  "aggregations" : {
    "tag" : {
      "doc_count_error_upper_bound" : 0,
      "sum_other_doc_count" : 2803,
      "buckets" : [
        {
          "key" : "laborum",
          "doc_count" : 31
        },
        {
          "key" : "facilis",
          "doc_count" : 25
        },
        {
          "key" : "maiores",
          "doc_count" : 25
        }
      ]
    }
  }
}
```

The aggregation result is composed from several buckets with terms as follows:

- `key`: The term that's used to populate the bucket
- `doc_count`: The number of results with the `key` term

How it works...

During a search, there are a lot of phases that Elasticsearch executes. After the query execution, the aggregations are calculated and returned, along with the results.

In this recipe, we have seen the following parameters that the terms aggregation supports:

- `field`: This is the field to be used to extract the facets data. The `field` value can be a single string (as in the example tag) or a list of fields (that is, `field1`, `field2`).
- `size`: This controls the number of term values to be returned (default `10`).
- `min_doc_count`: This returns terms that have at least a minimum number of documents (optional).
- `include`: This defines the valid value to be aggregated using a regular expression (optional). This is evaluated before the `exclude` parameter. The regular expressions are controlled by the `flags` parameter, as follows:

  ```
  "include" : {
    "pattern" : ".*labor.*",
    "flags" : "CANON_EQ|CASE_INSENSITIVE"
  },
  ```

- `exclude`: This removes the terms that are contained in the `exclude` list (optional). The regular expressions are controlled by the `flags` parameter.
- `order`: This controls how to calculate the top *n* bucket values to be returned (optional, default `doc_count`). The `order` parameter can be one of the following types:
    - `_count`: Returns the aggregation values ordered by `count` (default).
    - `_term`: Returns the aggregation values ordered by term value; (that is, `"order" : { "_term" : "asc" }`).
- A sub-aggregation name, such as the following example:

  ```
  {
    "aggs": {
      "genders": {
        "terms": {
          "field": "tag",
          "order": {
            "avg_val": "desc"
          }
  ```

```
        },
        "aggs": {
          "avg_age": {
            "avg": {
              "field": "age"
            }
          }
        }
      }
    }
  }
}
```

Term aggregation is very useful to represent an overview of values used for further filtering.

In the following graph, the term aggregation results are shown as a bar chart:

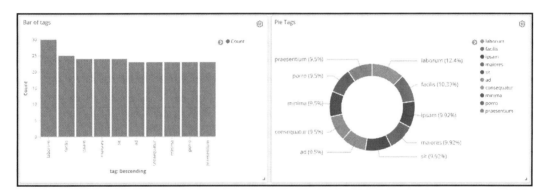

There's more...

Sometimes, we need to have much more control of terms aggregation: this can be achieved by adding an Elasticsearch script in the `script` field.

With scripting, it is possible to modify the term being used for the aggregation to generate a new value to be used. The following is a simple example, in which we append `123` to all terms:

```
{
  "aggs": {
    "tag": {
      "terms": {
        "field": "tag",
        "script": "_value + '123'"
```

```
                }
              }
           }
        }
     }
```

In the previous terms aggregation examples, we have provided the `field` or `fields` parameter to select the field to be used to compute the aggregation. It's also possible to pass a `script` parameter, which replaces `field` and `fields`, to define the field to be used to extract the data. The `script` can extract the term value from the `doc` script variable that's available in the script context.

In the case of `doc`, the first example can be rewritten as follows:

```
POST /index-agg/_search?size=0
{
  "aggs": {
    "tag": {
      "terms": {
        "script": {
          "source": """doc['tag'].value"""
        }
      }
    }
  }
}
```

See also

Refer to `Chapter 8`, *Scripting in Elasticsearch*, which covers how to use scripting languages in Elasticsearch.

Executing significant terms aggregation

Significant terms aggregation is an evolution of the previous one, in that it's able to cover several scenarios, such as the following:

- Suggesting relevant terms related to current query text
- Discovering relations of terms
- Discovering common patterns in text

In these scenario, the result must not be as simple as the previous terms aggregations; it must be computed as a variance between a foreground set (generally the query) and a background one (a large bulk of data).

Getting ready

You need an up and running Elasticsearch installation, as we described in the *Downloading and installing Elasticsearch* recipe in `Chapter 1`, *Getting Started*.

To execute the commands, any HTTP client can be used, such as curl (`https://curl.haxx.se/`), Postman (`https://www.getpostman.com/`), or similar. Using the Kibana Console is recommended, as it provides code completion and better character escaping for Elasticsearch.

To correctly execute the following commands, you will need an index populated with the `ch07/populate_aggregation.txt` commands available in the online code.

The index that's used in this recipe is `index-agg`.

How to do it...

For executing a significant term aggregation, we will perform the following steps:

1. We want to calculate the significant terms `tag` given some tags. The `REST` call should be as follows:

```
POST /index-agg/_search?size=0
{
  "query": {
    "terms": {
      "tag": [
        "ullam",
        "in",
        "ex"
      ]
    }
  },
  "aggs": {
    "significant_tags": {
      "significant_terms": {
        "field": "tag"
      }
    }
```

```
      }
   }
```

2. The result returned by Elasticsearch, if everything is okay, should be as
   follows:

```
{
  ...truncated...
   "aggregations" : {
     "significant_tags" : {
       "doc_count" : 45,
       "bg_count" : 1000,
       "buckets" : [
          {
            "key" : "ullam",
            "doc_count" : 17,
            "score" : 8.017283950617283,
            "bg_count" : 17
          },
   ...
   ...

          {
            "key" : "vitae",
            "doc_count" : 3,
            "score" : 0.13535353535353536,
            "bg_count" : 22
          }
       ]
     }
   }
}
```

The aggregation result is composed from several buckets with:

- key: The term used to populate the bucket
- doc_count: The number of results with the key term
- score: The score for this bucket
- bg_count: The number of background documents that contain the key
  term

How it works...

The execution of the aggregation is similar to the previous ones. Internally, two terms aggregations are computed: one related to the documents matched with the query or parent aggregation and the other based on all the documents on the knowledge base. Then, the two result datasets are scored to compute the significant result.

This kind of aggregation is very CPU intensive due to the large cardinality of terms queries and the cost of significant relevance computation.

The significant aggregation returns terms that are evaluated as significant for the current query.

This aggregation works only on `Keyword` mapping fields that are indexed in Elasticsearch with the field data flags. To be able to use the same functionality on text mapping fields, there is the `significant_text`. Because text fields have no field data (a special structure that keeps all the field values in memory), the distribution of the terms must be computed on the fly and this requires a lot of resources (CPU and RAM).

To speed up the process, generally you select a random subset of the documents to not waste resources. The best practise is to use a sampler to collect some hits and then extract the more significant terms from the text as shown in the following example:

```
POST /index-agg/_search?size=0
{
    "aggregations" : {
        "my_sample" : {
            "sampler" : {
                "shard_size" : 100
            },
            "aggregations": {
                "keywords" : {
                    "significant_text" : { "field" : "description" }
                }
            }
        }
    }
}
```

Executing range aggregations

The previous recipe describes an aggregation type that can be very useful if buckets must be computed on fixed terms or on a limited number of items. Otherwise, it's often required to return the buckets aggregated in ranges: the **range aggregations** meet this requirement. Commons scenarios are as follows:

- Price range (used in shops)
- Size range
- Alphabetical range

Getting ready

You need an up and running Elasticsearch installation, as we described in the *Downloading and installing Elasticsearch* recipe in `Chapter 1`, *Getting Started*.

To execute the commands, any HTTP client can be used, such as curl (`https://curl.haxx.se/`), Postman (`https://www.getpostman.com/`), or similar. Using the Kibana Console is recommended, as it provides code completion and better character escaping for Elasticsearch.

To correctly execute the following commands, you will need an index populated with the `ch07/populate_aggregation.txt` commands available in the online code.

The index that's used in this recipe is `index-agg`.

How to do it...

For executing range aggregations, we will perform the following steps:

1. We want to provide the following three types of aggregation ranges:
    - Price aggregation, which aggregates the price of items in ranges.
    - Age aggregation, which aggregates the age contained in a document in four ranges of 25 years.
    - Date aggregation, the ranges of 6 months of the previous year and all this year.

2. To obtain this result, we need to execute a query similar to the following:

```
POST /index-agg/_search?size=0
{
  "aggs": {
    "prices": {
      "range": {
        "field": "price",
        "ranges": [
          {"to": 10},
          {"from": 10, "to": 20},
          {"from": 20, "to": 100},
          {"from": 100}
        ]
      }
    },
    "ages": {
      "range": {
        "field": "age",
        "ranges": [
          {"to": 25},
          {"from": 25, "to": 50},
          {"from": 50, "to": 75},
          {"from": 75}
        ]
      }
    },
    "range": {
      "range": {
        "field": "date",
        "ranges": [
          {"from": "2016-01-01", "to": "2016-07-01"},
          {"from": "2017-07-01", "to": "2017-12-31"},
          {"from": "2018-01-01", "to": "2018-12-31"}
        ]
      }
    }
  }
}
```

3. The result returned by Elasticsearch, if everything is okay, should be:

```
{
  ...truncated...
  "aggregations" : {
    "range" : {
      "buckets" : [
        {
```

```
            "key" :
"2016-01-01T00:00:00.000Z-2016-07-01T00:00:00.000Z",
            "from" : 1.4516064E12,
            "from_as_string" : "2016-01-01T00:00:00.000Z",
            "to" : 1.4673312E12,
            "to_as_string" : "2016-07-01T00:00:00.000Z",
            "doc_count" : 42
...
...
          { "key" : "20.0-100.0", "from" : 20.0, "to" : 100.0,
"doc_count" : 788 },
          { "key" : "100.0-*", "from" : 100.0, "doc_count" : 0 }
        ]
      }
    }
  }
```

All aggregation results have the following fields:

- `to`, `to_as_string`, `from`, and `from_as_string`: Which define the original range of the aggregation.
- `doc_count`: Which is the number of results in this range.
- `key`: Which is a string representation of the range.

How it works...

This kind of aggregation is generally executed against numerical data types (`integer`, `float`, `long`, and `dates`). It can be considered as a list of range filters executed against the result of the query.

The `date` or `datetime` values, when used in a filter or query, must be expressed in string format: the valid string formats are `yyyy-MM-dd'T'HH:mm:ss` or `yyyy-MM-dd`.

Each range is computed independently, so in their definition they can overlap.

There's more...

There are two special range aggregations used for targeting—date and IPv4 ranges. They are similar to the preceding range aggregation, but they provide special functionalities to control the range on the date and IP address.

The date range aggregation (`date_range`) allows for defining `from` and `to` in date math expressions. For example, to execute an aggregation of hits in the previous 6 months and after, the aggregation will be as follows:

```
POST /index-agg/_search?size=0
{
  "aggs": {
    "range": {
      "date_range": {
        "field": "date",
        "format": "MM-yyyy",
        "ranges": [
          {
            "to": "now-6M/M"
          },
          {
            "from": "now-6M/M"
          }
        ]
      }
    }
  }
}
```

The result will be the following:

```
{
  ...truncated...
  "aggregations" : {
    "range" : {
      "buckets" : [
        {
          "key" : "*-06-2018",
          "to" : 1.5278112E12,
          "to_as_string" : "06-2018",
          "doc_count" : 894
        },
        {
          "key" : "06-2018-*",
          "from" : 1.5278112E12,
          "from_as_string" : "06-2018",
          "doc_count" : 106
        }
      ]
    }
  }
}
```

In this sample, the buckets will be formatted in the form month-year (MM–YYYY), in two ranges. now means the actual datetime, −6M means minus 6 months, and /M is a shortcut for dividing for months.

 A complete reference of date math expressions and codes is available at: https://www.elastic.co/guide/en/elasticsearch/ reference/current/search-aggregations-bucket-daterange-aggregation.html

The IPv4 range aggregation (ip_range) allows for defining the ranges as follows:

- IP range form:

```
{
  "aggs": {
    "ip_ranges": {
      "ip_range": {
        "field": "ip",
        "ranges": [
          {
            "to": "192.168.1.1"
          },
          {
            "from": "192.168.2.255"
          }
        ]
      }
    }
  }
}
```

- CIDR masks:

```
{
  "aggs": {
    "ip_ranges": {
      "ip_range": {
        "field": "ip",
        "ranges": [
          {
            "mask": "192.168.1.0/25"
          },
          {
            "mask": "192.168.1.127/25"
          }
        ]
      }
```

```
            }
          }
        }
```

See also

Refer to the *Using range query* recipe in `Chapter 5`, *Text and Numeric Queries*, for details of using range queries, and the official documentation for IP aggregation at: `https://www.elastic.co/guide/en/elasticsearch/reference/master/search-aggregations-bucket-iprange-aggregation.html`

Executing histogram aggregations

Elasticsearch numerical values can be used to process histogram data. The histogram representation is a very powerful way to show data to end users, mainly using bar charts.

Getting ready

You need an up and running Elasticsearch installation, as we described in the *Downloading and installing Elasticsearch* recipe in `Chapter 1`, *Getting Started*.

To execute the commands, any HTTP client can be used, such as curl (`https://curl.haxx.se/`), Postman (`https://www.getpostman.com/`), or similar. Using the Kibana Console is recommended, as it provides code completion and better character escaping for Elasticsearch.

To correctly execute the following commands, you will need an index populated with the `ch07/populate_aggregation.txt` commands available in the online code.

The index that's used in this recipe is `index-agg`.

How to do it...

For executing histogram aggregations, we will perform the following steps:

1. Using the items populated with the script, we will calculate the following aggregations:

   - age with an interval of 5 years
   - price with an interval of 10$
   - date with an interval of 6 months

   The query will be as follows:

   ```
   POST /index-agg/_search?size=0
   {
     "aggregations": {
       "age": {
         "histogram": {
           "field": "age",
           "interval": 5
         }
       },
       "price": {
         "histogram": {
           "field": "price",
           "interval": 10
         }
       }
     }
   }
   ```

2. The result returned by Elasticsearch, if everything is okay, should be as follows:

   ```
   {
     ...truncated...
     "aggregations" : {
       "price" : {
         "buckets" : [
           { "key" : 0.0, "doc_count" : 105 },
           { "key" : 10.0, "doc_count" : 107 },
           { "key" : 20.0, "doc_count" : 79 },
           ...truncated...
         ]
       },
       "age" : {
         "buckets" : [
   ```

```
                    { "key" : 0.0, "doc_count" : 34 },
                    { "key" : 5.0, "doc_count" : 41 },
                    { "key" : 10.0, "doc_count" : 42 },
                    { "key" : 15.0, "doc_count" : 43 },
                    { "key" : 20.0, "doc_count" : 50 },
                    ...truncated...
                    { "key" : 100.0, "doc_count" : 9 }
                  ]
                }
              }
            }
```

The aggregation result is composed by `buckets`: a list of aggregation results. These results are composed by the following:

- `key`: The value that is always on the x axis in the histogram graph
- `doc_count`: The document bucket size

How it works...

This kind of aggregation is calculated in a distributed manner in each shard with search results and then the aggregation results are aggregated in the search node server (arbiter) and returned to the user. The histogram aggregation works only on numerical fields (`boolean`, `integer`, `long integer`, and `float`) and `date` or `datetime` fields (these are internally represented as long).

To control the histogram generation on a defined `field`, the `interval` parameter is required, which is used to generate an interval to aggregate the hits.

The following are special parameters to control the histogram creation:

- `min_doc_count`: This allows you to set the minimum number of documents that there must be in the bucket for emitting it in the aggregation (default 1).
- `order`: This is used to change the key sorting. For a full reference, see the *Term Aggregation* recipe.
- `offset`: This is used to shift the keys by the defined offset (default 0).
- `missing`: This allows you to provide a default value if it's not available in the document. It can be very handy where you have a document with a missing field value and you need to provide a default one for your analytics.

- `extended_bounds`: This is used to set the minimum or maximum value to be considered in the histogram. Because Elasticsearch doesn't emit buckets if they don't contain documents, the histogram could contain holes in the X-axis. This option also allows Elasticsearch to emit empty buckets to prevent holes in the distribution:

```
POST /index-agg/_search?size=0 {
        "aggs" : {
        "prices" : {
            "histogram" : {
                "field" : "price",
                "interval" : 5,
                "extended_bounds" : {
                    "min" : 0,
                    "max" : 150
                }
            }
        }
    }
}
```

In this case, we have prices up to 100, but using max 150 in `extended_bounds`, we will generate empty buckets up to 150.

The general representation of a histogram could be a bar chart, similar to the following:

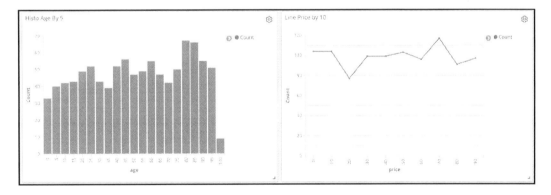

There's more...

The histogram aggregation can be also improved using Elasticsearch scripting functionalities. It is possible to script both, using _value if a field is stored or using the doc variable.

An example of a scripted aggregation histogram, using _value, is as follows:

```
POST /index-agg/_search?size=0
{
  "aggs": {
    "age": {
      "histogram": {
        "field": "age",
        "script": "_value*3",
        "interval": 5
      }
    }
  }
}
```

An example of a scripted aggregation histogram, using _doc, is as follows:

```
{
  ... truncated ...
  "aggregations" : {
    "age" : {
      "buckets" : [
        { "key" : 0.0, "doc_count" : 8 },
        { "key" : 5.0, "doc_count" : 17 },
        { "key" : 10.0, "doc_count" : 9 },
        { "key" : 15.0, "doc_count" : 19 },
... truncated ...
        { "key" : 295.0, "doc_count" : 11 },
        { "key" : 300.0, "doc_count" : 9 }
      ]
    }
  }
}
```

See also

Refer to the *Executing date histogram aggregations* recipe in this chapter for histogram aggregations based on date or time values.

Executing date histogram aggregations

The previous recipe used mainly numeric fields; Elasticsearch provides special functionalities to compute the date histogram aggregation, which operates on `date` or `datetime` values.

This aggregation is required because date values need more customization to solve problems, such as timezone conversion and special time intervals.

Getting ready

You need an up and running Elasticsearch installation, as we described in the *Downloading and installing Elasticsearch* recipe in `Chapter 1`, *Getting Started*.

To execute these commands, any HTTP client can be used, such as curl (`https://curl.haxx.se/`), Postman (`https://www.getpostman.com/`), or similar. Using the Kibana Console is recommended, as it provides code completion and better character escaping for Elasticsearch.

To correctly execute the following commands, you will need an index populated with the `ch07/populate_aggregation.txt` commands available in the online code.

The index that's used in this recipe is `index-agg`.

How to do it...

To execute date histogram aggregations, we will perform the following steps:

1. We need two different date or time aggregations that are as follows:

    - An annual aggregation
    - A quarter aggregation, but with a time zone +1:00

    The query will be as follows:

    ```
    POST /index-agg/_search?size=0
    {
      "aggs": {
        "date_year": {
          "date_histogram": {
            "field": "date",
            "interval": "year"
    ```

```
            }
          },
          "date_quarter": {
            "date_histogram": {
              "field": "date",
              "interval": "quarter",
              "time_zone": "+01:00"
            }
          }
        }
      }
```

2. The result returned by Elasticsearch, if everything is okay, should be as follows:

```
{
  ... truncated ...
  "aggregations" : {
    "date_year" : {
      "buckets" : [
        {
          "key_as_string" : "2012-01-01T00:00:00.000Z",
          "key" : 1325376000000,
          "doc_count" : 190
        },
        {
          "key_as_string" : "2013-01-01T00:00:00.000Z",
          "key" : 1356998400000,
          "doc_count" : 180
        },
        ...truncated...
      ]
    },
    "date_quarter" : {
      "buckets" : [
        {
          "key_as_string" : "2012-01-01T00:00:00.000+01:00",
          "key" : 1325372400000,
          "doc_count" : 48
        },
        {
          "key_as_string" : "2012-04-01T00:00:00.000+01:00",
          "key" : 1333234800000,
          "doc_count" : 52
        },
        ... truncated...
      ]
    }
```

```
        }
    }
```

The aggregation result is composed by `buckets`: As a list of aggregation results. These results are composed by the following:

- `key`: The value that is always on the x axis in the histogram graph
- `key_as_string`: A string representation of the `key` value
- `doc_count`: The document bucket size

How it works...

The main difference from the previous recipe histogram is that the interval is not numerical, as generally, date intervals are defined time constants. All the parameters that we have used in the histogram aggregation can be used in the datetime.

The `interval` parameter allows you to use several values; the most commonly used ones are as follows::

- `year`
- `quarter`
- `month`
- `week`
- `day`
- `hour`
- `minute`

When working with date values, it's important to use the correct timezone to prevent query time offset errors. By default, Elasticsearch uses the UTC milliseconds as the epoch to store datetime values. To better handle the correct timestamp, there are some parameters that can be used, such as the following:

- `time_zone` (or `pre_zone`): This allows you to define a timezone offset to be used in the value calculation (optional). This value is used to preprocess the datetime value for the aggregation. The value can be expressed in numeric form (that is, -3) if specifying hours, or if minutes must be defined in the timezone, a string representation can be used (that is, +07:30).
- `post_zone`: This takes the result and applies the timezone offset (optional).
- `pre_zone_adjust_large_interval`: This applies the `hour` interval for `day` or larger intervals (default: `false`) (optional).

There's more...

Estimating the number of buckets that a date histogram aggregation will produce is very hard. Often, it's very common to generate a large number of buckets and have memory and performances issues, not only at the Elasticsearch side, but also at the application level.

To prevent this problem, Elasticsearch introduced a date histogram aggregation that autosizes the interval to generate the wanted number of buckets: `auto_date_histogram`.

The extra parameter that it requires is `bucket`, along with the number of buckets to be generated. To test this, we can execute the following query:

```
POST /index-agg/_search?size=0
{
  "aggs": {
    "10_buckets_date": {
      "auto_date_histogram": {
        "field": "date",
        "buckets": 10,
        "format": "yyyy-MM-dd"
      }
    }
  }
}
```

The result will be as follows:

```
{
  ... truncated...
  "aggregations" : {
    "10_buckets_date" : {
      "buckets" : [
        {
          "key_as_string" : "2012-01-01",
          "key" : 1325376000000,
          "doc_count" : 190
        },
        ... truncated ...
  {
          "key_as_string" : "2018-01-01",
          "key" : 1514764800000,
          "doc_count" : 182
        }
      ],
      "interval" : "1y"
```

```
            }
        }
    }
```

As you can see, this aggregation returns the interval that was used for this aggregation!

 The maximum number of buckets is 333.

See also

You can refer to the following documentation for further reference to what we covered in this recipe:

- The official Elasticsearch documentation on date histogram aggregation at: `https://www.elastic.co/guide/en/elasticsearch/reference/current/search-aggregations-bucket-datehistogram-aggregation.html` for more details on managing time zone issues.
- The official Elasticsearch documentation on auto date histogram aggregation at: `https://www.elastic.co/guide/en/elasticsearch/reference/master/search-aggregations-bucket-autodatehistogram-aggregation.html`

Executing filter aggregations

Sometimes, we need to reduce the number of hits in our aggregation to satisfy a particular filter. To obtain this result, filter aggregation is used.

The filter is one of the simpler ways to manipulate the bucket when filtering out values.

Getting ready

You need an up and running Elasticsearch installation, as we described in the *Downloading and installing Elasticsearch* recipe in `Chapter 1`, *Getting Started*.

To execute these commands, any HTTP client can be used, such as curl (`https://curl.haxx.se/`), Postman (`https://www.getpostman.com/`), or similar. Using the Kibana Console is recommended, as it provides code completion and better character escaping for Elasticsearch.

To correctly execute the following commands, you will need an index populated with the `ch07/populate_aggregation.txt` commands available in the online code.

The index that's used in this recipe is `index-agg`.

How to do it...

To execute filter aggregations, we will perform the following steps:

1. We need to compute two different filter aggregations, as follows:

- The count of documents that have `"ullam"` as a tag
- The count of documents that have age equal to 37

The query to execute these aggregations is as follows:

```
POST /index-agg/_search?size=0
{
  "aggregations": {
    "ullam_docs": {
      "filter": {
        "term": {
          "tag": "ullam"
        }
      }
    },
    "age37_docs": {
      "filter": {
        "term": {
          "age": 37
        }
      }
    }
  }
}
```

In this case, we have used simple filters, but they can be more complex if needed.

2. The result returned by Elasticsearch, if everything is okay, should be as follows:

```
{
    ... truncated ...
    "aggregations" : {
      "age37_docs" : {
        "doc_count" : 6
      },
      "ullam_docs" : {
        "doc_count" : 17
      }
    }
}
```

How it works...

The filter aggregation is very trivial: it executes a count on a filter on a matched element. You can consider this aggregation as a count query on the results. As we can see from the preceding result, the aggregation contains one value: doc_count, the count result.

It could be a very simple aggregation: generally users tend not to use it as they prefer the statistic one, which also provides a count, or in the worst cases, they execute another search generating more server workload.

The big advantage of this kind of aggregation is that the count, if possible, is executed using a filter: that is by far faster than iterating all the results. Another important advantage is that the filter can be composed by every possible valid Query DSL element.

There's more...

It's often required to have the count of the document that doesn't match a filter or generally doesn't have a particular field (or is null). For this kind of scenario, there is a special aggregation type: missing.

For example, to count the number of documents that have a missing code field, the query will be as follows:

```
POST /index-agg/_search?size=0
{
```

```
      "aggs": {
        "missing_code": {
          "missing": {
            "field": "code"
          }
        }
      }
    }
```

The result will be as follows:

```
    {
      ... truncated ...
      "aggregations" : {
        "missing_code" : {
          "doc_count" : 1000
        }
      }
    }
```

See also

Refer to the *Counting matched results* recipe in `Chapter 4`, *Exploring Search Capabilities*, for a standard count query.

Executing filters aggregations

The filters aggregation answers the common requirement to split buckets documents using custom filters, which can be every kind of query supported by Elasticsearch.

Getting ready

You need an up and running Elasticsearch installation, as we described in the *Downloading and installing Elasticsearch* recipe in `Chapter 1`, *Getting Started*.

To execute the commands, any HTTP client can be used, such as Curl (`https://curl.haxx.se/`), Postman (`https://www.getpostman.com/`), or similar. Using the Kibana Console is recommended, as it provides code completion and better character escaping for Elasticsearch.

To correctly execute the following commands, you will need an index populated with the `ch07/populate_aggregation.txt` commands available in the online code.

The index used in this recipe is `index-agg`.

How to do it...

To execute filters aggregations, we will perform the following steps:

1. We need to compute a filters aggregation composed of the following queries:

    - Date greater than 2016/01/01 and price greater or equal to 50
    - Date lower than 2016/01/01 and price greater or equal to 50
    - All the documents that are not matched

    The query to execute these aggregations is as follows:

    ```
    POST /index-agg/_search?size=0
    {
      "aggs": {
        "expensive_docs": {
          "filters": {
            "other_bucket": true,
            "other_bucket_key": "other_documents",
            "filters": {
              "2016_over_50": {
                "bool": {
                  "must": [
                    {
                      "range": {
                        "date": {
                          "gte": "2016-01-01"
                        }
                      }
                    },
                    {
                      "range": {
                        "price": {
                          "gte": 50
                        }
                      }
                    }
                  ]
                }
    ```

```
          },
          "previous_2016_over_50": {
            "bool": {
              "must": [
                {
                  "range": {
                    "date": {
                      "lt": "2016-01-01"
                    }
                  }
                },
                {
                  "range": {
                    "price": {
                      "gte": 50
                    }
                  }
                }
              ]
            }
          }
        }
      }
    }
  }
}
```

2. The result returned by Elasticsearch, if everything is okay, should be as follows:

```
{
  ... truncated ...
  "aggregations" : {
    "expensive_docs" : {
      "buckets" : {
        "2016_over_50" : {
          "doc_count" : 137
        },
        "previous_2016_over_50" : {
          "doc_count" : 374
        },
        "other_documents" : {
          "doc_count" : 489
        }
      }
    }
  }
}
```

How it works...

The filters aggregation is a very handy one, because it provides a convenient way to generate data buckets. The filters that compose the aggregation can be every kind of query that Elasticsearch supports. For this reason, this aggregation can be used to achieve complex relation management using children and nested queries.

Every query in the `filters` object generates a new bucket. Because the queries can be overlapped, the generated buckets can have overlapping documents. To collect all the documents that are not matched in filters, it's possible to use the `other_bucket` and `other_bucket_key` parameters. The `other_bucket` is a `boolean` parameter: if it's `true`, it will return all the unmatched documents in `_other_` bucket.

The `other_bucket_key` is a string parameter that contains the label name of the other bucket, which is used to control the name of the residual document bucket. If `other_bucket_key` is defined, it automatically implies that `other_bucket` is equal to `true`.

Executing global aggregations

The aggregations are generally executed on query search results; Elasticsearch provides a special aggregation `global` that is executed globally on all the documents without being influenced by the query.

Getting ready

You need an up and running Elasticsearch installation, as we described in the *Downloading and installing Elasticsearch* recipe in `Chapter 1`, *Getting Started*.

To execute the commands, any HTTP client can be used, such as Curl (`https://curl.haxx.se/`), Postman (`https://www.getpostman.com/`), or similar. Using the Kibana Console is recommended, as it provides the code completion and better character escaping for Elasticsearch.

To correctly execute the following commands, you will need an index populated with the `ch07/populate_aggregation.txt` commands available in the online code.

The index used in this recipe is `index-agg`.

How to do it...

For executing global aggregations, we will perform the following steps:

1. Compare a global average with a query; the call will be something similar to the following:

```
POST /index-agg/_search?size=0
{
  "query": {
    "term": {
      "tag": "ullam"
    }
  },
  "aggregations": {
    "query_age_avg": {
      "avg": {
        "field": "age"
      }
    },
    "all_persons": {
      "global": {},
      "aggs": {
        "age_global_avg": {
          "avg": {
            "field": "age"
          }
        }
      }
    }
  }
}
```

2. The result returned by Elasticsearch, if everything is okay, should be as follows:

```
{
  ... truncated ...
  "aggregations" : {
    "all_persons" : {
      "doc_count" : 1000,
      "age_global_avg" : {
        "value" : 53.243
      }
    },
    "query_age_avg" : {
      "value" : 53.470588235294116
    }
```

```
          }
     }
```

In the preceding example, `query_age_avg` is computed on the query and the `age_global_avg` is computed on all the documents.

How it works...

This kind of aggregation is mainly used as top aggregation as a start point for other sub-aggregations. The JSON body of the global aggregations is empty: it doesn't have any optional parameters.

The most frequent use cases are comparing aggregations that are executed on filters with the ones without them, as like we did in the preceding example.

Executing geo distance aggregations

Among the other standard types that we have seen in the previous aggregations, Elasticsearch allows you to execute aggregations against a GeoPoint: the geo distance aggregations. This is an evolution of the previously discussed range aggregations that have been built to work on geo locations.

Getting ready

You need an up and running Elasticsearch installation, as we described in the *Downloading and installing Elasticsearch* recipe in `Chapter 1`, *Getting Started*.

To execute the commands, any HTTP client can be used, such as Curl (`https://curl.haxx.se/`), Postman (`https://www.getpostman.com/`), or similar. Using the Kibana Console is recommended, as it provides code completion and better character escaping for Elasticsearch.

To correctly execute the following commands, you will need an index populated with the `ch07/populate_aggregation.txt` commands available in the online code.

The index used in this recipe is `index-agg`.

How to do it...

To execute geo distance aggregations, we will perform the following steps:

1. Using the `position` field that's available in the documents, we'll aggregate the other documents in the following five ranges:

   - Less than 10 kilometers
   - From 10 kilometers to 20
   - From 20 kilometers to 50
   - From 50 kilometers to 100
   - Above 100 kilometers

2. To achieve these goals, we will create a geo distance aggregation with a code similar to following:

```
POST /index-agg/_search?size=0
{
  "aggs": {
    "position": {
      "geo_distance": {
        "field": "position",
        "origin": {
          "lat": 83.76,
          "lon": -81.2
        },
        "ranges": [
          { "to": 10 },
          { "from": 10, "to": 20 },
          { "from": 20, "to": 50 },
          { "from": 50, "to": 100 },
          { "from": 100 }
        ]
      }
    }
  }
}
```

3. The result returned by Elasticsearch, if everything is okay, should be as follows:

```
{
  ... truncated ...
  "aggregations" : {
    "position" : {
```

```
        "buckets" : [
          {
            "key" : "*-10.0",
            "from" : 0.0,
            "to" : 10.0,
            "doc_count" : 0
          },
          {
            "key" : "10.0-20.0",
            "from" : 10.0,
            "to" : 20.0,
            "doc_count" : 0
          },
          {
            "key" : "20.0-50.0",
            "from" : 20.0,
            "to" : 50.0,
            "doc_count" : 0
          },
          {
            "key" : "50.0-100.0",
            "from" : 50.0,
            "to" : 100.0,
            "doc_count" : 0
          },
          {
            "key" : "100.0-*",
            "from" : 100.0,
            "doc_count" : 1000
          }
        ]
      }
    }
  }
```

How it works...

The geo range aggregation is an extension of the range aggregations that works on
geo localizations. It works only if a field is mapped as a `geo_point`. The field can
contain a single or multivalue geo points.

The aggregation requires at least the following three parameters:

- `field`: The field of the geo point to work on
- `origin`: The geo point to be used for computing the distances
- `ranges`: A list of ranges to collect documents based on their distance from the target point

The geo point can be defined in one of the following accepted formats:

- latitude and longitude as properties, that is, `{"lat": 83.76, "lon": -81.20 }`
- longitude and latitude as an array, that is, `[-81.20, 83.76]`
- latitude and longitude as a string, that is, `83.76, -81.20`
- geohash, that is, `fnyk80`

The ranges are defined as a couple of `from`/`to` values. If one of them is missing, they are considered unbound.

The values that are used for the range are set to kilometers by default, but by using the `unit` property , it's possible to set them as follows:

- `mi` or `miles`
- `in` or `inch`
- `yd` or `yard`
- `km` or `kilometers`
- `m` or `meters`
- `cm` or `centimeter`
- `mm` or `millimeters`

It's also possible to set how the distance is computed with the `distance_type` parameter. Valid values for this parameter are as follows:

- `arc`: This uses the arc length formula. It is the most precise (see `http://en.wikipedia.org/wiki/Arc_length` for more details on the arc length algorithm).
- `plane`: This is used for the plane distance formula. It is the fastest and most CPU-intensive, but it's also the least precise.

As for the range filter, the range values are treated independently, so the overlapping ranges are allowed. When the results are returned, this aggregation provides a lot of information in its fields as follows:

- `from` or `to`: Defines the analyzed range
- `key`: Defines the string representation of the range
- `doc_count`: Defines the number of documents in the bucket that matches the range

See also

You can refer to the following for recipes further reference to what we covered in this recipe:

- Refer to the *Executing range aggregations* recipe in this chapter for common functionalities of range aggregations
- Refer to the *Mapping a GeoPoint field* recipe in `Chapter 2`, *Managing Mapping*, to correctly define a GeoPoint field for executing geo aggregations
- Refer to the *GeoHash grid Aggregation* recipe at: `https://www.elastic.co/guide/en/elasticsearch/reference/current/search-aggregations-bucket-geohashgrid-aggregation.html` to learn how to aggregations on a geohash

Executing children aggregations

Children aggregation allows you to execute analytics based on parent documents and child documents. When working with complex structures, nested objects are very common.

Getting ready

You need an up and running Elasticsearch installation, as we described in the *Downloading and installing Elasticsearch* recipe in `Chapter 1`, *Getting Started*.

To execute these commands, any HTTP client can be used, such as Curl (`https://curl.haxx.se/`), Postman (`https://www.getpostman.com/`), or similar. Using the Kibana Console is recommended, as it provides code completion and better character escaping for Elasticsearch.

To correctly execute the following commands, you will need an index populated with the ch07/populate_aggregation.txt commands, which is available in the online code.

The index used in this recipe is index-agg.

How to do it...

To execute children aggregations, we will perform the following steps:

1. Index documents with child or parent relations, as discussed in the *Managing a child document* recipe in Chapter 2, *Managing Mapping*. For this example, we will use the same dataset as the child query.

2. Execute a terms aggregation on the uuid of the parent, and for every uuid collecting the terms of the children, value, we create a children aggregation with code similar to following:

```
POST /mybooks-join/_search?size=0
{
  "aggs": {
    "uuid": {
      "terms": {
        "field": "uuid",
        "size": 10
      },
      "aggs": {
        "to-children": {
          "children": {
            "type": "author"
          },
          "aggs": {
            "top-values": {
              "terms": {
                "field": "name.keyword",
                "size": 10
              }
            }
          }
        }
      }
    }
  }
}
```

3. The result returned by Elasticsearch, if everything is okay, should be as follows:

```
{
    ... truncated ...
    "aggregations" : {
      "uuid" : {
        "doc_count_error_upper_bound" : 0,
        "sum_other_doc_count" : 0,
        "buckets" : [
          {
            "key" : "11111",
            "doc_count" : 1,
            "to-children" : {
              "doc_count" : 2,
              "top-values" : {
                "doc_count_error_upper_bound" : 0,
                "sum_other_doc_count" : 0,
                "buckets" : [
                  {
                    "key" : "Mark",
                    "doc_count" : 1
                  },
                  {
                    "key" : "Peter",
                    "doc_count" : 1
                  }
                ]
              }
            }
          },
          ... truncated ...
        ]
      }
    }
}
```

How it works...

The children aggregation works by following these steps:

1. All the parent IDs are collected by the matched query or by previous bucket aggregations.
2. The parent IDs are used to filter the children, and the matching document results are used to compute the children aggregation.

This type of aggregation, similar to the nested one, allows us to aggregate on different documents on searched ones. Because children documents are stored in the same shard of the parents, they are very fast.

Executing nested aggregations

Nested aggregation allows you to execute analytics on nested documents. When working with complex structures, nested objects are very common.

Getting ready

You need an up and running Elasticsearch installation, as we described in the *Downloading and installing Elasticsearch* recipe in `Chapter 1`, *Getting Started*.

To execute these commands, any HTTP client can be used, such as Curl (`https://curl.haxx.se/`), Postman (`https://www.getpostman.com/`), or similar. Using the Kibana Console is recommended, as it provides code completion and better character escaping for Elasticsearch.

To correctly execute the following commands, you will need an index populated with the `ch07/populate_aggregation.txt` commands, which is available in the online code.

The index used in this recipe is `index-agg`.

How to do it...

To execute nested aggregations, we will perform the following steps:

1. Create a nested aggregation to return the minimum size of the product
   version that can be purchased using the following code:

```
POST /mybooks-join/_search?size=0
{
  "aggs": {
    "versions": {
      "nested": {
        "path": "versions"
      },
      "aggs": {
        "min_size": {
          "min": {
            "field": "versions.size"
          }
        }
      }
    }
  }
}
```

2. The result returned by Elasticsearch, if everything is okay, should be as
   follows:

```
{
  ... truncated ...
  "aggregations" : {
    "versions" : {
      "doc_count" : 5,
      "min_size" : {
        "value" : 2.0
      }
    }
  }
}
```

In this case, the result aggregation is a simple min metric that we have already seen in the second recipe of this chapter.

How it works...

The nested aggregation requires only the `path` of the field, relative to the parent, which contains the nested documents.

After having defined the nested aggregation, all the other kinds of aggregations can be used in the sub-aggregations.

There's more...

Elasticsearch provides a way to aggregate values from nested documents to their parent: this aggregation is called `reverse_nested`.

For the preceding example, we can aggregate the top tags for the reseller with a similar query, as follows:

```
POST /mybooks-join/_search?size=0
{
  "aggs": {
    "versions": {
      "nested": {
        "path": "versions"
      },
      "aggs": {
        "top_colors": {
          "terms": {
            "field": "versions.color"
          },
          "aggs": {
            "version_to_book": {
              "reverse_nested": {},
              "aggs": {
                "top_uuid_per_version": {
                  "terms": {
                    "field": "uuid"
                  }
                }
              }
            }
          }
        }
      }
    }
  }
}
```

In this example, there are several steps:

1. We aggregate initially for nested `versions`.
2. Having activated the nested versions documents, we are able to term the aggregate by the `color` field (`versions.color`).
3. From the top versions aggregation, we go back to aggregate on the parent using `"reverse_nested"`.
4. Now, we can aggregate the `uuid` of the parent document.

The response will be similar to this one:

```
{
    ... truncated ...
  "aggregations" : {
    "versions" : {
      "doc_count" : 5,
      "top_colors" : {
        "doc_count_error_upper_bound" : 0,
        "sum_other_doc_count" : 0,
        "buckets" : [
          {
            "key" : "blue",
            "doc_count" : 2,
            "version_to_book" : {
              "doc_count" : 2,
              "top_uuid_per_version" : {
                "doc_count_error_upper_bound" : 0,
                "sum_other_doc_count" : 0,
                "buckets" : [
                  { "key" : "11111", "doc_count" : 1 },
                  { "key" : "22222", "doc_count" : 1 }
                ]
              }
            }
          },
          ... truncated ...
        ]
      }
    }
  }
}
```

Executing top hit aggregations

The top hit aggregation is different from the other aggregation types: all the previous aggregations have metric (simple values) or bucket values; the top hit aggregation returns buckets of search hits (documents).

Generally, the top hit aggregation is used as a sub-aggregation, so that the top matching documents can be aggregated in buckets. The most common scenario for this aggregation is to have, for example, the top *n* documents grouped by category (very common in search results in e-commerce websites).

Getting ready

You need an up and running Elasticsearch installation, as we described in the *Downloading and installing Elasticsearch* recipe in `Chapter 1`, *Getting Started*.

To execute these commands, any HTTP client can be used, such as Curl (`https://curl.haxx.se/`), Postman (`https://www.getpostman.com/`), or similar. Using the Kibana Console is recommended, as it provides code completion and better character escaping for Elasticsearch.

To correctly execute the following commands, you will need an index populated with the `ch07/populate_aggregation.txt` commands, which is available in the online code.

The index used in this recipe is `index-agg`.

How to do it...

To execute a top hit aggregation, we will perform the following steps:

1. Aggregate the document hits by the tag (`tags`) and return only the `name` field of the document with the maximum age (`top_tag_hits`). The search and aggregation will be executed with the following command:

```
POST /index-agg/_search?size=0
{
  "aggs": {
    "tags": {
      "terms": {
        "field": "tag",
        "size": 2
```

```
        },
        "aggs": {
          "top_tag_hits": {
            "top_hits": {
              "sort": [
                {
                  "age": {
                    "order": "desc"
                  }
                }
              ],
              "_source": {
                "includes": [
                  "name"
                ]
              },
              "size": 1
            }
          }
        }
      }
    }
```

2. The result returned by Elasticsearch, if everything is okay, should be as follows:

```
{
  ... truncated ...
  "aggregations" : {
    "tags" : {
      "doc_count_error_upper_bound" : 0,
      "sum_other_doc_count" : 2828,
      "buckets" : [
        {
          "key" : "laborum",
          "doc_count" : 31,
          "top_tag_hits" : {
            "hits" : {
              "total" : 31,
              "max_score" : null,
              "hits" : [
                {
                  "_index" : "index-agg",
                  "_type" : "_doc",
                  "_id" : "730",
                  "_score" : null,
                  "_source" : { "name" : "Gladiator"},
```

```
                    "sort" : [ 90]
                  }
                ]
              }
            }
          },
          ... truncated ...
        ]
      }
    }
  }
```

How it works...

The top hit aggregation allows you to collect buckets of hits of another aggregation. It provides optional parameters to control the results slicing. They are as follows:

- from: This is the starting position of the hits in the bucket (default: 0).
- size: This is the hit bucket size (default: the parent bucket size).
- sort: This allows us to sort for different values (default: score). Its definition is similar to the search sort of Chapter 5, *Text and Numeric Queries*.

To control the returned hits, it's possible to use the same parameters that were used for the search, as follows:

- _source: This allows us to control the returned source. It can be disabled (false), partially returned (obj.*), or have multiple exclude or include rules. In the preceding example, we have returned only the name field, as follows:

  ```
  "_source": {
    "include": [
      "name"
    ]
  },
  ```

- highlighting: This allows us to define the fields and settings to be used for calculating a query abstract
- stored_fields: This allows us to return stored fields

- `explain`: This returns information on how the score is calculated for a particular document
- `version`: This adds the version of a document in the results (default: `false`)

> The top hit aggregation can be used for implementing a field collapsing feature, first using a `terms` aggregation on the field that we want to collapse, and then collecting the documents with a top hit aggregation.

See also

Refer to the *Executing a search* recipe in `Chapter 4`, *Exploring Search Capabilities*, for common parameters that can be used during search.

Executing a matrix stats aggregation

Elasticsearch 5.x or above provided a special module called `aggs-matrix-stats` that automatically computes advanced statistics on several fields.

Getting ready

You need an up and running Elasticsearch installation, as we described in the *Downloading and installing Elasticsearch* recipe in `Chapter 1`, *Getting Started*.

To execute these commands, any HTTP client can be used, such as Curl (`https://curl.haxx.se/`), Postman (`https://www.getpostman.com/`), or similar. Using the Kibana Console is recommended, as it provides code completion and better character escaping for Elasticsearch.

To correctly execute the following commands, you will need an index populated with the `ch07/populate_aggregation.txt` commands, which is available in the online code.

The index used in this recipe is `index-agg`.

How to do it...

To execute a top hot aggregation, we will perform the following steps:

1. First, we will evaluate statistics related to price and age in our knowledge base. The search and aggregation will be executed with the following command:

```
POST /index-agg/_search?size=0
{
  "aggs": {
    "matrixstats": {
      "matrix_stats": {
        "fields": [
          "age",
          "price"
        ]
      }
    }
  }
}
```

2. The result returned by Elasticsearch, if everything is okay, should be as follows:

```
{
  ... truncated ...
  "aggregations" : {
    "matrixstats" : {
      "doc_count" : 1000,
      "fields" : [
        {
          "name" : "price",
          "count" : 1000,
          "mean" : 50.29545117592628,
          "variance" : 834.2714234338575,
          "skewness" : -0.04757692114597182,
          "kurtosis" : 1.808483274482735,
          "covariance" : {
            "price" : 834.2714234338575,
            "age" : 2.523682208250993
          },
          "correlation" : {
            "price" : 1.0,
            "age" : 0.003051775248782358
          }
        },
```

```
        ... truncated ...
      ]
    }
  }
}
```

How it works...

The matrix xtats aggregation allows us to compute different metric on numeric fields, as follows:

- count: This is the number of per field samples included in the calculation.
- mean: This is the average value for each field.
- variance: This is the per field measurement for how spread out the samples are from the mean.
- skewness: This is the per field measurement quantifying the asymmetric distribution around the mean.
- kurtosis: This is the per field measurement quantifying the shape of the distribution.
- covariance: This is a matrix that quantitatively describes how changes in one field are associated with another.
- correlation: This is the covariance matrix scaled to a range of -1 to 1, inclusive. It describes the relationship between field distributions. The higher the value of the correlation, the more the numeric fields are correlated.

The matrix stats aggregation is also a good code sample for developing custom aggregation plugins to extend the power of the aggregation framework of Elasticsearch.

Executing geo bounds aggregations

It's a very common scenario to have a set of documents that match a query, and you need to know the box that contains them. The solution to this scenario is the metric aggregation geo bounds.

Getting ready

You need an up and running Elasticsearch installation, as we described in the *Downloading and installing Elasticsearch* recipe in `Chapter 1`, *Getting Started*.

To execute these commands, any HTTP client can be used, such as Curl (`https://curl.haxx.se/`), Postman (`https://www.getpostman.com/`), or similar. Using the Kibana Console is recommended, as it provides code completion and better character escaping for Elasticsearch.

To correctly execute the following commands, you will need an index populated with the `ch07/populate_aggregation.txt` commands, which is available in the online code.

The index used in this recipe is `index-agg`.

How to do it...

To execute geo bounds aggregations, we will perform the following steps:

1. Execute a query and calculate the geo bounds on the results using the following code:

```
POST /index-agg/_search?size=0
{
  "aggs": {
    "box": {
      "geo_bounds": {
        "field": "position",
        "wrap_longitude": true
      }
    }
  }
}
```

2. The result returned by Elasticsearch, if everything is okay, should be as follows:

```
{
  ... truncated ...
  "aggregations" : {
    "box" : {
      "bounds" : {
        "top_left" : {
          "lat" : 89.97587876860052,
```

```
            "lon" : 0.7563168089836836
          },
          "bottom_right" : {
            "lat" : -89.8060692474246,
            "lon" : -0.2987125888466835
          }
        }
      }
    }
  }
}
```

How it works...

The geo bounds aggregation is a metric aggregation that is able to compute the box of all the documents that are in a bucket.

It allows you to use the following parameters:

- `field`: This is the field that contains the geo point of the document.
- `wrap_longitude`: This is an optional parameter that specifies whether the bounding box should be allowed to overlap the International Date Line (default `true`).

The returned box (square) is given by two geo points: the top-left and the bottom-right.

See also

Refer to the *Mapping a GeoPoint field* recipe in `Chapter 2`, *Managing Mapping,* to correctly define a GeoPoint field for executing geo aggregations.

Executing geo centroid aggregations

If you have a lot of geo localized events and you need to know the center of these events, the geo centroid aggregation allows you to compute this geo point.

Common scenarios could be as follows:

- During Twitter monitoring for events (earthquakes, tsunamis, and so on), in order to detect the center of the event by monitoring the first top *n* events tweets.
- Having documents that have coordinates, in order to find the common center of these documents.

Getting ready

You need an up and running Elasticsearch installation, as we described in the *Downloading and installing Elasticsearch* recipe in `Chapter 1`, *Getting Started*.

To execute the commands, any HTTP client can be used, such as curl (`https://curl.haxx.se/`), Postman (`https://www.getpostman.com/`), or similar. Using Kibana Console is recommended, as it provides the code completion and better character escaping for Elasticsearch.

To correctly execute the following commands, you will need an index populated with the `ch07/populate_aggregation.txt` commands available in the online code.

The index used in this recipe is the `index-agg`.

How to do it...

To execute geo centroid aggregations, we will perform the following steps:

1. Execute a query and calculate the `geo_centroid` on the results using the following code:

```
POST /index-agg/_search?size=0
{
  "aggs": {
    "centroid": {
      "geo_centroid": {
        "field": "position"
      }
    }
  }
}
```

2. The result returned by Elasticsearch, if everything is okay, should be as follows:

```
{
    ... documents ...
    "aggregations" : {
      "centroid" : {
        "location" : {
          "lat" : 3.0941622890532017,
          "lon" : 0.5758556071668863
        },
        "count" : 1000
      }
    }
}
```

How it works...

The geo centroid aggregation is a metric aggregation that is able to compute the geo point centroid of a bucket of documents. It allows you to define only a single parameter in the `field` that contains the geo point of the document.

The returned result is a geo point that is the centroid of the document distribution. For example, if your document contains earthquake events, by using the geo centroid aggregation, you are able to compute the epicenter of the earthquake.

See also

Refer to the *Mapping a GeoPoint field* recipe in `Chapter 2`, *Managing Mapping*, to correctly define a GeoPoint field for executing geo aggregations.

Executing pipeline aggregations

Elasticsearch allows you to define aggregations that are a mix of the results of other aggregations (for example, by comparing the results of two metric aggregations): these are **pipeline** aggregations.

They are very common when you need to compute results from different aggregations, such as statistics on results.

Getting ready

You need an up and running Elasticsearch installation, as we described in the *Downloading and installing Elasticsearch* recipe in Chapter 1, *Getting Started*.

To execute the commands, any HTTP client can be used, such as curl (https://curl.haxx.se/), Postman (https://www.getpostman.com/), or similar. Using Kibana Console is recommended, as it provides the code completion and better character escaping for Elasticsearch.

To correctly execute the following commands, you will need create the index-pipagg with the following command:

```
PUT /index-pipagg
{
  "mappings": {
    "_doc": {
      "properties": {
        "type": {
          "type": "keyword"
        },
        "date": {
          "type": "date"
        }
      }
    }
  }
}
```

And populate it with some documents as follows:

```
PUT /_bulk
{"index":{"_index":"index-pipagg"}}
{"date": "2019-01-01", "price": 200, "promoted": true, "rating": 1,
"type": "hat"}
{"index":{"_index":"index-pipagg"}}
{"date": "2019-01-01", "price": 200, "promoted": true, "rating": 1,
"type": "t-shirt"}
{"index":{"_index":"index-pipagg"}}
{"date": "2019-01-01", "price": 150, "promoted": true, "rating": 5,
"type": "bag"}
{"index":{"_index":"index-pipagg"}}
{"date": "2019-02-01", "price": 50, "promoted": false, "rating": 1,
"type": "hat"}
{"index":{"_index":"index-pipagg"}}
{"date": "2019-02-01", "price": 10, "promoted": true, "rating": 4,
"type": "t-shirt"}
```

```
{"index":{"_index":"index-pipagg"}}
{"date": "2019-03-01", "price": 200, "promoted": true, "rating": 1,
"type": "hat"}
{"index":{"_index":"index-pipagg"}}
{"date": "2019-03-01", "price": 175, "promoted": false, "rating":2,
"type": "t-shirt"}
```

How to do it...

To execute a pipeline aggregations, we will perform the following steps:

1. Execute a query and calculate a composed aggregation that will divide the sales in the month, and for every month, we will compute the incoming (price). To get the extended aggregation on these sales, we will execute the following code:

```
POST /index-pipagg/_search?size=0
{
    "aggs" : {
        "sales_per_month" : {
            "date_histogram" : {
                "field" : "date",
                "interval" : "month"
            },
            "aggs": {
                "sales": {
                    "sum": {
                        "field": "price"
                    }
                }
            }
        },
        "stats_monthly_sales": {
            "extended_stats_bucket": {
                "buckets_path": "sales_per_month>sales"
            }
        }
    }
}
```

2. The result returned by Elasticsearch, if everything is okay, should be as follows:

```
{
    ... truncated ...
    "aggregations" : {
      "sales_per_month" : {
        "buckets" : [
          {
            "key_as_string" : "2019-01-01T00:00:00.000Z",
            "key" : 1546300800000,
            "doc_count" : 3,
            "sales" : {
              "value" : 550.0
            }
          },
          {
            "key_as_string" : "2019-02-01T00:00:00.000Z",
            "key" : 1548979200000,
            "doc_count" : 2,
            "sales" : {
              "value" : 60.0
            }
          },
          {
            "key_as_string" : "2019-03-01T00:00:00.000Z",
            "key" : 1551398400000,
            "doc_count" : 2,
            "sales" : {
              "value" : 375.0
            }
          }
        ]
      },
      "stats_monthly_sales" : {
        "count" : 3,
        "min" : 60.0,
        "max" : 550.0,
        "avg" : 328.3333333333333,
        "sum" : 985.0,
        "sum_of_squares" : 446725.0,
        "variance" : 41105.55555555556,
        "std_deviation" : 202.74505063146563,
        "std_deviation_bounds" : {
          "upper" : 733.8234345962646,
          "lower" : -77.15676792959795
        }
      }
```

```
        }
    }
```

How it works...

The pipeline aggregation is able to compute an aggregation based on another one. You can consider the pipeline aggregation similar to a metric (see the *Executing stats aggregations* recipe in this chapter) that is working on the results of other aggregations.

The most used types of pipeline aggregation are as follows:

- `avg_bucket`: Used to compute the average of parent aggregations.
- `derivative`: Used to compute the derivative of parent aggregations.
- `max_bucket`: Used to compute the maximum of related aggregations.
- `min_bucket`: Used to compute the minimum of related aggregations.
- `sum_bucket`: Used to compute the sum of related aggregations.
- `stats_bucket`: Used to compute the statistic of related aggregations.
- `extended_stats_bucket`: Used to compute the statistic of related aggregations.
- `percentile_bucket`: Used to compute the percentile of related aggregations.
- `moving_fn`: A moving function, which is used to compute the percentile of related aggregations.
- `cumulative_sum`: Used to compute the derivative of parent aggregations.
- `bucket_script`: Used to define the operation between related aggregations. This is the most powerful one if you need to customize complex value computations between aggregation metrics.
- `bucket_select`: Used to filter out parent bucket aggregation.
- `bucket_sort`: Used to sort parent bucket aggregation.

Every pipeline type aggregation has additional parameters that relate to how the metric is computed: the online official documentation covers all the corners cases of these usages.

See also

The official Elasticsearch documentation on pipeline aggregations at: `https://www.elastic.co/guide/en/elasticsearch/reference/master/search-aggregations-pipeline.html`

8
Scripting in Elasticsearch

Elasticsearch has a powerful way of extending its capabilities by using custom scripts, which can be written in several programming languages. The most common ones are Painless, Express, and Mustache. In this chapter, we will explore how it's possible to create custom scoring algorithms, specially-processed return fields, custom sorting, and complex update operations on records. The scripting concept of Elasticsearch is an advanced stored-procedure system in the NoSQL world; due to this, every advanced user of Elasticsearch should learn how to master it.

Elasticsearch natively provides scripting in Java (that is, a Java code compiled in JAR), Painless, Express, and Mustache; however, a lot of other interesting languages are also available as plugins, such as Kotlin and Velocity. In older Elasticsearch releases, prior to version 5.0, the official scripting language was **Groovy**. But for better sandboxing and performance, the official language is now Painless, which is provided in Elasticsearch by default.

In this chapter, we will cover the following recipes:

- Painless scripting
- Installing additional script plugins
- Managing scripts
- Sorting data using scripts
- Computing return fields with scripting
- Filtering a search using scripting
- Using scripting in aggregations
- Updating a document using scripts
- Reindexing with a script

Painless scripting

Painless is a simple, secure scripting language that is available in Elasticsearch by default. It was designed by the Elasticsearch team to be used specifically with Elasticsearch and can safely be used with inline and stored scripting. Its syntax is similar to Groovy.

Getting ready

You will need an up-and-running Elasticsearch installation – similar to the one that we described in the *Downloading and installing Elasticsearch* recipe in Chapter 1, *Getting Started*.

In order to execute the commands, any HTTP client can be used, such as Curl (https://curl.haxx.se/) or Postman (https://www.getpostman.com/). You can use the Kibana console as it provides code completion and better character escaping for Elasticsearch.

To correctly execute the following commands, you will need an index that is populated with the ch07/populate_aggregation.txt commands – these are available in the online code.

To be able to use regular expressions in Painless scripting, you will need to activate them in elasticsearch.yml by adding the following code:

```
script.painless.regex.enabled: true
```

The index used in this recipe is the index-agg index.

How to do it...

We'll use Painless scripting to compute the scoring by using the following steps:

1. We can execute a search with a scripting function in kibana using the following code:

```
POST /index-agg/_search
{
  "query": {
    "function_score": {
      "script_score": {
        "script": {
```

```
                    "lang": "painless",
                    "source": "doc['price'].value * 1.2"
                }
            }
        }
    }
}
```

2. If everything works correctly, the result will be as follows:

```
{
    ...truncated ...
    "hits" : {
        "total" : 1000,
        "max_score" : 119.97963,
        "hits" : [
            {
                "_index" : "index-agg",
                "_type" : "_doc",
                "_id" : "857",
                "_score" : 119.97963,
                "_source" : {
                    ... truncated ...
                    "price" : 99.98302508488757,
                    ... truncated ...
                },
                {
                "_index" : "index-agg",
                "_type" : "_doc",
                "_id" : "136",
                "_score" : 119.90164,
                "_source" : {
                    ...truncated ...
                    "price" : 99.91804048691392,
    ... truncated ...
            ]
        }
}
```

You can see that, in this case, using the scripting has the same meaning as sorting by price!

How it works...

Painless is a scripting language that was developed for Elasticsearch for rapid data processing and security (it is sandboxed in order to prevent a malicious code injection). The syntax is based on Groovy, and it's provided by default in every installation. Painless is marked as experimental by the Elasticsearch team, because some features may change in the future—however, it is the preferred language for scripting.

Elasticsearch processes the scripting language in two steps:

1. The script code is compiled in an object in order to be used in a script call; if the scripting code is invalid, then an exception is raised.
2. For each element, the script is called and the result is collected; if the script fails on some elements, then the search or computation may fail.

 Using scripting is a powerful Elasticsearch functionality, but it costs a lot in terms of memory and CPU cycles. The best practice, if possible, is to optimize the indexing of data to search or aggregate – and to avoid using scripting completely.

The method that is used to define a script in Elasticsearch is always the same; the script is contained in an `script` object using the following format:

```
"script": {
    "lang":    "...",
    "source" | "id": "...",
    "params": { ... }
}
```

It accepts several parameters, as follows:

- `source`/`id`: These are the references for the script, which can be defined as follows:
    - `source`: If the string with your script code is provided with the call.
    - `id`: If the script is stored in the cluster, then it refers to the `id` parameter, which is used to save the script in the cluster.

- `params` (an optional JSON object): This defines the parameters to be passed, which are, in the context of scripting, available using the `params` variable.
- `lang` (the default is `painless`): This defines the scripting language that is to be used.

> For complex scripts that contain the special character " in the text, I suggest using kibana and a triple " to escape the script text (similar to Python and Scala special `"""`). In this way you can improve the readability of your script code.

There's more...

Painless is the preferred choice if the script is not too complex; otherwise, a native plugin provides a better environment in order to implement complex logic and data management.

For accessing document properties in Painless scripts, the same approach works as with other scripting languages:

- `doc._score`: This stores the document score; it's generally available in searching, sorting, and aggregations.
- `doc._source`: This allows access to the source of the document. Use it wisely because it requires the entire source to be fetched and it's very CPU-and-memory-intensive.
- `_fields['field_name'].value`: This allows you to load the value from the stored field (in mapping, the field has the `stored:true` parameter).
- `doc['field_name']`: This extracts the document field value from the `doc` values of the field. In Elasticsearch, the `doc` values are automatically stored for every field that is not of the `text` type.
- `doc['field_name'].value`: This extracts the value of the `field_name` field from the document. If the value is an array, or if you want to extract the value as an array, then you can use `doc['field_name'].values`.
- `doc['field_name'].empty`: This returns `true` if the `field_name` field has no value in the document.
- `doc['field_name'].multivalue`: This returns `true` if the `field_name` field contains multiple values.

For performance, the fastest access method for a field value is through the `doc` value, then the stored field, and, finally, from the source.

If the field contains a GeoPoint value, then additional methods are available, such as the following:

- `doc['field_name'].lat`: This returns the latitude of a GeoPoint value. If you need the value as an array, then you can use `doc['field_name'].lats`.
- `doc['field_name'].lon`: This returns the longitude of a GeoPoint value. If you need the value as an array, then you can use `doc['field_name'].lons`.
- `doc['field_name'].distance(lat,lon)`: This returns the plane distance in miles from a latitude/longitude point.
- `doc['field_name'].arcDistance(lat,lon)`: This returns the arc distance in miles, which is given as a latitude/longitude point.
- `doc['field_name'].geohashDistance(geohash)`: This returns the distance in miles, which is given as a geohash value.

By using these helper methods, it is possible to create advanced scripts in order to boost a document by a distance, which can be very handy for developing geospatial-centered applications.

See also

You can refer to the following URLs for further reference, which are related to this recipe:

- The official announcement by Jack Conradson about the Painless development at `https://www.elastic.co/blog/painless-a-new-scripting-language`
- The Elasticsearch official page of Painless at `https://www.elastic.co/guide/en/elasticsearch/reference/master/modules-scripting-painless.html` to learn about its main functionalities
- The Painless syntax reference at `https://www.elastic.co/guide/en/elasticsearch/reference/master/modules-scripting-painless.html` to learn about Painless powerful syntax

Installing additional script plugins

Elasticsearch provides native scripting (that is, Java code compiled in JAR) and Painless, but a lot of other interesting languages are also available, such as Kotlin.

 At the time of writing this book, there are no available language plugins as part of Elasticsearch's official ones. Usually, plugin authors will take up to a week or a month to update their plugins to the new version after a major release.

As previously stated, the official language is now Painless, and this is provided by default in Elasticsearch for better sandboxing and performance.

Getting ready

You will need an up-and-running Elasticsearch installation – similar to the one that we described in the *Downloading and installing Elasticsearch* recipe in Chapter 1, *Getting Started*.

How to do it...

In order to install the JavaScript language support for Elasticsearch, we will perform the following steps:

1. From the command line, simply call the following command:

```
bin/elasticsearch-plugin install lang-kotlin
```

2. It will print the following output:

```
-> Downloading lang-kotlin from elastic
[=============================================] 100%??
@@@@@@@@@@@@@@@@@@@@@@@@@@@@@@@@@@@@@@@@@@@@@@@@@@@@@@@@@@
@ WARNING: plugin requires additional permissions @
@@@@@@@@@@@@@@@@@@@@@@@@@@@@@@@@@@@@@@@@@@@@@@@@@@@@@@@@@@
* java.lang.RuntimePermission createClassLoader
* org.elasticsearch.script.ClassPermission <<STANDARD>>
* org.elasticsearch.script.ClassPermission
org.mozilla.javascript.ContextFactory
* org.elasticsearch.script.ClassPermission
org.mozilla.javascript.Callable
* org.elasticsearch.script.ClassPermission
org.mozilla.javascript.NativeFunction
```

```
* org.elasticsearch.script.ClassPermission
org.mozilla.javascript.Script
* org.elasticsearch.script.ClassPermission
org.mozilla.javascript.ScriptRuntime
* org.elasticsearch.script.ClassPermission
org.mozilla.javascript.Undefined
* org.elasticsearch.script.ClassPermission
org.mozilla.javascript.optimizer.OptRuntime
See http://docs.oracle.com/javase/8/docs/technotes/
guides/security/permissions.html
for descriptions of what these permissions allow and the
associated risks.

Continue with installation? [y/N]y
-> Installed lang-javascript
```

If the installation is successful, the output will end with `Installed`; otherwise, an error is returned. You can refer to `http://docs.oracle.com/javase/8/docs/technotes/guides/security/permissions.html` for descriptions about what these permissions allow and their associated risks:

1. Restart your Elasticsearch server in order to check that the scripting plugins are loaded:

```
[...][INFO ][o.e.n.Node ] [] initializing ...
[...][INFO ][o.e.e.NodeEnvironment ] [R2Gp0ny] using [1]
data paths, mounts [[/ (/dev/disk1)]], net usable_space
[82.4gb], net total_space [930.7gb], spins? [unknown], types
[hfs]
[...][INFO ][o.e.e.NodeEnvironment ] [R2Gp0ny] heap size
[1.9gb], compressed ordinary object pointers [true]
[...][INFO ][o.e.n.Node ] [R2Gp0ny] node name
[R2Gp0ny] derived from node ID; set [node.name] to override
[...][INFO ][o.e.n.Node ] [R2Gp0ny]
version[5.0.0-beta1], pid[58291], build[7eb6260/2016-09-
20T23:10:37.942Z], OS[Mac OS X/10.12/x86_64], JVM[Oracle
Corporation/Java HotSpot(TM) 64-Bit Server
VM/1.8.0_101/25.101-
b13]
[...][INFO ][o.e.p.PluginsService ] [R2Gp0ny] loaded module
[aggs-matrix-stats]
[...][INFO ][o.e.p.PluginsService ] [R2Gp0ny] loaded module
[ingest-common]
[...][INFO ][o.e.p.PluginsService ] [R2Gp0ny] loaded module
[lang-expression]
[...][INFO ][o.e.p.PluginsService ] [R2Gp0ny] loaded module
[lang-groovy]
```

```
[...][INFO ][o.e.p.PluginsService ] [R2Gp0ny] loaded module
[lang-mustache]
[...][INFO ][o.e.p.PluginsService ] [R2Gp0ny] loaded module
[lang-painless]
[...][INFO ][o.e.p.PluginsService ] [R2Gp0ny] loaded module
[percolator]
[...][INFO ][o.e.p.PluginsService ] [R2Gp0ny] loaded module
[reindex]
[...][INFO ][o.e.p.PluginsService ] [R2Gp0ny] loaded module
[transport-netty3]
[...][INFO ][o.e.p.PluginsService ] [R2Gp0ny] loaded module
[transport-netty4]
[...][INFO ][o.e.p.PluginsService ] [R2Gp0ny] loaded plugin
[lang-javascript]
[...][INFO ][o.e.p.PluginsService ] [R2Gp0ny] loaded plugin
[lang-python]
[...][INFO ][o.e.n.Node ] [R2Gp0ny] initialized
[...][INFO ][o.e.n.Node ] [R2Gp0ny] starting ...
```

How it works...

Language plugins allow an extension for the number of supported languages that can be used in scripting. During installation, they require special permissions in order to access classes and methods that are banned by the Elasticsearch security layer, such as access to ClassLoader or class permissions.

During the Elasticsearch start-up, an internal Elasticsearch service, known as PluginService, loads all the installed language plugins.

 Installing or upgrading a plugin requires the restarting of a node.

From version 7.x, all the plugins have the same version of Elasticsearch.

The Elasticsearch community provides a number of common scripting languages (a full list is available on the Elasticsearch site plugin page at http://www.elastic.co/ guide/en/elasticsearch/reference/current/modules-plugins.html), while other languages are available in the GitHub repository (a simple search on GitHub will allow you to find them).

There's more...

The plugin manager that we used to install the plugins also provides the following commands:

- `list`: This command is used to list all the installed plugins.

  For example, you can execute the following command:

  ```
  bin/elasticsearch-plugin list
  ```

  The result of the preceding command will be as follows:

  ```
  lang-kotlin@7.0.0
  ```

- `remove`: This command is used to remove an installed plugin.

  For example, you can execute the following command:

  ```
  bin/elasticsearch-plugin remove lang-kotlin
  ```

  The result of the preceding command will be as follows:

  ```
  -> Removing lang-kotlin...
  ```

Managing scripts

Depending on your scripting usage, there are several ways of customizing Elasticsearch in order to use your script extensions.

In this recipe, we will demonstrate how you can provide scripts to Elasticsearch using files, indexes, or in lines.

Getting ready

You will need an up-and-running Elasticsearch installation – similar to the one that we described in the *Downloading and installing Elasticsearch* recipe in `Chapter 1`, *Getting Started*.

In order to execute the commands, any HTTP client can be used, such as Curl (`https://curl.haxx.se/`) or Postman (`https://www.getpostman.com/`). You can use the Kibana console as it provides code completion and better character escaping for Elasticsearch.

To correctly execute the following commands, you will need an index populated with the ch08/populate_aggregation.txt commands – these are available in the online code.

In order to be able to use regular expressions in Painless scripting, you will need to activate them in elasticsearch.yml by adding the following code:

```
script.painless.regex.enabled: true
```

The index used in this recipe is the index-agg index.

How to do it...

To manage scripting, we will perform the following steps:

1. Dynamic scripting (except Painless) is disabled by default for security reasons. We need to activate it in order to use dynamic scripting languages such as JavaScript and Python. To do this, we need to enable the scripting flags in the Elasticsearch configuration file (config/elasticseach.yml), and then restart the cluster:

   ```
   script.inline: true
   script.stored: true
   ```

2. If the dynamic script is enabled (as done in the first step), Elasticsearch lets us store the scripts in a special part of the cluster state: "_scripts". In order to put my_script in the cluster state, execute the following code:

   ```
   POST /_scripts/my_script
   {
     "script": {
       "source": """doc['price'].value * params.factor""",
       "lang":"painless"
     }
   }
   ```

3. The script can be used by simply referencing it in the script/id field:

   ```
   POST /index-agg/_search?size=2
   {
     "sort": {
       "_script": {
         "script": {
           "id": "my_script",
           "params": {
   ```

```
                    "factor": 1.2
                }
            },
            "type": "number",
            "order": "desc"
        }
    },
    "_source": {
      "includes": [
        "price"
      ]
    }
  }
}
```

How it works...

Elasticsearch permits different ways in which to load your script, and each approach has its pros and cons. The scripts can also be available in the special _script cluster state. The REST endpoints are as follows:

```
POST http://<server>/_scripts/<id> (to retrieve a script)
PUT http://<server>/_scripts/<id> (to store a script)
DELETE http://<server>/_scripts/<id> (to delete a script)
```

The stored script can be referenced in the code using `"script":{"id": "id_of_the_script"}`.

The following sections of the book will use inline scripting because it's easier to use during the development and testing phases.

Generally, a good workflow is to do the development using inline dynamic scripting on request – this is because it's faster to prototype. Once the script is ready and no more changes are required, then it should be stored in the index, so that it will be simpler to call and manage in all the cluster nodes. In production, the best practice is to disable dynamic scripting and to store the script on a disk (by dumping the indexed script to the disk) in order to improve security.

When you are storing files on a disk, pay attention to the file extension; the following table summarizes the status of the plugins:

Language	Provided as	File extension	Status
Painless	Built-in/module	`painless`	Default
Expression	Built-in/module	`expression`	Deprecated
Mustache	Built-in/module	`mustache`	Default

The other scripting parameters that can be set in `config/elasticsearch.yml` are as follows:

- `script.max_compilations_per_minute` (the default is 25): This default scripting engine has a global limit for how many compilations can be done per minute. You can change this to a higher value, for example, `script.max_compilations_per_minute: 1000`.

- `script.cache.max_size` (the default is 100): This defines how many scripts are cached; it depends on context, but, in general, it's better to increase this value.

- `script.max_size_in_bytes` (the default is 65535): This defines the maximum text size for a script; for large scripts, the best practice is to develop native plugins.

- `script.cache.expire` (the default is disabled): This defines a time-based expiration for the cached scripts.

There's more...

In the preceding example, we activated Elasticsearch scripting for all the engines, but Elasticsearch provides fine-grained settings in order to control them.

In Elasticsearch, the scripting can be used in following different contexts:

Context	Description
`aggs`	Aggregations
`search`	The search API, percolator API, and suggest API
`update`	The update API
`plugin`	The special scripts under the generic `plugin` category

Here, scripting is enabled, by default, for all the contexts.

You can disable all the scripting by setting the `script.allowed_contexts: none` value in `elasticsearch.yml`.

To activate the scripting only for `update` and `search`, then you can use `script.allowed_contexts: search, update`.

For more fine-grained control, scripting can be controlled by the active type of scripting using the `elasticsearch.yml` entry: `script.allowed_types`.

In order to only enable inline scripting, then we can use the following command:

```
script.allowed_types: inline
```

See also

You can refer to the following URLs for further reference, which are related to this recipe:

- The scripting page on the Elasticsearch website at `https://www.elastic.co/guide/en/elasticsearch/reference/current/modules-scripting.html` for general information about scripting
- The scripting security page at `https://www.elastic.co/guide/en/elasticsearch/reference/current/modules-scripting-security.html` for other borderline cases on security management

Sorting data using scripts

Elasticsearch provides scripting support for sorting functionality. In real-world applications, there is often a need to modify the default sorting using an algorithm that is dependent on the context and some external variables. Some common scenarios are as follows:

- Sorting places near a point
- Sorting by most read articles
- Sorting items by custom user logic
- Sorting items by revenue

Because the computing of scores on a large dataset is very CPU-intensive, if you use scripting, then it's better to execute it on a small dataset using standard score queries for detecting the top documents, and then execute a rescoring on the top subset.

Getting ready

You will need an up-and-running Elasticsearch installation – similar to the one that we described in the *Downloading and installing Elasticsearch* recipe in `Chapter 1`, *Getting Started*.

To execute the commands, any HTTP client can be used, such as curl (`https://curl.haxx.se/`) or postman (`https://www.getpostman.com/`). You can use the `Kibana` console as it provides code completion and better character escaping for Elasticsearch.

To correctly execute the following commands, you will need an index that is populated with the `ch07/populate_aggregation.txt` commands – these are available in the online code.

To be able to use regular expressions in Painless scripting, you will need to activate them in `elasticsearch.yml` by adding `script.painless.regex.enabled: true`.

The index used in this recipe is the `index-agg` index.

How to do it...

For sorting using scripting, we will perform the following steps:

1. If we want to order our documents by the `price` field multiplied by a `factor` parameter (that is, sales tax), then the search will be as follows:

```
POST /index-agg/_search?size=3
{
  "sort": {
    "_script": {
      "script": {
        "source": """
Math.sqrt(doc["price"].value *
params.factor)
""",
        "params": {
```

```
            "factor": 1.2
          }
        },
        "type": "number",
        "order": "desc"
      }
    },
    "_source": {
      "includes": [
        "price"
      ]
    }
  }
}
```

Here, we have used a `sort` script; in real-world applications, the documents that are to be sorted should not have a high cardinality.

2. If everything's correct, then the result that is returned by Elasticsearch will be as follows:

```
{
  ... deprecated ...
  "hits" : {
    "total" : 1000,
    "max_score" : null,
    "hits" : [
      {
        "_index" : "index-agg",
        "_type" : "_doc",
        "_id" : "857",
        "_score" : null,
        "_source" : {
          "price" : 99.98302508488757
        },
        "sort" : [
          10.953521329536066
        ]
      },
      {
        "_index" : "index-agg",
        "_type" : "_doc",
        "_id" : "136",
        "_score" : null,
        "_source" : {
          "price" : 99.91804048691392
        },
        "sort" : [
          10.949960954152345
```

```
      ]
    },
    {
      "_index" : "index-agg",
      "_type" : "_doc",
      "_id" : "762",
      "_score" : null,
      "_source" : {
        "price" : 99.86804119988182
      },
      "sort" : [
        10.947221126414913
      ]
    }
  ]
 }
}
```

How it works...

The sort parameter, which we discussed in Chapter 4, *Exploring Search Capabilities*, can be extended with the help of scripting.

The sort scripting allows you to define several parameters, such as the following:

- order (default "asc") ("asc" or "desc"): This determines whether the order must be ascending or descending
- type: This defines the type in order to convert the value
- script: This contains the script object that is to be executed

Extending the sort parameter using scripting allows you to use a broader approach to score your hits.

Elasticsearch scripting permits the use of any code that you want to use; for instance, you can create custom complex algorithms for scoring your documents.

There's more...

Painless and Groovy provide a lot of built-in functions (mainly taken from the Java `Math` class) that can be used in scripts, such as the following:

Function	Description
`time()`	This is the current time in milliseconds
`sin(a)`	This returns the trigonometric sine of an angle
`cos(a)`	This returns the trigonometric cosine of an angle
`tan(a)`	This returns the trigonometric tangent of an angle
`asin(a)`	This returns the arc sine of a value
`acos(a)`	This returns the arc cosine of a value
`atan(a)`	This returns the arc tangent of a value
`toRadians(angdeg)`	This converts an angle that is measured in degrees to an approximately equivalent angle that is measured in radians
`toDegrees(angrad)`	This converts an angle that is measured in radians to an approximately equivalent angle that is measured in degrees
`exp(a)`	This returns Euler's number raised to the power of a value
`log(a)`	This returns the natural logarithm (base e) of a value
`log10(a)`	This returns the base 10 logarithm of a value
`sqrt(a)`	This returns the correctly rounded positive square root of a value
`cbrt(a)`	This returns the cube root of a double value
`IEEEremainder(f1, f2)`	This computes the remainder operation on two arguments as prescribed by the IEEE 754 standard
`ceil(a)`	This returns the smallest (closest to negative infinity) value that is greater than or equal to the argument and is equal to a mathematical integer
`floor(a)`	This returns the largest (closest to positive infinity) value that is less than or equal to the argument and is equal to a mathematical integer
`rint(a)`	This returns the value that is closest in value to the argument and is equal to a mathematical integer

`atan2(y, x)`	This returns the angle, theta, from the conversion of rectangular coordinates (x, y_) to polar coordinates (r, _theta)
`pow(a, b)`	This returns the value of the first argument raised to the power of the second argument
`round(a)`	This returns the closest integer to the argument
`random()`	This returns a random double value
`abs(a)`	This returns the absolute value of a value
`max(a, b)`	This returns the greater of two values
`min(a, b)`	This returns the smaller of two values
`ulp(d)`	This returns the size of the unit in the last place of the argument
`signum(d)`	This returns the signum function of the argument
`sinh(x)`	This returns the hyperbolic sine of a value
`cosh(x)`	This returns the hyperbolic cosine of a value
`tanh(x)`	This returns the hyperbolic tangent of a value
`hypot(x,y)`	This returns $sqrt(x^2+y^2)$ without intermediate overflow or underflow
`acos(a)`	This returns the arc cosine of a value
`atan(a)`	This returns the arc tangent of a value

If you want to retrieve records in a random order, then you can use a script with a random method, as shown in the following code:

```
POST /index-agg/_search?&size=2
{
  "sort": {
    "_script": {
      "script": {
        "source": "Math.random()"
      },
      "type": "number",
      "order": "asc"
    }
  }
}
```

In this example, for every hit, the new sort value is computed by executing the `Math.random()` scripting function.

Computing return fields with scripting

Elasticsearch allows us to define complex expressions that can be used to return a new calculated field value.

These special fields are called `script_fields`, and they can be expressed with a script in every available Elasticsearch scripting language.

Getting ready

You will need an up-and-running Elasticsearch installation – similar to the one that we described in the *Downloading and installing Elasticsearch* recipe in `Chapter 1`, *Getting Started*.

To execute the commands, any HTTP client can be used, such as Curl (`https://curl.haxx.se/`) or postman (`https://www.getpostman.com/`). You can use the Kibana console as it provides code completion and better character escaping for Elasticsearch.

In order to correctly execute the following commands, you will need an index that is populated with the `ch07/populate_aggregation.txt` commands—these are available in the online code.

To be able to use regular expressions in Painless scripting, you need to activate them in `elasticsearch.yml` by adding `script.painless.regex.enabled: true`.

The index used in this recipe is the `index-agg` index.

How to do it...

For computing return fields with scripting, we will perform the following steps:

1. Return the following script fields:

   - `"my_calc_field"`: This concatenates the texts of the `"name"` and `"description"` fields
   - `"my_calc_field2"`: This multiplies the `"price"` value by the `"discount"` parameter

2. From the command line, we will execute the following code:

```
POST /index-agg/_search?size=2
{
  "script_fields": {
    "my_calc_field": {
      "script": {
        "source": """params._source.name + " -- " +
params._source.description"""
      }
    },
    "my_calc_field2": {
      "script": {
        "source": """doc["price"].value * params.discount""",
        "params": {
          "discount": 0.8
        }
      }
    }
  }
}
```

3. If everything is all right, then the result that is returned by Elasticsearch will be as follows:

```
{
  ... truncated ...
  "hits" : {
    "total" : 1000,
    "max_score" : 1.0,
    "hits" : [
      {
        "_index" : "index-agg",
        "_type" : "_doc",
        "_id" : "1",
        "_score" : 1.0,
        "fields" : {
          "my_calc_field" : [
            "Valkyrie -- ducimus nobis harum doloribus
voluptatibus libero nisi omnis officiis exercitationem amet
odio odit dolor perspiciatis minima quae voluptas dignissimos
facere ullam tempore temporibus laboriosam ad doloremque
blanditiis numquam placeat accusantium at maxime consectetur
esse earum velit officia dolorum corporis nemo consequatur
perferendis cupiditate eum illum facilis sunt saepe"
          ],
          "my_calc_field2" : [
            15.696847534179689
```

```
                    ]
                }
            },
            {
               "_index" : "index-agg",
               "_type" : "_doc",
               "_id" : "2",
               "_score" : 1.0,
               "fields" : {
                 "my_calc_field" : [
                     "Omega Red -- quod provident sequi rem placeat
        deleniti exercitationem veritatis quasi accusantium accusamus
        autem repudiandae"
                 ],
                 "my_calc_field2" : [
                     56.201733398437504
                 ]
               }
            }
         ]
      }
   }
```

How it works...

The script fields are similar to executing an SQL function on a field during a select. In Elasticsearch, after a search phase is executed and the hits to be returned are calculated, if some fields (standard or script) are defined, then they are calculated and returned.

The script field, which can be defined using all supported languages, is processed by passing a value to the source of the document and, if some other parameters are defined in the script (such as the discount factor), then they are passed to the script function.

The script function is a code snippet, so it can contain everything that the language allows to be written; however, it must be evaluated to a value (or a list of values).

See also

You can refer to the following recipes for further reference:

- The *Installing additional script plugins* recipe in this chapter to install additional languages for scripting
- The *Sorting data using scripts* recipe in this chapter for a reference to extra built-in functions for Painless scripts

Filtering a search using scripting

In `Chapter 4`, *Exploring Search Capabilities*, we explored many filters. Elasticsearch scripting allows the extension of a traditional filter by using custom scripts.

Using scripting to create a custom filter is a convenient way to write scripting rules that are not provided by Lucene or Elasticsearch, and to implement business logic that is not available in a DSL query.

Getting ready

You will need an up-and-running Elasticsearch installation – similar to the one that we described in the *Downloading and installing Elasticsearch* recipe in `Chapter 1`, *Getting Started*.

To execute the commands, any HTTP client can be used, such as curl (`https://curl.haxx.se/`) or postman (`https://www.getpostman.com/`). You can use the Kibana console as it provides code completion and better character escaping for Elasticsearch.

To correctly execute the following commands, you will need an index that is populated with the `ch07/populate_aggregation.txt` commands – these are available in the online code.

In order to be able to use regular expressions in Painless scripting, you will need to activate them in `elasticsearch.yml` by adding `script.painless.regex.enabled: true`.

The index used in this recipe is the `index-agg` index.

How to do it...

For filtering a search using script, we will perform the following steps:

1. We'll write a search using a filter that filters out a document with a price value that is less than a parameter value:

```
POST /index-agg/_search?pretty&size=3
{
  "query": {
    "bool": {
      "filter": {
        "script": {
          "script": {
            "source": """doc['price'].value >
params.param1""",
            "params": {
              "param1": 80
            }
          }
        }
      }
    }
  },
  "_source": {
    "includes": [
      "name",
      "price"
    ]
  }
}
```

In this example, all the documents, where the age value is greater than `param1`, are taken as qualified for return.

This script filter is done for demonstration purposes – in real-world applications it can be replaced with a `range` query, which is much faster.

2. If everything is correct, the result that is returned by Elasticsearch will be as follows:

```
{
  ... truncated ...
  "hits" : {
    "total" : 190,
    "max_score" : 0.0,
    "hits" : [
```

```
        {
          "_index" : "index-agg",
          "_type" : "_doc",
          "_id" : "7",
          "_score" : 0.0,
          "_source" : {
            "price" : 86.65705393127125,
            "name" : "Bishop"
          }
        },
        {
          "_index" : "index-agg",
          "_type" : "_doc",
          "_id" : "14",
          "_score" : 0.0,
          "_source" : {
            "price" : 84.9516714617024,
            "name" : "Crusader"
          }
        },
        {
          "_index" : "index-agg",
          "_type" : "_doc",
          "_id" : "15",
          "_score" : 0.0,
          "_source" : {
            "price" : 98.22030937628774,
            "name" : "Stacy, George"
          }
        }
      ]
    }
  }
```

How it works...

The script filter is a language script that returns a Boolean value (true or false). For every hit, the script is evaluated and, if it returns true, then the hit passes the filter. This type of scripting can only be used as Lucene filters and not as queries because it doesn't affect the search.

The script code can be any code in your preferred supported scripting language that returns a Boolean value.

See also

You can refer to the following recipes for further reference:

- The *Installing additional script plugins* recipe in this chapter to install additional languages for scripting
- The *Sorting data using script* recipe for a reference to extra built-in functions that are available for Painless scripts

Using scripting in aggregations

Scripting can be used in aggregations for extending its analytics capabilities in order to change the values used in metric aggregations or to define new rules to create buckets.

Getting ready

You will need an up-and-running Elasticsearch installation – similar to the one that we described in the *Downloading and installing Elasticsearch* recipe in `Chapter 1`, *Getting Started*.

To execute the commands, any HTTP client can be used, such as curl (`https://curl.haxx.se/`) or postman (`https://www.getpostman.com/`). You can use the Kibana console as it provides code completion and better character escaping for Elasticsearch.

To correctly execute the following commands, you will need an index that is populated with the `ch07/populate_aggregation.txt` commands – these are available in the online code.

In order to be able to use regular expressions in Painless scripting, you will need to activate them in `elasticsearch.yml` by adding `script.painless.regex.enabled: true`.

The index used in this recipe is the `index-agg` index.

How to do it...

For using a scripting language in aggregation, we will perform the following steps:

1. Write a metric aggregation that selects the field using `script`:

```
POST /index-agg/_search?size=0
{
  "aggs": {
    "my_value": {
      "sum": {
        "script": {
          "source": """doc["price"].value *
doc["price"].value"""
        }
      }
    }
  }
}
```

2. If everything is correct, then the result that is returned by Elasticsearch will be as follows:

```
{
  ... truncated ...
  "hits" : {
    "total" : 1000,
    "max_score" : null,
    "hits" : [ ]
  },
  "aggregations" : {
    "my_value" : {
      "value" : 3363069.561000406
    }
  }
}
```

3. Then, write a metric aggregation that uses the value field using `script`:

```
POST /index-agg/_search?size=0
{
  "aggs": {
    "my_value": {
      "sum": {
        "field": "price",
        "script": {
          "source": "_value * _value"
        }
```

```
            }
          }
        }
      }
```

4. If everything is correct, then the result that is returned by Elasticsearch will be as follows:

```
{
    ... truncated ...
    "hits" : {
      "total" : 1000,
      "max_score" : null,
      "hits" : [ ]
    },
    "aggregations" : {
      "my_value" : {
        "value" : 3363069.561000406
      }
    }
}
```

5. Again, write a term bucket aggregation that changes the terms using `script`:

```
POST /index-agg/_search?size=0
{
  "aggs": {
    "my_value": {
      "terms": {
        "field": "tag",
        "size": 5,
        "script": {
          "source": """
if(params.replace.containsKey(_value.toUpperCase())) {
  params.replace[_value.toUpperCase()]
} else {
  _value.toUpperCase()
}
""",
          "params": {
            "replace": {
              "LABORUM": "Result1",
              "MAIORES": "Result2",
              "FACILIS": "Result3"
            }
          }
        }
      }
```

```
            }
          }
        }
      }
    }
```

6. If everything is correct, then the result that is returned by Elasticsearch will
   be as follows:

```
{
   ... truncated ...
   "aggregations" : {
     "my_value" : {
       "doc_count_error_upper_bound" : 0,
       "sum_other_doc_count" : 2755,
       "buckets" : [
         {
           "key" : "Result1",
           "doc_count" : 31
         },
         {
           "key" : "Result2",
           "doc_count" : 25
         },
         {
           "key" : "Result3",
           "doc_count" : 25
         },
         {
           "key" : "IPSAM",
           "doc_count" : 24
         },
         {
           "key" : "SIT",
           "doc_count" : 24
         }
       ]
     }
   }
}
```

How it works...

Elasticsearch provides two kinds of aggregation, as follows:

- Metrics that compute some values
- Buckets that aggregate documents in a bucket

In both cases, you can use script or value script (if you define the field to be used in the aggregation). The object accepted in aggregation is the standard `script` object; the value that is returned by the script will be used for the aggregation.

If a `field` value is defined in the aggregation, then you can use the value script aggregation. In this case, in the context of the script, there is a special `_value` variable available that contains the value of the field.

 Using scripting in aggregation is a very powerful feature; however, using it on large cardinality aggregation could be very CPU-intensive and could slow down query times.

Updating a document using scripts

Elasticsearch allows you to update a document in-place. Updating a document using scripting reduces network traffic (otherwise, you need to fetch the document, change the field or fields, and then send them back) and improves performance when you need to process a large number of documents.

Getting ready

You will need an up-and-running Elasticsearch installation – similar to the one that we described in the *Downloading and installing Elasticsearch* recipe in `Chapter 1`, *Getting Started*.

To execute the commands, any HTTP client can be used, such as curl (`https://curl.haxx.se/`) or postman (`https://www.getpostman.com/`). You can use the Kibana console as it provides code completion and better character escaping for Elasticsearch.

To correctly execute the following commands, you will need an index that is populated with the `ch07/populate_aggregation.txt` commands – these are available in the online code.

In order to be able to use regular expressions in Painless scripting, you will need to activate them in `elasticsearch.yml` by adding the following code:

```
script.painless.regex.enabled: true
```

The index used in this recipe is `index-agg` index.

How to do it...

For updating using scripting, we will perform the following steps:

1. Write an `update` action that adds a tag value to the list of tags that are available in the source of the document:

```
POST /index-agg/_doc/10/_update
{
  "script": {
    "source": "ctx._source.age = ctx._source.age +
params.sum",
    "params": {
      "sum": 2
    }
  }
}
```

2. If everything is correct, then the result that is returned by Elasticsearch will be as follows:

```
{
  "_index" : "index-agg",
  "_type" : "_doc",
  "_id" : "10",
  "_version" : 3,
  "result" : "updated",
  "_shards" : {
    "total" : 2,
    "successful" : 1,
    "failed" : 0
  },
  "_seq_no" : 2002,
  "_primary_term" : 3
}
```

3. If we now retrieve the document, we will have the following code:

```
GET /index-agg/_doc/10
{
  "_index" : "index-agg",
  "_type" : "_doc",
  "_id" : "10",
  "_version" : 3,
```

```
        "found" : true,
        "_source" : {
          ...truncated...
          "age" : 102, ...truncated...
        }
```

From the preceding result, we can see that the version number has increased by one.

How it works...

The REST HTTP method that is used to update a document is POST. The URL contains only the index name, the type, the document ID, and the action:

```
http://<server>/<index_name>/_doc/<document_id>/_update
```

The update action is composed of three different steps, as follows:

1. **The Get API Call is very fast**: This operation works on real-time data (there is no need to refresh) and retrieves the record
2. **The script execution**: The script is executed in the document and, if required, it is updated
3. **Saving the document**: The document, if needed, is saved

The script execution follows the workflow in the following manner:

- The script is compiled and the result is cached to improve re-execution. The compilation depends on the scripting language; that is, it detects errors in the script such as typographical errors, syntax errors, and language-related errors. The compilation step can also be CPU-bound, so that Elasticsearch caches the compilation results for further execution.
- The document is executed in the script context; the document data is available in the ctx variable in the script.

The update script can set several parameters in the ctx variable; the most important parameters are as follows:

- ctx._source: This contains the source of the document.
- ctx._timestamp: If it's defined, this value is set to the document timestamp.

- `ctx.op`: This defines the main operation type to be executed. There are several available values, such as the following:
  - `index`: This is the default value; the record is reindexed with the update values.
  - `delete`: The document is deleted and not updated (that is, this can be used for updating a document or removing it if it exceeds a quota).
  - `none`: The document is skipped without reindexing the document.

 If you need to execute a large number of update operations, then it's better to perform them in bulk in order to improve your application's performance.

There's more...

In the following example, we'll execute an update that adds new `tags` and `labels` values to an object; however, we will mark the document for indexing only if the `tags` or `labels` values are changed:

```
POST /index-agg/_doc/10/_update
{
  "script": {
    "source": """
    ctx.op = "none";
    if(ctx._source.containsValue("tags")){
      for(def item : params.new_tags){
        if(!ctx._source.tags.contains(item)){
          ctx._source.tags.add(item);
          ctx.op = "index";
        }
      }
    }else{
      ctx._source.tags=params.new_tags;
      ctx.op = "index"
    }
    if(ctx._source.containsValue("labels")){
      for(def item : params.new_labels){
        if(!ctx._source.labels.contains(item)){
          ctx._source.labels.add(item);
          ctx.op = "index"
        }
```

```
        }
    }else{
      ctx._source.labels=params.new_labels;
      ctx.op = "index"
    }
""",
    "params": {
      "new_tags": [
        "cool",
        "nice"
      ],
      "new_labels": [
        "red",
        "blue",
        "green"
      ]
    }
  }
}
```

The preceding script uses the following steps:

1. It marks the operation to none to prevent indexing if, in the following steps, the original source is not changed.
2. It checks whether the tags field is available in the source object.
3. If the tags field is available in the source object, then it iterates all the values of the new_tags list. If the value is not available in the current tags list, then it adds it and updates the operation to the index.
4. It the tags field doesn't exist in the source object, then it simply adds it to the source and marks the operation to the index.
5. The steps from 2 to 4 are repeated for the labels value. The repetition is present in this example to show the Elasticsearch user how it is possible to update multiple values in a single update operation.

You can consolidate different script operations into a single script. To do this, use the previously explained workflow of building the script, adding sections in the script, and changing ctx.op only if the record is changed.

This script can be quite complex, but it shows Elasticsearch's powerful scripting capabilities.

Reindexing with a script

Reindexing is a new functionality that was introduced in Elasticsearch 5.x for automatically reindexing your data in a new index. This action is often done for a variety of reasons, mainly for mapping changes that require a full reindex of your data.

Getting ready

You will need an up-and-running Elasticsearch installation—similar to the one that we described in the *Downloading and installing Elasticsearch* recipe in Chapter 2, *Managing Mapping*.

To execute `curl` using the command line, then you will need to install `curl` for your operating system.

In order to correctly execute the following commands, you will need an index that is populated with the `chapter_09/populate_for_scripting.sh` script—available in the online code—and the JavaScript or Python language scripting plugins installed.

How to do it...

For reindexing with a script, we will perform the following steps:

1. Create the destination index as this is not created by the `reindex` API:

```
PUT /reindex-scripting
{
  "mappings": {
    "test-type": {
      "properties": {
        "name": {
          "term_vector": "with_positions_offsets",
          "boost": 1,
          "store": true,
          "type": "text"
        },
        "title": {
          "term_vector": "with_positions_offsets",
          "boost": 1,
          "store": true,
          "type": "text"
```

```
      },
      "parsedtext": {
        "term_vector": "with_positions_offsets",
        "boost": 1,
        "store": true,
        "type": "text"
      },
      "tag": {
        "type": "keyword",
        "store": true
      },
      "processed": {
        "type": "boolean"
      },
      "date": {
        "type": "date",
        "store": true
      },
      "position": {
        "type": "geo_point",
        "store": true
      },
      "uuid": {
        "boost": 1,
        "store": true,
        "type": "keyword"
      }
    }
  }
 }
}
```

2. Write a reindex action that adds a `processed` field (a Boolean field set to `true`); it should look as follows:

```
POST /_reindex
{
  "source": {
    "index": "index-agg"
  },
  "dest": {
    "index": "reindex-scripting"
  },
  "script": {
    "source": """
if(!ctx._source.containsKey("processed")){
  ctx._source.processed=true
}
```

```
    """
      }
    }
```

3. If everything is correct, then the result that is returned by Elasticsearch should be as follows:

```
{
  "took" : 386,
  "timed_out" : false,
  "total" : 1000,
  "updated" : 0,
  "created" : 1000,
  "deleted" : 0,
  "batches" : 1,
  "version_conflicts" : 0,
  "noops" : 0,
  "retries" : {
    "bulk" : 0,
    "search" : 0
  },
  "throttled_millis" : 0,
  "requests_per_second" : -1.0,
  "throttled_until_millis" : 0,
  "failures" : [ ]
}
```

4. Now if we retrieve the same documents, we will have the following code:

```
GET /reindex-scripting/_doc/10
{
  "_index" : "reindex-scripting",
  "_type" : "_doc",
  "_id" : "10",
  "_version" : 1,
  "found" : true,
  "_source" : {
    "date" : "2012-06-21T16:46:01.689622",
    "processed" : true,
    ... truncated ...
  }
}
```

From the preceding result, we can see that the script is applied.

How it works...

The scripting in `reindex` offers a very powerful functionality, because it allows the execution of a lot of useful actions, such as the following:

- Computing new fields
- Removing fields from a document
- Adding a new field with default values
- Modifying the field values

The scripting works as for `update`, but during reindexing you can also change the following document metadata fields:

- `_id`: This is the ID of the document
- `_type`: This is the type of the document
- `_index`: This is the destination index of the document
- `_version`: This is the version of the document
- `_routing`: This is the routing value to send the document in a specific shard
- `_parent`: This is the parent of the document

The possibility of changing these values provides a lot of options during reindexing; for example, splitting a type into two different indices, or partitioning an index into several indices and changing the `_index` value.

Managing Clusters

9

In the **Elasticsearch** ecosystem, it's important to monitor nodes and clusters in order to manage and improve their performance and state. There are several issues that can arise at the cluster level, such as the following:

- **Node overheads**: Some nodes can have too many shards allocated and become a bottleneck for the entire cluster.
- **Node shutdown**: This can happen due to a number of reasons, for example, full disks, hardware failures, and power problems.
- **Shard relocation problems or corruptions**: Some shards can't get an online status.
- **Shards that are too large**: If a shard is too big, then the index performance decreases due to the merging of massive Lucene segments.
- **Empty indices and shards**: These waste memory and resources; however, because each shard has a lot of active threads, if there are a large number of unused indices and shards, then the general cluster performance is degraded.

Detecting malfunctioning or poor performance at the cluster level can be done through an API or frontends (as we will see in `Chapter 11`, *User Interfaces*). These allow users to have a working web dashboard on their Elasticsearch data; it works by monitoring the cluster health, backing up or restoring data, and allowing the testing of queries before implementing them in the code.

In this chapter, we will explore the following topics:

- Using the health API to check the health of the cluster
- Using the task API that controls jobs a cluster level
- Using hot threads to check inside nodes for problems due to a high CPU usage
- Learning how to monitor Lucene segments so as not to reduce the performance of a node due to there being too many of them

In this chapter, we will cover the following recipes:

- Controlling the cluster health using an API
- Controlling the cluster state using an API
- Getting cluster node information using an API
- Getting node statistics using an API
- Using the task management API
- Hot Threads API
- Managing the shard allocation
- Monitoring segments with the segment API
- Cleaning the cache

Controlling the cluster health using an API

Elasticsearch provides a convenient way in which to manage the cluster state, and this is one of the first things to check if any problems do occur.

Getting ready

You will need an up-and-running Elasticsearch installation—similar to the one that we described in the *Downloading and installing Elasticsearch* recipe in Chapter 1, *Getting Started*.

To execute the commands, any HTTP client can be used, such as Curl (https://curl.haxx.se/) or Postman (https://www.getpostman.com/). You can use the Kibana console as it provides code completion and better character escaping for Elasticsearch.

How to do it...

To control the cluster health, we will perform the following steps:

1. In order to view the cluster health, the HTTP method that we use is GET:

```
GET /_cluster/health
```

2. The result will be as follows:

```
{
  "cluster_name" : "elasticsearch",
  "status" : "yellow",
  "timed_out" : false,
  "number_of_nodes" : 1,
  "number_of_data_nodes" : 1,
  "active_primary_shards" : 17,
  "active_shards" : 17,
  "relocating_shards" : 0,
  "initializing_shards" : 0,
  "unassigned_shards" : 15,
  "delayed_unassigned_shards" : 0,
  "number_of_pending_tasks" : 0,
  "number_of_in_flight_fetch" : 0,
  "task_max_waiting_in_queue_millis" : 0,
  "active_shards_percent_as_number" : 53.125
}
```

How it works...

Every Elasticsearch node keeps the cluster's status. The `status` value of the cluster can be of three types, as follows:

- `green`: This means that everything is okay.
- `yellow`: This means that some nodes or shards are missing, but they don't compromise the cluster's functionality. For instance, some replicas could be missing (either a node is down or there are insufficient nodes for replicas), but there is a least one copy of each active shard; additionally, read and write functions are working. The yellow state is very common during the development stage when users typically start a single Elasticsearch server.
- `red`: This indicates that some primary shards are missing and these indices are in the red status. You cannot write to indices that are in the red status and, additionally, the results may not be complete, or only partial results may be returned. Usually, you'll need to restart the node that is down and possibly create some replicas.

 The yellow or red states could be transient if some nodes are in recovery mode. In this case, just wait until the recovery completes.

The cluster health API contains an enormous amount of information, as follows:

- `cluster_name`: This is the name of the cluster.

- `timeout`: This is a Boolean value indicating whether the REST API hits the timeout set in the call.

- `number_of_nodes`: This indicates the number of nodes that are in the cluster.

- `number_of_data_nodes`: This indicates the number of nodes that can store data (you can refer to Chapter 2, *Managing Mapping*, and the *Downloading and Setup* recipe in order to set up different node types for different types of nodes).

- `active_primary_shards`: This shows the number of active primary shards; the primary shards are the masters of writing operations.

- `active_shards`: This shows the number of active shards; these shards can be used for searches.

- `relocating_shards`: This shows the number of shards that are relocating or migrating from one node to another node – this is mainly due to cluster-node balancing.

- `initializing_shards`: This shows the number of shards that are in the initializing status. The initializing process is done at shard startup. It's a transient state before becoming active and it's composed of several steps; the most important steps are as follows:
  - Copy the shard data from a primary one if its translation log is too old or a new replica is needed
  - Check the Lucene indices
  - Process the transaction log as needed

- `unassigned_shards`: This shows the number of shards that are not assigned to a node. This is usually due to having set a replica number that is larger than the number of nodes. During startup, shards that are not already initialized or initializing will be counted here.

- `delayed_unassigned_shards`: This shows the number of shards that will be assigned, but their nodes are configured for a delayed assignment. You can find more information about delayed shard assignments at `https://www.elastic.co/guide/en/elasticsearch/reference/5.0/delayed-allocation.html`.

- `number_of_pending_tasks`: This is the number of pending tasks at the cluster level, such as updates to the cluster state, the creation of indices, and shard relocations. It should rarely be anything other than 0.

- `number_of_in_flight_fetch`: This is the number of cluster updates that must be executed in the shards. As the cluster updates are asynchronous, this number tracks how many updates still have to be executed in the shards.
- `task_max_waiting_in_queue_millis`: This is the maximum amount of time that some cluster tasks have been waiting in the queue. It should rarely be anything other than 0. If the value is different to 0, then it means that there is some kind of cluster saturation of resources or a similar problem.
- `active_shards_percent_as_number`: This is the percentage of active shards that are required by the cluster. In a production environment, it should rarely differ from 100 percent – apart from some relocations and shard initializations.

Installed plugins play an important role in shard initialization; for example, if you use a mapping type that is provided by a native plugin and you remove the plugin (or if the plugin cannot be initialized due to API changes), then the shard initialization will fail. These issues are easily detected by reading the Elasticsearch log file.

When upgrading your cluster to a new Elasticsearch release, make sure that you upgrade your mapping plugins or, at the very least, check that they work with the new Elasticsearch release. If you don't do this, you risk your shards failing to initialize and giving a red status to your cluster.

There's more...

This API call is very useful; it's possible to execute it against one or more indices in order to obtain their health in the cluster. This approach allows the isolation of those indices that have problems; the API call to execute this is as follows:

```
GET /_cluster/health/index1,index2,indexN
```

The previous call also has additional request parameters in order to control the health of the cluster. These additional parameters are as follows:

- `level`: This controls the level of the health information that is returned. This parameter accepts only `cluster`, `index`, and `shards`.
- `timeout`: This is the wait time for a `wait_for_*` parameter (the default is `30s`).

- `wait_for_status`: This allows the server to wait for the provided status (`green`, `yellow`, or `red`) until timeout.
- `wait_for_relocating_shards`: This allows the server to wait until the provided number of relocating shards has been reached, or until the timeout period has been reached (the default is `0`).
- `wait_for_nodes`: This waits until the defined number of nodes are available in the cluster. The value for this parameter can also be an expression, such as *>N*, *>=N*, *<N*, *<=N*, *ge(N)*, *gt(N)*, *le(N)*, and *lt(N)*.

If the number of pending tasks is different to zero, then it's good practice to investigate what these pending tasks are. They can be shown using the following API URL:

```
GET /_cluster/pending_tasks
```

The return value is a list of pending tasks; beware that Elasticsearch applies cluster changes very quickly, so many of these tasks have a lifespan of some milliseconds to apply those that show themselves to you.

See also

You can refer to the following recipe and web page for more information:

- The *Setting up different node types* recipe in `Chapter 1`, *Getting Started*, in order to set up nodes as masters.
- The official documentation about pending cluster tasks at `https://www.elastic.co/guide/en/elasticsearch/reference/current/cluster-pending.html`, `for example, the returned value from this call.`

Controlling the cluster state using an API

The previous recipe returns information only about the health of the cluster. If you need more details on your cluster, then you need to query its state.

Getting ready

You will need an up-and-running Elasticsearch installation – similar to the one that we described in the *Downloading and installing Elasticsearch* recipe in `Chapter 1`, *Getting Started*.

In order to execute the commands, any HTTP client can be used, such as curl (`https://curl.haxx.se/`) or postman (`https://www.getpostman.com/`). You can use the Kibana console as it provides code completion and better character escaping for Elasticsearch.

How to do it...

To check the cluster state, we will perform the following steps:

1. In order to view the cluster state, the HTTP method that you can use is GET, and the `curl` command is as follows:

   ```
   GET /_cluster/state
   ```

2. The result will contain the following data sections

3. The general cluster information is as follows:

   ```
   {
     "cluster_name" : "elastic-cookbook",
     "compressed_size_in_bytes" : 4714,
     "cluster_uuid" : "02UhFNltQXOqtz1JH6ec8w",
     "version" : 9,
     "state_uuid" : "LZcYMc3PRdKSJ9MMAyM-ew",
     "master_node" : "-IFjP29_TOGQF-1axtNMSg",
     "blocks" : { },
   ```

4. The node address information is as follows:

   ```
   "nodes" : {
     "-IFjP29_TOGQF-1axtNMSg" : {
       "name" : "5863a2552d84",
       "ephemeral_id" : "o6xo1mowRIGVZ7ZfXkClww",
       "transport_address" : "172.18.0.2:9300",
       "attributes" : {
         "xpack.installed" : "true"
       }
     }
   },
   ```

5. The cluster metadata information (such as templates, indices with mappings, and the aliases) is as follows:

```
"metadata" : {
    "cluster_uuid" : "02UhFNltQXOqtz1JH6ec8w",
    "cluster_coordination" : {
      "term" : 0,
      "last_committed_config" : [ ],
      "last_accepted_config" : [ ],
      "voting_config_exclusions" : [ ]
    },
    "templates" : {
      "kibana_index_template:.kibana" : {
        "index_patterns" : [
          ".kibana"
        ],
        "order" : 0,
        "settings" : {
          "index" : {
            "number_of_shards" : "1",
            "auto_expand_replicas" : "0-1"
          }
        },
        "mappings" : {
          "doc" : {
            "dynamic" : "strict",
            "properties" : {
              "server" : {
                "properties" : {
                  "uuid" : {
                    "type" : "keyword"
                  }
                }
              },
              ... truncated ...
    },
    "index-graveyard" : {
      "tombstones" : [ ]
    }
  },
```

6. You can route the tables in order to find the shards by using the following code:

```
"routing_table" : {
  "indices" : {
    ".kibana_1" : {
      "shards" : {
```

```
                    "0" : [
                      {
                        "state" : "STARTED",
                        "primary" : true,
                        "node" : "-IFjP29_TOGQF-1axtNMSg",
                        "relocating_node" : null,
                        "shard" : 0,
                        "index" : ".kibana_1",
                        "allocation_id" : {
                          "id" : "QjMusIOIRRqOIsL8kEdudQ"
                        }
                      }
                    ]
                  }
                }
              }
            },
```

7. You can route the nodes by using the following code:

```
"routing_nodes" : {
    "unassigned" : [ ],
    "nodes" : {
      "-IFjP29_TOGQF-1axtNMSg" : [
        {
          "state" : "STARTED",
          "primary" : true,
          "node" : "-IFjP29_TOGQF-1axtNMSg",
          "relocating_node" : null,
          "shard" : 0,
          "index" : ".kibana_1",
          "allocation_id" : {
            "id" : "QjMusIOIRRqOIsL8kEdudQ"
          }
        }
      ]
    }
}
```

How it works...

The cluster state contains information about the whole cluster; the fact that its output is very large is normal.

The call output also contains common fields, and they are as follows:

- `cluster_name`: This is the name of the cluster.
- `master_node`: This is the identifier of the master node. The master node is the primary node that is used for cluster management.
- `blocks`: This section shows the active blocks in a cluster.
- `nodes`: This shows the list of nodes in the cluster. For each node, we have the following information:
    - `id`: This is the hash that is used to identify the node in Elasticsearch (for example, `7NwnFF1JTPOPhOYuP1AVN`).
    - `name`: This is the name of the node.
    - `transport_address`: This is the IP address and port used to connect to this node.
    - `attributes`: These are additional node attributes.
- `metadata`: This is the definition of the indices (including their settings and mappings), ingest pipelines, and `stored_scripts`.
- `routing_table`: These are the indices or shards routing tables, which are used to select primary and secondary shards and their nodes.
- `routing_nodes`: This is the routing for the nodes.

The metadata section is the most used field because it contains all the information that is related to the indices and their mappings. This is a convenient way in which to gather all the indices mappings in one go; otherwise, you'll need to call the `get` mapping instance for every type.

The metadata section is composed of several sections, as follows:

- `templates`: These are the templates that control the dynamic mapping for your created indices.
- `indices`: These are the indices that exist in the cluster.
- `* ingest`: This stores all the ingest pipelines that are defined in the system.
- `stored_scripts`: This stores the scripts, which are usually in the form of `language#script_name`.

The indices subsection returns a full representation of all the metadata descriptions for each index; it contains the following:

- `state` (open or closed): This describes whether an index is open (that is, it can be searched and can index data) or closed (you can refer to the *Opening/closing an index* recipe in `Chapter 3`, *Basic Operations*).
- `settings`: These are the index settings. The most important ones are as follows:
    - `index.number_of_replicas`: This is the number of replicas of this index; it can be changed using an update index settings call.
    - `index.number_of_shards`: This is the number of shards in this index. This value cannot be changed in an index.
    - `index.codec`: This is the codec that is used to store index data; `default` is not shown, but the LZ4 algorithm is used. If you want a high compression rate, then use `best_compression` and the DEFLATE algorithm (this will slow down the writing performances slightly).
    - `index.version.created`: This is the index version.
- `mappings`: These are defined in the index. This section is similar to the `get` mapping response (you can refer to the *Getting a Mapping* recipe in `Chapter 3`, *Basic Operations*).
- `alias`: This is a list of index aliases, which allows the aggregation of indices in a single name or the definition of alternative names for an index.

The routing records for the index and shards have similar fields and they are as follows:

- `state (UNASSIGNED, INITIALIZING, STARTED, RELOCATING)`: This shows the state of the shard or the index.
- `primary (true/false)`: This shows whether the shard or node is primary.
- `node`: This shows the ID of the node.
- `relocating_node`: This field, if validated, shows the `id` node in which the shard is relocated.
- `shard`: This shows the number of the shard.
- `index`: This shows the name of the index in which the shard is contained.

There's more...

The cluster state call returns a lot of information, and it's possible to filter out the different section parts through the URL.

The complete URL of the cluster state API is as follows:

```
http://{elasticsearch_server}/_cluster/state/{metrics}/{indices}
```

The `metrics` value could be used to return only parts of the response; it consists of a comma-separated list and includes the following values:

- `* version`: This is used to show the version part of the response.
- `blocks`: This is used to show the blocks part of the response.
- `master_node`: This is used to show the master node part of the response.
- `nodes`: This is used to show the node part of the response.
- `metadata`: This is used to show the metadata part of the response.
- `routing_table`: This is used to show the `routing_table` part of the response.

The `indices` value is a comma-separated list of index names to include in the metadata.

See also

You can refer to the following recipes for more information:

- The *Opening or* closing an index recipe in `Chapter 3`, *Basic Operations*, for APIs on opening and closing indices—remember that closed indices cannot be searched.
- The *Getting a mapping* recipe in `Chapter 3`, *Basic Operations*, for returning single mappings.

Getting cluster node information using an API

The previous recipe allows information to be returned to the cluster level; Elasticsearch provides calls to gather information at the node level. In production clusters, it's very important to monitor nodes using this API in order to detect misconfiguration and any problems relating to different plugins and modules.

Getting ready

You will need an up-and-running Elasticsearch installation—similar to the one that we described in the *Downloading and installing Elasticsearch* recipe in `Chapter 1`, *Getting Started*.

In order to execute the commands, any HTTP client can be used, such as curl (`https://curl.haxx.se/`) or postman (`https://www.getpostman.com/`). You can use the Kibana console as it provides code completion and better character escaping for Elasticsearch.

How to do it...

To get the cluster node information, we will perform the following steps:

1. To retrieve the node information, the HTTP method you can use is GET, and the `curl` command is as follows:

   ```
   GET /_nodes

   GET /_nodes/<nodeId1>,<nodeId2>
   ```

2. The result will contain a lot of information about the node; it's huge, so the repetitive parts have been truncated:

   ```
   {
     "_nodes" : {
       "total" : 1,
       "successful" : 1,
       "failed" : 0
     },
     "cluster_name" : "elastic-cookbook",
     "nodes" : {
   ```

```
"-IFjP29_TOGQF-1axtNMSg" : {
  "name" : "5863a2552d84",
  "transport_address" : "172.18.0.2:9300",
  "host" : "172.18.0.2",
  "ip" : "172.18.0.2",
  "version" : "7.0.0",
  "build_flavor" : "default",
  "build_type" : "tar",
  "build_hash" : "a30e8c2",
  "total_indexing_buffer" : 103887667,
  "roles" : [
    "master",
    "data",
    "ingest"
  ],
  "attributes" : {
    "xpack.installed" : "true"
  },
  "settings" : {
    "cluster" : {
      "name" : "elastic-cookbook"
    },
    "node" : {
      "attr" : {
        "xpack" : {
          "installed" : "true"
        }
      },
      "name" : "5863a2552d84"
    },
    "path" : {
      "logs" : "/usr/share/elasticsearch/logs",
      "home" : "/usr/share/elasticsearch"
    },
    "discovery" : {
      "type" : "single-node",
      "zen" : {
        "minimum_master_nodes" : "1"
      }
    },
    "client" : {
      "type" : "node"
    },
    "http" : {
      "type" : {
        "default" : "netty4"
      }
    },
```

```
                    "transport" : {
                      "type" : {
                        "default" : "netty4"
                      },
                      "features" : {
                        "x-pack" : "true"
                      }
                    },
                    "xpack" : ... truncated ...
                    "network" : {
                      "host" : "0.0.0.0"
                    }
                  },
                  "os" : {
                    "refresh_interval_in_millis" : 1000,
                    "name" : "Linux",
                    "pretty_name" : "CentOS Linux 7 (Core)",
                    "arch" : "amd64",
                    "version" : "4.9.125-linuxkit",
                    "available_processors" : 4,
                    "allocated_processors" : 4
                  },
                  "process" : {
                    "refresh_interval_in_millis" : 1000,
                    "id" : 1,
                    "mlockall" : false
                  },
                  "jvm" :... truncated ...
                  },
                  "thread_pool" : {
                    "force_merge" : {
                      "type" : "fixed",
                      "size" : 1,
                      "queue_size" : -1
                    },
        ... truncated ...
                  },
                  "transport" : {
                    "bound_address" : [
                      "0.0.0.0:9300"
                    ],
                    "publish_address" : "172.18.0.2:9300",
                    "profiles" : { }
                  },
                  "http" : {
                    "bound_address" : [
                      "0.0.0.0:9200"
                    ],
```

```
                   "publish_address" : "172.18.0.2:9200",
                   "max_content_length_in_bytes" : 104857600
                },
                "plugins" : [
                   {
                     "name" : "analysis-icu",
                     "version" : "7.0.0-alpha2",
                     "elasticsearch_version" : "7.0.0",
                     "java_version" : "1.8",
                     "description" : "The ICU Analysis plugin integrates
         Lucene ICU module into elasticsearch, adding ICU relates
         analysis components.",
                     "classname" :
         "org.elasticsearch.plugin.analysis.icu.AnalysisICUPlugin",
                     "extended_plugins" : [ ],
                     "has_native_controller" : false
                   },
         ... truncated ...
                 ],
                "ingest" : {
                   "processors" : [
                     {
                        "type" : "append"
                     },
         ... truncated...
                   }
                }
              }
            }
```

How it works...

The cluster node information call provides an overview of the node configuration. It covers a lot of information; the most important sections are as follows:

- hostname: This is the name of the host.
- ip: This is the IP address of the host.
- version: This is the Elasticsearch version; it's best practice for all the nodes of a cluster to have the same Elasticsearch version.
- roles: This is a list of roles that this node can cover. The developer nodes usually support three roles: master, data, and ingest.
- settings: This section contains information about the current cluster and the path of the Elasticsearch node. The most important fields are as follows:
    - cluster_name: This is the name of the cluster.

- `node.name`: This is the name of the node.
- `path.*`: This is the configured path of this Elasticsearch instance.
- `script`: This section is useful to check the `script` configuration of the node.
- `os`: This section provides the **operating system (OS)** information about the node that is running Elasticsearch, including the processors that are available or allocated, and the OS version.
- `process`: This section contains information about the currently-running Elasticsearch process:
    - `id`: This is the PID ID of the process.
    - `mlockall`: This flag defines whether Elasticsearch can use direct memory access; in production, this must be set to active.
- `max_file_descriptors`: This is the max file descriptor number.
- `jvm`: This section contains information about the **Java Virtual Machine (JVM)** node; this includes the version, vendor, name, PID, and memory (heaps and non-heaps).

It's highly recommended to run all the nodes on the same JVM version and type.

- `thread_pool`: This section contains information about several types of thread pools running in a node.
- `transport`: This section contains information about the transport protocol. The transport protocol is used for intra-cluster communication, or by the native client in order to communicate with a cluster. The response format is similar to the HTTP one, as follows:
    - `bound_address`: If a specific IP is not set in the configuration, then Elasticsearch binds all the interfaces together.
    - `publish_address`: This is the address that is used for publishing the native transport protocol.

- `http`: This section gives information about the HTTP configuration
- `max_content_length_in_bytes` (the default is `104857600` of 100 MB): This is the maximum size of HTTP content that Elasticsearch will allow to be received; HTTP payloads that are bigger than this size are rejected.

 The default 100 MB HTTP limit, which can be changed in elasticsearch.yml, can result in a malfunction due to a large payload (often in conjunction with a mapper plugin attachment), so it's important to bear this limit in mind when doing bulk actions or working with attachments.

- `publish_address`: This is the address that is used to publish the Elasticsearch node.
- `plugins`: This section lists every plugin installed in the node and provides information about the following:
    - `name`: This is the plugin name.
    - `description`: This is the plugin description.
    - `version`: This is the plugin version.
    - `classname`: This is the Java class used to load the plugin.

 - All the nodes must have the same plugin version; different plugin versions in a node bring unexpected failures.

- `modules`: This section lists every module installed in the node. The structure is the same as the plugin section.
- `ingest`: This section contains the list of active processors in the ingest node.

There's more...

The API call allows you to filter the section that must be returned. In this example, we've returned the whole section. Alternatively, we could select one or more of the following sections:

- http
- thread_pool
- transport
- jvm
- os
- process
- plugins
- modules
- ingest
- settings

For example, if you need only the os and plugins information, the call will be as follows:

```
GET /_nodes/os,plugins
```

See also

You can refer to the following recipes for more information:

- The *Networking setup* recipe in Chapter 1, *Getting Started,* about how to configure networking for Elasticsearch
- Chapter 13, *Using the Ingest Module,* for more information about Elasticsearch ingestion

Getting node statistics via the API

The node statistics call API is used to collect real-time metrics of your node, such as memory usage, threads usage, the number of indices, and searches.

Getting ready

You will need an up-and-running Elasticsearch installation – similar to the one that we described in the *Downloading and installing Elasticsearch* recipe in `Chapter 1`, *Getting Started*.

In order to execute the commands, any HTTP client can be used, such as curl (`https://curl.haxx.se/`) or postman (`https://www.getpostman.com/`). You can use the Kibana console as it provides code completion and better character escaping for Elasticsearch.

How to do it...

To get the node statistics, we will perform the following steps:

1. To retrieve the node statistics, the HTTP method that we will use is `GET`, and the command is as follows:

   ```
   GET /_nodes/stats
   GET /_nodes/<nodeId1>,<nodeId2>/stats
   ```

2. The result will be a long list of all the node statistics. The most significant parts of the results can be broken up as follows.

   First, a header that describes the cluster name and the nodes section, as follows:

   ```
   {
     "_nodes" : {
       "total" : 1,
       "successful" : 1,
       "failed" : 0
     },
     "cluster_name" : "elastic-cookbook",
     "nodes" : {
       "-IFjP29_TOGQF-1axtNMSg" : {
         "timestamp" : 1545580226575,
         "name" : "5863a2552d84",
         "transport_address" : "172.18.0.2:9300",
         "host" : "172.18.0.2",
         "ip" : "172.18.0.2:9300",
         "roles" : [
           "master",
           "data",
           "ingest"
   ```

```
        ],
        "attributes" : {
          "xpack.installed" : "true"
        },
```

Here are the statistics that are related to the indices:

```
"indices" : {
        "docs" : {
          "count" : 3,
          "deleted" : 0
        },
        "store" : {
          "size_in_bytes" : 12311
        },
        ... truncated...
        },
```

Here are the statistics that are related to the OS:

```
        "os" : {
          "timestamp" : 1545580226579,
          "cpu" : {
            "percent" : 0,
            "load_average" : {
              "1m" : 0.0,
              "5m" : 0.02,
              "15m" : 0.0
            }
          },
          "mem" : {
            "total_in_bytes" : 2095869952,
            "free_in_bytes" : 87678976,
            "used_in_bytes" : 2008190976,
            "free_percent" : 4,
            "used_percent" : 96
          },
...truncated ...
          "memory" : {
            "control_group" : "/",
            "limit_in_bytes" : "9223372036854771712",
            "usage_in_bytes" : "1360773120"
          }
        }
        },
```

Here are the statistics that are related to the current Elasticsearch process:

```
"process" : {
        "timestamp" : 1545580226580,
        "open_file_descriptors" : 257,
        "max_file_descriptors" : 1048576,
        "cpu" : {
          "percent" : 0,
          "total_in_millis" : 50380
        },
        "mem" : {
          "total_virtual_in_bytes" : 4881367040
        }
    },
```

Here are the statistics that are related to the current JVM:

```
"jvm" : {
    "timestamp" : 1545580226581,
    "uptime_in_millis" : 3224543,
    "mem" : {
      "heap_used_in_bytes" : 245981600,
      "heap_used_percent" : 23,
      "heap_committed_in_bytes" : 1038876672,
      "heap_max_in_bytes" : 1038876672,
      "non_heap_used_in_bytes" : 109403072,
      "non_heap_committed_in_bytes" : 119635968,
... truncated ...
    },
```

Here are the statistics related to thread pools:

```
"thread_pool" : {
    "analyze" : {
      "threads" : 0,
      "queue" : 0,
      "active" : 0,
      "rejected" : 0,
      "largest" : 0,
      "completed" : 0
    },
... truncated ...
    },
```

Here are the node filesystem statistics:

```
"fs" : {
    "timestamp" : 1545580226582,
    "total" : {
```

```
        "total_in_bytes" : 62725623808,
        "free_in_bytes" : 59856470016,
        "available_in_bytes" : 56639754240
      },
      ... truncated ...
    },
```

Here are the statistics relating to the communications between the nodes:

```
    "transport" : {
      "server_open" : 0,
      "rx_count" : 0,
"rx_size_in_bytes" : 0,
      "tx_count" : 0,
      "tx_size_in_bytes" : 0
    },
```

Here are the statistics related to the HTTP connections:

```
    "http" : {
      "current_open" : 4,
      "total_opened" : 175
    },
```

Here are the statistics related to the breaker caches:

```
    "breakers" : {
      "request" : {
        "limit_size_in_bytes" : 623326003,
        "limit_size" : "594.4mb",
        "estimated_size_in_bytes" : 0,
        "estimated_size" : "0b",
        "overhead" : 1.0,
        "tripped" : 0
      },
... truncated ...
    },
```

Here are the statistics related to the script:

```
    "script" : {
      "compilations" : 0,
      "cache_evictions" : 0,
      "compilation_limit_triggered" : 0
    },
```

Here is the cluster state queue:

```
"discovery" : { },
```

Here are the `ingest` statistics:

```
"ingest" : {
  "total" : {
    "count" : 0,
    "time_in_millis" : 0,
    "current" : 0,
    "failed" : 0
  },
  "pipelines" : { }
},
```

Here are the `adaptive_selection` statistics:

```
"adaptive_selection" : {
  "-IFjP29_TOGQF-1axtNMSg" : {
    "outgoing_searches" : 0,
    "avg_queue_size" : 0,
    "avg_service_time_ns" : 7479391,
    "avg_response_time_ns" : 13218805,
    "rank" : "13.2"
  }
}
```

How it works...

During execution, each Elasticsearch node collects statistics about several aspects of node management; these statistics are accessible using the statistics API call. In the next recipe, we will see an example of a monitoring application that uses this information to provide the real-time status of a node or a cluster.

The main statistics collected by this API are as follows:

- `fs`: This section contains statistics about the filesystem; this includes the free space that is on devices, the mount points, and reads and writes. It can also be used to remotely control the disk usage of your nodes.
- `http`: This gives the number of current open sockets and their maximum number.

- `indices`: This section contains statistics about several indexing aspects:
  - The use of fields and caches.
  - Statistics about operations such as `get`, `indexing`, `flush`, `merges`, `refresh`, and `warmer`.
- `jvm`: This section provides statistics about buffers, pools, garbage collectors (this refers to the creation or destruction of objects and their memory management), memory (such as used memory, heaps, and pools), threads, and uptime. You should check to see whether the node is running out of memory.
- `network`: This section provides statistics about **transmission control protocol** (**TCP**) traffic, such as open connections, closed connections, and data I/O.
- `os`: This section collects statistics about the OS, such as the following:
  - CPU usage
  - Node load
  - Virtual and swap memory
  - Uptime
- `process`: This section contains statistics about the CPU that is used by Elasticsearch, memory, and open file descriptors.

- It's very important to monitor the open file descriptors; this is because if you run out of them, then the indices may be corrupted.

- `thread_pool`: This section monitors all the thread pools that are available in Elasticsearch. It's important, in the case of low performance, to control whether there are pools that have an excessive overhead. Some of them can be configured to a new maximum value.
- `transport`: This section contains statistics about the transport layer and, in particular, the bytes that are read and transmitted.
- `breakers`: This section monitors the circuit breakers. This must be checked to see whether it's necessary to optimize resources, queries, or aggregations to prevent them from being called.

- `adaptive_selection`: This section contains information about the adaptive node selection that is used for executing searches. Adaptive selection allows you to choose the best replica node from a coodinator node to execute searches.

There's more...

The API response is very large. It's possible to limit it by requesting only the parts that are required. In order to do this, you will need to pass a query parameter to the API call specifying the following desired sections:

- `fs`
- `http`
- `indices`
- `jvm`
- `network`
- `os`
- `process`
- `thread_pool`
- `transport`
- `breaker`
- `discovery`
- `script`
- `ingest`
- `breakers`
- `adaptive_selection`

For example, to request only `os` and `http` statistics, then the call will be as follows:

```
GET /_nodes/stats/os,http
```

Using the task management API

Elasticsearch 5.x and later versions allow you to define the actions that are executed to the server side. These actions can take some time to complete and they can use huge cluster resources. The most common ones are as follows:

- `delete_by_query`
- `update_by_query`
- `reindex`

When these actions are called, they create a server-side task that executes the job; the task management API allows you to control these jobs.

Getting ready

You will need an up-and-running Elasticsearch installation – similar to the one that we described in the *Downloading and installing Elasticsearch* recipe in `Chapter 1`, *Getting Started*.

In order to execute the commands, any HTTP client can be used, such as curl (`https://curl.haxx.se/`) or postman (`https://www.getpostman.com/`). You can use the Kibana console as it provides code completion and better character escaping for Elasticsearch.

How to do it...

To get task information, we will perform the following steps:

1. Retrieve the node information using the HTTP GET method; the command is as follows:

```
GET /_tasks
GET /_tasks?nodes=nodeId1,nodeId2'
GET /_tasks?nodes=nodeId1,nodeId2&actions=cluster:'
```

2. The result will be as follows:

```
{
  "nodes" : {
    "-IFjP29_TOGQF-1axtNMSg" : {
      "name" : "5863a2552d84",
```

```
          "transport_address" : "172.18.0.2:9300",
          "host" : "172.18.0.2",
          "ip" : "172.18.0.2:9300",
          "roles" : [
            "master",
            "data",
            "ingest"
          ],
          "attributes" : {
            "xpack.installed" : "true"
          },
          "tasks" : {
            "-IFjP29_TOGQF-1axtNMSg:92797" : {
              "node" : "-IFjP29_TOGQF-1axtNMSg",
              "id" : 92797,
              "type" : "transport",
              "action" : "cluster:monitor/tasks/lists",
              "start_time_in_millis" : 1545642518460,
              "running_time_in_nanos" : 7937700,
              "cancellable" : false,
              "headers" : { }
            },
            "-IFjP29_TOGQF-1axtNMSg:92798" : {
              "node" : "-IFjP29_TOGQF-1axtNMSg",
              "id" : 92798,
              "type" : "direct",
              "action" : "cluster:monitor/tasks/lists[n]",
              "start_time_in_millis" : 1545642518462,
              "running_time_in_nanos" : 5701400,
              "cancellable" : false,
              "parent_task_id" : "-IFjP29_TOGQF-1axtNMSg:92797",
              "headers" : { }
            }
          }
        }
      }
    }
  }
}
```

How it works...

Every task that is executed in Elasticsearch is available in the task list.

The most important properties for the tasks are as follows:

- node: This defines the node that is executing the task.
- id: This defines the unique ID of the task.
- action: This is the name of the action; it's generally composed by an action type, the : separator, and the detailed action.
- cancellable: This defines whether the task can be canceled; some tasks, such as delete/update by query or reindex, can be canceled; however, other tasks are mainly management tasks and so they cannot be canceled.
- parent_task_id: This defines the group of tasks; some tasks can be split and executed in several subtasks. This value can be used to group these tasks by the parent.

The id property of the task can be used to filter the response through the node_id parameter of the API call:

```
GET /_tasks/-IFjP29_TOGQF-1axtNMSg:92797
```

If you need to monitor a group of tasks, you can filter according to their parent_task_id property using an API call, as follows:

```
GET /_tasks?parent_task_id=-IFjP29_TOGQF-1axtNMSg:92797
```

There's more...

In general, canceling a task could produce some data inconsistency in Elasticsearch due to the partial updating or deleting of documents; however, when reindexing, it can make good sense. When you are reindexing a large amount of data, it's common to change the mapping or to reindex a script in the middle of it. So, in order to not waste time and CPU usage, canceling the reindexing is a sensible solution.

To cancel a task, the API URL is as follows:

```
POST /_tasks/task_id:1/_cancel
```

In the case of a group of tasks, then they can be stopped with a single cancel call using query arguments to select them as follows:

```
POST /_tasks/_cancel?nodes=nodeId1,nodeId2&actions=*reindex
```

See also

- The official documentation regarding task management for some more borderline cases is available at `https://www.elastic.co/guide/en/elasticsearch/reference/current/tasks.html`.

Using the hot threads API

Sometimes, your cluster will slow down due to high levels of CPU usage and you will need to understand why. Elasticsearch provides the ability to monitor hot threads in order to be able to understand where the problem is.

In Java, hot threads are threads that use a lot of CPU and take a long time to execute.

Getting ready

You will need an up-and-running Elasticsearch installation – similar to the one that we described in the *Downloading and installing Elasticsearch* recipe in `Chapter 1`, *Getting Started*.

In order to execute the commands, any HTTP client can be used, such as curl (`https://curl.haxx.se/`) or postman (`https://www.getpostman.com/`). You can use the Kibana console as it provides code completion and better character escaping for Elasticsearch.

How to do it...

To get the task information, we will perform the following steps:

1. To retrieve the node information, the HTTP method that we use is `GET`, and the `curl` command is as follows:

   ```
   GET /_nodes/hot_threads
   GET /_nodes/{nodesIds}/hot_threads'
   ```

2. The result will be as follows:

   ```
   ::: {5863a2552d84}{-
   IFjP29_TOGQF-1axtNMSg}{o6xo1mowRIGVZ7ZfXkClww}{172.18.0.2}{172
   .18.0.2:9300}{xpack.installed=true}
   ```

```
    Hot threads at 2018-12-24T09:22:30.481, interval=500ms,
busiestThreads=3, ignoreIdleThreads=true:
    16.1% (80.6ms out of 500ms) cpu usage by thread
'elasticsearch[5863a2552d84][write][T#2]'
      10/10 snapshots sharing following 2 elements
java.base@11.0.1/java.util.concurrent.ThreadPoolExecutor$Worke
r.run(ThreadPoolExecutor.java:628)
        java.base@11.0.1/java.lang.Thread.run(Thread.java:834)
    8.7% (43.3ms out of 500ms) cpu usage by thread
'elasticsearch[5863a2552d84][write][T#3]'
      2/10 snapshots sharing following 35 elements
app//org.elasticsearch.index.mapper.DocumentMapper.parse(Docum
entMapper.java:264)
app//org.elasticsearch.index.shard.IndexShard.prepareIndex(Ind
exShard.java:733)
app//org.elasticsearch.index.shard.IndexShard.applyIndexOperat
ion(IndexShard.java:710)
app//org.elasticsearch.index.shard.IndexShard.applyIndexOperat
ionOnPrimary(IndexShard.java:691)
app//org.elasticsearch.action.bulk.TransportShardBulkAction.la
mbda$executeIndexRequestOnPrimary$3(TransportShardBulkAction.j
ava:462)
    ... truncated ...
```

How it works...

The hot threads API is quite particular; it works by returning a text representation of the currently-running hot threads, so that it's possible to check the causes of the slowdown of every single thread by using the stack trace.

To control the returned values, there are additional parameters that can be provided as query arguments:

- threads: This is the number of hot threads to provide (the default is 3).
- interval: This is the interval for the sampling of threads (the default is 500ms).
- type: This allows the control of different types of hot threads, for example, to check, wait, and block states (the default is cpu; the possible values are cpu, wait, and block).
- ignore_idle_threads: This is used to filter out any known idle threads (the default is true).

The hot threads API is an advanced monitor feature that is provided by Elasticsearch; it's very handy in helping you to debug the slow speed of a production cluster as it can be used as a runtime debugger. If your nodes or clusters have performance problems, then the hot threads API is the only call that can help you to understand how the CPU is being used.

It's common to have a high overhead in computation due to the wrong regex usage, or due to scripting problems.

Managing the shard allocation

During normal Elasticsearch usage, it is not generally necessary to change the shard allocation, because the default settings work very well with all standard scenarios. Sometimes, however, due to massive relocation, nodes restarting, or some other cluster issues, it's necessary to monitor or define a custom shard allocation.

Getting ready

You will need an up-and-running Elasticsearch installation – similar to the one that we described in the *Downloading and installing Elasticsearch* recipe in `Chapter 1`, *Getting Started*.

In order to execute the commands, any HTTP client can be used, such as curl (`https://curl.haxx.se/`) or postman (`https://www.getpostman.com/`). You can use the Kibana console as it provides code completion and better character escaping for Elasticsearch.

How to do it...

To get information about the current state of unassigned shard allocations, we will perform the following steps:

1. To retrieve the cluster allocation information, the HTTP method that we use is GET, and the command is as follows:

```
GET /_cluster/allocation/explain
```

2. The result will be as follows:

```
{
  "index" : "mybooks",
  "shard" : 0,
  "primary" : false,
  "current_state" : "unassigned",
  "unassigned_info" : {
    "reason" : "INDEX_CREATED",
    "at" : "2018-12-24T09:47:23.192Z",
    "last_allocation_status" : "no_attempt"
  },
  "can_allocate" : "no",
  "allocate_explanation" : "cannot allocate because allocation
is not permitted to any of the nodes",
  "node_allocation_decisions" : [
    {
      "node_id" : "-IFjP29_TOGQF-1axtNMSg",
      "node_name" : "5863a2552d84",
      "transport_address" : "172.18.0.2:9300",
      "node_attributes" : {
        "xpack.installed" : "true"
      },
      "node_decision" : "no",
      "weight_ranking" : 1,
      "deciders" : [
        {
          "decider" : "same_shard",
          "decision" : "NO",
          "explanation" : "the shard cannot be allocated to
the same node on which a copy of the shard already exists
[[mybooks][0], node[-IFjP29_TOGQF-1axtNMSg], [P], s[STARTED],
a[id=4IEkiR-JS7adyFCHN_GGTw]]"
        }
      ]
    }
  ]
}
```

How it works...

Elasticsearch allows for different shard allocation mechanisms. Sometimes, your shards are not assigned to nodes, and it's useful to investigate why Elasticsearch has not allocated them by querying the cluster allocation explain API.

The call returns a lot of information about the unassigned shard, but the most important one is `decisions`. This is a list of objects that explain why the shard cannot be allocated in the node. In the preceding example, the result was `the shard cannot be allocated on the same node id [-IFjP29_TOGQF-1axtNMSg] on which it already exists`, which is returned because the shard needs a replica. However, in this case, the cluster is composed of only one node, so it's not possible to initialize the replicated shard in the cluster.

There's more...

The cluster allocation explain API provides capabilities to filter the result for searching for a particular shard; this is very useful if your cluster has a lot of shards. This can be done by adding parameters to be used as a filter in the `get` body; these parameters are as follows:

- `index`: This is the index that the shard belongs to.
- `shard`: This is the number of the shard; shard numbers start from 0.
- `primary` (`true` or `false`): This indicates whether the shard to be checked is the primary one or not.

The preceding example shard can be filtered using a similar call as follows:

```
GET /_cluster/allocation/explain
{
  "index": "mybooks",
  "shard": 0,
  "primary": false
}
```

To manually relocate shards, Elasticsearch provides a cluster reroute API that allows the migration of shards between nodes. The following is an example of this API:

```
POST /_cluster/reroute
{
  "commands": [
    {
      "move": {
        "index": "test-index",
        "shard": 0,
        "from_node": "node1",
        "to_node": "node2"
      }
    }
```

```
    ]
  }
```

In this case, the `0` shard of the `test-index` index is migrated from `node1` to `node2`. If you force a shard migration, the cluster starts moving the other shard in order to rebalance itself.

See also

You can refer to the following web pages for more information related to this recipe:

- The official documentation about shard allocations and the settings that control it can be found at `https://www.elastic.co/guide/en/ elasticsearch/reference/current/shards-allocation.html`.
- The cluster reroute API official documentation can be found at `https:// www.elastic.co/guide/en/elasticsearch/reference/current/cluster- reroute.html`. It describes the complexity of the manual relocation of shards in depth.

Monitoring segments with the segment API

Monitoring the index segments means monitoring the health of an index. It contains information about the number of segments and the data that is stored in them.

Getting ready

You will need an up-and-running Elasticsearch installation – similar to the one that we described in the *Downloading and installing Elasticsearch* recipe in `Chapter 1`, *Getting Started*.

In order to execute the commands, any HTTP client can be used, such as curl (`https://curl.haxx.se/`) or postman (`https://www.getpostman.com/`). You can use the Kibana console as it provides code completion and better character escaping for Elasticsearch.

How to do it...

To get information about index segments, we will perform the following steps:

1. To retrieve the index segments, the HTTP method that we use is GET, and the curl command is as follows:

```
GET /mybooks/_segments
```

2. The result will be as follows:

```
{
  "_shards" : {
    "total" : 2,
    "successful" : 1,
    "failed" : 0
  },
  "indices" : {
    "mybooks" : {
      "shards" : {
        "0" : [
          {
            "routing" : {
              "state" : "STARTED",
              "primary" : true,
              "node" : "-IFjP29_TOGQF-1axtNMSg"
            },
            "num_committed_segments" : 1,
            "num_search_segments" : 1,
            "segments" : {
              "_0" : {
                "generation" : 0,
                "num_docs" : 3,
                "deleted_docs" : 0,
                "size_in_bytes" : 5688,
                "memory_in_bytes" : 2137,
                "committed" : true,
                "search" : true,
                "version" : "8.0.0",
                "compound" : true,
                "attributes" : {
                  "Lucene50StoredFieldsFormat.mode" :
"BEST_SPEED"
                }
              }
            }
          }
        }, ...truncated...
      ]
```

```
                }
              }
            }
          }
```

In Elasticsearch, there is the special `alias` `_all` value, which
defines all the indices. This can be used in all the APIs that require a
list of index names.

How it works...

The indices segment API returns statistics about the segments in an index. This is an
important indicator of the health of an index. It returns the following information:

- `num_docs`: The number of documents that are stored in the index.
- `deleted_docs`: The number of deleted documents in the index. If this
  value is high, then a lot of space is wasted to tombstone documents in the
  index.
- `size_in_bytes`: The size of the segments in bytes. If this value is too high,
  the writing speed will be very low.
- `memory_in_bytes`: The memory taken up, in bytes, by the segment.
- `committed`: This indicates whether the segment is committed to the disk.
- `search`: This indicates whether the segment is used for searching. During
  force merge or index optimization, new segments are created and returned
  by the API, but they are not available for searching until the end of the
  optimization.
- `version`: The Lucene version that is used for creating the index.
- `compound`: This indicates whether the index is a compound one.
- `attributes`: This is a key-value list of attributes about the current
  segment.

The most important elements that are needed to monitor the segments are
`deleted_docs` and `size_in_bytes`. This is because they either mean a waste of
disk space or that the shard is too large. If the shard is too large (that is, it is over 10
GB), then for improved performances in writing the best solution is to reindex the
index with a large number of shards.

Having large shards also creates a problem in relocating, due to massive data moving
between nodes.

It's impossible to define the perfect size for a shard. In general, a good size for a shard that doesn't need to be frequently updated is between 10 GB and 25 GB.

See also

You can refer to the following recipes for more information related to this recipe:

- The *ForceMerge an index* recipe in `Chapter 3`, *Basic Operations*, is about how to optimize an index with a small number of fragments in order to improve search performances.
- The *Shrinking an index* recipe in `Chapter 3`, *Basic Operations*, is about how to reduce the number of shards if too large a number of shards are defined for an index.

Cleaning the cache

During its execution, Elasticsearch caches data in order to speed up searching, such as results, items, and filter results.

Automatically, Elasticsearch frees up memory by following internal indicators such as the percentage size of the cache regarding the memory (that is, 20%). If you want to start some performance tests or free up memory manually, then it's necessary to call the cache API.

Getting ready

You will need an up-and-running Elasticsearch installation – similar to the one that we described in the *Downloading and installing Elasticsearch* recipe in `Chapter 1`, *Getting Started*.

In order to execute the commands, any HTTP client can be used, such as curl (`https://curl.haxx.se/`) or postman (`https://www.getpostman.com/`). You can use the Kibana console as it provides code completion and better character escaping for Elasticsearch.

How to do it...

For cleaning the cache, we will perform the following steps:

1. We call the `_cache/clean` API on an index as follows:

    ```
    POST /mybooks/_cache/clear
    ```

2. If everything is okay, then the result that is returned by Elasticsearch will be as follows:

    ```
    {
      "_shards" : {
        "total" : 2,
        "successful" : 1,
        "failed" : 0
      }
    }
    ```

How it works...

The cache clean API frees the memory used to cache values in Elasticsearch – both queries and aggregations.

Generally, it's not a good idea to clean the cache because Elasticsearch manages the cache internally by itself and cleans obsolete values. However, it can be very handy if your node is running out of memory or if you want to force a complete cache clean up.

If you have done a performance test, then before firing a query you can execute a clean cache API to have a real-time sample of query execution, without the boost due to the caching.

Backups and Restoring Data **10**

Elasticsearch is commonly used as a data store for logs and other kinds of data. Therefore, if you store valuable data, then you will also need tools to back up and restore this data to support disaster recovery.

In the earlier versions of Elasticsearch, the only viable solution was to dump your data with a complete scan and then reindex it. As Elasticsearch matured as a complete product, it supported native functionalities to back up the data and restore it.

In this chapter, we'll explore how you can configure a shared storage using **Network File System** (**NFS**) for storing your backups, and how to execute and restore a backup.

In the last recipe of the chapter, we will demonstrate how to use the reindex functionality to clone data between different Elasticsearch clusters. This approach is very useful if you are not able to use standard backup or restore functionalities due to moving from an old Elasticsearch version to the new one.

In this chapter, we will cover the following recipes:

- Managing repositories
- Executing a snapshot
- Restoring a snapshot
- Setting up an NFS share for backups
- Reindexing from a remote cluster

Managing repositories

Elasticsearch provides a built-in system to rapidly back up and restore your data. When working with live data, keeping a backup is complex, due to the large number of concurrency problems.

An Elasticsearch snapshot allows you to create snapshots of individual indices (or aliases), or an entire cluster, in a remote repository.

Before starting to execute a snapshot, a repository must be created – this is where your backups or snapshots will be stored.

Getting ready

You will need an up-and-running Elasticsearch installation – similar to the one that we described in the *Downloading and installing Elasticsearch* recipe in Chapter 1, *Getting Started*.

In order to execute the commands, any HTTP client can be used, such as Curl (https://curl.haxx.se/) or Postman (https://www.getpostman.com/). You can use the Kibana console as it provides code completion and better character escaping for Elasticsearch.

We need to edit config/elasticsearch.yml and add the directory of your backup repository – path.repo: /backup/.

Generally, in a production cluster, the /backup directory should be a shared repository.

 If you are using the Docker Compose that was provided in Chapter 1, *Getting Started*, then everything is already configured for you.

How to do it...

To manage a repository, we will perform the following steps:

1. To create a repository called `my_repository`, the HTTP method that we use is `PUT`, and the command will be as follows:

    ```
    PUT /_snapshot/my_repository
    {
      "type": "fs",
      "settings": {
        "location": "/backup/my_repository",
        "compress": true
      }
    }
    ```

    The result will be as follows:

    ```
    {"acknowledged":true}
    ```

If you check on your filesystem, the `/backup/my_repository` directory will be created as follows:

2. To retrieve repository information, the HTTP method that we use is `GET`, and the `curl` command is as follows:

    ```
    GET /_snapshot/my_repository
    ```

    The result will be as follows:

    ```
    {
      "my_repository" : {
        "type" : "fs",
        "settings" : {
          "compress" : "true",
          "location" : "/backup/my_repository"
        }
      }
    }
    ```

3. To delete a repository, the HTTP method that we use is `DELETE`, and the `curl` command is as follows:

    ```
    DELETE /_snapshot/my_repository
    ```

The result will be as follows:

```
{
    "acknowledged" : true
}
```

How it works...

Before taking a snapshot of our data, we must create a repository – that is, a place where we can store our backup data. The parameters that can be used to create a repository are as follows:

- `type`: This is used to define the type of shared filesystem repository (it is generally `fs`).
- `settings`: These are options that we can use to set up the shared filesystem repository.

In the case of the `fs` type usage, the settings are as follows:

- `location`: This is the location on the filesystem for storing snapshots.
- `compress`: This turns on the compression for the snapshot files. Compression is applied only to metadata files (that is, index mapping and settings); data files are not compressed (the default is `true`).
- `chunk_size`: This defines the size of the chunks of files during snapshotting. The chunk size can be specified in bytes or by using size value notation (that is, 1 g, 10 m, or 5 k; the default is disabled).
- `max_restore_bytes_per_sec`: This controls the throttle per node restore rate (the default is `20mb`).
- `max_snapshot_bytes_per_sec`: This controls the throttle per node snapshot rate (the default is `20mb`).
- `readonly`: This flag defines the repository as read-only (the default is `false`). It is possible to return all the defined repositories by executing `GET` without providing the repository name:

  ```
  GET /_snapshot
  ```

The default values for `max_restore_bytes_per_sec` and `max_snapshot_bytes_per_sec` are too low for production environments. Usually, production systems use SSDs or more efficient solutions, so it's better to configure these values related to your real networks and storage performance.

There's more...

The most common type for a repository backend is a filesystem, but there are other official repository backends, such as the following:

- **S3 repository**: `https://www.elastic.co/guide/en/elasticsearch/plugins/master/repository-s3.html`
- **HDFS**: `https://www.elastic.co/guide/en/elasticsearch/plugins/master/repository-hdfs.html` for Hadoop environments
- **Azure Cloud**: `https://www.elastic.co/guide/en/elasticsearch/plugins/master/repository-azure.html` for Azure storage repositories
- **Google Cloud**: `https://www.elastic.co/guide/en/elasticsearch/plugins/master/repository-gcs.html` for Google Cloud storage repositories

When a repository is created, it's immediately verified on all the data nodes in order to make sure that it's functional.

Elasticsearch also provides a manual way in which to verify the node status repository, which is very useful in order to check the status of the cloud repository storage. The command to manually verify a repository is as follows:

```
POST /_snapshot/my_repository/_verify
```

See also

- The official Elasticsearch documentation at `https://www.elastic.co/guide/en/elasticsearch/reference/master/modules-snapshots.html` provides a lot of information about borderline cases for repository usage.

Executing a snapshot

In the previous recipe, we defined a repository – that is, the place where we will store the backups. Now we can create snapshots of indices (using the full backup of an index) in the exact instant that the command is called.

For every repository it's possible to define multiple snapshots.

Getting ready

You will need an up-and-running Elasticsearch installation – similar to the one that we described in the *Downloading and installing Elasticsearch* recipe in `Chapter 1`, *Getting Started*.

To execute the commands, any HTTP client can be used, such as Curl (`https://curl.haxx.se/`) or Postman (`https://www.getpostman.com/`). You can use the Kibana console as it provides code completion and better character escaping for Elasticsearch.

To correctly execute the following commands, the repository that was created in the previous recipe is required.

How to do it...

To manage a snapshot, we will perform the following steps:

1. To create a snapshot called `snap_1` for the `index*`, `mybooks*` and `mygeo*` indices, the HTTP method that we use is `PUT`, and the command is as follows:

```
PUT /_snapshot/my_repository/snap_1?wait_for_completion=true
{
  "indices": "index*,mybooks*,mygeo*",
  "ignore_unavailable": "true",
  "include_global_state": false
}
```

The result will be as follows:

```
{
  "snapshot" : {
    "snapshot" : "snap_1",
    "uuid" : "9-LLrAHAT_KmmxLTmtF38w",
```

```
        "version_id" : 7000099,
        "version" : "7.0.0",
        "indices" : [
          "mybooks-join",
          "mybooks",
          "index-agg",
          "mygeo-index"
        ],
        "include_global_state" : false,
        "state" : "SUCCESS",
        "start_time" : "2019-01-06T13:00:24.328Z",
        "start_time_in_millis" : 1546779624328,
        "end_time" : "2019-01-06T13:00:24.441Z",
        "end_time_in_millis" : 1546779624441,
        "duration_in_millis" : 113,
        "failures" : [ ],
        "shards" : {
          "total" : 4,
          "failed" : 0,
          "successful" : 4
        }
      }
    }
  }
```

2. If you check your filesystem, then the /backup/my_repository directory will be populated with a number of files, such as index (a directory that contains our data), metadata-snap_1, and snapshot-snap_1.

3. To retrieve the snapshot information, the HTTP method that we use is GET, and the command is as follows:

```
GET /_snapshot/my_repository/snap_1
```

The result will be the same as the previous step.

4. To delete a snapshot, the HTTP method that we use is DELETE, and the command is as follows:

```
DELETE /_snapshot/my_repository/snap_1
```

The result will be as follows:

```
{
  "acknowledged" : true
}
```

How it works...

The minimum configuration that is required to create a snapshot is the name of the repository and the name of the snapshot (that is, `snap_1`).

If no other parameters are set, then the snapshot command will dump all the cluster data. To control the snapshot process, the following parameters are available:

- `indices` (a comma-delimited list of indices; wildcards are accepted): This controls the indices that must be dumped.
- `ignore_unavailable` (the default is `false`): This prevents the snapshot from failing if some indices are missing.
- `include_global_state` (this defaults to `true`; the available values are `true`, `false`, and `partial`): This controls the storing of the global state in the snapshot. If a primary shard is not available, then the snapshot fails.

The `wait_for_completion` query argument allows you to wait for the snapshot to end before returning the call. It's very useful if you want to automate your snapshot script to sequentially back up indices.

If the `wait_for_completion` argument is not set, then in order to check the snapshot status a user must monitor it using the snapshot GET call.

The snapshots are incremental; this means that only changed files are copied between two snapshots of the same index. This approach reduces both the time and disk usage during snapshots.

The snapshot process is designed to be as fast as possible, so it implements a direct copy of the Lucene index segments in the repository. In order to prevent changes and index corruption that may occur during the copy, all the segments that need to be copied are blocked from changing until the end of the snapshot.

Lucene's segment copy is at the shard level, so if you have a cluster of several nodes and you have a local repository, then the snapshot is spread through all the nodes. For this reason, in a production cluster the repository must be shared in order to easily collect all the backup fragments.

Elasticsearch takes care of everything during a snapshot, including preventing writing data to files that are in the snapshot process, and managing cluster events (such as shard relocating, failures, and more).

To retrieve all the available snapshots for a repository the command is as follows:

```
GET /_snapshot/my_repository/_all
```

There's more...

The snapshot process can be monitored using the _status endpoint, which provides a complete overview of the snapshot status.

For the current example, the snapshot _status API call will be as follows:

```
GET /_snapshot/my_repository/snap_1/_status
```

The result is very long and consists of the following sections:

- Here is the information about the snapshot:

```
"snapshots" : [
  {
    "snapshot" : "snap_1",
    "repository" : "my_repository",
    "uuid" : "h50pswT-Qw642VUi4aandQ",
    "state" : "SUCCESS",
    "include_global_state" : false,
```

- Here are the global shard's statistics:

```
"shards_stats" : {
      "initializing" : 0,
      "started" : 0,
      "finalizing" : 0,
      "done" : 4,
      "failed" : 0,
      "total" : 4
    },
```

- Here are the snapshot's global statistics:

```
"stats" : {
    "incremental" : {
      "file_count" : 16,
      "size_in_bytes" : 837344
```

```
        },
        "total" : {
          "file_count" : 16,
          "size_in_bytes" : 837344
        },
        "start_time_in_millis" : 1546779914447,
        "time_in_millis" : 52
      },
```

- Here is a drill down of the snapshot index statistics:

```
      "indices" : {
          "mybooks-join" : {
            "shards_stats" : {
              "initializing" : 0,
              "started" : 0,
              "finalizing" : 0,
              "done" : 1,
              "failed" : 0,
              "total" : 1
            },
            "stats" : {
              "incremental" : {
                "file_count" : 4,
                "size_in_bytes" : 10409
              },
              "total" : {
                "file_count" : 4,
                "size_in_bytes" : 10409
              },
              "start_time_in_millis" : 1546779914449,
              "time_in_millis" : 15
            },
```

- Here are the statistics for each index and shard:

```
      "shards" : {
              "0" : {
                "stage" : "DONE",
                "stats" : {
                  "incremental" : {
                    "file_count" : 4,
                    "size_in_bytes" : 10409
                  },
                  "total" : {
                    "file_count" : 4,
                    "size_in_bytes" : 10409
                  },
```

```
                    "start_time_in_millis" : 1546779914449,
                    "time_in_millis" : 15
                  }
                }
              }
            }, ... truncated ...
```

The status response is very rich, and it can also be used to estimate the performance of the snapshot and the size that is required in time for the incremental backups.

Restoring a snapshot

Once you have snapshots of your data, it can be restored. The restore process is very fast – the indexed shard data is simply copied on the nodes and activated.

Getting ready

You will need an up-and-running Elasticsearch installation—similar to the one that we described in the *Downloading and installing Elasticsearch* recipe in Chapter 1, *Getting Started*.

To execute the commands, any HTTP client can be used, such as Curl (https://curl.haxx.se/) or Postman (https://www.getpostman.com/). You can use the Kibana console as it provides code completion and better character escaping for Elasticsearch.

In order to correctly execute the following commands, the backup that was created in the previous recipe is required.

How to do it...

To restore a snapshot, we will perform the following steps:

1. To restore a snapshot called snap_1 for the mybooks-* indices, the HTTP method that we use is POST, and the command is as follows:

```
POST /_snapshot/my_repository/snap_1/_restore
{
  "indices": "mybooks-*",
  "ignore_unavailable": "true",
  "include_global_state": false,
  "rename_pattern": "mybooks-(.+)",
```

```
        "rename_replacement": "copy_$1"
    }
```

The result will be as follows:

```
    {
    "accepted" : true
    }
```

2. The restore is finished when the cluster state changes from `red` to `yellow` or `green`.

In this example, the `"mybooks-*"` index pattern matches `mybooks-join`. The `rename_pattern` parameter captures `"join"`, and the new index will be generated by `rename_placement` and `"copy-join"`.

How it works...

The restore process is very fast; the process comprises the following steps:

1. The data is copied on the primary shard of the restored index (during this step, the cluster is in the `red` state).
2. The primary shards are recovered (during this step, the cluster turns from `red` to `yellow` or `green`).
3. If a replica is set, then the primary shards are copied onto other nodes.

It's possible to control the restore process using some parameters, as follows:

- `indices`: This controls the indices that must be restored. If not defined, then all indices in the snapshot are restored (a comma-delimited list of indices; wildcards are accepted).
- `ignore_unavailable`: This stops the restore from failing if some indices are missing (the default is `false`).
- `include_global_state`: This allows the restoration of the global state from the snapshot (this defaults to `true`; the available values are `true` and `false`).
- `rename_pattern` and `rename_replacement`: The first one is a pattern that must be matched, and the second one uses regular expression replacement to define a new index name.
- `partial`: If set to `true`, it allows the restoration of indices with missing shards (the default is `false`).

Setting up an NFS share for backups

Managing the repository (where the data is stored) is the most crucial part in Elasticsearch backup management. Due to its native distributed architecture, the snapshot and the restore are designed in a cluster style.

During a snapshot, the shards are copied to the defined repository. If this repository is local to the nodes, then the backup data is spread across all the nodes. For this reason, it's necessary to have shared repository storage if you have a multinode cluster.

A common approach is to use an NFS, as it's very easy to set up and it's a very quick solution (additionally, standard Windows Samba shares can be used.)

Getting ready

We have a network with the following nodes:

- **Host server**: 192.168.1.30 (where we will store the backup data)
- **Elasticsearch master node 1**: 192.168.1.40
- **Elasticsearch data node 1**: 192.168.1.50
- **Elasticsearch data node 2**: 192.168.1.51

You will need an up-and-running Elasticsearch installation – similar to the one that we described in the *Downloading and installing Elasticsearch* recipe in Chapter 1, *Getting Started*.

In order to execute the commands, any HTTP client can be used, such as curl (https://curl.haxx.se/) or postman (https://www.getpostman.com/). You can use the Kibana console as it provides code completion and better character escaping for Elasticsearch.

The following instructions are for the standard Debian or Ubuntu distributions; they can be easily changed for another Linux distribution.

How to do it...

To create an NFS shared repository, we need to execute the following steps on the NFS server:

1. Install the NFS server (using the `nfs-kernel-server` package) on the host server. On the `192.168.1.30` host server, we will execute the following commands:

   ```
   sudo apt-get update
   sudo apt-get install nfs-kernel-server
   ```

2. Once the package is installed, create a directory to be shared among all the clients:

   ```
   sudo mkdir /mnt/shared-directory
   ```

3. Give access permissions for this directory to the `nobody` user and the `nogroup` group. The nobody/nogroup are special user/group values to used to allow to share read/write permissions. To apply them you need root access and execute the following command:

   ```
   sudo chown -R nobody:nogroup /mnt/shared-directory
   ```

4. Then, we need to configure the NFS exports, where we can specify that this directory will be shared with certain machines. Edit the `/etc/exports` file (`sudo nano /etc/exports`) and add the following lines containing the directory that is to be shared and a list of client IP that are allowed to access the exported directory:

   ```
   /mnt/shared-directory 192.168.1.40(rw,sync,no_subtree_check)

   192.168.1.50(rw,sync,no_subtree_check)

   192.168.1.51(rw,sync,no_subtree_check)
   ```

5. To refresh the NFS table that holds the export of the share, the following command must be executed:

   ```
   sudo exportfs -a
   ```

6. Finally, we can start the NFS service by running the following command:

   ```
   sudo service nfs-kernel-server start
   ```

After the NFS server is up-and-running, we need to configure the clients. We'll repeat the following steps on each Elasticsearch node:

1. Install the NFS client on our Elasticsearch node:

```
sudo apt-get update
sudo apt-get install nfs-common
```

2. Now create a directory on the client machine and we'll try to mount the remote shared directory:

```
sudo mkdir /mnt/nfs
sudo mount 192.168.1.30:/mnt/shared-directory /mnt/nfs
```

3. If everything is fine, we can add the mount directory to our node /etc/fstab file, so that it will be mounted during the next boot:

```
sudo nano /etc/fstab
```

4. Then, add the following lines into this file:

```
192.168.1.30:/mnt/shared-directory /mnt/nfs/ nfs
auto,noatime,nolock,bg,nfsvers=4,sec=krb5p,intr,tcp,actimeo=18
00 0 0
```

5. We update our Elasticsearch node configuration (config/elasticsearch.yml) of path.repo as follows:

```
path.repo: /mnt/nfs/
```

6. After having restarted all the Elasticsearch nodes, we can create our share repository on the cluster using a single standard repository creation call:

```
PUT /_snapshot/my_repository
{
  "type": "fs",
  "settings": {
    "location": "/ mnt/nfs/my_repository",
    "compress": true
  }
}
```

How it works...

NFS is a distributed filesystem protocol that is very common in the Unix world – it allows you to mount remote directories on your server. The mounted directories look like the local directory of the server, and therefore, by using NFS, multiple servers can write to same directory.

This is very handy if you need to do a shared backup; this is because all the nodes will write/read from the same shared directory.

 If you need to snapshot an index that will be rarely updated, such as an old time-based index, the best practice is to optimize it before backing it up, cleaning up deleted documents, and reducing the Lucene segments.

Reindexing from a remote cluster

The snapshot and restore APIs are very fast and are the preferred way to back up data, but they do have some limitations:

- The backup is a safe Lucene index copy, so it depends on the Elasticsearch version that is used. If you are switching from a version of Elastisearch that is prior to version 5.x, then it's not possible to restore the old indices.
- It's not possible to restore the backups of a newer Elasticsearch version in an older version; the restore is only forward-compatible.
- It's not possible to restore partial data from a backup.

To be able to copy data in this scenario, the solution is to use the reindex API using a remote server.

Getting ready

You will need an up-and-running Elasticsearch installation – similar to the one that we described in the *Downloading and installing Elasticsearch* recipe in `Chapter 1`, *Getting Started*.

In order to execute the commands, any HTTP client can be used, such as curl (`https://curl.haxx.se/`) or postman (`https://www.getpostman.com/`). You can use the Kibana console as it provides code completion and better character escaping for Elasticsearch.

How to do it...

To copy an index from a remote server, we need to execute the following steps:

1. We need to add the remote server address in the `config/elasticsearch.yml` section using `reindex.remote.whitelist` as follows:

   ```
   reindex.remote.whitelist: ["192.168.1.227:9200"]
   ```

2. After having restarted the Elasticsearch node to take the new configuration, we can call the reindex API to copy a `test-source` index data in `test-dest` using the remote REST endpoint in this way:

   ```
   POST /_reindex
   {
     "source": {
       "remote": {
         "host": "http://192.168.1.227:9200"
       },
       "index": "test-source"
     },
     "dest": {
       "index": "test-dest"
     }
   }
   ```

The result will be similar to a local reindex that we have already seen in the *Reindexing an index* recipe in `Chapter 3`, *Basic Operations*.

How it works...

The reindex API allows you to call a remote cluster. Every version of the Elasticsearch server is supported (mainly version 1.x or later).

The reindex API executes a scan query on the remote index cluster and puts the data in the current cluster. This process can take a lot of time, depending on the amount of data that needs to be copied and the time that is required to index the data.

The source section contains important parameters to control the fetched data, such as the following:

- `remote`: This is a section that contains information on the remote cluster connection.
- `index`: This is the remote index that has to be used to fetch the data; it can also be an alias or multiple indices via GLOB patterns.
- `query`: This parameter is optional; it's a standard query that can be used to select the document that must be copied.
- `size`: This parameter is optional and the buffer is up to 200 MB – the number of the documents to be used for the bulk read and write.

The `remote` section of the configuration is composed of the following parameters:

- `host`: The remote REST endpoint of the cluster.
- `username`: The username to be used for copying the data (this is an optional parameter).
- `password`: The password for the user to access the remote cluster (this is optional).

There are a lot advantages to using this approach on standard snapshot and restore, including the following:

- The ability to copy data from older clusters (from version 1.x or later).
- The ability to use a query to copy from a selection of documents. This is very handy for copying data from a production cluster to a development or test one.

See also

- The *Reindex an index* recipe in Chapter 3, *Basic Operations,* and the official Elasticsearch documentation at `https://www.elastic.co/guide/en/elasticsearch/reference/master/docs-reindex.html`, which provides more detailed information about the reindex API and some borderline cases in using this API

11
User Interfaces

In an Elasticsearch ecosystem, it can be immensely useful to monitor nodes and clusters in order to manage and improve their performance and state. There are several issues that can arise at the cluster level, such as the following:

- There can be node overheads; for instance, where some nodes can have too many shards allocated and can become a bottleneck for the entire cluster
- Node shutdown can occur due to many reasons, such as, full disks, hardware failures, and power problems
- Shard relocation problems or corruptions, in which some shards are unable to be initialized and go online due to some issues.
- Having very large shards can also be an issue; index performance can decrease due to large Lucene segments merging
- Empty indices and shards waste memory and resources; however, because every shard has a lot of active threads, if there is a huge number of unused indices and shards, then general cluster performance is degraded
- There can be other node-related problems such as high CPU usage or full disks

Detecting malfunction or bad performance can be done through the API or through some frontends that are designed to be used in Elasticsearch.

Some of the frontends introduced in this chapter will allow you to have a working web dashboard in your Elasticsearch data; these work by monitoring cluster health, backing up or restoring your data, and allowing test queries before implementing them in the code. In this chapter, we will only briefly examine these frontends; this is due to their complexity and large number of features, which are beyond the scope of this book. For an in-depth description, I suggest that you have a look at the official documentation of Kibana, which is available at `https://www.elastic.co/guide/en/kibana/current/index.html`.

In this chapter, we will explore Cerebro, ElasticSearchHQ, and some aspects of Kibana (covering all Kibana's functionalities is beyond the scope of this book).

Grafana (`https://grafana.com/`) is another open source solution, which is used to visualize Elasticsearch data and monitor **public key infrastruture** (**PKI**), however, it is not covered in this book.

In this chapter, we will cover the following recipes:

- Installing and using Cerebro
- Installing and using Elasticsearch HQ
- Installing Kibana
- Managing Kibana Discovery
- Visualizing data with Kibana
- Using Kibana Dev Tools

Installing and using Cerebro

Cerebro is the evolution of the previous Elasticsearch plugin, Elasticsearch Kopf (`https://github.com/lmenezes/elasticsearch-kopf`) – this doesn't work in Elasticsearch version 5.x or later versions due to the removal of site plugins.

Cerebro is one of the most useful interfaces for looking at shard allocations and executing common index operations through a graphic interface. It's completely open source, and it allows you to add a user, password, or LDAP authentication for accessing the web interface.

Cerebro is a partial rewrite of the previous plugin, and it is available as a self-working application server, based on Scala's Play Framework.

Getting ready

You will need an up-and-running Elasticsearch installation—similar to the one that we described in the *Downloading and installing Elasticsearch* recipe in `Chapter 1`, *Getting Started*.

Java JVM version 8.x, or a later version, must be installed in order to run Cerebro.

If you are installing using Docker Compose, which is available in the `ch01` directory, then you don't need to manually install it.

How to do it...

In order to install Cerebro, you will need to download and install it manually. Then, we will perform the following steps:

1. You can download a binary distribution of Cerebro at `https://github.com/lmenezes/cerebro/releases`. For Linux or macOSX, we can use the following command:

   ```
   wget -c
   https://github.com/lmenezes/cerebro/releases/download/v0.8.3/c
   erebro-0.8.3.tgz
   ```

2. Now, you can extract it, using the following command:

   ```
   tar xfvz cerebro-0.8.3.tgz
   ```

3. Now, you can execute it using the following command:

   ```
   cerebro-0.8.3/bin/cerebro
   ```

4. Alternatively, for Windows, use the following command:

   ```
   cerebro-0.8.3/bin/cerebro.bat
   ```

5. In the console, you should see the following output:

   ```
   [info] play.api.Play - Application started (Prod)
   [info] p.c.s.AkkaHttpServer - Listening for HTTP on
   /0.0.0.0:9000
   ```

6. To access the web interface, you will need to navigate to the following address, using your browser,:

   ```
   http://0.0.0.0:9000/
   ```

How it works...

Cerebro is a modern reactive application; it is written in Scala using the Play Framework for backend REST and Elasticsearch communications. Additionally, it uses a **Single Page Application (SPA)** frontend that is written in JavaScript with AngularJS.

By default, Cerebro binds to port `9000`. You can navigate to the `http://0.0.0.0:9000` address using a browser in order to view the following start page:

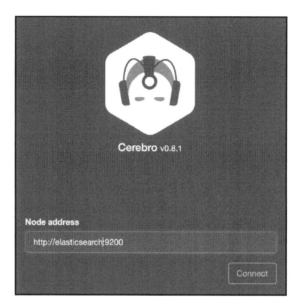

On the start page, you can select a predefined host or you can manually insert the address of your Elasticsearch server. If required, you can provide credentials for accessing your Elasticsearch cluster.

After clicking on **Connect**, if everything is okay, you can then access the Cerebro main page using the **nodes** view, as shown in the following screenshot:

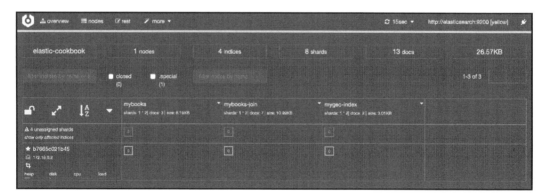

The Cerebro main page provides a very large overview of your cluster and data; from top to bottom we have the following:

- **The menu**: This is where **overview** is a link to the home page, **rest** allows you to send generic REST calls, and by clicking on **more**, we have additional admin functionalities, as shown in the following screenshot:

- **The status line**: This is either green, yellow, or red; in this case, it is yellow because my cluster requires more nodes.
- **The line of cluster global statistics**: This includes the name of the cluster, the number of nodes, the number of indices, the number of shards, the number of documents, and the size of your data.
- **The filter indices line**: This is where you can do the following:
    - Filter the indices by name
    - Show or hide any closed indices
    - Show or hide any special indices (such as index names that start for . (dot) character)
    - Filter by node names
    - Control the indices' pagination
- **The main grid block that contains the node and indices information**: In the first column, we have the following:
    - **The general cluster control functionalities**: Here, the lock symbol allows you to lock the shard relocation at the cluster level (this is useful for cluster restart management). The second symbol allows you to show extra node information, such as the JVM version and Elasticsearch version. The sorting simply allows you to sort the nodes by name.

- The arrow symbol allows you to execute actions on all the selected indices, such as **close**, **open**, **refresh,** and **cache clear**.

  - **The unassigned shards line**: This allows you to check the unassigned shard for the affected indices.
  - **The node information**: Here, in a single cell we have the **node name**, **node IP**, and the **heap**, **disk**, **cpu**, or **load** on the node. If these values are too high, then they appear in red.

- **In the other columns, we have the indices information**:
  - This includes the index name, the number of shards, the number of documents, and the total size; from the arrow, you can access an action that can be executed against the index:

  - The **shards** are represented as a box with a number; by clicking on it, you can view any additional shard information.

The main page or **overview** view is very rich with useful data. Using only a single glance, you can scope nodes that have high loads or a full disk, view how the shards are distributed in your cluster, and determine whether there are problems with some indices.

When you click on **index settings**, a form opens that allows you to change some of the index options, as shown in the following screenshot:

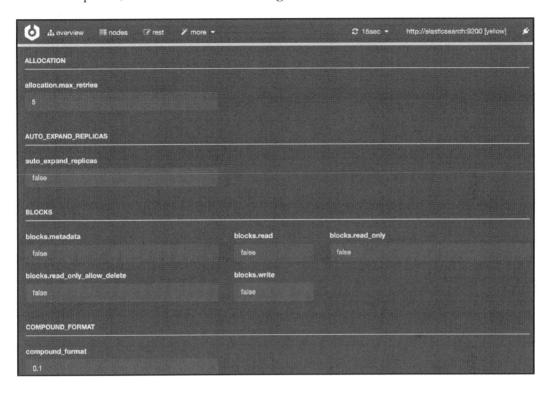

The **create index** page allows you to easily create an index defining shards, replicas, or templates, as shown in the following screenshot:

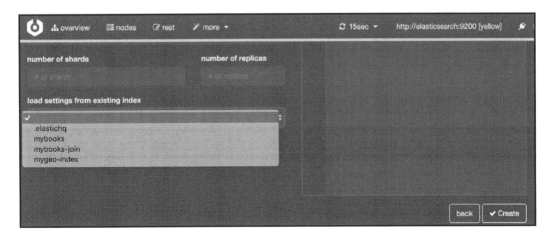

The **cluster settings** page allows you to change the cluster's mutable parameters from a simple interface. This is advanced usage, but the simplicity of the form speeds up the management of the cluster, as shown in the following screenshot:

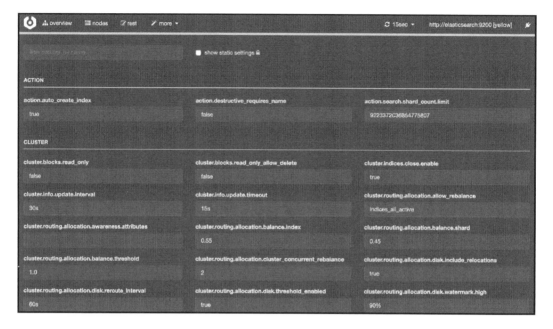

Managing the repository can be achieved by using the **repositories** menu; the page allows you to define the name and type of repository that you want to use for future backup or restore actions, as shown in the following screenshot:

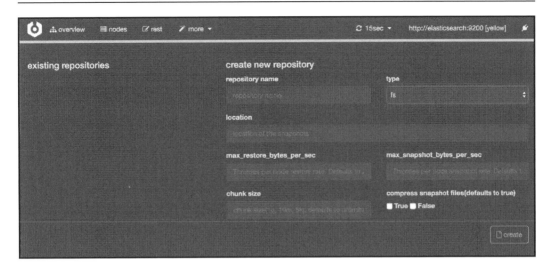

If a repository is created using the interface or API, then it can be used to execute backup and restore actions. By clicking on the **shapshot** menu, you can access a page that allows you to perform the following actions:

- On the right-side, you can create a snapshot by selecting the repository, giving it a name, and selecting the indices that need to be backed up
- On the left-side, there is a list of available snapshots that can be restored, as shown in the following screenshot:

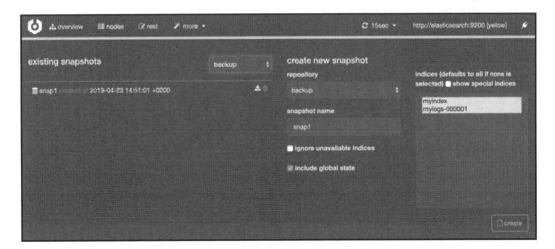

There's more...

The initial part of Cerebro allows you to cover special aspects of Elasticsearch management. For example, in the **rest** menu, you can access a page that allows you to execute raw REST calls against Elasticsearch, as shown in the following screenshot:

Cerebro doesn't provide data visualization or discovery like Kibana, but it can execute raw REST calls against an Elasticsearch endpoint. With this functionality, queries can be tested against an Elasticsearch server. This is very useful in order to work with a low-level client using Elasticsearch.

The rest interface also allows you to export the call as a curl command. The Cerebro interface is relatively new; the new features are currently in development and will be released in the near future.

Installing and using Elasticsearch HQ

ElasticSearch HQ (`http://www.elastichq.org`) is a monitoring and management application, which manages both instances and clusters. It's an open source solution, and it is free for both private and commercial use.

Getting ready

You will need an up-and-running Elasticsearch installation – similar to the one that we described in the *Downloading and installing Elasticsearch* recipe in `Chapter 1`, *Getting Started*.

Python version 3.4, or a later version, must be installed in order to run ElasticSearch HQ.

If you are installing using Docker Compose, which is available in the `ch01` directory, then you don't need to manually install it.

How to do it...

In order to install ElasticSearch HQ, you will need to download and install it manually. Then, we will perform the following steps:

1. You can download a ZIP file or `tar.gz` distribution of ElasticSearch HQ at `https://github.com/ElasticHQ/elasticsearch-HQ/releases`. For Linux or macOSX, we can use the following command:

```
wget -c
https://github.com/ElasticHQ/elasticsearch-HQ/archive/v3.5.0.t
ar.gz
```

2. Now you can extract it, using the following command:

```
tar xfvz v3.5.0.tar.gz
```

3. Now you can execute it, using the following commands:

```
cd v3.5.0
pip install -r requirements.txt
./manage.py runserver
```

4. In the console, you should see the following output:

    2019-02-16 18:22:26,972 CRIT Supervisor running as root (no user in config file)
    2019-02-16 18:22:26,977 INFO supervisord started with pid 1
    2019-02-16 18:22:27,980 INFO spawned: 'gunicorn' with pid 8
    2019-02-16 18:22:28,983 INFO success: gunicorn entered RUNNING state, process
    has stayed up for > than 1 seconds (startsecs)
    loading config /src/elastichq/config/logger.json
    2019-02-16 18:22:30,250 INFO engineio server.__init__:140 Server initialized for
    eventlet.

5. To access the web interface, you will need to navigate, using your browser, to the following address:

    `http://0.0.0.0:5000/`

How it works...

ElasticSearch HQ is a modern reactive application. It was composed by a backend written in Python using the Flask framework (`http://flask.pocoo.org/`) and a SPA frontend that was written in JavaScript using AngularJS.

By default, ElasticSearch HQ binds to port `5000`. You can navigate to the `http://0.0.0.0:5000` address using a browser in order to view the following start page:

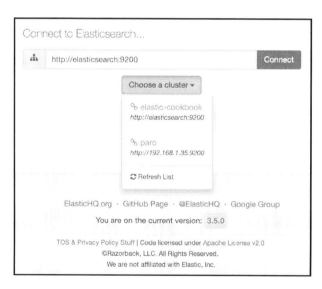

On the start page, you can select a predefined host or you can manually insert the address of your Elasticsearch server. In this case, my instance is able to suggest clusters that I've already used.

After clicking on **Connect**, if everything is okay, then you can access the **ElasticHQ** main page displaying your **Nodes** view and **Indices** view, as shown in the following screenshot:

The **ElasticHQ** main page provides an extensive overview of your cluster and data; from top to bottom, we have the following:

- **The menu on the top-right**: Here, you can choose from the following options:
  - **Indices:** This allows you to perform actions on the indices (such as alias, restore, open, or close)
  - **Metrics**: This offers you metrics about the cluster
  - **Nodes**: This is a list of nodes that you can use to check node information or the state of a node
  - **Diagnostics**: This is a page that provides checks on common Elasticsearch parameters
  - **REST**: This allows you to execute test REST calls
  - **Query**: This allows you to execute searches on the data

- **Counters**: These display the more important items of the cluster, such as **Nodes**, **Indices**, **Documents**, and the **Size** of the data
- A line that displays the status of the number of shards
- The list of **Nodes**
- The list of **Indices**: The color on the left-side refers to the index state (yellows means that some replicas are missing)

If you access the **Indices | Indices Summary** menu, then you will be taken to an index overview page, as follows:

As you can see from the preceding screenshot, many useful actions are available at the single click of a button:

- **Refresh**: This is to refresh the indices in order to speed up the search of new items, without waiting for the automatic refresh
- **Force Merge**: This button reduces the index segments
- **Flush**: This writes all the index data onto a disk
- **Clear Cache**: This frees the memory
- **Expunge Deleted**: This executes a fast force merge that only removes deleted segments
- **Create Index**: This adds a new index
- **Re-Index**: This moves data between the indices

By selecting an index name, you have access to the information of that particular
index and its actions:

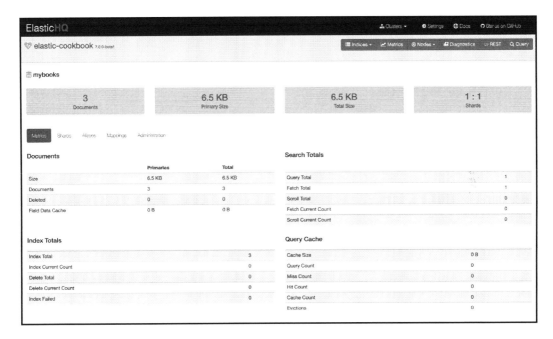

From this view, you can access more index details as follows:

- **Metrics** (the default page): This provides metrics level information
- **Shards**: This provides details about the shards
- **Alias**: This allows you to manage the alias for the current index
- **Mappings**: This allows you to view the mappings
- **Administration**: This allows you to execute administrative commands only
  on this index

The index administrative view is displayed in the following screenshot:

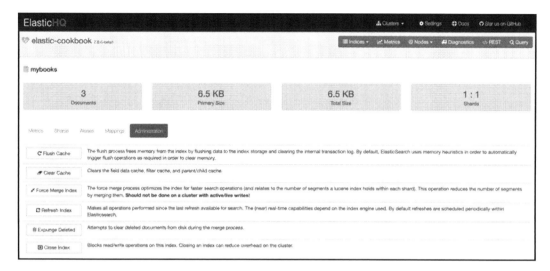

If you need to understand server loads or monitor the Elasticsearch KPI, then by using the **Metrics** button, you can access a real-time graph:

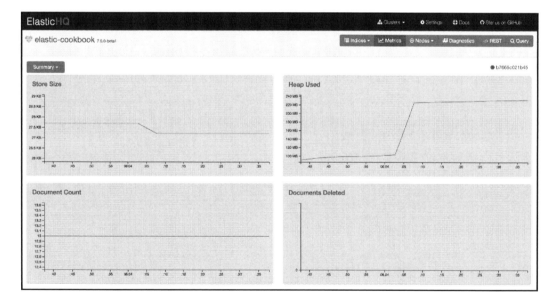

To monitor the nodes' configuration and parameters, you can access details from the **Nodes** menu:

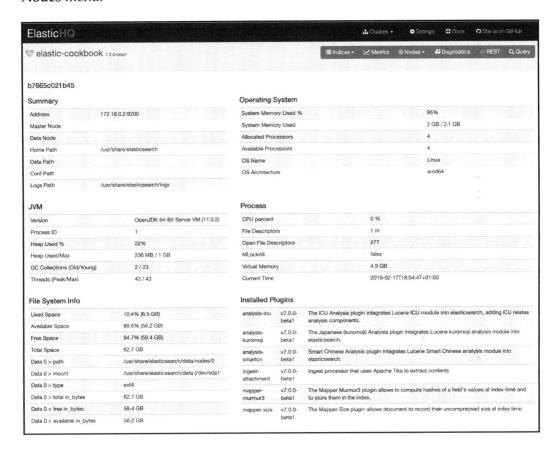

ElasticHQ is the only **user interface** (**UI**) that provides a **Diagnostic** page, which collects all the node information and marks their states using colors. This page is accessible from the **Diagnostic** button:

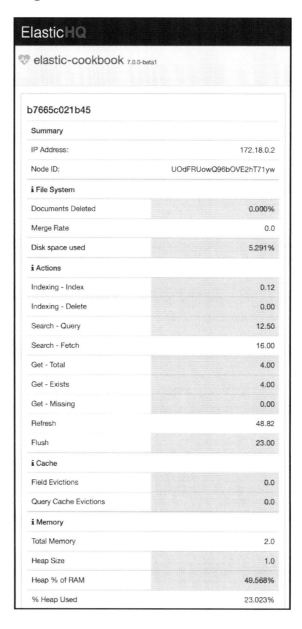

Another useful feature of ElasticSearch HQ is the ability to call all the REST entries of Elasticsearch from the **REST** button. Simply by clicking on a link, the relative REST entry is executed:

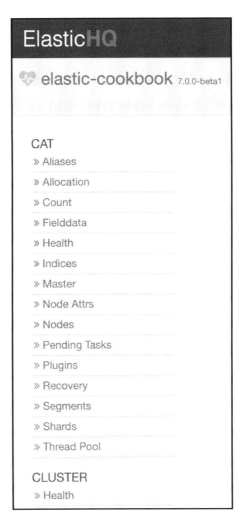

ElasticHQ also provides a useful REST interface in order to test your queries:

For every ElasticSearch user, ElasticSearch HQ is a good UI that provides a lot of features that help with the everyday maintenance and monitoring of Elasticsearch.

Installing Kibana

The most famous Elasticsearch interface is Kibana; from Elasticsearch version 7.x, they share the same version number. Kibana is an open source pluggable interface and is free to use with Elasticsearch. It provides data visualization and it can be extended with a commercial product called X-Pack that provides security, graph capabilities, and cluster monitoring.

In this chapter, we will mainly cover the Kibana open source components. Kibana with X-Pack offers a lot of functionalities and as these are beyond the scope of this book, I suggest that you look for books related to Kibana for a full description of all Kibana's capabilities.

Getting ready

You will need an up-and-running Elasticsearch installation – similar to the one that we described in the *Downloading and installing Elasticsearch* recipe in `Chapter 1, Getting Started`.

If you are installing using Docker Compose, which is available in the `ch01` directory, then you don't need to manually install it.

 The Kibana version must be the same version of Elasticsearch, so if you update your Elasticsearch cluster, then it's best practice to update the Kibana nodes as well.

How to do it...

To install Kibana, we will perform the following steps:

1. Download a binary version of the Elasticsearch website and unpack it. For Linux, the commands are as follows:

```
wget
https://artifacts.elastic.co/downloads/kibana/kibana-7.0.0-bet
a1-linux-x86_64.tar.gz
tar xfvz kibana-7.0.0-beta1-linux-x86_64.tar.gz
```

2. On macOSX, you can install Kibana using the following command:

```
brew install kibana
```

3. If Kibana or X-Pack is hard to get ready, then there is a Docker image that you can use to simplify the process (this is available at `http://elk-docker. readthedocs.io/#installation`). Using two commands on Linux, you can have the stack up and running.

How it works...

Kibana is the official Elasticsearch frontend. It's an open source analytics and visualization platform based on AngularJS that works with Elasticsearch. It's served by a Node.js backend webserver. The development of Kibana is highly connected to Elasticsearch ones and the best practice is to use a Kibana version that is aligned to Elasticsearch versions.

Kibana allows you to navigate data in Elasticsearch and organize it in dashboards that are created, shared, and updated in real time.

After setting up and starting Elasticsearch and Kibana, you can navigate to Kibana using `http://localhost:5601`, as shown in the following screenshot:

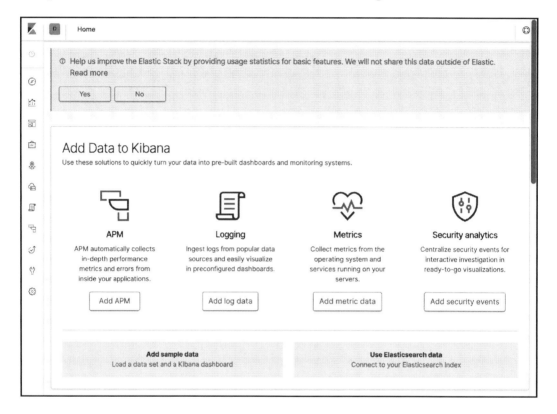

Before playing with Kibana, I suggest that you load some datasets, which are provided in the installation. Just click on **Load a data set and a Kibana dashboard** on the **Add sample data** tile:

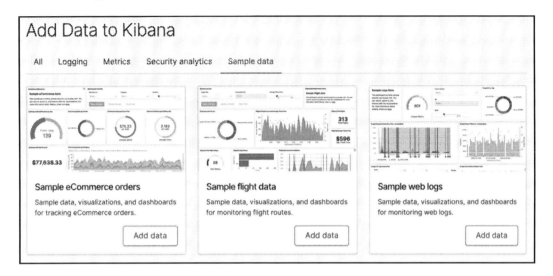

The Kibana installation provides some data samples that you can start to use; these datasets are very handy because they show many of the advanced Kibana dashboard capabilities; just click on **Add data** to initialize them.

If you select the first one, you will gain access to a full feature dashboard as follows:

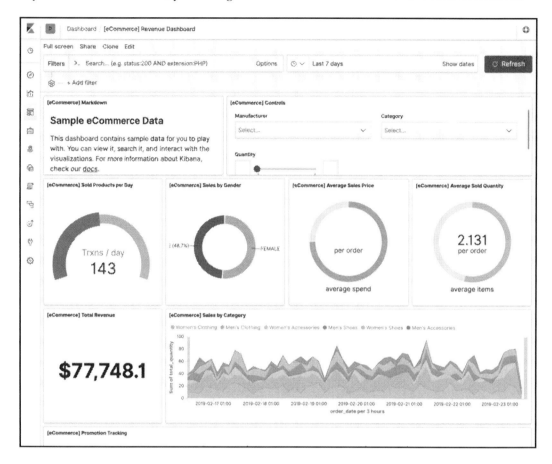

On the left-side of the dashboard, you have the navigation bar:

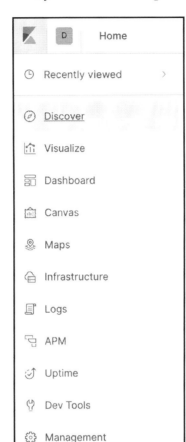

From the navigation bar, you have access to the following icons:

- **Spaces** (the green **D**): This is a way to group your interface in its defined own spaces
- **Discovery**: This is used to navigate your data in order to discover information
- **Visualize**: This is used to create visualizations that can be used to populate pages
- **Dashboard**: This section hosts your **Space** dashboards
- **Canvas**: This section allows you to create pixel art dashboards that are similar to infographics

- **Maps**: This section allows you to manage maps
- **Infrastructure**: This section allows you to configure an infrastructure that you can later monitor
- **Logs**: This section is used to manage logs
- **Application Performance Monitoring (APM)**: This section is used to create visualizations
- **Uptime**: This section is used to manage the uptime of applications
- **Dev Tools**: This section contains the `dev` tool components
- **Management**: This section allows you to configure Kibana
- **Monitor**: This is used to monitor your node functionalities and the cluster overall
- **Graph**: This provides the graph API for Elasticsearch—that is, a graph-based approach for data discovery
- **Watcher**: This is a system providing registered queries, which allows you to monitor and keep an alert on your data
- **Reporting**: This is a module that is able to create reports from your dashboards

See also

- An overview of Kibana is available at ;`https://www.elastic.co/products/kibana`.

Managing Kibana discovery

One of the most popular aspects of Kibana is the discovery dashboard. This is because it allows you to dynamically navigate your data. With the evolution of Kibana, a lot of new features have been added to the Discovery dashboard in order to allow you to easily filter and analyze your data.

Getting ready

You will need an up-and-running Elasticsearch installation – similar to the one that we described in the *Downloading and installing Elasticsearch* recipe in `Chapter 1`, *Getting Started.* Additionally, a working Kibana instance is required, as described in the *Installing Kibana* recipe of this chapter.

If you have used Docker Compose, which is available in the `ch01` directory, then everything should be correctly installed.

How to do it...

For managing Kibana dashboards, we will perform the following steps:

1. We access the **Discovery** section of Kibana, as shown in the following screenshot:

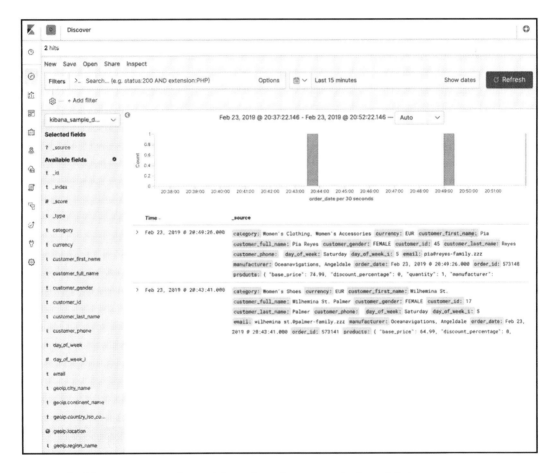

2. Now, you can play with and analyze your indexed data.

How it works...

The **Discovery** section is designed to allow you to explore your data.

You can save and share your created discovery dashboard—this can then be reused to build other dashboards. In the middle of the screen, you should be able to view your documents, which are available in tabular and JSON formats:

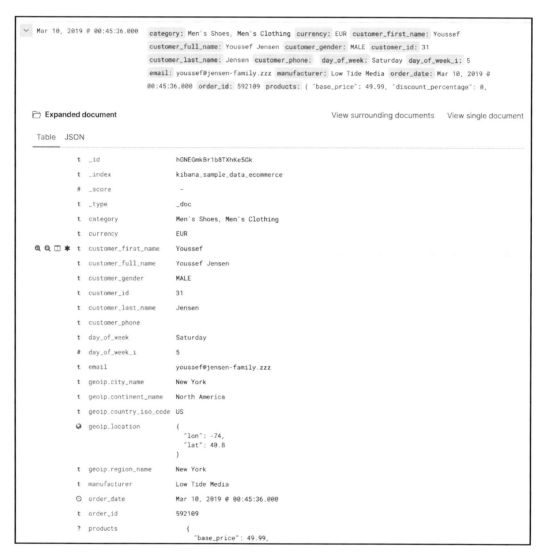

As you can see, from the preceding screenshot, when you hover over a field, special actions are enabled:

- **Filter using this value**
- **Filter not using this value**
- **Toggle column in table**
- **Filter for field present** (exists query)

Sometimes, your data is not shown; this is mainly because you have selected the wrong date range.

You can change it easily from the calendar drop-down menu, as follows:

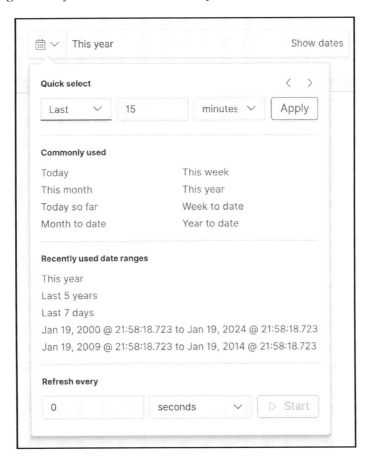

The core of the filtering is done from the search box; here, you can provide Google-like syntax in order to search for your data quickly:

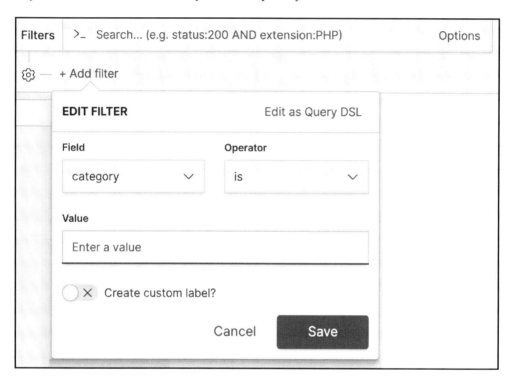

You can add a filter using the following two options:

- Using the web interface: This is for simple filters. All the fields are available in the drop-down menus; in this way, building the query should be very easy.
- Using **Edit as Query DSL**: This allows you to input your complex JSON.

You can also create filters using the facets created automatically when you select a field on the left-side of the screen:

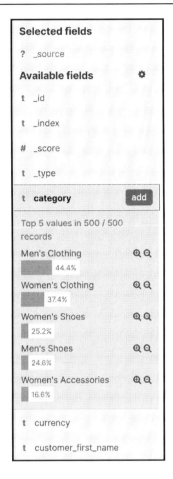

For every field, the interface suggests the most used values in order to easily use them as filter. Using the + and - symbols you can choose to filter or unfilter values.

Visualizing data with Kibana

Kibana allows you to create reusable data representations called visualizations. These are representations of aggregations and can be used to power up the dashboard using custom graphs. In general, you can consider visualization as a building block for your dashboard.

Getting ready

You will need an up-and-running Elasticsearch installation – similar to the one that we described in the *Downloading and installing Elasticsearch* recipe in `Chapter 1`, *Getting Started.* Additionally, a working Kibana instance is required, as described in the *Installing Kibana* recipe of this chapter.

If you have used Docker Compose, which is available in the `ch01` directory, then everything should be correctly installed.

How to do it...

To use Kibana to create custom widgets, we will perform the following steps:

1. We access the **Visualize** section of Kibana, as shown in the following screenshot:

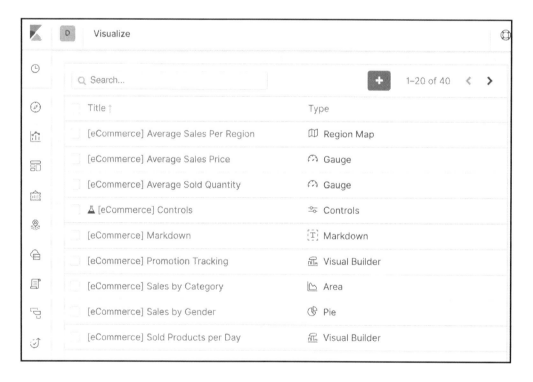

2. Now, we can choose the visualization that we want to create, as shown in the following screenshot:

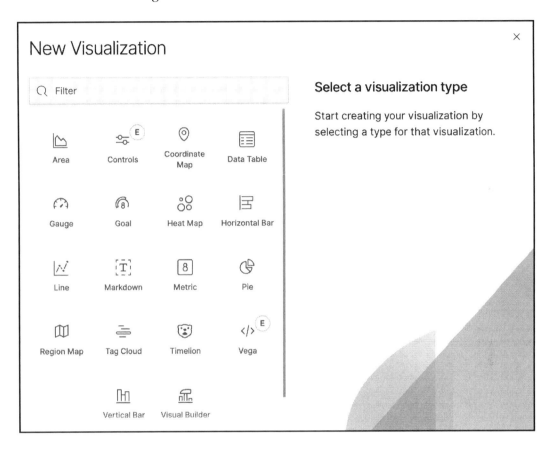

3. If we want to create a **Tag cloud** visualization, then we select it and populate the required fields, as shown in the following screenshot:

How it works...

Aggregations and searches can be grouped in the visualization widgets, which can be used as building blocks for creating custom interfaces.

The built-in visualizations are as follows:

- **Area chart**: This is useful for representing stacked timelines
- **Controls**: These are useful for extending filtering
- **Coordinate Map**: This is used to manage geodata
- **Data table**: This allows you to create a data table using the aggregation results
- **Gauge**: This is useful for showing range values
- **Goal**: This is useful for showing the number count
- **Heat Map**: This shows data in heat maps
- **Horizontal/Vertical bar chart**: This is the general purpose bar representation for histograms
- **Line charts**: This is useful for representing time-based hits and comparing them
- **Markdown widget**: This is useful for displaying explanations or instructions for dashboards
- **Metric**: This represents a numeric metric value
- **Pie**: This is useful for representing low cardinality values
- **Region Map**: This is useful for displaying geographical boxed data
- **Tag cloud**: This is useful for representing term values such as tags and labels
- **Time series/ Timelion**: This allows you to use Timelion expression language to create time series chart
- **Vega**: This is a customizable JavaScript canvas (`https://vega.github.io/vega/`)
- **Visual Builder**: This allows you to create custom visualization using a predefined builder

After selecting a visualization, a custom form is presented on the left, which allows you to populate all the required values. On the right, we have the widget representation that is updated in near-real time with the result of the queries and aggregations.

After the configuration of the visualization is completed, it must be saved in order to be used as a widget in the dashboard:

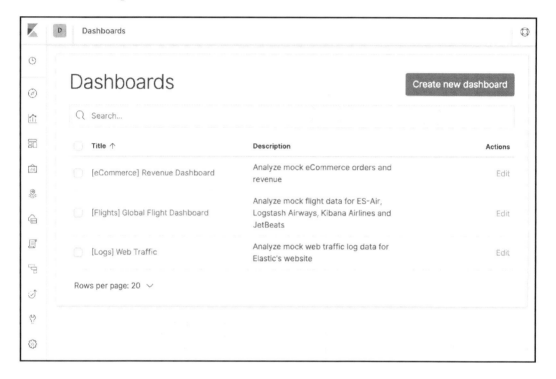

After selecting **Create new dashboard**, you can start editing it by adding your saved visualizations, as show, in the following screenshot:

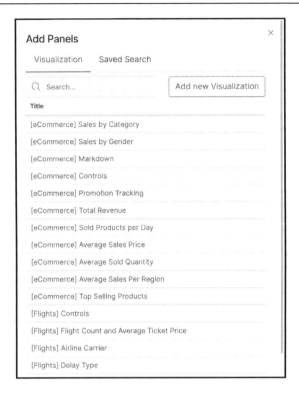

The dashboard top menu allows you to do the following:

- Create a new dashboard starting from scratch using the **New** menu entry.
- **Save** the current dashboard or query giving it a name.
- Open the dashboards that you have already saved.
- **Share** a dashboard or a dashboard snapshot (with the date/time value fixed) using a link.
- Generate a PDF from the current dashboard using the **Reporting** menu entry. In order to generate a report, your dashboard must be saved; the reporting entry is available only if X-Pack is activated.
- If you are using autorefresh dashboards, then you can pause autorefresh using the pause icon. By clicking on the refresh interval, you can change it.
- Change or define the time interval range by clicking on the time range value.

Internally, the Kibana dashboards are stored in an Elasticsearch .kibana special index; for any kind of asynchronous task, the data is read from this index.

In this recipe, we have only scratched the surface of the powerful Kibana dashboard. I suggest that you buy a book related to Kibana, or refer to online documentation or videos on Kibana because it is a tool that has very rich capabilities.

Using Kibana Dev tools

Kibana provides a very handy section for developers: Dev Tools. In the open source version, this section is composed of three tools:

- **Dev-Console**: The place where the developer tests and execute commands
- **Search Profiler**: A tool that is used to profile queries
- **Grok Debugger**: This is useful for debugging Grok regular expressions

Getting ready

You will need an up-and-running Elasticsearch installation—similar to the one that we described in the *Downloading and installing Elasticsearch* recipe in Chapter 1, *Getting Started.* Additionally, a working Kibana instance is required, as described in the *Installing Kibana* recipe of this chapter.

If you have used Docker Compose, which is available in the ch01 directory, then everything should be correctly installed.

How to do it...

To use Dev-Console, we will perform the following steps:

1. We access the **Dev Tools** section of Kibana, as shown in the following screenshot:

---

2. Now we can use the Dev-Console to create, execute, and test queries and other Elasticsearch HTTP APIs that are using it, as shown in the following screenshot:

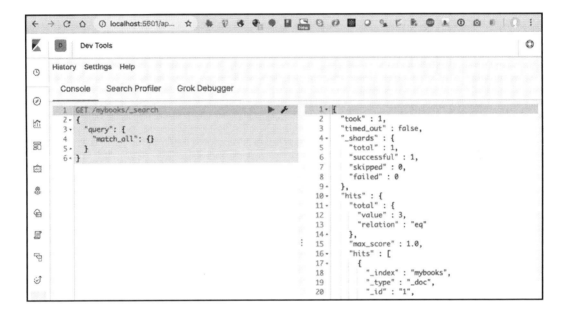

How it works...

The Kibana Dev-Console is very similar to the Cerebro interface that we mentioned previously. It allows you to execute every kind of REST API call through the `http` interface to Elasticsearch. It can be used for several purposes, including the following:

- Creating complex queries and aggregations: The console interface helps the user by providing code completion and syntax checking during editing.
- Analyzing the returned results: This is very useful for checking particular aggregation responses or the structure of the API answers.
- Testing or debugging queries before embedding them in your application code.
- Executing REST services that are now wrapped in Elasticsearch interfaces, such as repository, snapshot, and restore services.

Kibana Dev-Console's autocompletion of any queries helps users to build complex queries quickly.

There's more...

The Kibana Dev Tools also provides support to drill down the times needed to execute a particular query using the **Profiler ;**section. It's available in the open source part of Kibana, as shown in the following screenshot:

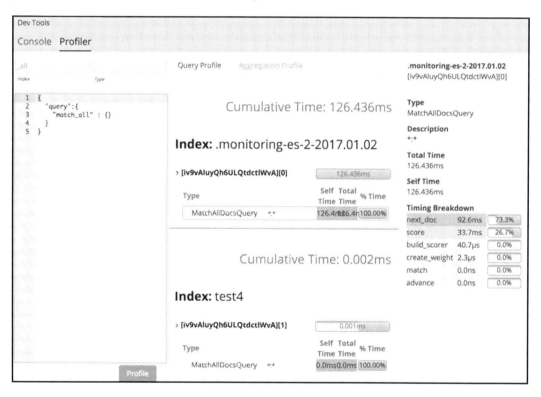

As the execution of a query with some aggregation can be very complex and it can take a lot of time to profile the query, this is the most advanced interface available in Elasticsearch for profiling query executions.

12
Using the Ingest Module

Elasticsearch 5.x introduces a set of powerful functionalities that target the problems that arise during ingestion of documents via the ingest node.

In `Chapter 1`, *Getting Started*, we discussed that the Elasticsearch node can be `master`, `data`, or `ingest`; the idea to split the ingest component from the others is to create a more stable cluster due to problems that can arise when preprocessing documents.

To create a more stable cluster, the ingest nodes should be isolated by the master nodes (and possibly also from the data ones) in the event that some problems may occur, such as a crash due to an attachment plugin and high loads due to complex type manipulation.

 The ingestion node can replace a `Logstash` installation in simple scenarios.

In this chapter, we will cover the following recipes:

- Pipeline definition
- Inserting an ingest pipeline
- Getting an ingest pipeline
- Deleting an ingest pipeline
- Simulating a pipeline
- Built-in processors
- The grok processor
- Using the ingest attachment plugin
- Using the ingest GeoIP plugin

Pipeline definition

The job of ingest nodes is to pre-process the documents before sending them to the data nodes. This process is called a pipeline definition and every single step of this pipeline is a processor definition.

Getting ready

You need an up-and-running Elasticsearch installation, as we described in the *Downloading and installing Elasticsearch* recipe in `Chapter 1`, *Getting Started*.

To execute these commands, any HTTP client can be used, such as curl (`https://curl.haxx.se/`), postman (`https://www.getpostman.com/`), or similar. We will use the Kibana console, as it provides code completion and better character escaping for Elasticsearch.

How to do it...

To define an ingestion pipeline, you need to provide a description and some processors, as follows:

1. Define a pipeline that adds a field called `user` with the value, `john`:

```
{
  "description": "Add user john field",
  "processors": [
    {
      "set": {
        "field": "user",
        "value": "john"
      }
    }
  ],
  "version": 1
}
```

How it works...

The generic template representation is as follows:

```
{
  "description" : "...",
  "processors" : [ ... ],
  "version": 1,
  "on_failure" : [ ... ],
}
```

The `description` contains a definition of the activities done by this pipeline. It's very useful if you store a lot of pipelines in your cluster.

The `processors` field contains a list of processor actions. They will be executed in order.

In the preceding example, we have used a simple processor action called `set` that allows us to set a field with a value. The `version` field is optional, but it is very useful in keeping track of your pipeline versions. The optional `on_failure` field allows us to define a list of processors to be applied if there are failures during normal pipeline execution.

There's more...

To prevent failure in the case of missing fields or similar constraints, some processors provide the `ignore_failure` property.

For example, a pipeline with a `rename` field that handles the missing field should be defined in this way:

```
{
  "description": "my pipeline with handled exceptions",
  "processors": [
    {
      "rename": {
        "field": "foo",
        "target_field": "bar",
        "ignore_failure": true
      }
    }
  ]
}
```

In case of failure, you can configure an `on_failure` entry to manage the error.

For example, the error can be saved in a field in the following way:

```
{
  "description": "my pipeline with handled exceptions",
  "processors": [
    {
      "rename": {
        "field": "foo",
        "target_field": "bar",
        "on_failure": [
          {
            "set": {
              "field": "error",
              "value": "{{ _ingest.on_failure_message }}"
            }
          }
        ]
      }
    }
  ]
}
```

 Many of the processors allow us to define an `if` statement using Painless script or Regular Expression. This property is very handy to build more complex pipelines.

See also

The official documentation about the conditionals in the pipeline can be found at https://www.elastic.co/guide/en/elasticsearch/reference/master/ingest-conditional-complex.html, https://www.elastic.co/guide/en/elasticsearch/reference/master/conditionals-with-multiple-pipelines.html, and https://www.elastic.co/guide/en/elasticsearch/reference/master/conditionals-with-regex.html.

Inserting an ingest pipeline

The power of the pipeline definition is the ability for it to be updated and created without a node restart (compared to Logstash). The definition is stored in a cluster state via the `put` pipeline API.

Now that we've defined a pipeline, we need to provide it to the Elasticsearch cluster.

Getting ready

You need an up-and-running Elasticsearch installation, as we described in the *Downloading and installing Elasticsearch* recipe in `Chapter 1`, *Getting Started*.

To execute the commands, every HTTP client can be used, such as curl (`https://curl.haxx.se/`), postman (`https://www.getpostman.com/`), or similar. Use the Kibana console, as it provides the code completion and better character escaping for Elasticsearch.

How to do it...

To store or update an ingestion pipeline in Elasticsearch, we will perform the following steps:

1. Store the ingest pipeline using a PUT call:

```
PUT /_ingest/pipeline/add-user-john
{
  "description": "Add user john field",
  "processors": [
    {
      "set": {
        "field": "user",
        "value": "john"
      }
    }
  ],
  "version": 1
}
```

2. The result that's returned by Elasticsearch, if everything is okay, should be as follows:

```
{
    "acknowledged" : true
}
```

How it works...

The PUT pipeline method works both for creating a pipeline as well as updating an existing one.

The pipelines are stored in a cluster state, and they are immediately propagated to all ingest nodes. When the ingest nodes receive the new pipeline, they will update their node in an in-memory pipeline representation, and the pipeline changes take effect immediately.

When you store a pipeline in the cluster, pay attention and provide a meaningful name (in the example, add-user-john) so that you can easily understand what the pipeline does. The name of the pipeline used in the put call will be the ID of the pipeline in other pipeline flows.

After storing your pipeline in Elasticsearch, you can index a document providing the pipeline name as a query argument. For example:

```
PUT /my_index/my_type/my_id?pipeline=add-user-john
{}
```

The document will be enriched by the pipeline before being indexed:

```
{
  "_index" : "my_index",
  "_type" : "_doc",
  "_id" : "my_id",
  "_version" : 1,
  "found" : true,
  "_source" : {
    "user" : "john"
  }
}
```

Getting an ingest pipeline

After having stored your pipeline, it is common to retrieve its content, so that you can check its definition. This action can be done via the `get` pipeline API.

Getting ready

You need an up-and-running Elasticsearch installation, as we described in the *Downloading and installing Elasticsearch* recipe in `Chapter 1`, *Getting Started*.

To execute the commands, every HTTP client can be used, such as curl (`https://curl.haxx.se/`), postman (`https://www.getpostman.com/`), or similar. Use the Kibana console, as it provides the code completion and better character escaping for Elasticsearch.

How to do it...

To retrieve an ingestion pipeline in Elasticsearch, we will perform the following steps:

1. We can retrieve the ingest pipeline using a GET call:

   ```
   GET /_ingest/pipeline/add-user-
   ```

2. The result that's returned by Elasticsearch, if everything is okay, should be as follows:

   ```
   {
     "add-user-john" : {
       "description" : "Add user john field",
       "processors" : [
         {
           "set" : {
             "field" : "user",
             "value" : "john"
           }
         }
       ],
       "version" : 1
     }
   }
   ```

How it works...

To retrieve an ingestion pipeline, you need its name or ID. For each returned pipeline, all the data is returned: the source and the version, if they are defined.

The GET pipeline allows us to use a wildcard in names, so you can do the following:

- Retrieve all pipelines using *:

```
GET /_ingest/pipeline/*
```

- Retrieve a partial pipeline:

```
GET /_ingest/pipeline/add-*
```

 In case you have a lot of pipelines, using a good name convention helps a lot in their management.

There's more...

If you need only a part of the pipeline, such as the version, you can use filter_path to filter the pipeline only for the parts that are needed. Take a look at the following code example:

```
GET /_ingest/pipeline/add-user-john?filter_path=*.version
```

It will return only the version part of the pipeline:

```
{
  "add-user-john" : {
    "version" : 1
  }
}
```

Deleting an ingest pipeline

To clean up our Elasticsearch cluster for obsolete or unwanted pipelines, we need to call the delete pipeline API with the ID of the pipeline.

Getting ready

You need an up-and-running Elasticsearch installation, as we described in the *Downloading and installing Elasticsearch* recipe in `Chapter 1`, *Getting Started*.

To execute the commands, every HTTP client can be used, such as curl (`https://curl.haxx.se/`), postman (`https://www.getpostman.com/`), or similar. Use the Kibana console, as it provides the code completion and better character escaping for Elasticsearch.

How to do it...

To delete an ingestion pipeline in Elasticsearch, we will perform the following steps:

1. We can delete the ingest pipeline using a `DELETE` call:

```
DELETE /_ingest/pipeline/add-user-john
```

2. The result that's returned by Elasticsearch, if everything is okay, should be as follows:

```
{
   "acknowledged" : true
}
```

How it works...

The `delete` pipeline API removes the named pipeline from Elasticsearch.

Since the pipelines are kept in memory in every node due to their cluster-level storage and the pipelines are always up and running in the ingest node, it's good practice to keep only the necessary pipelines in the cluster.

 The `delete pipeline` API does not allow you to use wildcards in pipeline names or IDs.

Simulating an ingest pipeline

The ingest part of every architecture is very sensitive, so the Elasticsearch team has created the possibility of simulating your pipelines without the need to store them in Elasticsearch.

The `simulate` pipeline API allows a user to test, improve, and check functionalities of your pipeline without deployment in the Elasticsearch cluster.

Getting ready

You need an up-and-running Elasticsearch installation, as we described in the *Downloading and installing Elasticsearch* recipe in Chapter 1, *Getting Started*.

To execute the commands, every HTTP client can be used, such as curl (https://curl.haxx.se/), postman (https://www.getpostman.com/), or similar. Use the Kibana console, as it provides the code completion and better character escaping for Elasticsearch.

How to do it...

To simulate an ingestion pipeline in Elasticsearch, we will perform the following steps:

1. Execute a call for passing both the pipeline and a sample subset of a document that you can test the pipeline against:

```
POST /_ingest/pipeline/_simulate
{
  "pipeline": {
    "description": "Add user john field",
    "processors": [
      {
        "set": {
          "field": "user",
          "value": "john"
        }
      },
      {
        "set": {
          "field": "job",
          "value": 10
```

```
        }
      }
    ],
    "version": 1
  },
  "docs": [
    {
      "_index": "index",
      "_type": "type",
      "_id": "1",
      "_source": {
        "name": "docs1"
      }
    },
    {
      "_index": "index",
      "_type": "type",
      "_id": "2",
      "_source": {
        "name": "docs2"
      }
    }
  ]
}
```

2. The result returned by Elasticsearch, if everything is okay, should be a list of documents with the pipeline processed:

```
{
  "docs" : [
    {
      "doc" : {
        "_index" : "index",
        "_type" : "type",
        "_id" : "1",
        "_source" : {
          "name" : "docs1",
          "job" : 10,
          "user" : "john"
        },
        "_ingest" : {
          "timestamp" : "2019-01-06T14:14:49.805621Z"
        }
      }
    },
    {
      "doc" : {
        "_index" : "index",
```

```
                    "_type" : "type",
                    "_id" : "2",
                    "_source" : {
                      "name" : "docs2",
                      "job" : 10,
                      "user" : "john"
                    },
                    "_ingest" : {
                      "timestamp" : "2019-01-06T14:14:49.805651Z"
                    }
                  }
                }
              ]
            }
```

How it works...

In a single call, the `simulated` pipeline API is able to test a pipeline on a subset of documents. It internally executes the following steps:

1. It parses the provided pipeline definition, creating an in-memory representation of the pipeline
2. It reads the provided documents by applying the pipeline
3. It returns the processed results

The only required sections are `pipeline one` and `docs` containing a list of documents. The documents (provided in `docs`) must be formatted with metadata fields and the source field, similar to a query result.

There are processors that are able to modify the metadata fields; for example, they are able to change _index or _type based on its contents. The metadata fields are _index, _type, _id, _routing, and _parent.

For debugging purposes, it is possible to add the URL query argument verbosely to return all the intermediate steps of the pipeline. For example, let's say we change the call of the previous simulation in the code:

```
POST /_ingest/pipeline/_simulate
{..truncated ...}
```

The result will be expanded for every pipeline step:

```
{
  "docs" : [
    {
      "processor_results" : [
        {
          "doc" : {
            "_index" : "index",
            "_type" : "type",
            "_id" : "1",
            "_source" : {
              "name" : "docs1",
              "user" : "john"
            },
            "_ingest" : {
              "timestamp" : "2019-01-06T14:17:46.739584Z"
            }
          }
        },
        {
          "doc" : {
            "_index" : "index",
            "_type" : "type",
            "_id" : "1",
            "_source" : {
              "name" : "docs1",
              "job" : 10,
              "user" : "john"
            },
            "_ingest" : {
              "timestamp" : "2019-01-06T14:17:46.739584Z"
            }
          }
        }
      ]
    },
    ... truncated ...
}
```

There's more...

The `simulate` pipeline API is very handy when a user needs to check a complex pipeline that uses special fields access, such as:

- **Ingest metadata fields**: These are special metadata fields, such as `_ingest.timestamp`, and are available during ingestion. This kind of field allows values to be added in the document; for example:

```
{
  "set": {
    "field": "received",
    "value": "{{_ingest.timestamp}}"
  }
}
```

- **Field replace templating**: Using the templating with `{{}}`, it's possible to inject other fields or join their values:

```
{
  "set": {
    "field": "full_name",
    "value": "{{name}} {{surname}}"
  }
}
```

The ingest metadata fields (accessible using `_ingest`) are as follows:

- `timestamp`: This contains the current pipeline timestamp.
- `on_failure_message`: This is available only in the `on_failure` block in case of failure. It contains the failure message.
- `on_failure_processor_type`: This is available only in the `on_failure` block in case of failure. It contains the failure processor type that has generated the failure.
- `on_failure_processor_tag`: This is available only in the `on_failure` block in case of failure. It contains the failure tag that has generated the failure.

Built-in processors

Elasticsearch provides a large set of ingest processors by default. Their number and functionalities can also change from minor versions to extended versions for new scenarios.

In this recipe, we will look at the most commonly used ones.

Getting ready

You need an up-and-running Elasticsearch installation, as we described in the *Downloading and installing Elasticsearch* recipe in `Chapter 1`, *Getting Started*.

To execute the commands, every HTTP client can be used, such as curl (`https://curl.haxx.se/`), postman (`https://www.getpostman.com/`), or similar. Use the Kibana console, as it provides the code completion and better character escaping for Elasticsearch.

How to do it...

To use several processors in an ingestion pipeline in Elasticsearch, we will perform the following steps:

1. Execute a `simulate` pipeline API call using several processors with a sample subset of a document that you can test the pipeline against:

```
POST /_ingest/pipeline/_simulate
{
  "pipeline": {
    "description": "Testing some build-processors",
    "processors": [
      {
        "dot_expander": {
          "field": "extfield.innerfield"
        }
      },
      {
        "remove": {
          "field": "unwanted"
        }
      },
      {
        "trim": {
```

```
                    "field": "message"
                }
            },
            {
                "set": {
                    "field": "tokens",
                    "value": "{{message}}"
                }
            },
            {
                "split": {
                    "field": "tokens",
                    "separator": "\\s+"
                }
            },
            {
                "sort": {
                    "field": "tokens",
                    "order": "desc"
                }
            },
            {
                "convert": {
                    "field": "mynumbertext",
                    "target_field": "mynumber",
                    "type": "integer"
                }
            }
        ]
    },
    "docs": [
        {
            "_index": "index",
            "_type": "type",
            "_id": "1",
            "_source": {
                "extfield.innerfield": "booo",
                "unwanted": 32243,
                "message": "155.2.124.3 GET /index.html 15442 0.038",
                "mynumbertext": "3123"
            }
        }
    ]
}
```

The result will be as follows:

```json
{
  "docs" : [
    {
      "doc" : {
        "_index" : "index",
        "_type" : "type",
        "_id" : "1",
        "_source" : {
          "mynumbertext" : "3123",
          "extfield" : {
            "innerfield" : "booo"
          },
          "tokens" : [
            "GET",
            "155.2.124.3",
            "15442",
            "0.038",
            "/index.html"
          ],
          "message" : "155.2.124.3 GET /index.html 15442
0.038",
          "mynumber" : 3123
        },
        "_ingest" : {
          "timestamp" : "2019-01-06T15:08:45.489069Z"
        }
      }
    }
  ]
}
```

How it works...

The preceding example shows how to build a complex pipeline in order to preprocess a document. There are a lot of built-in processors to cover the most common scenarios in log and text processing. More complex ones can be done using scripting.

At the time of writing this book, Elasticsearch provides built-in pipelines. The following are the most used processors:

Name	Description
Append	Appends values to a field. If required, it converts them into an array
Convert	Converts a field value into a different type
Date	Parses a date and uses it as a timestamp for the document
Date index name	Allows us to set the `_index` name based on the date field
Drop	Drops the following document without raising an error
Fail	Raises a failure
Foreach	Processes the element of an array with the provided processor
Grok	Applies `grok` pattern extraction
Gsub	Executes a regular expression `replace` on a field
Join	Joins an array of values using a separator
JSON	Converts a JSON string into a JSON object
Lowercase	Lowercases a field
Remove	Removes a field
Pipeline	Allows us to execute other pipelines
Rename	Renames a field
Script	Allows us to execute a script
Set	Sets the value of a field
Split	Splits a field in an array using regular expression
Sort	Sorts the values of an array field
Trim	Trims whitespaces from a field
Uppercase	Uppercases a field
Dot expander	Expands a field with a dot in the objects

See also

In `Chapter 16`, *Plugin Development*, we will cover how to write a custom processor in Java to extend the capabilities of Elasticsearch.

Grok processor

Elasticsearch provides a large number of built-in processors that increases with every release. In the preceding examples, we have seen the set and the replace ones. In this recipe, we will cover one that's mostly used for log analysis: the grok processor, which is well-known to Logstash users.

Getting ready

You need an up-and-running Elasticsearch installation, as we described in the *Downloading and installing Elasticsearch* recipe in Chapter 1, *Getting Started*.

To execute the commands, every HTTP client can be used, such as curl (https://curl.haxx.se/), postman (https://www.getpostman.com/), or similar. Use the Kibana console, as it provides the code completion and better character escaping for Elasticsearch.

How to do it...

To test a grok pattern against some log lines, we will perform the following steps:

1. Execute a call by passing both the pipeline with our grok processor and a sample subset of a document to test the pipeline against:

```
POST /_ingest/pipeline/_simulate
{
  "pipeline": {
    "description": "Testing grok pattern",
    "processors": [
      {
        "grok": {
          "field": "message",
          "patterns": [
            "%{IP:client} %{WORD:method}
%{URIPATHPARAM:request} %{NUMBER:bytes} %{NUMBER:duration}"
          ]
        }
      }
    ]
  },
  "docs": [
    {
```

```
        "_index": "index",
        "_type": "type",
        "_id": "1",
        "_source": {
          "message": "155.2.124.3 GET /index.html 15442 0.038"
        }
      }
    ]
  }
```

2. The result returned by Elasticsearch, if everything is okay, should be a list of documents with the pipeline processed:

```
{
  "docs" : [
    {
      "doc" : {
        "_index" : "index",
"_type" : "type",
"_id" : "1",
"_source" : {
"duration" : "0.038",
          "request" : "/index.html",
          "method" : "GET",
          "bytes" : "15442",
          "client" : "155.2.124.3",
          "message" : "155.2.124.3 GET /index.html 15442
0.038"
        },
        "_ingest" : {
          "timestamp" : "2019-01-06T15:17:02.784882Z"
        }
      }
    }
  ]
}
```

How it works...

The grok processor allows you to extract structure fields out of a single text field in a document. A grok pattern is like a regular expression that supports aliased expressions that can be reused. It was used mainly in another piece of Elastic software, Logstash, for its powerful syntax for log data extraction.

Elastisearch has about 120 built-in grok expressions (you can analyze them at `https://github.com/elastic/elasticsearch/tree/master/modules/ingest-common/src/main/resources/patterns`).

Defining a grok expression is quite simple, since the syntax is human readable. If we want to extract colors from an expression (`pattern`) and check if their value is in a subset of RED, YELLOW, and BLUE using `pattern_definitions`, we can define a similar processor:

```
POST /_ingest/pipeline/_simulate
{
  "pipeline": {
    "description": "custom grok pattern",
    "processors": [
      {
        "grok": {
          "field": "message",
          "patterns": [
            "my favorite color is %{COLOR:color}"
          ],
          "pattern_definitions": {
            "COLOR": "RED|GREEN|BLUE"
          }
        }
      }
    ]
  },
  "docs": [
    {
      "_source": {
        "message": "my favorite color is RED"
      }
    },
    {
      "_source": {
        "message": "happy fail!!"
      }
    }
  ]
}
```

The result will be as follows:

```
{
  "docs" : [
    {
```

```
      "doc" : {
        "_index" : "_index",
        "_type" : "_type",
        "_id" : "_id",
        "_source" : {
          "message" : "my favorite color is RED",
          "color" : "RED"
        },
        "_ingest" : {
          "timestamp" : "2019-01-06T15:18:53.8785Z"
        }
      }
    },
    {
      "error" : {
        "root_cause" : [
          {
            "type" : "exception",
            "reason" : "java.lang.IllegalArgumentException:
java.lang.IllegalArgumentException: Provided Grok expressions do not
match field value: [happy fail!!]",
            "header" : {
              "processor_type" : "grok"
            }
          }
        ],
        "type" : "exception",
        "reason" : "java.lang.IllegalArgumentException:
java.lang.IllegalArgumentException: Provided Grok expressions do not
match field value: [happy fail!!]",
        "caused_by" : {
          "type" : "illegal_argument_exception",
          "reason" : "java.lang.IllegalArgumentException: Provided
Grok expressions do not match field value: [happy fail!!]",
          "caused_by" : {
            "type" : "illegal_argument_exception",
            "reason" : "Provided Grok expressions do not match field
value: [happy fail!!]"
          }
        },
        "header" : {
          "processor_type" : "grok"
        }
      }
    }
  ]
}
```

In real applications, the failing grok processor exceptions will prevent your document from being indexed. For this reason, when you design your grok pattern, be sure to test it on a large subset.

See also

There are online sites where you can test your grok expressions, such as `http://grokdebug.herokuapp.com` and `http://grokconstructor.appspot.com`.

Using the ingest attachment plugin

It's easy to make a cluster non-responsive in Elasticsearch prior to 5.x, by using the attachment mapper. The metadata extraction from a document requires a very high CPU operation and if you are ingesting a lot of documents, your cluster is under-loaded.

To prevent this scenario, Elasticsearch introduces the ingest node. An ingest node can be held under very high pressure without causing problems to the rest of the Elasticsearch cluster.

The attachment processor allows us to use the document extraction capabilities of Tika in an ingest node.

Getting ready

You need an up-and-running Elasticsearch installation, as we described in the, *Downloading and installing Elasticsearch* recipe in `Chapter 1`, *Getting Started*.

To execute the commands, every HTTP client can be used, such as curl (`https://curl.haxx.se/`), postman (`https://www.getpostman.com/`), or similar. Use the Kibana console, as it provides the code completion and better character escaping for Elasticsearch.

How to do it...

To be able to use the ingest attachment processor, perform the following steps:

1. Install `ingest-attachment` as a plugin, by using the following command:

```
bi

n/elasticsearch-plugin install ingest-attachment
```

The

output will be something similar to the following:

```
-> Downloading ingest-attachment from elastic
[=========================================] 100%??
@@@@@@@@@@@@@@@@@@@@@@@@@@@@@@@@@@@@@@@@@@@@@@@@@@@@@@@@@@@@@@@@@
@@@@
 @ WARNING: plugin requires additional permissions @
@@@@@@@@@@@@@@@@@@@@@@@@@@@@@@@@@@@@@@@@@@@@@@@@@@@@@@@@@@@@@@@@@
@@@@
 * java.lang.RuntimePermission getClassLoader
 * java.lang.reflect.ReflectPermission suppressAccessChecks
 * java.security.SecurityPermission createAccessControlContext
 * java.security.SecurityPermission insertProvider
 * java.security.SecurityPermission putProviderProperty.BC
Continue with the installation? [y/n] y
-> Installed ingest-attachment
```

You must accept the security permissions to successfully complete the installation.

 See `http://docs.oracle.com/javase/8/docs/technotes/guides/ security/permissions.html`for more details on the allowed permissions and the associated risks.

2. After installing a new plugin, your node must be restarted to be able to load it. Now, you can create a pipeline ingest with the attachment processor:

```
PUT /_ingest/pipeline/attachment
{
  "description": "Extract data from an attachment via Tika",
  "processors": [
    {
      "attachment": {
```

```
          "field": "data"
        }
      }
    ],
    "version": 1
}
```

If everything is okay, you should receive the following message:

```
{
  "acknowledged" : true
}
```

3. Now, we can index a document using a pipeline:

```
PUT /my_index/my_type/my_id?pipeline=attachment
{
  "data":
"e1xydGYxXGFuc2kNCkxvcmVtIGlwc3VtIGRvbG9yIHNpdCBhbWV0DQpccGFyI
H0="
}
```

4. Now, we can recall it:

```
GET /my_index/_doc/my_id
```

The result will be as follows:

```
{
  "_index" : "my_index",
  "_type" : "_doc",
  "_id" : "my_id",
  "_version" : 1,
  "found" : true,
  "_source" : {
    "data" :
"e1xydGYxXGFuc2kNCkxvcmVtIGlwc3VtIGRvbG9yIHNpdCBhbWV0DQpccGFyI
H0=",
    "attachment" : {
      "content_type" : "application/rtf",
      "language" : "ro",
      "content" : "Lorem ipsum dolor sit amet",
      "content_length" : 28
    }
  }
}
```

How it works...

The attachment ingest processor is provided by a separate plugin that must be installed. After installing it, it works like every other processor. The properties that control it are as follows:

- `field`: This is the field that will contain the base 64 representation of the binary data.
- `target_field`: This will hold the attachment information (default `attachment`).
- `indexed_char`: This is the number of characters to be extracted to prevent very huge fields. If it is set to `-1`, all the characters are extracted (default `100000`).
- `properties`: Other metadata fields of the document that need to be extracted. They can be `content`, `title`, `name`, `author`, `keywords`, `date`, `content_type`, `content_length`, and `language` (default `all`).

Using the ingest GeoIP plugin

Another interesting processor is the GeoIP plugin that allows us to map an IP address to a GeoPoint and other location data.

Getting ready

You need an up-and-running Elasticsearch installation, as we described in the *Downloading and installing Elasticsearch* recipe in `Chapter 1`, *Getting Started*.

To execute the commands, every HTTP client can be used, such as curl (`https://curl.haxx.se/`), postman (`https://www.getpostman.com/`), or similar. Use the Kibana console, as it provides the code completion and better character escaping for Elasticsearch.

How to do it...

To be able to use the ingest GeoIP processor, perform the following steps:

1. Install the ingest GeoIP processor as a plugin using the following command:

   ```
   bin/elasticsearch-plugin install ingest-geoip
   ```

   The output will be something like the following:

   -> Downloading ingest-geoip from elastic
   [==] 100%??
   @@@
   @ WARNING: plugin requires additional permissions @
   @@@
   * java.lang.RuntimePermission accessDeclaredMembers
   See http://docs.oracle.com/javase/8/docs/technotes/guides/
   security/permissions.html
   for descriptions of what these permissions allow and the
   associated risks.
   Continue with the installation? [y/n] y.
   -> Installed ingest-geoip

   You must accept the security permissions to successfully complete the installation.

2. After installing a new plugin, your node must be restarted to be able to load it.

3. Now, you can create a pipeline ingest with the attachment processor:

   ```
   PUT /_ingest/pipeline/geoip
   {
     "description": "Extract geopoint from an IP",
     "processors": [
       {
         "geoip": {
           "field": "ip"
         }
       }
     ],
     "version": 1
   }
   ```

4. If everything is okay, you should receive the following message:

```
{
  "acknowledged" : true
}
```

5. Now, we can index a document using a pipeline:

```
PUT /my_index/_doc/my_id?pipeline=geoip
{
  "ip": "8.8.8.8"
}
```

6. Then, we can recall it:

```
GET /my_index/_doc/my_id
```

The result will be as follows:

```
{
  "_index" : "my_index",
  "_type" : "_doc",
  "_id" : "my_id",
  "_version" : 3,
  "found" : true,
  "_source" : {
    "geoip" : {
      "continent_name" : "North America",
      "country_iso_code" : "US",
      "location" : {
        "lon" : -97.822,
        "lat" : 37.751
      }
    },
    "ip" : "8.8.8.8"
  }
}
```

How it works...

The GeoIP ingest processor is provided by a separate plugin that must be installed.

It uses data from the MaxMind databases to extract information about the geographical location of IP addresses. This processor adds this information by default under the geoip field. The GeoIP processor can resolve both IPv4 and IPv6 addresses.

After installing it, it works like every other processor. The properties that control it are as follows:

- `field`: This is the field that will contain the IP from which the geo data is extracted.
- `target_field`: This will hold the `geoip` information (the default is `geoip`).
- `database_file`: This is the database file that contains maps from `ip` to geolocations. The default one is installed during the plugin's installation (default `GeoLite2-City.mmdb`).
- `properties`: The properties values depends on the database. You should refer to the database description for details on the extracted fields (the default is `all`).

See also

The official documentation about the GeoIP processor plugin and how to use it with other `GeoIP2` databases can be found at `https://www.elastic.co/guide/en/elasticsearch/plugins/master/ingest-geoip.html`.

13
Java Integration

Elasticsearch functionalities can be easily integrated in any Java application in a couple of ways: via a REST API and via native ones. In Java, it's easy to call a REST HTTP interface with one of the many of libraries available, such as the Apache HttpComponents client (see `http://hc.apache.org/` for more information). In this field, there's no such thing as the most used library; typically, developers choose the library that best suits their preferences or one that they know very well. From Elasticsearch 6.x onward, Elastic has provided a battle low/high-level HTTP for clients to use. In this chapter, we will mainly use these ones for all the examples that are provided.

Each JVM language can also use the native protocol to integrate Elasticsearch with their applications; however, we will not cover this because it has fallen out of use from Elasticsearch 7.x onward. New applications should rely on HTTP. In this chapter, we will learn how to initialize different clients and how to execute the commands that we have seen in the previous chapters. We will not cover every call in depth, as we have already described for the REST APIs. The Elasticsearch community recommends using the REST APIs when integrating them, as they are more stable between releases and are well-documented (the native one will be removed in Elasticsearch 8.x).

All the code presented in these recipes is available in this book's code repository, and can be built with Maven.

In this chapter, we will cover the following recipes:

- Creating a standard Java HTTP client
- Creating a low-level Elasticsearch client
- Creating a high-level Elasticsearch client
- Managing indices
- Managing mappings
- Managing documents

- Managing bulk actions
- Building a query
- Executing a standard search
- Executing a search with aggregations
- Executing a scroll search

Creating a standard Java HTTP client

An HTTP client is one of the easiest clients to create. It's very handy because it allows for the calling, not only of the internal methods, as the native protocol does, but also of third-party calls, implemented in plugins that can only be called via HTTP.

Getting ready

You need an up-and-running Elasticsearch installation, as we described in the *Downloading and installing Elasticsearch* recipe in Chapter 1, *Getting Started*.

To correctly execute the following commands, you will need an index populated with the ch04/populate_kibana.txt commands that are available in the online code.

A Maven tool or an IDE that natively supports it for Java programming, such as Eclipse or IntelliJ IDEA, must be installed.

The code for this recipe is in the chapter_13/http_java_client directory.

How to do it...

To create an HTTP client, we will perform the following steps:

1. For these examples, we have chosen the Apache HttpComponents library, which is one of the most widely used libraries for executing HTTP calls. This library is available in the main Maven repository called search.maven.org.

   To enable the compilation in your Maven pom.xml project, just add the following code:

   ```
   <dependency>
       <groupId>org.apache.httpcomponents</groupId>
   ```

```
        <artifactId>httpclient</artifactId>
        <version>4.5.6</version>
    </dependency>
```

2. If we want to instantiate a client and fetch a document with a `get` method, the code will look like the following:

```java
package com.packtpub;

import org.apache.http.HttpEntity;
import org.apache.http.HttpStatus;
import org.apache.http.client.methods.CloseableHttpResponse;
import org.apache.http.client.methods.HttpGet;
import org.apache.http.impl.client.CloseableHttpClient;
import org.apache.http.impl.client.HttpClients;
import org.apache.http.util.EntityUtils;

import java.io.IOException;

public class App {

    private static String wsUrl = "http://127.0.0.1:9200";


    public static void main(String[] args) {
        CloseableHttpClient client = HttpClients.custom()
                .setRetryHandler(new
MyRequestRetryHandler()).build();
        HttpGet method = new HttpGet(wsUrl +
"/mybooks/_doc/1");
        // Execute the method.

        try {
            CloseableHttpResponse response =
client.execute(method);

            if (response.getStatusLine().getStatusCode() !=
HttpStatus.SC_OK) {
                System.err.println("Method failed: " +
response.getStatusLine());
            } else {
                HttpEntity entity = response.getEntity();
                String responseBody =
EntityUtils.toString(entity);
                System.out.println(responseBody);
            }

        } catch (IOException e) {
```

```
                    System.err.println("Fatal transport error: " +
        e.getMessage());
                    e.printStackTrace();
            } finally {
                // Release the connection.
                method.releaseConnection();
            }
        }
    }
```

The result will be as follows:

```
{"_index":"mybooks","_type":"_doc","_id":"1","_version":1,"fou
nd":true,"_source":{"uuid":"11111","position":1,"title":"Joe
Tester","description":"Joe Testere nice
guy","date":"2015-10-22","price":4.3,"quantity":50}}
```

How it works...

We performed the previous steps to create and use an HTTP client. Let's look at them in a little more detail:

1. The first step is to initialize the HTTP client object. In the previous code, this is done via the following code fragment:

```
CloseableHttpClient client = HttpClients.custom()
        .setRetryHandler(new MyRequestRetryHandler()).build();
```

2. Before using the client, it is good practice to customize it. In general, the client can be modified to provide extra functionalities, such as retry support. Retry support is very important for designing robust applications; the IP network protocol is never 100% reliable, so it automatically retries an action if something goes bad (HTTP connection closed, server overhead, and so on).

3. In the previous code, we defined an `HttpRequestRetryHandler`, which monitors the execution and repeats it three times before raising an error.

4. Once we have set up the client, we can define the `call` method.

5. In the previous example, we want to execute the GET REST call. The used method will be for HttpGet and the URL will be the item named index/type/id (similar to the CURL example in the *Getting a document* recipe in Chapter 3, *Basic Operations*). To initialize the method, use the following code:

```
HttpGet method = new HttpGet(wsUrl + "/mybooks/_doc/1");
```

6. To improve the quality of our REST call, it's good practice to add extra controls to the method, such as authentication and custom headers.

7. By default, the Elasticsearch server doesn't require authentication, so we need to provide a security layer at the top of our architecture.

8. A typical scenario is using your HTTP client with the search guard plugin (https://github.com/floragunncom/search-guard) or the shield plugin, which is part of X-Pack (https://www.elastic.co/products/x-pack), which allows the Elasticsearch REST to be extended with authentication and SSL. After one of these plugins is installed and configured on the server, the following code adds a host entry that allows the credentials to be provided only if context calls are targeting that host.

9. The authentication is simply basicAuth, but works very well for noncomplex deployments, as you can see in the following code:

```
HttpHost targetHost = new HttpHost("localhost", 9200, "http");
CredentialsProvider credsProvider = new
BasicCredentialsProvider();

credsProvider.setCredentials(
        new AuthScope(targetHost.getHostName(),
targetHost.getPort()),
        new UsernamePasswordCredentials("username",
"password"));
// Create AuthCache instance

AuthCache authCache = new BasicAuthCache();

// Generate BASIC scheme object and add it to local auth cache

BasicScheme basicAuth = new BasicScheme();
authCache.put(targetHost, basicAuth);
```

10. The create `context` must be used in executing the call, as shown in the following code:

```
// Add AuthCache to the execution context
HttpClientContext context = HttpClientContext.create();
context.setCredentialsProvider(credsProvider);
```

11. Custom headers allow us to pass extra information to the server to execute a call. Some examples could be API keys or hints about supported formats.

12. A typical example is using `gzip` data compression over HTTP to reduce bandwidth usage. To do that, we can add a custom header to the call informing the server that our client accepts encoding. An example custom header can be made from the phrases `Accept-Encoding` and `gzip`, as shown in the following code:

```
request.addHeader("Accept-Encoding", "gzip");
```

13. After configuring the call with all the parameters, we can fire up the request as follows:

```
response = client.execute(method, context);
```

14. Every response object must be validated on its return status: if the call is `OK`, the return status should be `200`. In the previous code, the check is done in the `if` statement, as follows:

```
if (response.getStatusLine().getStatusCode() !=
HttpStatus.SC_OK)
```

15. If the call was `OK` and the status code of the response is `200`, we can read the answer, as follows:

```
HttpEntity entity = response.getEntity();
String responseBody = EntityUtils.toString(entity);
```

The response is wrapped in `HttpEntity`, which is a stream.

The HTTP client library provides a helper method called `EntityUtils.toString` that reads all the content of `HttpEntity` as a string; otherwise, we'd need to create some code to read from the string and build the string.

Obviously, all the read parts of the call are wrapped in a `try-catch` block to collect all possible errors created by networking errors.

See also

You can refer to the following URLs for further reference, which are related to this recipe:

- The Apache `HttpComponents` library at `http://hc.apache.org/` for a complete reference and more examples about this library
- The search guard plugin to provide authenticated Elasticsearch access at `https://github.com/floragunncom/search-guard` or the Elasticsearch official shield plugin at `https://www.elastic.co/products/x-pack`
- The *Getting a document* recipe in `Chapter 3`, *Basic Operations*, which covers the API call that was used in these examples

Creating an HTTP Elasticsearch client

With Elasticsearch 6.x, the Elasticsearch team has provided a custom low-level HTTP client to communicate with Elasticsearch. Its main features are as follows:

- Minimal dependencies
- Load balancing across all available nodes
- Failover in the case of node failures and upon specific response codes
- Failed connection penalization (whether a failed node is retried depends on how many consecutive times it failed; the more failed attempts, the longer the client will wait before trying that same node again)
- Persistent connections
- Trace logging of requests and responses
- Optional automatic discovery of cluster nodes

Getting ready

You need an up-and-running Elasticsearch installation, which can be obtained as described in the *Downloading and installing Elasticsearch* recipe in `Chapter 1`, *Getting Started*.

To correctly execute the following commands, you will need an index populated with the `ch04/populate_kibana.txt` commands that are available in the online code.

A Maven tool or an IDE that natively supports it for Java programming, such as Eclipse or IntelliJ IDEA, must be installed.

The code for this recipe is in the `ch13/http_es_client` directory.

How to do it...

For creating `RestClient`, we will perform the following steps:

1. For these examples, we need to add the Elasticsearch HTTP client library that's used to execute HTTP calls. This library is available in the main Maven repository at `search.maven.org`. To enable compilation in your `Maven pom.xml` project, just add the following code:

```
<dependency>
    <groupId>org.elasticsearch.client</groupId>
    <artifactId>elasticsearch-rest-client</artifactId>
    <version>7.0.0-alpha2</version>
</dependency>
```

2. If we want to instantiate a client and fetch a document with a `get` method, the code will look like the following:

```
package com.packtpub;

import org.apache.http.HttpEntity;
import org.apache.http.HttpHost;
import org.apache.http.HttpStatus;
import org.apache.http.util.EntityUtils;
import org.elasticsearch.client.Request;
import org.elasticsearch.client.Response;
import org.elasticsearch.client.RestClient;

import java.io.IOException;

public class App {

    public static void main(String[] args) {
        RestClient client = RestClient.builder(
                new HttpHost("localhost", 9200,
"http")).build();
```

```
        try {
            Request request=new Request("GET",
"/mybooks/_doc/1");
            Response response =
client.performRequest(request);

            if (response.getStatusLine().getStatusCode() !=
HttpStatus.SC_OK) {
                System.err.println("Method failed: " +
response.getStatusLine());
            } else {
                HttpEntity entity = response.getEntity();
                String responseBody =
EntityUtils.toString(entity);
                System.out.println(responseBody);
            }

        } catch (IOException e) {
            System.err.println("Fatal transport error: " +
e.getMessage());
            e.printStackTrace();
        } finally {
            // Release the connection.
            try {
                client.close();
            } catch (IOException e) {
                e.printStackTrace();
            }
        }
    }
}
```

The result will be as follows:

```
{"_index":"mybooks","_type":"_doc","_id":"1","_version":1,"fou
nd":true,"_source":{"uuid":"11111","position":1,"title":"Joe
Tester","description":"Joe Testere nice
guy","date":"2015-10-22","price":4.3,"quantity":50}}
```

How it works...

Internally, the Elasticsearch RestClient uses the Apache HttpComponents library and wraps it with more convenient methods.

We performed the previous steps to create and use a `RestClient`. Let's look at them in a little more detail:

1. The first step is to initialize the `RestClient` object.
2. In the previous code, this is done via the following code fragment:

    ```
    RestClient client = RestClient.builder(
            new HttpHost("localhost", 9200, "http")).build();
    ```

3. The `builder` method accepts a multivalue `HttpHost` (in this way, you can pass a list of HTTP addresses) and returns `RestClientBuilder` under the hood.
4. The `RestClientBuilder` allows client communication to be customized by several methods, such as the following:

    -   `setDefaultHeaders(Header[] defaultHeaders)`: This allows the custom headers that must be sent for every request to be provided.
    -   `setMaxRetryTimeoutMillis(int maxRetryTimeoutMillis)`: This allows the max retry timeout to be defined if there are multiple attempts for the same request.
    -   `setPathPrefix(String pathPrefix)`: This allows a custom path prefix to be defined for every request.
    -   `setFailureListener(FailureListener failureListener)`: This allows a custom failure listener to be provided, which is called in an instance of node failure. This can be used to provide user-defined behavior in the case of node failure.
    -   `setHttpClientConfigCallback(RestClientBuilder.HttpClientConfigCallback httpClientConfigCallback)`: This allows the modification of the HTTP client communication, such as adding compression or an encryption layer.
    -   `setRequestConfigCallback(RestClientBuilder.RequestConfigCallback requestConfigCallback)`: This allows the configuration of request authentications, timeouts, and other properties that can be set at a request level.

5. After creating the `RestClient`, we can execute some requests against it via the several kinds of `performRequest` for synchronous calls and `performRequestAsync` methods for asynchronous ones.

6. These methods allow you to set parameters, such as the following:
    - `String method`: This is the HTTP method or verb to be used in the call (required).
    - `String endpoint`: This is the API endpoint (required). In the previous example, it is `/test-index/test-type/1`.
    - `Map<String, String> params`: This is a map of values to be passed as query parameters.
    - `HttpEntity entity`: This is the body of the request. It's a `org/apache/http/HttpEntity` (see `http://hc.apache.org/httpcomponents-core-ga/httpcore/apidocs/org/apache/http/HttpEntity.html?is-external=true` for more details).
    - `HttpAsyncResponseConsumer<HttpResponse> responseConsumer`: This is used to manage responses in an asynchronous request (see `http://hc.apache.org/httpcomponents-core-ga/httpcore-nio/apidocs/org/apache/http/nio/protocol/HttpAsyncResponseConsumer.html` for more details). By default, it's used to keep all the responses in heap memory (the top memory limit is 100 MB).
    - `ResponseListener responseListener`: This is used to register callbacks during asynchronous calls.
    - `Header... headers`: These are additional headers passed during the call.

7. In the previous example, we executed the GET REST call with the following code:

```
Request request=new Request("GET", "/mybooks/_doc/1");
Response response = client.performRequest(request);
```

8. The response object is an `org.elasticsearch.client.Response` that wraps the Apache `HttpComponents` response; for this reason, the code to manage the response is the same as it was in the previous recipe.

 The `RestClient` is a low-level one; it has no helpers on build queries or actions. For now, using it consists of building the JSON string of the request and then parsing the JSON response string.

See also

You can refer to the following URLs for further reference, which are related to this recipe:

- The official documentation about the RestClient at `https://www.elastic.co/guide/en/elasticsearch/client/java-rest/current/index.html` for more usage examples and more about the Sniffer extension at `https://www.elastic.co/guide/en/elasticsearch/client/java-rest/current/sniffer.html` to support node discovery
- The Apache HttpComponents library at `http://hc.apache.org/` for a complete reference and more examples about this library
- The *Getting a document* recipe in `Chapter 3`, *Basic Operations*, which covers the API call used in these examples.

Creating a high-level REST client

A Java high-level REST client is built on top of low-level ones and provides automatic marshaling of requests and responses.

Initially released with ElasticSearch 6.x, this client depends on main Elasticsearch libraries to provide many extra functionalities, such as the following:

- JSON support
- Request/response marshaling/unmarshaling that provides stronger typed programming
- Support for both synchronous and asynchronous calls

Getting ready

You need an up-and-running Elasticsearch installation, as we described in the *Downloading and installing Elasticsearch* recipe in `Chapter 1`, *Getting Started*.

To correctly execute the following commands, you will need an index populated with the `ch04/populate_kibana.txt` commands available in the online code.

A Maven tool or an IDE that natively supports it for Java programming, such as Eclipse or IntelliJ IDEA, must be installed

The code for this recipe is in the `ch13/high-level-client` directory.

How to do it...

To create a native client, we will perform the following steps:

1. Before starting, we must be sure that Maven loads the Elasticsearch JAR by adding the following lines to the `pom.xml`:

```
<dependency>
    <groupId>org.elasticsearch.client</groupId>
    <artifactId>elasticsearch-rest-high-level-
client</artifactId>
    <version>7.0.0-alpha2</version>
</dependency>
```

 I always suggest using the latest available release of Elasticsearch or, in the case of a connection to a specific cluster, using the same version of Elasticsearch that the cluster is using. Native clients only work well if the client and the server have the same Elasticsearch version.

2. Now, there are two ways to create a client.

The first is to get the client from the transport protocol, which is the simplest way to get an Elasticsearch client. We can do this using the following code:

```
import org.apache.http.HttpHost;
import org.elasticsearch.client.RestClient;
import org.elasticsearch.client.RestHighLevelClient;

// on startup
RestHighLevelClient client= new RestHighLevelClient(
        RestClient.builder(
                new HttpHost("localhost", 9200, "http"),
                new HttpHost("localhost", 9201, "http")));

// on shutdown
//we need to close the client to free resources high-level-
client.close();
```

How it works...

Let's look at the steps to create the `RestHighLevelClient` in a little more detail:

1. In your Maven `pom.xml`, the transport plugin must be defined as follows:

```
<dependency>
    <groupId>org.elasticsearch.client</groupId>
    <artifactId>elasticsearch-rest-high-level-
client</artifactId>
    <version>7.0.0-alpha1</version>
</dependency>
```

2. We can create one or more instances of `HttpHost` that contain the addresses and ports of the nodes of our cluster, as follows:

```
HttpHost httpHost = new HttpHost("localhost", 9200, "http")
```

3. A `RestClientBuilder` must be provided with all the required `HttpHost` elements, as follows:

```
RestClientBuilder restClient = RestClient.builder(httpHost);
```

4. Now a `RestHighLevelClient` can be initialized with the `RestClient`, as shown in the following code:

```
RestHighLevelClient client = new
RestHighLevelClient(restClient);
```

5. At the end, before closing the application, we need to free the resource that is needed by the node; this can be done by calling the `close()` method on the `client`, as shown in the following code:

```
client.close();
```

See also

The official Elasticsearch documentation about *RestHighLevelClient* at `https://www.elastic.co/guide/en/elasticsearch/client/java-api/current/transport-client.html`

Managing indices

In the previous recipe, we learned how to initialize a client to send calls to an Elasticsearch cluster. In this recipe, we will learn how to manage indices via client calls.

Getting ready

You need an up-and-running Elasticsearch installation, which we described how to get in the *Downloading and installing Elasticsearch* recipe in `Chapter 1`, *Getting Started*.

A Maven tool or an IDE that natively supports it for Java programming, such as Eclipse or IntelliJ IDEA, must be installed.

The code for this recipe is in the `ch13/high-level-client` directory and the referred class is `IndicesOperations`.

How to do it...

An Elasticsearch client maps all index operations under the `indices` object of the client, such as `create`, `delete`, `exists`, `open`, `close`, and `optimize`.The following steps retrieve a client and execute the main operations on the indices:

1. First, we import the required classes, as shown in the following code:

```
import
org.elasticsearch.action.admin.indices.close.CloseIndexRequest
;
import
org.elasticsearch.action.admin.indices.create.CreateIndexReque
st;
import
org.elasticsearch.action.admin.indices.delete.DeleteIndexReque
st;
import
org.elasticsearch.action.admin.indices.get.GetIndexRequest;
import
org.elasticsearch.action.admin.indices.mapping.put.PutMappingR
equest;
import
org.elasticsearch.action.admin.indices.open.OpenIndexRequest;
import org.elasticsearch.client.RequestOptions;
import org.elasticsearch.client.RestHighLevelClient;
```

2. Then, we define an `IndicesOperations` class that manages the index operations, as shown in the following code:

```
public class IndicesOperations {
    private final RestHighLevelClient client;

    public IndicesOperations(RestHighLevelClient client) {
        this.client = client;
    }
```

3. Next, we define a function that is used to check whether the index is there, as shown in the following code:

```
public boolean checkIndexExists(String name) throws
IOException {
    return client.indices().exists(new
GetIndexRequest().indices(name), RequestOptions.DEFAULT);
}
```

4. Then, we define a function that can be used to create an index, as shown in the following code:

```
public void createIndex(String name) throws IOException {
    client.indices().create(new CreateIndexRequest(name),
RequestOptions.DEFAULT);
}
```

5. We then define a function that can be used to delete an index, as follows:

```
public void deleteIndex(String name) throws IOException {
    client.indices().delete(new DeleteIndexRequest(name),
RequestOptions.DEFAULT);
}
```

6. Then, we define a function that can be used to close an index, as follows:

```
public void closeIndex(String name) throws IOException {
    client.indices().close(new
CloseIndexRequest().indices(name), RequestOptions.DEFAULT);
}
```

7. Next, we define a function that can be used to open an index, as follows:

```
public void openIndex(String name) throws IOException {
    client.indices().open(new
OpenIndexRequest().indices(name), RequestOptions.DEFAULT);
}
```

8. Then, we test all the previously defined functions, as follows:

```
public static void main(String[] args) throws
InterruptedException, IOException {
    RestHighLevelClientHelper nativeClient = new
RestHighLevelClientHelper();
    RestHighLevelClient client = nativeClient.getClient();
    IndicesOperations io = new IndicesOperations(client);
    String myIndex = "test";
    if (io.checkIndexExists(myIndex))
        io.deleteIndex(myIndex);
    io.createIndex(myIndex);
    Thread.sleep(1000);
    io.closeIndex(myIndex);
    io.openIndex(myIndex);
    io.deleteIndex(myIndex);

    //we need to close the client to free resources
    nativeClient.close();

}
```

How it works...

Before executing every index operation, a client must be available (we saw how to create one in the previous recipe).

The client has a lot of methods grouped by functionalities, as shown in the following list:

- In the root `client.*`, we have record-related operations, such as index, deletion of records, search, and update
- Under `indices.*`, we have index-related methods, such as create index, delete index, and so on
- Under `cluster.*`, we have cluster-related methods, such as state and health

Client methods usually follow the following conventions:

- Methods that end with an `Async` postfix (such as `createAsync`) require a build request and optional action listener.
- Methods that do not end with `Async` require a request and some instances of `RequestOption` to execute the call in a synchronous way.

In the previous example, we have several index calls, as shown in the following list:

- The method call to check the existence if the is `exists`. It takes a `GetIndexRequest` element and returns a `boolean`, which contains information about whether the index exists, as shown in the following code:

```
return client.indices().exists(new
GetIndexRequest().indices(name), RequestOptions.DEFAULT);
```

- You can create an index with the `create` call, as follows:

```
client.indices().create(new CreateIndexRequest(name),
RequestOptions.DEFAULT);
```

- You can close an index with the `close` call, as follows:

```
client.indices().close(new CloseIndexRequest().indices(name),
RequestOptions.DEFAULT);
```

- You can open an index with the `open` call, as follows:

```
client.indices().open(new OpenIndexRequest().indices(name),
RequestOptions.DEFAULT);
```

- You can delete an index with the `delete` call, as follows:

```
client.indices().delete(new DeleteIndexRequest(name),
RequestOptions.DEFAULT);
```

 We have put a delay of 1 second (`Thread.wait(1000)`) in the code to prevent fast actions on indices because their shard allocations are asynchronous, and they requires a few milliseconds to be ready. The best practice is to not use a similar hack, but to poll an index's state before you perform further operations, and to only perform those operations when it goes green.

See also

You can refer to the following URLs for further reference, which are related to this recipe:

- The *Creating an index* recipe in `Chapter 3`, *Basic Operations*, for details on index creation
- The *Deleting an index* recipe in `Chapter 3`, *Basic Operations*, for details on index deletion
- The *Opening/closing an index* recipe in `Chapter 3`, *Basic Operations*, for the description of opening/closing index APIs

Managing mappings

After creating an index, the next step is to add some mappings to it. We have already seen how to add a mapping via the REST API in `Chapter 3`, *Basic Operations*. In this recipe, we will look at how to manage mappings via a native client.

Getting ready

You need an up-and-running Elasticsearch installation, which we described how to get in the *Downloading and installing Elasticsearch* recipe in `Chapter 1`, *Getting Started*.

A Maven tool or an IDE that natively supports it for Java programming, such as Eclipse or IntelliJ IDEA, must be installed.

The code for this recipe is in the `ch13/high-level-client` directory and the referred class is `MappingOperations`.

How to do it...

In the following steps, we add a `mytype` mapping to a `myindex` index via the native client:

1. Import the required classes using the following code:

   ```
   import
   org.elasticsearch.action.admin.indices.mapping.put.PutMappingR
   equest;
   ```

```
import
org.elasticsearch.action.support.master.AcknowledgedResponse;
import org.elasticsearch.client.RequestOptions;
import org.elasticsearch.client.RestHighLevelClient;
import org.elasticsearch.common.xcontent.XContentBuilder;

import java.io.IOException;
import java.net.UnknownHostException;

import static
org.elasticsearch.common.xcontent.XContentFactory.jsonBuilder;
```

2. Define a class to contain our code and to initialize `client` and `index`, as follows:

```
public class MappingOperations {

    public static void main(String[] args) {
        String index = "mytest";
        String type = "mytype";
        RestHighLevelClient client =
RestHighLevelClientHelper.createHighLevelClient();
        IndicesOperations io = new IndicesOperations(client);
        try {
            if (io.checkIndexExists(index))
                io.deleteIndex(index);
            io.createIndex(index);
```

3. Prepare the JSON mapping to put in the index, as follows:

```
XContentBuilder builder = null;
try {
    builder = jsonBuilder().
            startObject().
            field("type1").
            startObject().
            field("properties").
            startObject().
            field("nested1").
            startObject().
            field("type").
            value("nested").
            endObject().
            endObject().
            endObject().
            endObject();
```

4. Put the mapping in `index`, as follows:

```
    AcknowledgedResponse response = client.indices()
            .putMapping(new
PutMappingRequest(index).type(type).source(builder),
RequestOptions.DEFAULT);
    if (!response.isAcknowledged()) {
        System.out.println("Something strange happens");
    }
} catch (IOException e) {
    System.out.println("Unable to create mapping");
}
```

5. We remove `index`, as follows:

```
    io.deleteIndex(index);
```

6. Now, we can close the client to free up resources, as follows:

```
} finally {

    //we need to close the client to free resources
    try {
        client.close();
    } catch (IOException e) {
        e.printStackTrace();
    }
}
```

How it works...

Before executing a mapping operation, a client must be available and the index must be created.

In the previous example, if the index exists, it's deleted and a new one is recreated, so we are sure that we are starting from scratch. This can be seen in the following code:

```
RestHighLevelClient client =
RestHighLevelClientHelper.createHighLevelClient();
IndicesOperations io = new IndicesOperations(client);
try {
    if (io.checkIndexExists(index))
        io.deleteIndex(index);
    io.createIndex(index);
```

Now, we have a fresh `index` to put the mapping that we need in order to create it. The mapping, as with every standard object in Elasticsearch, is a JSON object. Elasticsearch provides a convenient way to create JSON programmatically via `XContentBuilder.jsonBuilder`.

To use this, you need to add the following imports to your Java file:

```
import org.elasticsearch.common.xcontent.XContentBuilder;
import static
org.elasticsearch.common.xcontent.XContentFactory.jsonBuilder;
```

The `XContentBuilder.jsonBuilder` method allows JSON to be built programmatically, since it's the Swiss Army knife of JSON generation in Elasticsearch because of its ability to be chained, and it has a lot of methods. These methods always return a builder, so they can be easily chained. The most important ones are as follows:

- `startObject()` and `startObject(name)`: Here, `name` is the name of the JSON object. It starts the definition of a JSON object. The object must be closed with an `endObject()`.
- `field(name)` or `field(name, value)`: The `name` must always be a string, and the `value` must be a valid value that can be converted to JSON. It's used to define a field in a JSON object.
- `value(value)`: The `value` in parentheses must be a valid value that can be converted into JSON. It defines a single value in a field.
- `startArray ()` and `startArray(name)`: Here, `name` is the name of the JSON array. It starts the definition of a JSON array and must be ended with an `endArray()`.

Generally, in Elasticsearch, every method that accepts a JSON object as a parameter also accepts a JSON builder.

Now that we have the mapping in the builder, we need to call the `Put` mapping API. This API is in the `client.indices()` namespace, and you need to define the index, the type, and the mapping to execute this call, as follows:

```
AcknowledgedResponse response = client.indices()
        .putMapping(new
PutMappingRequest(index).type(type).source(builder),
RequestOptions.DEFAULT);
```

If everything is okay, you can check the status in the `response.isAcknowledged()` that must be `true` (Boolean value); otherwise, an error is raised.

If you need to update a mapping, then you must execute the same call, but you should only put the fields that you need to add in the mapping .

There's more...

There is another important call that is used to manage the mapping—the `Get` mapping API. The call is like `delete`, and returns a `GetMappingResponse`:

```
GetMappingsResponse resp = client.indices().getMapping(new
GetMappingsRequest().indices(index), RequestOptions.DEFAULT);
```

The `response` contains the mapping information. The data that's returned is structured as it would be in an index map; it contains mapping as the name and `MappingMetaData`.

The `MappingMetaData` is an object that contains all the mapping information and all the sections that we discussed in `Chapter 3`, *Basic Operations*.

See also

You can refer to the following URLs for further reference, which are related to this recipe:

- The *Putting a mapping in an index* recipe in `Chapter 3`, *Basic Operations*, for more details about the `Put` mapping API
- The *Getting a mapping* recipe in `Chapter 3`, *Basic Operations*, for more details about the `Get` mapping API

Managing documents

The native APIs for managing documents (`index`, `delete`, and `update`) are the most important after the search APIs. In this recipe, we will learn how to use them. In the next recipe, we will proceed to bulk actions to improve performance.

Getting ready

You need an up-and-running Elasticsearch installation, which we described how to get in the *Downloading and installing Elasticsearch* recipe in `Chapter 1`, *Getting Started*.

A Maven tool, or an IDE that natively supports it for Java programming such as Eclipse or IntelliJ IDEA, must be installed.

The code for this recipe is in the `ch13/high-level-client` directory and the referred class is `DocumentOperations`.

How to do it...

For managing documents, we will perform the following steps:

1. We'll need to import the required classes to execute all the document CRUD operations via the high-level client, as follows:

```
import
org.elasticsearch.action.admin.indices.create.CreateIndexReque
st;
import org.elasticsearch.action.delete.DeleteRequest;
import org.elasticsearch.action.delete.DeleteResponse;
import org.elasticsearch.action.get.GetRequest;
import org.elasticsearch.action.get.GetResponse;
import org.elasticsearch.action.index.IndexRequest;
import org.elasticsearch.action.index.IndexResponse;
import org.elasticsearch.action.update.UpdateRequest;
import org.elasticsearch.action.update.UpdateResponse;
import org.elasticsearch.client.RequestOptions;
import org.elasticsearch.client.RestHighLevelClient;
import org.elasticsearch.common.xcontent.XContentFactory;
import org.elasticsearch.script.Script;

import java.io.IOException;
```

2. The following code will create the client and remove the index that contains our data, if it exists:

```
public class DocumentOperations {

    public static void main(String[] args) {
        String index = "mytest";
        String type = "mytype";
        RestHighLevelClient client =
```

```
RestHighLevelClientHelper.createHighLevelClient();
        IndicesOperations io = new IndicesOperations(client);
        try {
            if (io.checkIndexExists(index))
                io.deleteIndex(index);
```

3. We will call the create `index` by providing the required mapping, as follows:

```
try {
    client.indices().create(
            new CreateIndexRequest()
                    .index(index)
                    .mapping(type,
XContentFactory.jsonBuilder()
                            .startObject()
                            .startObject(type)
                            .startObject("properties")
                            .startObject("text").field("type",
"text").field("store", "yes").endObject()
                            .endObject()
                            .endObject()
                            .endObject()),
            RequestOptions.DEFAULT
    );
} catch (IOException e) {
    System.out.println("Unable to create mapping");
}
```

4. Now, we can store a document in Elasticsearch via the `index` call, as follows:

```
IndexResponse ir = client.index(new IndexRequest(index, type,
"2").source("text", "unicorn"), RequestOptions.DEFAULT);
System.out.println("Version: " + ir.getVersion());
```

5. Let's retrieve the stored document via the `get` call, as follows:

```
GetResponse gr = client.get(new GetRequest(index, type, "2"),
RequestOptions.DEFAULT);
System.out.println("Version: " + gr.getVersion());
```

6. We can update the stored document via the `update` call using a script in `painless`, as follows:

```
UpdateResponse ur = client.update(new UpdateRequest(index,
type, "2").script(new Script("ctx._source.text = 'v2'")),
RequestOptions.DEFAULT);
System.out.println("Version: " + ur.getVersion());
```

7. We can delete the stored document via the `delete` call, as follows:

```
DeleteResponse dr = client.delete(new DeleteRequest(index,
type, "2"), RequestOptions.DEFAULT);
```

8. We can now free up the resources that were used, as follows:

```
        io.deleteIndex(index);
} catch (IOException e) {
    e.printStackTrace();
} finally {

    //we need to close the client to free resources
    try {
        client.close();
    } catch (IOException e) {
        e.printStackTrace();
    }
}
```

9. The console output result will be as follows:

```
Version: 1
Version: 1
Version: 2
```

10. The document version, after an update action and if the document is reindexed with new changes, is always incremented by `1`.

How it works...

Before executing a document action, the client and the index must be available and document mapping should be created (the mapping is optional because it can be inferred from the indexed document).

To index a document via the native client, the `index` method is created. It requires the index and the type as arguments. If an ID is provided, it will be used; otherwise, a new one will be created.

In the previous example, we put the source in the form of a key and value, but many forms are available to pass as the source. They are as follows:

- A JSON string, such as `{"field": "value"}`
- A string and a value (from one up to four couples), such as `field1, value1, field2,` or `value2, field3, value3, field4, value4`
- A builder, such as `jsonBuilder().startObject().field(field,value).endObject()`
- A byte array

Obviously, it's possible to add all the parameters that we looked at in the *Indexing a document* recipe in `Chapter 3`, *Basic Operations*, such as `parent`, `routing`, and so on. In the previous example, the call was as follows:

```
IndexResponse ir = client.index(new IndexRequest(index, type,
"2").source("text", "unicorn"), RequestOptions.DEFAULT);
```

The `IndexResponse` return value can be used in the following ways:

- To check whether the index was successful
- To get the ID of the indexed document, if it was not provided during the index action
- To retrieve the document version

To retrieve a document, you need to know the index/type/ID. The client method is `get`. It requires the usual triplet (`index`, `type`, `id`), but a lot of other methods are available to control the routing (such as `souring` and `parent`) or the fields that we have saw in the *Getting a document* recipe in `Chapter 3`, *Basic Operations*. In the previous example, the call is as follows:

```
GetResponse gr = client.get(new GetRequest(index, type, "2"),
RequestOptions.DEFAULT);
```

The `GetResponse` return type contains all the requests (if the document exists) and document information (`source`, `version`, `index`, `type`, and `id`).

To update a document, you need to know the index/type/ID and provide a script or a document to be used for the update. The client method is `update`.

In the previous example, there is the following:

```
UpdateResponse ur = client.update(new UpdateRequest(index, type,
"2").script(new Script("ctx._source.text = 'v2'")),
RequestOptions.DEFAULT);
```

The script code must be a string. If the script language is not defined, the default `painless` method is used.

The returned response contains information about the execution and the new version value to manage concurrency.

To delete a document (without needing to execute a query), we need to know the index/type/ID triple, and we can use the `delete` client method to create a delete request. In the previous code, we used the following:

```
DeleteResponse dr = client.delete(new DeleteRequest(index, type, "2"),
RequestOptions.DEFAULT);
```

The delete request allows all the parameters to be passed to it that we saw in the *Deleting a document* recipe in `Chapter 3`, *Basic Operations*, to control the routing and version.

See also

In our recipes, we have used all the CRUD operations on a document. For more details about these actions, refer to the following:

- The *Indexing a document* recipe in `Chapter 3`, *Basic Operations*, for information on how to index a document
- The *Getting a document* recipe in `Chapter 3`, *Basic Operations*, for information on how to retrieve a stored document
- The *Deleting a document* recipe in `Chapter 3`, *Basic Operations*, for information on how to delete a document
- The *Updating a document* recipe in `Chapter 3`, *Basic Operations*, for information on how to update a document

Managing bulk actions

Executing automatic operations on items via a single call will often be the cause of a bottleneck if you need to index or delete thousands/millions of records. The best practice in this case is to execute a bulk action.

We have discussed bulk actions via the REST API in the *Speeding up atomic operations (bulk)* recipe in `Chapter 3`, *Basic Operations*.

Getting ready

You need an up-and-running Elasticsearch installation, which you can get using the *Downloading and installing Elasticsearch* recipe in `Chapter 1`, *Getting Started*.

A Maven tool or an IDE that natively supports it for Java programming, such as Eclipse or IntelliJ IDEA, must be installed.

The code of this recipe is in the `ch13/high-level-client` directory and the referred class is `BulkOperations`.

How to do it...

To manage a bulk action, we will perform these steps:

1. We'll need to import the required classes to execute bulk actions via the high-level `client`, as follows:

```
import
org.elasticsearch.action.admin.indices.create.CreateIndexReque
st;
import org.elasticsearch.action.bulk.BulkRequest;
import org.elasticsearch.action.delete.DeleteRequest;
import org.elasticsearch.action.index.IndexRequest;
import org.elasticsearch.action.update.UpdateRequest;
import org.elasticsearch.client.RequestOptions;
import org.elasticsearch.client.RestHighLevelClient;
import org.elasticsearch.common.xcontent.XContentFactory;
import org.elasticsearch.script.Script;

import java.io.IOException;
```

2. Next, we'll create the `client`, remove the old index if it exists, and create a new one, as follows:

```
public class BulkOperations {

    public static void main(String[] args) {
        String index = "mytest";
        String type = "mytype";
        RestHighLevelClient client =
RestHighLevelClientHelper.createHighLevelClient();
        IndicesOperations io = new IndicesOperations(client);
        try {
            if (io.checkIndexExists(index))
                io.deleteIndex(index);
            try {
                client.indices().create(
                        new CreateIndexRequest()
                                .index(index)
                                .mapping(type,
XContentFactory.jsonBuilder()
                                        .startObject()
                                        .startObject(type)
.startObject("properties")
.startObject("position").field("type",
"integer").field("store", "yes").endObject()
                                        .endObject()
                                        .endObject()
                                        .endObject()),
                        RequestOptions.DEFAULT);
                ;
            } catch (IOException e) {
                System.out.println("Unable to create
mapping");
            }
```

3. Now, we can bulk index 1000 documents, adding the bulk `index` actions to the `bulker`, as follows:

```
BulkRequest bulker = new BulkRequest();
for (int i = 1; i < 1000; i++) {
    bulker.add(new IndexRequest(index, type,
Integer.toString(i)).source("position", Integer.toString(i)));
}
System.out.println("Number of actions for index: " +
bulker.numberOfActions());

client.bulk(bulker, RequestOptions.DEFAULT);
```

4. We can bulk update the previously created 1000 documents via a script, adding the bulk update action to the `bulker`, as follows:

```
bulker = new BulkRequest();
for (int i = 1; i <= 1000; i++) {
    bulker.add(new UpdateRequest(index, type,
Integer.toString(i)).script(new Script("ctx._source.position
+= 2")));
}
System.out.println("Number of actions for update: " +
bulker.numberOfActions());
client.bulk(bulker, RequestOptions.DEFAULT);
```

5. We can bulk delete 1000 documents, adding the bulk delete actions to the `bulker`, as follows:

```
bulker = new BulkRequest();
for (int i = 1; i <= 1000; i++) {
    bulker.add(new DeleteRequest(index, type,
Integer.toString(i)));
}
System.out.println("Number of actions for delete: " +
bulker.numberOfActions());
client.bulk(bulker, RequestOptions.DEFAULT);
```

6. We can now free up the resources that were used, as follows:

```
        io.deleteIndex(index);
} catch (IOException e) {
    e.printStackTrace();
} finally {
    //we need to close the client to free resources
    try {
        client.close();
    } catch (IOException e) {
        e.printStackTrace();
    }
}
```

7. The result will be as follows:

```
Number of actions for index: 1000
Number of actions for update: 1000
Number of actions for delete: 1000
```

How it works...

Before executing these bulk actions, a client must be available and an index must be created. I you wish, you can also create document mapping.

We can consider `BulkRequest` as a collector of the following different actions:

- `IndexRequest`
- `UpdateRequest`
- `DeleteRequest`
- A bulk-formatted array of bytes

Generally, when used in code, we can consider it as a `List` in which we add the actions of the supported types. Let's go through the following steps:

1. To initialize `bulkBuilder`, we use the following code:

   ```
   BulkRequest bulker = new BulkRequest();
   ```

2. In the previous example, we added 1,000 index actions, as follows:

   ```
   for (int i = 1; i < 1000; i++) {
       bulker.add(new IndexRequest(index, type,
   Integer.toString(i)).source("position", Integer.toString(i)));
   }
   ```

3. After adding all the actions, we can print (for example) the number of actions and then execute them, as follows:

   ```
   System.out.println("Number of actions for index: " +
   bulker.numberOfActions());
   client.bulk(bulker, RequestOptions.DEFAULT);
   ```

4. We have populated the bulk with 1,000 update actions, as follows:

   ```
   bulker = new BulkRequest();
   for (int i = 1; i <= 1000; i++) {
       bulker.add(new UpdateRequest(index, type,
   Integer.toString(i)).script(new Script("ctx._source.position
   += 2")));
   }
   ```

5. After adding all the update actions, we can execute them in bulk using `bulker.execute().actionGet();`, as follows:

```
System.out.println("Number of actions for update: " +
bulker.numberOfActions());
client.bulk(bulker, RequestOptions.DEFAULT);
```

6. Next, the same step is performed with the delete action, as follows:

```
bulker = new BulkRequest();
for (int i = 1; i <= 1000; i++) {
    bulker.add(new DeleteRequest(index, type,
Integer.toString(i)));
}
```

7. To commit the delete, we need to execute the bulk, as follows:

```
client.bulk(bulker, RequestOptions.DEFAULT);
```

 In this example, to simplify it, I created bulk actions with the same type of actions, but, as I described previously, you can put any supported type of action into the same bulk operation.

Building a query

Before a search, a query must be built. Elasticsearch provides several ways to build these queries. In this recipe, we will learn how to create a query object via `QueryBuilder` and simple strings.

Getting ready

You need an up-and-running Elasticsearch installation, which you can get as described in the *Downloading and installing Elasticsearch* recipe in Chapter 1, *Getting Started*.

A Maven tool or an IDE that natively supports it for Java programming, such as Eclipse or IntelliJ IDEA, must be installed.

The code for this recipe is in the `ch13/high-level-client` directory and the referred class is `QueryCreation`.

How to do it...

To create a query, we will perform the following steps:

1. We need to import the `QueryBuilders` using the following code:

    ```
    import static org.elasticsearch.index.query.QueryBuilders.*;
    ```

2. Next, we'll create a query using `QueryBuilder`, as follows:

    ```
    TermQueryBuilder filter = termQuery("number2", 1);
    RangeQueryBuilder range = rangeQuery("number1").gt(500);
    BoolQueryBuilder query =
    boolQuery().must(range).filter(filter);
    SearchSourceBuilder searchSourceBuilder = new
    SearchSourceBuilder();
    searchSourceBuilder.query(query);
    SearchRequest searchRequest = new
    SearchRequest().indices(index).source(searchSourceBuilder);
    ```

3. Now, we can execute a search, as follows (searching via a native API will be discussed in the following recipes):

    ```
    SearchResponse response = client.search(searchRequest,
    RequestOptions.DEFAULT);
    System.out.println("Matched records of elements: " +
    response.getHits().getTotalHits());
    ```

4. I've removed the redundant parts that are similar to the example of the previous recipe. The result will be as follows:

    ```
    Matched records of elements: 250
    ```

How it works...

There are several ways to define a query in Elasticsearch.

Generally, a query can be defined as the following:

*   `QueryBuilder`: A helper to build a query.
*   `XContentBuilder`: A helper to create JSON code. We discussed this in the *Managing mapping* recipe in this chapter. The JSON code to be generated is similar to the previous REST, but is converted into programmatic code.

- `Array of Bytes` or `String`: In this case, it's usually the JSON to be executed, as we have seen in REST calls.
- `Map`: This contains the query and the value of the query.

In the previous example, we created a query via `QueryBuilders`. The first step is to import the `QueryBuilder` from the namespace, as follows:

```
import static org.elasticsearch.index.query.QueryBuilders.*;
```

The query of the example is a Boolean query with a `termQuery` as a filter. The goal of the example is to show how to mix several query types to create a complex query.

We need to define a filter, as shown in the following code. In this case, we have used a term query, which is one of the most used kinds of query:

```
TermQueryBuilder filter = termQuery("number2", 1);
```

The `termQuery` accepts a field and a value, which must be a valid Elasticsearch type.

The previous code is similar to the JSON REST `{"term": {"number2":1}`.

The Boolean query contains a `must` clause with a `range` query. We can start to create the `range` query as follows:

```
RangeQueryBuilder range = rangeQuery("number1").gt(500);
```

This `range` query matches all the values that are greater than or equal to (`gte`) 500 in the `number1` field.

After creating the `range` query, we can add it to a Boolean query in the `must` block and the `filter` query in the `filter` block, as follows:

```
BoolQueryBuilder query = boolQuery().must(range).filter(filter);
```

In real-world complex queries, you can have a lot of nested queries in a Boolean query or filter.

Before executing a query, the index must be refreshed so that you don't miss any results.

In our example, this is done using the following code:

```
client.indices().refresh(new RefreshRequest(index),
RequestOptions.DEFAULT);
```

There's more...

The possible native queries/filters are the same as REST ones, and have the same parameters: the only difference is that they are accessible via builder methods.

The most common query builders are as follows:

- `matchAllQuery`: This allows all the documents to be matched
- `matchQuery` and `matchPhraseQuery`: These are used to match against text strings
- `termQuery` and `termsQuery`: These are used to match a term value(s) against a specific field
- `boolQuery`: This is used to aggregate other queries with Boolean logic
- `idsQuery`: This is used to match a list of IDs
- `fieldQuery`: This is used to match a field with text
- `wildcardQuery`: This is used to match terms with wildcards (*?.)
- `regexpQuery`: This is used to match terms via a regular expression
- Span query family (`spanTermsQuery`, `spanTermQuery`, `spanORQuery`, `spanNotQuery`, `spanFirstQuery`, and so on): These are a few examples of the span query family, which are used in building span queries
- `hasChildQuery`, `hasParentQuery`, and `nestedQuery`: These are used to manage related documents

The previous list is not exhaustive, because it will constantly evolve throughout the life of Elasticsearch. New query types will be added to cover new search cases, or they are occasionally renamed, such as text query changing to match query.

Executing a standard search

In the previous recipe, we learned how to build queries. In this recipe, we will execute a query to retrieve some documents.

Getting ready

You need an up-and-running Elasticsearch installation, as we described in the *Downloading and installing Elasticsearch* recipe in Chapter 1, *Getting Started*.

A Maven tool or an IDE that natively supports it for Java programming, such as Eclipse or IntelliJ IDEA, must be installed.

The code for this recipe is in the `ch13/high-level-client` directory and the referred class is the `QueryExample`.

How to do it...

To execute a standard query, we will perform the following steps:

1. We need to import `QueryBuilders` to create the query, as follows:

```
import static org.elasticsearch.index.query.QueryBuilders.*;
```

2. We can create an `index` and populate it with some data, as follows:

```
String index = "mytest";
String type = "mytype";
QueryHelper qh = new QueryHelper();
qh.populateData(index, type);
RestHighLevelClient client = qh.getClient();
```

3. Now, we will build a query with the `number1` field greater than or equal to `500` and filter it for `number2` equal to 1, as follows:

```
QueryBuilder query =
boolQuery().must(rangeQuery("number1").gte(500)).filter(termQu
ery("number2", 1));
```

4. After creating a query, it is enough to execute it using the following code:

```
SearchSourceBuilder searchSourceBuilder = new
SearchSourceBuilder();
searchSourceBuilder.query(query).highlighter(new
HighlightBuilder().field("name"));
SearchRequest searchRequest = new
SearchRequest().indices(index).source(searchSourceBuilder);
SearchResponse response = client.search(searchRequest,
RequestOptions.DEFAULT);
```

5. When we have `SearchResponse`, we need to check its status and iterate it on `SearchHit`, as follows:

```
if (response.status().getStatus() == 200) {
    System.out.println("Matched number of documents: " +
response.getHits().getTotalHits());
```

```
        System.out.println("Maximum score: " +
    response.getHits().getMaxScore());

        for (SearchHit hit : response.getHits().getHits()) {
            System.out.println("hit: " + hit.getIndex() + ":" +
    hit.getType() + ":" + hit.getId());
        }
    }
```

6. The result should be similar to the following:

```
Number of actions for index: 999
Matched number of documents: 999
Maximum score: 1.0
hit: mytest:mytype:499
hit: mytest:mytype:501
hit: mytest:mytype:503
hit: mytest:mytype:505
hit: mytest:mytype:507
hit: mytest:mytype:509
hit: mytest:mytype:511
hit: mytest:mytype:513
hit: mytest:mytype:515
hit: mytest:mytype:517
```

How it works...

The call to execute a search is prepareSearch, which returns a SearchResponse, as follows:

```
import org.elasticsearch.action.search.SearchResponse;

SearchSourceBuilder searchSourceBuilder = new SearchSourceBuilder();
searchSourceBuilder.query(query).highlighter(new
HighlightBuilder().field("name"));

SearchResponse response = client.search(searchRequest,
RequestOptions.DEFAULT);
```

The SearchSourceBuilder has a lot of methods that can set of all the parameters that we have already seen in the *Executing a search* recipe in Chapter 4, *Exploring Search Capabilities*. The most used ones are as follows:

- indices: This allows the indices to be defined.
- query: This allows the query that is to be executed to be set.

- `storedField`/`storedFields`: These allow setting fields to be returned (used to reduce the bandwidth by returning only the needed fields).
- `aggregation`: This allows us to compute any added aggregations.
- `highlighter`: This allows us to return any added highlighting.
- `scriptField`: This allows a scripted field to be returned. A scripted field is a field that is computed by server-side scripting using one of the available scripting languages. For example, it can be as follows:

```
Map<String, Object> params = MapBuilder.<String,
Object>newMapBuilder().put("factor", 2.0).map();
.scriptField("sNum1", new Script("_doc.num1.value * factor", params))
```

After executing a search, a response object is returned.

It's good practice to check whether the search has been successful by checking the returned status, and optionally the number of hits. If the search was executed correctly, the return status will be 200, as shown in the following code:

```
if (response.status().getStatus() == 200) {
```

The response object contains a lot of sections that we analyzed in the *Executing a search* recipe in `Chapter 4`, *Exploring Search Capabilities*. The most important one is the hits section that contains our results. The main accessor methods of this section are as follows:

- `totalHits`: This allows the total number of results to be obtained, as shown in the following code:

```
System.out.println("Matched number of documents: " +
response.getHits().getTotalHits());
```

- `maxScore`: This gives the maximum score for the documents. It is the same score value of the first `SearchHit`, as shown in the following code:

```
System.out.println("Maximum score: " +
response.getHits().getMaxScore());
```

- `hits`: This is an array of `SearchHit`, which contains the results, if available.

The `SearchHit` is the result object. It has a lot of methods, of which the most important ones are as follows:

- `getIndex()`: This is the index that contains the document.
- `getId()`: This is the ID of the document.
- `getScore()`: This is the query score of the document, if available.
- `getVersion()`: This is the version of the document, if available.
- `getSource()`, `getSourceAsString()`, `getSourceAsMap()`, and so on: These return the source of the document in different forms, if available.
- `getExplanation()`: If available (required in the search), this contains the query explanation.
- `getFields`, `getField(String name)`: These return the fields that were requested if they were passed fields to search for an object.
- `getSortValues()`: This is the value/values that are used to sort this record. It's only available if `sort` is specified during the search phase.
- `getShard()`: This is the shard of the search hit. This value is very important for custom routing.

In the preceding example, we have printed only the index, type, and ID of each hit, as shown in the following code:

```
for (SearchHit hit : response.getHits().getHits()) {
    System.out.println("hit: " + hit.getIndex() + ":" + hit.getType()
+ ":" + hit.getId());
}
```

The number of returned hits, if not defined, is limited to 10. To retrieve more hits, you need to define a larger value in the `size` method or paginate using the `from` method.

See also

The *Executing a search* recipe in `Chapter 4`, *Exploring Search Capabilities*

Executing a search with aggregations

The previous recipe can be extended to support aggregations in order to retrieve analytics on indexed data.

Getting ready

You need an up-and-running Elasticsearch installation, which you can get as described in the *Downloading and installing Elasticsearch* recipe in `Chapter 1`, *Getting Started*.

A Maven tool or an IDE that natively supports it for Java programming, such as Eclipse or IntelliJ IDEA, must be installed.

The code for this recipe is in the `ch13/high-level-client` directory and the referred class is `AggregationExample`.

How to do it...

To execute a search with aggregations, we will perform the following steps:

1. We need to import the necessary classes for the aggregations using the following code:

```
import
org.elasticsearch.search.aggregations.AggregationBuilder;
import
org.elasticsearch.search.aggregations.bucket.terms.Terms;
import
org.elasticsearch.search.aggregations.metrics.ExtendedStats;
import
org.elasticsearch.search.aggregations.metrics.ExtendedStatsAgg
regationBuilder;
import org.elasticsearch.search.builder.SearchSourceBuilder;
import static
org.elasticsearch.index.query.QueryBuilders.matchAllQuery;
import static
org.elasticsearch.search.aggregations.AggregationBuilders.*;
```

2. We can create an index and populate it with some data that we will use for the aggregations, as follows:

```
String index = "mytest";
String type = "mytype";
QueryHelper qh = new QueryHelper();
qh.populateData(index, type);
RestHighLevelClient client = qh.getClient();
```

3. We then calculate two different aggregations (terms and extended statistics), as shown in the following code::

```
AggregationBuilder aggsBuilder = terms("tag").field("tag");
ExtendedStatsAggregationBuilder aggsBuilder2 =
extendedStats("number1").field("number1");
```

4. Now, we can execute a search, and pass the aggregations using the following code. We use `size(0)` because we don't need the hits:

```
SearchSourceBuilder searchSourceBuilder = new
SearchSourceBuilder();
searchSourceBuilder.query(matchAllQuery()).aggregation(aggsBui
lder).
        aggregation(aggsBuilder2).size(0);
SearchRequest searchRequest = new
SearchRequest().indices(index).source(searchSourceBuilder);
SearchResponse response = client.search(searchRequest,
RequestOptions.DEFAULT);
```

5. We need to check the response validity and wrap the aggregation results, as shown in the following code:

```
if (response.status().getStatus() == 200) {
    System.out.println("Matched number of documents: " +
response.getHits().getTotalHits());
    Terms termsAggs = response.getAggregations().get("tag");
    System.out.println("Aggregation name: " +
termsAggs.getName());
    System.out.println("Aggregation total: " +
termsAggs.getBuckets().size());
    for (Terms.Bucket entry : termsAggs.getBuckets()) {
        System.out.println(" - " + entry.getKey() + " " +
entry.getDocCount());
    }
    ExtendedStats extStats =
response.getAggregations().get("number1");
    System.out.println("Aggregation name: " +
extStats.getName());
    System.out.println("Count: " + extStats.getCount());
    System.out.println("Min: " + extStats.getMin());
    System.out.println("Max: " + extStats.getMax());
    System.out.println("Standard Deviation: " +
extStats.getStdDeviation());
    System.out.println("Sum of Squares: " +
extStats.getSumOfSquares());
    System.out.println("Variance: " + extStats.getVariance());
}
```

6. The result should be as follows:

```
Matched number of documents: 1000
Aggregation name: tag
Aggregation total: 4
- bad 264
- amazing 246
- cool 245
- nice 245
Aggregation name: number1
Count: 1000
Min: 2.0
Max: 1001.0
Standard Deviation: 288.6749902572095
Sum of Squares: 3.348355E8
Variance: 83333.25
```

How it works...

The search part is similar to the previous example. In this case, we have used a matchAllQuery, which matches all the documents.

To execute an aggregation, first you need to create it. There are three ways to do so:

- Using a string that maps a JSON object
- Using a XContentBuilder, which will be used to produce a JSON object
- Using a AggregationBuilder

The first two ways are trivial; the third one needs the builders to be imported, as follows:

```
import static
org.elasticsearch.search.aggregations.AggregationBuilders.*;
```

There are several types of aggregation, as we have already seen in Chapter 5, *Text and Numeric Queries*.

The first one, which we created with AggregationBuilder, is a Terms aggregation, which collects and counts all terms occurrences in buckets, as shown in the following code:

```
AggregationBuilder aggsBuilder = terms("tag").field("tag");
```

The required value for every aggregation is the name, which is passed in the builder constructor. In the case of a `terms` aggregation, the field is required to be able to process the request. There are a lot of other parameters; see the *Executing terms aggregations* recipe in `Chapter 7`, *Aggregations*, for full details.

The second `aggregationBuilder` that we created is an extended statistical aggregation based on the `number1` numeric field, as follows:

```
ExtendedStatsAggregationBuilder aggsBuilder2 =
extendedStats("number1").field("number1");
```

Now that we have created `aggregationBuilders`, we can add them on a `SearchSourceBuilder` object via the `aggregation` method, as follows:

```
SearchSourceBuilder searchSourceBuilder = new SearchSourceBuilder();
searchSourceBuilder.query(matchAllQuery()).aggregation(aggsBuilder).
        aggregation(aggsBuilder2).size(0);
SearchRequest searchRequest = new
SearchRequest().indices(index).source(searchSourceBuilder);
SearchResponse response = client.search(searchRequest,
RequestOptions.DEFAULT);
```

Now, the response holds information about our aggregations. To access them, we need to use the `getAggregations` method of the response.

The aggregation's results are contained in a hash-like structure, and you can retrieve them with the names that you have previously defined in the request.

To retrieve the first aggregation results, we need to get them, as follows:

```
Terms termsAggs = response.getAggregations().get("tag");
```

Now that we have an aggregation result of type `Terms` (see the *Executing terms aggregations* recipe in `Chapter 7`, *Aggregations*), we can get the aggregation properties and iterate in buckets, as follows:

```
System.out.println("Aggregation name: " + termsAggs.getName());
System.out.println("Aggregation total: " +
termsAggs.getBuckets().size());
for (Terms.Bucket entry : termsAggs.getBuckets()) {
    System.out.println(" - " + entry.getKey() + " " +
entry.getDocCount());
}
```

To retrieve the second aggregation result, because the result is of type `ExtendedStats`, you need to cast to it, as shown in the following code:

```
ExtendedStats extStats = response.getAggregations().get("number1");
```

Now, you can access the result properties of this kind of aggregation, as follows:

```
System.out.println("Aggregation name: " + extStats.getName());
System.out.println("Count: " + extStats.getCount());
System.out.println("Min: " + extStats.getMin());
System.out.println("Max: " + extStats.getMax());
System.out.println("Standard Deviation: " +
extStats.getStdDeviation());
System.out.println("Sum of Squares: " + extStats.getSumOfSquares());
System.out.println("Variance: " + extStats.getVariance());
```

 Using aggregations with a native client is quite easy, and you need only pay attention to the returned aggregation type to execute the correct type cast to access your results.

See also

You can refer to the following URLs for further reference, which are related to this recipe:

- The *Executing terms aggregations* recipe in `Chapter 7`, *Aggregations*, which describes the `terms` aggregation in depth
- The *Executing statistical aggregations* recipe in `Chapter 7`, *Aggregations* for more details about statistical aggregations

Executing a scroll search

Pagination with a standard query works very well if you are matching documents with documents that do not change too often; otherwise, performing pagination with live data returns unpredictable results. To bypass this problem, Elasticsearch provides an extra parameter in the query: `scroll`.

Getting ready

You need an up-and-running Elasticsearch installation, which you can get as described in the *Downloading and installing Elasticsearch* recipe in Chapter 1, *Getting Started*.

A Maven tool, or an IDE that natively supports it for Java programming such as Eclipse or IntelliJ IDEA, installed.

The code for this recipe is in the ch13/high-level-client directory and the referred class is ScrollQueryExample.

How to do it...

The search is done as it was shown in the *Execute a standard search* recipe. The main difference is the use of a setScroll timeout, which allows the resulting IDs to be stored in memory for a query for a defined period of time. The steps are like those that are used for a standard search, as you can see from the following steps:

1. We import the TimeValue object to define time in a more human way, as follows:

```
import org.elasticsearch.common.unit.TimeValue;
```

2. We execute the search by setting the scroll value. We can change the code of the *Execute a standard search* recipe to use scroll in the following way:

```
SearchSourceBuilder searchSourceBuilder = new
SearchSourceBuilder();
searchSourceBuilder.query(query).size(30);
SearchRequest searchRequest = new SearchRequest()
        .indices(index).source(searchSourceBuilder)
        .scroll(TimeValue.timeValueMinutes(2));
```

3. To manage the scrolling, we need to create a loop until the results are returned, as follows:

```
SearchResponse response = client.search(searchRequest,
RequestOptions.DEFAULT);

do {
    for (SearchHit hit : response.getHits().getHits()) {
        System.out.println("hit: " + hit.getIndex() + ":" +
hit.getType() + ":" + hit.getId());
```

```
        }
        response = client.scroll(new
SearchScrollRequest(response.getScrollId()).scroll(TimeValue.t
imeValueMinutes(2)), RequestOptions.DEFAULT);
        } while (response.getHits().getHits().length != 0); // Zero
hits mark the end of the scroll and the while loop.
```

4. The loop will iterate on all the results until records are available. The
   output will be similar to the following:

```
hit: mytest:mytype:499
hit: mytest:mytype:531
hit: mytest:mytype:533
hit: mytest:mytype:535
hit: mytest:mytype:555
hit: mytest:mytype:559
hit: mytest:mytype:571
hit: mytest:mytype:575
...truncated...
```

How it works...

To use the scrolling result, it's enough to add a `scroll` method with a timeout to the
`SearchRequest` object.

When using scrolling, the following behaviors must be kept in mind:

- The timeout defines the period of time that an Elasticsearch server keeps
  the results for. If you ask for a scroll after the timeout, the server returns an
  error. The user must be careful with short timeouts.
- The scroll consumes memory until it ends or a timeout is raised. Setting too
  large a timeout without consuming the data results in a big memory
  overhead. Using a large number of open scrollers consumes a lot of
  memory proportional to the number of IDs and their related data (score,
  order, and so on) in the results.
- With scrolling, it's not possible to paginate the documents as there is no
  start. Scrolling is designed to fetch consecutive results.

A standard `SearchRequest` is changed to a scroll in the following way:

```
SearchRequest searchRequest = new SearchRequest()
        .indices(index).source(searchSourceBuilder)
        .scroll(TimeValue.timeValueMinutes(2));
```

The response contains the same results as the standard search, plus a scroll ID, which is required to fetch the next set of results.

To execute the scroll, you need to call the `scroll` client method with a scroll ID and a new timeout. In this example, we are processing all the result documents, as shown in the following code:

```
do {
    // Process hits
    response = client.scroll(new
SearchScrollRequest(response.getScrollId()).scroll(TimeValue.timeValue
Minutes(2)), RequestOptions.DEFAULT);
} while (response.getHits().getHits().length != 0); // Zero hits mark
the end of the scroll and the while loop.
```

To understand that we are at the end of the scroll, we can check that no results are returned.

There are a lot of scenarios in which `scroll` is very important, but when working on big data solutions when the number of results is very large, it's easy to hit the timeout. In these scenarios, it is important to have good architecture in which you fetch the results as fast as possible and don't process the results iteratively in the loop but defer the manipulation result in a distributed way.

In this case, the best solution is to use the `search_after` functionality of Elasticsearch, sorting by `_uid`, as described in the *Using search_after functionality* recipe in `Chapter 4`, *Exploring Search Capabilities*.

See also

You can refer to the following URLs for further reference, which are related to this recipe:

- The *Executing a scroll query* recipe in `Chapter 4`, *Exploring Search Capabilities*
- The *Using search_after functionality* recipe in `Chapter 4`, *Exploring Search Capabilities*

Integrating with DeepLearning4j

DeepLearning4J (DL4J) is one of the most used opensource library in machine learning. It can be found at `https://deeplearning4j.org/`.

The best description for this library is available on its website, which says—*Deeplearning4j is the first commercial-grade, open-source, distributed deep learning library written for Java and Scala. Integrated with Hadoop and Apache Spark, DL4J brings AI to business environments for use on distributed GPUs and CPUs.*

In this recipe, we will see how it's possible to use Elasticsearch as a source for data to be trained in a machine learning algorithm.

Getting ready

You need an up and running Elasticsearch installation, as we described in the *Downloading and installing Elasticsearch* recipe in `Chapter 1`, *Getting Started*.

A Maven tool, or an IDE that natively supports Java programming, such as Eclipse or IntelliJ IDEA must be installed.

The code for this recipe is in the `ch13/deeplearning4j` directory.

How to do it...

We will use the famous `iris` dataset (`https://en.wikipedia.org/wiki/Iris_flower_data_set`) well known to every data scientist for creating an index with the data to be used in training the deep learning model.

To prepare your index dataset, we need to populate it by executing the `PopulatingIndex` class available in the source code. The `PopulatingIndex` class reads the `iris.txt` file and stores the rows of dataset with the following object format:

Field Name	Type	Description
f1	float	Feature 1 of the flower
f2	float	Feature 2 of the flower
f3	float	Feature 3 of the flower
f4	float	Feature 4 of the flower
label	int	Label of the Flower (valid values 0,1,2)

To use DL4J as a source data input for your models, you will perform the following steps:

1. Add the various DL4J dependencies to `pom.xml` of the Maven project:

```
<dependency>
    <groupId>org.nd4j</groupId>
    <artifactId>nd4j-native-platform</artifactId>
    <version>${nd4j.version}</version>
</dependency>

<!-- ND4J backend. You need one in every DL4J project.
Normally define artifactId as either "nd4j-native-platform" or
"nd4j-cuda-9.2-platform" -->
<dependency>
    <groupId>org.nd4j</groupId>
    <artifactId>${nd4j.backend}</artifactId>
    <version>${nd4j.version}</version>
</dependency>

<!-- Core DL4J functionality -->
<dependency>
    <groupId>org.deeplearning4j</groupId>
    <artifactId>deeplearning4j-core</artifactId>
    <version>${dl4j.version}</version>
</dependency>
```

2. Now we can write our `ElasticSearchD4J` class to train and test our model. As the first step, we need to initialize the Elasticsearch client:

```
HttpHost httpHost = new HttpHost("localhost", 9200, "http");
RestClientBuilder restClient = RestClient.builder(httpHost);
RestHighLevelClient client = new
RestHighLevelClient(restClient);
String indexName="iris";
```

3. After having the client, we can read our dataset. We will execute a query and collect the `Hit` results using a simple search:

```
SearchResponse searchResult=client.search(new
SearchRequest(indexName).source(SearchSourceBuilder.searchSour
ce().size(1000)), RequestOptions.DEFAULT);

SearchHit[] hits=searchResult.getHits().getHits();
```

4. We need to convert the hits in a DL4J dataset. We will do this by creating intermediate arrays and populating them:

```
//Convert the iris data into 150x4 matrix
int row=150;
int col=4;
double[][] irisMatrix=new double[row][col];
//Now do the same for the label data
int colLabel=3;
double[][] labelMatrix=new double[row][colLabel];

for(int r=0; r<row; r++){
    // we populate features
    Map<String, Object> source=hits[r].getSourceAsMap();
    irisMatrix[r][0]=(double)source.get("f1");
    irisMatrix[r][1]=(double)source.get("f2");
    irisMatrix[r][2]=(double)source.get("f3");
    irisMatrix[r][3]=(double)source.get("f4");
    // we populate labels
    int label=(Integer) source.get("label");
    labelMatrix[r][0]=0.0;
    labelMatrix[r][1]=0.0;
    labelMatrix[r][2]=0.0;
    if(label == 0) labelMatrix[r][0]=1.0;
    if(label == 1) labelMatrix[r][1]=1.0;
    if(label == 2) labelMatrix[r][2]=1.0;
}
//Check the array by printing it in the log
//Convert the data matrices into training INDArrays
INDArray training = Nd4j.create(irisMatrix);
INDArray labels = Nd4j.create(labelMatrix);

DataSet allData = new DataSet(training, labels);
```

5. Then, split the datasets into two—one for training and one for tests. After having them, we need to normalize the values. These actions can be done with the following code:

```
allData.shuffle();
SplitTestAndTrain testAndTrain =
allData.splitTestAndTrain(0.65); //Use 65% of data for
training

DataSet trainingData = testAndTrain.getTrain();
DataSet testData = testAndTrain.getTest();

//We need to normalize our data. We'll use
NormalizeStandardize (which gives us mean 0, unit variance):
```

```
DataNormalization normalizer = new NormalizerStandardize();
normalizer.fit(trainingData); //Collect the statistics
(mean/stdev) from the training data. This does not modify the
input data
normalizer.transform(trainingData); //Apply normalization to
the training data
normalizer.transform(testData); //Apply normalization to the
test data. This is using statistics calculated from the
*training* set
```

6. Now we can design the model to be used for the training:

```
final int numInputs = 4;
int outputNum = 3;
long seed = 6;
MultiLayerConfiguration conf = new
NeuralNetConfiguration.Builder()
        .seed(seed)
        .activation(Activation.TANH)
        .weightInit(WeightInit.XAVIER)
        .updater(new Sgd(0.1))
        .l2(1e-4)
        .list()
        .layer(0, new
DenseLayer.Builder().nIn(numInputs).nOut(3)
                .build())
        .layer(1, new DenseLayer.Builder().nIn(3).nOut(3)
                .build())
        .layer(2, new
OutputLayer.Builder(LossFunctions.LossFunction.NEGATIVELOGLIKE
LIHOOD)
                .activation(Activation.SOFTMAX)
                .nIn(3).nOut(outputNum).build())
        .backprop(true).pretrain(false)
        .build();
```

7. After having defined the model, we can finally train it with our dataset—we use 1000 iterations for the training. The training code is as follows:

```
MultiLayerNetwork model = new MultiLayerNetwork(conf);
model.init();
model.setListeners(new ScoreIterationListener(100));

for(int i=0; i<1000; i++ ) {
    model.fit(trainingData);
}
```

8. Now that we have a trained model, we need to evaluate its accuracy and we can do that using the test dataset:

```
Evaluation eval = new Evaluation(3);
INDArray output = model.output(testData.getFeatures());
eval.eval(testData.getLabels(), output);
log.info(eval.stats());
```

If you execute the model training, the output will be something similar as follows:

```
14:17:24.684 [main] INFO com.packtpub.ElasticSearchD4J -

========================Evaluation Metrics========================
 # of classes: 3
 Accuracy: 0.9811
 Precision: 0.9778
 Recall: 0.9833
 F1 Score: 0.9800
Precision, recall & F1: macro-averaged (equally weighted avg. of 3
classes)


========================Confusion Matrix========================
  0 1 2
 ----------
 19 0 0 | 0 = 0
  0 19 1 | 1 = 1
  0 0 14 | 2 = 2

Confusion matrix format: Actual (rowClass) predicted as (columnClass)
N times
==================================================================
```

How it works...

Eclipse Deeplearning4j is a deep learning programming library written for Java and the **Java Virtual Machine (JVM)**. It includes implementations of the restricted Boltzmann machine, deep belief net, deep autoencoder, stacked denoising autoencoder, and recursive neural tensor networks such as word2vec, doc2vec, and GloVe. These algorithms all include distributed parallel versions that integrate with Apache Hadoop and Spark.

DL4J is able to use both CPU and GPU to process deep learning workloads fast.

In the preceding example, we have stored out dataset in Elasticsearch and fetched it to build the DL4J dataset. Using Elasticsearch as dataset storage is very handy, because you can use the power of Elasticsearch to analyze, to clean it, and to filter the data before giving them to a machine learning algorithm.

The dataset was shuffled (`allData.shuffle();`) to provide a less bias on the training and test datasets. In this case, we have chosen a three layers deep learning model and we have trained the model with the data taken by Elasticsearch, iterating the training 1000 times. The result was a neural network model with accuracy of 0.98.

This example is every simple, but it shows how it's easy to use Elasticsearch as a data source for machine learning jobs. DL4J is a wonderful library that can be used outside Elasticsearch or can be embedded in a plugin to provide machine learning capabilities to Elasticsearch.

See also

You can refer to the following URLs for further reference, which are related to this recipe:

- The official site of DeepLearning4J (`https://deeplearning4j.org/`) for more example and references about this powerful library.
- A more detailed description of Iris dataset (`https://en.wikipedia.org/wiki/Iris_flower_data_set`)

14
Scala Integration

Scala is becoming one of the most used languages in big data scenarios. This language provides a lot of facilities for managing data, such as immutability and functional programming.

In Scala, you can simply use the libraries we saw in the previous chapter for Java, but they are not scalastic as they don't provide type safety (because many of these libraries take a JSON as a string) and it is easy to use asynchronous programming.

In this chapter, we will look at how to use **elastic4s**, a mature library, to use Elasticsearch in Scala. Its main features are as follows:

- Type-safe, concise DSL
- Integrates with standard Scala futures
- Uses the Scala collections library over Java collections
- Returns option where the Java methods would return `null`
- Uses Scala durations instead of strings/longs for time values
- Uses typeclass for marshalling and unmarshalling classes to/from Elasticsearch documents, and is backed by Jackson, Circe, Json4s, and PlayJson implementations
- Provides reactive-streams implementation
- Provides embedded nodes and testkit sub-projects, which are ideal for your tests

In this chapter, we will mainly see examples about standard elastic4s DSL usage and some helpers such as the `circe` extension for the easy marshalling/unmarshalling of documents in classes.

In this chapter, we will cover the following recipes:

- Creating a client in Scala
- Managing indices

- Managing mappings
- Managing documents
- Executing a standard search
- Executing a search with aggregations

Creating a client in Scala

The first step for working with elastic4s is to create a connection client to call ElasticSearch. Similar to Java, the connection client is native and can be a node or a transport one.

Similar to Java, the connection client can be both a native one and a HTTP one. In this recipe, we'll initialize an HTTP client because it can be put behind a proxy/balancer to increase the high availablity of your solution. This is good practice.

Getting ready

You need an up-and-running Elasticsearch installation, as we described in the *Downloading and installing Elasticsearch* recipe in `Chapter 1`, *Getting Started*.

An IDE that supports Scala programming, such as IntelliJ IDEA, with the Scala plugin should be installed globally.

The code for this recipe can be found in the `chapter_14/elastic4s_sample` directory and the reference file is `ClientSample.scala`.

How to do it...

To create an Elasticsearch client and for create/search a document, we will perform the following steps:

1. The first step is to add the `elastic4s` library to the `build.sbt` configuration via the following code:

```
libraryDependencies ++= {
  val elastic4sV = "7.0.0"
  val scalaTestV = "3.0.5"
  val Log4jVersion = "2.11.1"
  Seq(
```

```
      "com.sksamuel.elastic4s" %% "elastic4s-core" % elastic4sV,
      "com.sksamuel.elastic4s" %% "elastic4s-circe" %
elastic4sV,
      // for the http client
      "com.sksamuel.elastic4s" %% "elastic4s-http" % elastic4sV,

      // if you want to use reactive streams
      "com.sksamuel.elastic4s" %% "elastic4s-http-streams" %
elastic4sV,

      // testing
      "com.sksamuel.elastic4s" %% "elastic4s-testkit" %
elastic4sV % "test",
      "com.sksamuel.elastic4s" %% "elastic4s-embedded" %
elastic4sV % "test",
      "org.apache.logging.log4j" % "log4j-api" % Log4jVersion,
      "org.apache.logging.log4j" % "log4j-core" % Log4jVersion,
      "org.apache.logging.log4j" % "log4j-1.2-api" %
Log4jVersion,
      "org.scalatest" %% "scalatest" % scalaTestV % "test"
    )
}

resolvers ++= Seq(
  Resolver.sonatypeRepo("releases"),
  Resolver.jcenterRepo
)
```

2. To use the library, we need to import client classes and implicits:

```
import com.sksamuel.elastic4s.http.ElasticDsl._
import com.sksamuel.elastic4s.http.{ElasticClient,
ElasticProperties}
```

3. Now, we can initialize the client, by providing an Elasticsearch URI:

```
object ClientSample extends App {
  val client =
ElasticClient(ElasticProperties("http://127.0.0.1:9200"))
```

4. To index a document, we execute `indexInto` with the document in the following way:

```
client.execute {
  indexInto("bands" / "artists") fields "name" -> "coldplay"
}.await

Thread.sleep(2000)  //to be sure that the record is indexed
```

5. Now, we can search for the document we indexed earlier:

```
// now we can search for the document we indexed earlier
val resp = client.execute {
  search("bands") query "coldplay"
}.await
println(resp)
```

The result, if the document is available, will be as follows:

```
RichSearchResponse({"took":2,"timed_out":false,"_shards":{"tot
al":5,"successful":5,"failed":0},"hits":{"total":1,"max_score"
:0.2876821,"hits":[{"_index":"bands","_type":"artists","_id":"
AViBXXEWXe9IuvJzw-
HT","_score":0.2876821,"_source":{"name":"coldplay"}}]}})
```

How it works...

Elastic4s hides a lot of the boilerplate required for initializing an Elasticsearch client.

The simpler way to define a connection to Elasticsearch is via `ElasticProperties`, and this allows you to provide the following:

- Multiple server endpoints, separated by commas (that is, `http(s)://host:port,host:port(/prefix)?querystring`)
- The other settings to be provided to the client via a Map[String,String] (that is, `?cluster.name=elasticsearch`)

After having defined `ElasticProperties`, you can create `ElasticClient`, which is used for every Elasticsearch call.

You can initialize `ElasticClient` in several ways. We suggest the following:

- via `ElasticProperties`, which accepts a string similar to a JDBC connection. It is very handy because you can store it as a simple string in your application configuration file:

```
val client =
ElasticClient(ElasticProperties("http://127.0.0.1:9200"))
```

- By providing a Rest client:

```
val restClient = RestClient.builder(
    new HttpHost("localhost", 9200, "http"),
    new HttpHost("localhost", 9201, "http")).build();
val client = ElasticClient.fromRestClient(restClient)
```

See also

You can refer to the following URLs for further reference, which are related to this recipe:

- The official Elasticsearch documentation about the `RestClient` can be found at `https://www.elastic.co/guide/en/elasticsearch/client/java-api/current/transport-client.html`
- The official documentation of elastic4s is at `https://github.com/sksamuel/elastic4s` and provides more examples of client initialization

Managing indices

Now that we have a client, the first thing we need to do is to create a custom index with an optimized mapping for it. Elastic4s provides a powerful DSL to perform this kind of operation.

In this recipe, we will create a custom mapping using the **Domain Syntax Language** (**DSL**), which was developed by the author of elastic4s. This syntax is designed on the Elasticsearch JSON one, so it is very natural and easy to use.

Getting ready

You need an up-and-running Elasticsearch installation, as we described in the *Downloading and installing Elasticsearch* recipe in Chapter 1, *Getting Started*.

An IDE that supports Scala programming, such as IntelliJ IDEA, with the Scala plugin should be installed globally.

The code for this recipe can be found in the `ch14/elastic4s_sample` directory and the reference file is `IndicesExample`.

How to do it...

The Elasticsearch client maps all index operations under the `admin.indices` object of the client.

Here, you will find all the index operations (`create`, `delete`, `exists`, `open`, `close`, `forceMerge`, and so on).

The following code retrieves a client and executes the main operations on indices:

1. We need to import the required classes:

```
import com.sksamuel.elastic4s.http.ElasticDsl._
```

2. We define an `IndicesExample` class that manages the index operations:

```
object IndicesExample extends App with ElasticSearchClientTrait{
```

3. We check if the index exists. If `true`, we delete it:

```
val indexName="test"
if(client.execute{ indexExists(indexName) }.await.result.isExists){
  client.execute{ deleteIndex(indexName) }.await
}
```

4. We create an index, including a mapping:

```
client.execute{
  createIndex(indexName) shards 1 replicas 0 mappings (
    mapping("_doc") as (
  textField("name").termVector("with_positions_offsets").stored(
  true),
      keywordField("tag")
    )
    )
}.await

Thread.sleep(2000)
```

5. We can optimize the index to reduce the number of segments:

```
client.execute(forceMerge(indexName)).await
```

6. We close an index as follows:

```
client.execute(closeIndex(indexName)).await
```

7. We open an index as follows:

```
client.execute(openIndex(indexName)).await
```

8. We delete an index as follows:

```
client.execute(deleteIndex(indexName)).await
```

9. We close the client to clean up the resources as follows:

```
client.close()
```

How it works...

The Elasticsearch **Domain Script Language** (**DSL**) that uses elastic4s is very simple and easy to use. It models the standard Elasticsearch functionalities in a way that is more natural to work with. It is also strong-typed so it prevents common errors such as typographic errors or value type changes.

To simplify the code in these samples, we have created a trait that contains the code to initialize the `ElasticSearchClientTrait` client.

All the API calls in elastic4s are asynchronous, so they return `Future`. To materialize the result, we need to add `.wait` to the end of the call.

Under the hood, elastic4s uses the Java standard Elasticsearch client, but wraps it in the DSL so that the methods and the parameters have the same meaning as the standard Elasticsearch documentation.

In the code, we have put a delay of 1 second (`Thread.sleep(2000)`) to prevent fast actions on indices, because their shard allocations are asynchronous and they require some milliseconds to be ready. The best practice is not to have a similar hack, but to poll an index's state before performing further operations, and only to perform those operations when it goes green.

See also

In Chapter 3, *Basic Operations*, refer to the *Creating an index* recipe for details on index creation, to the *Deleting an index* recipe for details on index deletion, and to the *Opening/closing an index* recipe for a description of open/closed index APIs

Managing mappings

After creating an index, the next step is to add some mappings to it. We already saw how to include a mapping via the REST API in Chapter 3, *Basic Operations*. In this recipe, we will see how to manage mappings via a native client.

Getting ready

You need an up-and-running Elasticsearch installation, as we described in *Downloading and installing Elasticsearch* recipe in Chapter 1, *Getting Started*.

An IDE that supports Scala programming, such as IntelliJ IDEA, with the Scala plugin should be installed globally.

The code for this recipe can be found in the ch14/elastic4s_sample file and the referred class is MappingExample.

How to do it...

In the following code, we add a mytype mapping to a myindex index via the native client:

1. We need to import the required classes:

    ```
    package com.packtpub

    import com.sksamuel.elastic4s.http.ElasticDsl._
    ```

2. We define a class to contain our code and to initialize the client and the index:

    ```
    object MappingExample extends App with
    ElasticSearchClientTrait {
      val indexName = "myindex"
    ```

```
    if (client.execute { indexExists(indexName)
}.await.result.isExists) {
    client.execute { deleteIndex(indexName) }.await
}
```

3. We create the index by providing the _doc mapping:

```
client.execute {
    createIndex(indexName) shards 1 replicas 0 mappings (
        mapping("_doc") as (
    textField("name").termVector("with_positions_offsets").stored(
    true)
        )
    )
}.await
Thread.sleep(2000)
```

4. We add another field in the mapping via a putMapping call:

```
client.execute {
    putMapping(indexName / "_doc").as(
        keywordField("tag")
    )
}.await
```

5. We can now retrieve our mapping to test it:

```
val myMapping = client
    .execute {
        getMapping(indexName / "_doc")
    }
    .await
    .result
```

6. From the mapping, we extract the tag field:

```
val tagMapping = myMapping.seq.head
println(tagMapping)
```

7. We remove the index using the following command:

```
client.execute(deleteIndex(indexName)).await
```

8. Now, we can close the client to free up resources:

```
//we need to close the client to free resources
client.close()
```

How it works...

Before executing a mapping operation, a client must be available.

We can include the mapping during index creation via the `mappings` method in the `createIndex` builder:

```
createIndex(indexName) shards 1 replicas 0 mappings (
  mapping("_doc") as (
textField("name").termVector("with_positions_offsets").stored(true)
  )
)
```

 The elastic4s DSL provides a strong-typed definition for mapping fields.

If we forget to put a field in the mapping, or if during our application life we need to add a new field, `putMapping` can be called with the new field or a new complete type mapping:

```
putMapping(indexName / "_doc").as(
  keywordField("tag")
)
```

In this way, if the type exists, it is updated; otherwise, it is created. In the admin console, to check that our index types are stored in mappings, we need to retrieve them from the cluster state. The method that we have already seen is the `getMapping` method:

```
val myMapping = client
  .execute {
    getMapping(indexName / "_doc")
  }
  .await
  .result
```

The returned mapping object is a list of `IndexMapping` elements:

```
case class IndexMappings(index: String, mappings: Map[String,
Map[String, Any]])
```

To access our mapping, we take the first result:

```
val tagMapping = myMapping.seq.head
println(tagMapping)
```

See also

You can refer to the following URLs for further reference, which are related to this recipe:

- The *Putting a mapping in an index* recipe in `Chapter 3`, *Basic Operations*, for more details about the *Put Mapping API*
- The *Getting a mapping recipe* in `Chapter 3`, *Basic Operations*, for more details about the *Get Mapping API*

Managing documents

The APIs for managing documents (`index`, `delete`, and `update`) are the most important after the search ones. In this recipe, we will look at how to use them.

Getting ready

You need an up-and-running Elasticsearch installation, as we described in the *Downloading and installing Elasticsearch* recipe in `Chapter 1`, *Getting Started*.

An IDE that supports Scala programming, such as IntelliJ IDEA, with the Scala plugin should be installed globally.

The code for this recipe can be found in the `ch14/elastic4s_sample` file and the referred class is `DocumentExample`.

How to do it...

To manage documents, we will perform the following steps:

1. We'll need to import the required classes to execute all the document CRUD operations:

```
import com.sksamuel.elastic4s.http.ElasticDsl._
import com.sksamuel.elastic4s.circe._
```

2. We need to create the client and ensure that the index and mapping exists:

```
object DocumentExample extends App with
ElasticSearchClientTrait {
```

```
val indexName = "myindex"

ensureIndexMapping(indexName)
```

3. Now, we can store a document in Elasticsearch via the `indexInto` call:

```
client.execute {
  indexInto(indexName) id "0" fields (
    "name" -> "brown",
    "tag" -> List("nice", "simple")
  )
}.await
```

4. We can retrieve the stored document via the `get` call:

```
val bwn = client.execute {
  get("0") from indexName
}.await

println(bwn.result.sourceAsString)
```

5. We can update the stored document via the `update` call using a script in Painless:

```
client.execute {
  update("0").in(indexName).script("ctx._source.name = 'red'")
}.await
```

6. We can check if our update was applied:

```
val red = client.execute {
  get("0") from indexName
}.await

println(red.result.sourceAsString)
```

7. The console output result will be as follows:

```
{"name":"brown","tag":["nice","simple"]}
{"name":"red","tag":["nice","simple"]}
```

 The document version, following an update action and if the document is reindexed with new changes, is always incremented by 1.

How it works...

Before executing a document action, a client and the index must be available, and document mapping should be created (the mapping is optional, because it can be inferred from the indexed document).

To index a document, elastic4s allows us to provide the document content in several ways, such as via the following:

- `fields`:
    - A sequence of tuples (`String, Any`), as in the preceding example
    - A `Map[String, Any]`
    - An `Iterable[(String, Any)]`
- `doc/source`:
    - A string
    - A typeclass that derives `Indexable[T]`

Obviously, it's possible to add all the parameters that we saw in the *Indexing a document* recipe in `Chapter 3`, *Basic Operations*, such as parent, routing, and so on.

The return value, `IndexReponse`, is the object that's returned from the Java call.

To retrieve a document, we need to know the `index/id`; the method is `get`. It requires the `id` and the `index` that are provided in the `from` method. A lot of other methods are available to control the routing (such as sourcing, parent) or fields, as we have seen in the *Getting a document* recipe in `Chapter 3`, *Basic Operations*. In the preceding example, the call is as follows:

```
val bwn = client.execute {
  get("0") from indexName
}.await
```

The return type, `GetResponse`, contains all the requests (if the document exists) and the document information (`source`, `version`, `index`, `type`, and `id`).

To update a document, it's required to know the `index/id` and provide a script or a document to be used for the update. The client method is `update`. In the preceding example, we have used a script:

```
client.execute {
  update("0").in(indexName).script("ctx._source.name = 'red'")
}.await
```

The script code must be a string. If the script language is not defined, the default, Painless, is used.

The returned response contains information about the execution and the new version value to manage concurrency.

To delete a document (without the need to execute a query), we must know the `index/id`, and we can use the client method, `delete`, to create a `delete` request. In the preceding code, we used the following:

```
client.execute {
  delete("0") from indexName
}.await
```

The `delete` request allows all the parameters we saw in the *Deleting a document* recipe in `Chapter 3`, *Basic Operations*, which will control routing and versions, to be passed to it.

There's more...

Scala programmers love typeclass, automatic marshalling/unmarshalling from case classes, and a strong type management of the data. For this, `elastics4` provides additional support for the common JSON serialization library, such as the following:

- Circe (`https://circe.github.io/circe/`). To use this library, you need to add the following dependency:

  ```
  "com.sksamuel.elastic4s" %% "elastic4s-circe" % elastic4sV
  ```

- Jackson (`https://github.com/FasterXML/jackson-module-scala`). To use this library, you need to add the following dependency:

  ```
  "com.sksamuel.elastic4s" %% "elastic4s-jackson" % elastic4sV
  ```

- Json4s (`http://json4s.org/`). To use this library, you need to add the following dependency:

  ```
  "com.sksamuel.elastic4s" %% "elastic4s-json4s" % elastic4sV
  ```

For example, if you want to use Circe, perform the following steps:

1. You need to import the `circe` implicits:

```
import com.sksamuel.elastic4s.circe._
import io.circe.generic.auto._
import com.sksamuel.elastic4s.Indexable
```

2. You need to define the `case` class, which needs to be deserialized:

```
case class Place(id: Int, name: String)
case class Cafe(name: String, place: Place)
```

3. You need to force the implicit serializer:

```
implicitly[Indexable[Cafe]]
```

4. Now, you can index the case classes directly:

```
val cafe = Cafe("nespresso", Place(20, "Milan"))

client.execute {
  indexInto(indexName).id(cafe.name).source(cafe)
}.await
```

See also

In the preceding recipes, we have used all CRUD operations on a document. For more details about these actions, refer to:

- The *Indexing a document* recipe in Chapter 3, *Basic Operations*
- The *Getting a document* recipe in Chapter 3, *Basic Operations*, on retrieving a stored document
- The *Deleting a document* recipe in Chapter 3, *Basic Operations*
- The *Updating a document* recipe in Chapter 3, *Basic Operations*

Executing a standard search

Obviously, the most common action in Elasticsearch is searching. Elastic4s leverages the query DSL, which brings a type-safe definition for the queries to Scala. One of the most common advantages of this functionality is that, as Elasticsearch evolves, in Scala code via `elastic4s`, you can have deprecation or your compilation may break, requiring you to update your code.

In this recipe, we will see how to execute a search, retrieve the results, and convert them into typed Domain objects (classes) without the need to write a serializer/deserializer for our data.

Getting ready

You need an up-and-running Elasticsearch installation, as we described in the *Downloading and installing Elasticsearch* recipe in `Chapter 1`, *Getting Started.*

An IDE that supports Scala programming, such as IntelliJ IDEA, with the Scala plugin should be installed globally.

The code for this recipe can be found in the `ch14/elastic4s_sample` file and the referred class is `QueryExample`.

How to do it...

To execute a standard query, we will perform the following steps:

1. We need to import the classes and implicits that are required to index and search the data:

```
import com.sksamuel.elastic4s.http.ElasticDsl._
import com.sksamuel.elastic4s.circe._
import com.sksamuel.elastic4s.Indexable
import io.circe.generic.auto._
```

2. We will create an index and populate it with some data. We will use bulk calls for speedup:

```
object QueryExample extends App with ElasticSearchClientTrait
{
  val indexName = "myindex"
  val typeName = "_doc"
```

```scala
case class Place(id: Int, name: String)
case class Cafe(name: String, place: Place)

implicitly[Indexable[Cafe]]

ensureIndexMapping(indexName, typeName)

client.execute {
  bulk(
    indexInto(indexName / typeName)
      .id("0")
      .source(Cafe("nespresso", Place(20, "Milan")))),
    indexInto(indexName / typeName)
      .id("1")
      .source(Cafe("java", Place(60, "Rome")))),
    ... truncated...
    indexInto(indexName / typeName)
      .id("9")
      .source(Cafe("java", Place(89, "London")))
  )
}.await

Thread.sleep(2000)
```

3. We can use a `bool` filter for search documents with the `name` equal to `java` and `place.id` greater than or equal to 80:

```scala
val resp = client.execute {
  search(indexName).bool(
    must(termQuery("name", "java"),
  rangeQuery("place.id").gte(80)))
}.await
```

4. When we have the `response` parameter, we need to check its count and we can convert it back into a list of classes:

```scala
println(resp.result.size)

println(resp.result.to[Cafe].toList)
```

5. The result should be similar to the following:

```scala
List(Cafe(java,Place(80,Chicago)),
Cafe(java,Place(89,London)))
```

How it works...

The Elastic4s query DSL wraps the Elasticsearch one in a more human-readable way.

The `search` method allows us to define a complex query via DSL. The result is a wrapper of the original Java result and provides some helpers to be more productive.

The common methods of the Java result are available at a top level, but they also provide two interesting methods: `to` and `safeTo`.

They are able to convert the results in case classes via the implicit conversions available in the scope. In the case of the `to[T]` method, the result is an iterator of `T` (in the preceding example, we have the conversion back to a `List` of `Cafe`). In the case of `safeTo[T]`, the result is an `Either[Throwable, T]`; in this way, it's possible to collect the conversion errors/exceptions.

> Using the typeclass in Scala allows you to write a cleaner and easy-to-understand code, and also reduces errors due to string management in Elasticsearch.

See also

The *Executing a search* recipe in `Chapter 4`, *Exploring Search Capabilities*, has more detailed information about executing a query

Executing a search with aggregations

The next step after searching in Elasticsearch is to execute the aggregations. The elastic4s DSL also provides support for aggregation so that it can be built in a safer typed way.

Getting ready

You need an up-and-running Elasticsearch installation, as we described in the *Downloading and installing Elasticsearch* recipe in `Chapter 1`, *Getting Started*.

An IDE that supports Scala programming, such as IntelliJ IDEA, with the Scala plugin should be installed globally.

The code for this recipe can be found in the `ch14/elastic4s_sample` file and the referred class is `AggregationExample`.

How to do it...

To execute a search with aggregations, we will perform the following steps:

1. We need to import the classes that are needed for the aggregations:

```
import com.sksamuel.elastic4s.http.ElasticDsl._
```

2. We will create an index and populate it with some data that will be used for the aggregations:

```
val indexName = "myindex"
val typeName = "_doc"
ensureIndexMapping(indexName, typeName)
populateSampleData(indexName, typeName, 1000)
```

3. We already know how to execute a search with aggregation using `termsAggregation` with several sub-aggregations (extended statistics, geocentroid):

```
val resp = client
  .execute {
    search(indexName) size 0 aggregations
(termsAggregation("tag") field "tag" size 100 subAggregations
(
      extendedStatsAggregation("price") field "price",
extendedStatsAggregation(
        "size") field "size", geoBoundsAggregation("centroid")
field "location"
    ))
  }
  .await
  .result
```

4. The `resp` variable contains our query result. We can extract the aggregation results from it and show some values:

```
val tagsAgg = resp.aggregations.terms("tag")

println(s"Result Hits: ${resp.size}")
println(s"number of tags: ${tagsAgg.buckets.size}")
println(
  s"max price of first tag ${tagsAgg.buckets.head.key}:
```

```
${tagsAgg.buckets.head.extendedStats("price").max}")
println(
    s"min size of first tag ${tagsAgg.buckets.head.key}:
${tagsAgg.buckets.head.extendedStats("size").min}")
```

5. Finally, we clean up the used resources:

```
client.execute(deleteIndex(indexName)).await

client.close()
```

6. The result should look similar to the following:

```
number of tags: 5
 max price of first tag awesome: 10.799999999999999
 min size of first tag awesome: 0.0
```

How it works...

Elastic4s provides a powerful DSL for more type-safe aggregations.

In the preceding example, we used `termsAggregation` initially to aggregate the buckets by tag settings to collect at least 100 buckets (`termsAggregation("tag") size 100`). Then we have two types of sub-aggregations:

- `extendedStatsAggregation`: This is used to collect extended statistics on the price and size fields
- `geoBoundsAggregation`: This is used to compute the center of documents results

The elastic4s DSL provides all the official Elasticsearch aggregations.

Also, the aggregation result contains helpers for managing aggregations, such as automatic casing for some types. The most commonly used are:

- `StringTermsResult`: This wraps a string terms aggregation result
- `TermsResult`: This wraps a generic terms aggregation result
- `MissingResult`: This wraps a missing aggregation result
- `CardinalityResult`: This wraps a cardinality aggregation result
- `ExtendedStatsAggResult`: This wraps an extended stats result
- `AvgResult`: This wraps an average metric aggregation result
- `MaxResult`: This wraps a max metric aggregation result

- `SumResult`: This wraps a sum metric aggregation result
- `MinResult`: This wraps a min metric aggregation result
- `HistogramResult`: This wraps a histogram aggregation result
- `ValueCountResult`: This wraps a count aggregation result

If the aggregation result is not part of these aggregations results, a helper method, `get[T]:T`, allows you to retrieve a casted aggregation result.

See also

You can refer to the following URLs for further reference, which are related to this recipe:

- The *Executing term Aggregations* recipe in `Chapter 7`, *Aggregations*, which describes term aggregations
- The *Executing statistical aggregations* recipe in `Chapter 7`, *Aggregations*, for more details about statistical aggregations

Integrating with DeepLearning.scala

In the previous chapter, we learned to use DeepLearning4j with Java. This library can be used natively in Scala to provide deep learning capabilities to our Scala applications.

In this recipe, we will learn to use Elasticsearch as a source of training data in a machine learning algorithm.

Getting ready

You need an up and running Elasticsearch installation, as we described in the *Downloading and installing Elasticsearch* recipe in `Chapter 1`, *Getting Started*.

Maven, or an IDE that natively support Java programming, such as Eclipse or IntelliJ IDEA, must be installed.

The code for this recipe is in the `ch14/deeplearningscala` directory.

We will use the `iris` dataset (https://en.wikipedia.org/wiki/Iris_flower_data_set) that we have used in Chapter 13, *Java Integration*. To prepare your index dataset `iris`, we need to populate it executing the `PopulatingIndex` class available in the source code of Chapter 13, *Java Integration*.

How to do it...

To use DeepLearning4J as a source data input for your models, you will perform the following steps:

1. We need to add the DeepLearning4J dependencies to `build.sbt`:

```
"org.nd4j" % "nd4j-native-platform" % nd4jVersion,
"org.nd4j" % "nd4j-native-platform" % nd4jVersion,
"org.deeplearning4j" % "deeplearning4j-core" % dl4jVersion,
// ParallelWrapper & ParallelInference live here
"org.deeplearning4j" % "deeplearning4j-parallel-wrapper"%
dl4jVersion
```

2. Now, we can write our DeepLearning4J class to train and test our model. Initialize the Elasticsearch client:

```
lazy val client: ElasticClient = {
  ElasticClient(ElasticProperties("http://127.0.0.1:9200"))
}
lazy val indexName = "iris"
```

3. After having the client, we can read our dataset. We will execute a query and collect the Hit results using a simple search:

```
case class Iris(label: Int, f1: Double, f2: Double, f3:
Double, f4: Double)
implicitly[Indexable[Iris]]
val response = client.execute {
  search(indexName).size(1000)
}.await
val hits = response.result.to[Iris].toArray
```

4. We need to convert the hits in a DeepLearning4J dataset. To do this, create intermediate arrays and populate them:

```
//Convert the iris data into 150x4 matrix
val irisMatrix: Array[Array[Double]] = hits.map(r =>
Array(r.f1, r.f2, r.f3, r.f4))
//Now do the same for the label data
```

```
val labelMatrix: Array[Array[Double]] = hits.map { r =>
r.label match {
    case 0 => Array(1.0, 0.0, 0.0)
    case 1 => Array(0.0, 1.0, 0.0)
    case 2 => Array(0.0, 0.0, 1.0)
}
}

val training = Nd4j.create(irisMatrix)
val labels = Nd4j.create(labelMatrix)
val allData = new DataSet(training, labels)
```

5. We need to split the datasets in two parts—one for training and one for tests. Then, we need to normalize the values. These actions can be done with the following code:

```
allData.shuffle()
val testAndTrain = allData.splitTestAndTrain(0.65) //Use 65%
of data for training
val trainingData = testAndTrain.getTrain
val testData = testAndTrain.getTest
//We need to normalize our data. We'll use
NormalizeStandardize (which gives us mean 0, unit variance):
val normalizer = new NormalizerStandardize
normalizer.fit(trainingData) //Collect the statistics
(mean/stdev) from the training data. This does not modify the
input data
normalizer.transform(trainingData) //Apply normalization to
the training data
normalizer.transform(testData) //Apply normalization to the
test data. This is using statistics calculated from the
*training* set
```

6. Now we can design the model to be used for the training:

```
val numInputs = 4
val outputNum = 3
val seed = 6

logger.info("Build model....")
val conf = new NeuralNetConfiguration.Builder()
  .seed(seed)
  .activation(Activation.TANH)
  .weightInit(WeightInit.XAVIER)
  .updater(new Sgd(0.1))
  .l2(1e-4)
  .list
  .layer(0, new
```

```
DenseLayer.Builder().nIn(numInputs).nOut(3).build)
  .layer(1, new DenseLayer.Builder().nIn(3).nOut(3).build)
  .layer(2, new
OutputLayer.Builder(LossFunctions.LossFunction.NEGATIVELOGLIKE
LIHOOD)
  .activation(Activation.SOFTMAX).nIn(3).nOut(outputNum).build)
  .backprop(true)
  .pretrain(false)
  .build
```

7. After having defined the model, we can finally train it with our dataset—we use 1000 iterations for the training. The code is as follows:

```
//run the model
val model = new MultiLayerNetwork(conf)
model.init()
model.setListeners(new ScoreIterationListener(100))
0.to(1000).foreach{ _ => model.fit(trainingData) }
```

8. Now that we have a trained model, we need to evaluate its accuracy and we can do that using the test dataset:

```
//evaluate the model on the test set
val eval = new Evaluation(3)
val output = model.output(testData.getFeatures)
eval.eval(testData.getLabels, output)
logger.info(eval.stats)
```

How it works...

Elasticsearch can be used as a data store—using compact Scala code significantly reduces the amount of code required to fetch the dataset and use it. The best way to manage a dataset is to create a data model. In this case, we created `Iris` class for this purpose:

```
case class Iris(label: Int, f1: Double, f2: Double, f3: Double, f4:
Double)
```

We use Circe (`https://circe.github.io/circe/`) to derive the encoder and decoder for Elasticsearch search hits in an array of `Iris` objects:

```
  implicitly[Indexable[Iris]]
val response = client.execute {
  search(indexName).size(1000)
}.await
val hits = response.result.to[Iris].toArray
```

Using this approach, the code required to convert our data is reduced and we can work on a string type object for generating our deep learning model.

The final step for creating our dataset is to convert the `Iris` object to an array of value to be given to the algorithm. We have achieved this using some functional map on our Elasticsearch hits:

```
val irisMatrix: Array[Array[Double]] = hits.map(r => Array(r.f1, r.f2,
r.f3, r.f4))
```

The same is done with the labels, but in this case, we had to generate a 3-dimensional array depending on the label value:

```
val labelMatrix: Array[Array[Double]] = hits.map { r =>
  r.label match {
    case 0 => Array(1.0, 0.0, 0.0)
    case 1 => Array(0.0, 1.0, 0.0)
    case 2 => Array(0.0, 0.0, 1.0)
  }
}
```

Using a model `Iris` to populate our arrays, the code is simpler and readable. Another advantage is that, it allows to replace, in the future, hits with streamable structures without requiring a massive code refactory.

After having built the dataset, you can design your model, train it, and evaluate your hits quality—this approach is independent of the machine learning library that you use.

See also

You can refer to the following URLs, which are related to this recipe, for further reference:

- The official site of DeepLearning4J (`https://deeplearning4j.org/`) for more examples and references about this powerful library
- The official documentation for Circe at `https://circe.github.io/circe/`
- A more detailed description of Iris dataset at `https://en.wikipedia.org/wiki/Iris_flower_data_set`

15
Python Integration

In the previous chapter, we saw how it was possible to use a native client to access the Elasticsearch server via Java. This chapter is dedicated to the Python language and how to manage common tasks via its clients.

Apart from Java, the Elasticsearch team supports official clients for Perl, PHP, Python, .NET, and Ruby (see the announcement post on the Elasticsearch blog at `http://www.elasticsearch.org/blog/unleash-the-clients-ruby-python-php-perl/`). These clients have a lot of advantages over other implementations. A few of them are given in the following list:

- They are strongly tied to the Elasticsearch API. These clients are direct translations of the native Elasticsearch REST interface—the Elasticsearch team.
- They handle dynamic node detection and failovers. They are built with a strong networking base for communicating with the cluster.
- They have full coverage of the REST API. They share the same application approach for every language in which they are available, so switching from one language to another is fast.
- They are easily extensible.

The Python client plays very well with other Python frameworks, such as Django, web2py, and Pyramid. It allows very fast access to documents, indices, and clusters.

In this chapter, I'll try to describe the most important functionalities of the Elasticsearch official Python client; for additional examples, I suggest that you take a look at the online GitHub repository and documentation at `https://github.com/elastic/elasticsearch-py` and related documentation at `https://elasticsearch-py.readthedocs.io/en/master/`.

In this chapter, we will cover the following recipes:

- Creating a client
- Managing indices
- Managing mappings
- Managing documents
- Executing a standard search
- Executing a search with aggregations

Creating a client

The official Elasticsearch clients are designed to manage a lot of issues that are typically required to create solid REST clients, such as `retry` if there are network issues, autodiscovery of other nodes of the cluster, and data conversions for communicating on the HTTP layer.

In this recipe, we'll learn how to instantiate a client with varying options.

Getting ready

You need an up-and-running Elasticsearch installation, which we described how to get in the *Downloading and installing Elasticsearch* recipe in `Chapter 1`, *Getting Started*.

A Python 2.x or 3.x distribution should be installed. In Linux and the Mac OS X system, it's already provided in the standard installation. To manage Python, `pip` packages (`https://pypi.python.org/pypi/pip/`) must also be installed.

The full code for this recipe is in the `ch15/code/client_creation.py` file.

How to do it...

To create a client, we will perform the following steps:

1. Before using the Python client, we need to install it (possibly in a Python virtual environment). The client is officially hosted on PyPi (`http://pypi.python.org/`) and it's easy to install with the `pip` command, as shown in the following code:

   ```
   pip install elasticsearch
   ```

   This standard installation only provides HTTP.

2. If you need to use the requests library for HTTP communication, you need to install it, as follows:

   ```
   pip install requests
   ```

3. After installing the package, we can instantiate the client. It resides in the Python `elasticsearch` package and it must be imported to instantiate the client.

4. If you don't pass arguments to the `Elasticsearch` class, it instantiates a client that connects to the `localhost` and port `9200` (the default Elasticsearch HTTP one), as shown in the following code:

   ```
   es = elasticsearch.Elasticsearch()
   ```

5. If your cluster is composed of more than one node, you can pass the list of nodes as a round-robin connection between them and distribute the HTTP load, as follows:

   ```
   # client using two nodes
   es = elasticsearch.Elasticsearch(["search1:9200",
   "search2:9200"])
   ```

6. Often, the complete topology of the cluster is unknown; if you know at least one node IP, you can use the `sniff_on_start=True` option, as shown in the following code. This option activates the client's ability to detect other nodes in the cluster:

   ```
   # client using a node with sniffing
   es = elasticsearch.Elasticsearch("localhost:9200",
   sniff_on_start=True)
   ```

7. The default transport is `Urllib3HttpConnection`, but if you want to use the HTTP requests transport, you need to override the `connection_class` by passing `RequestsHttpConnection`, as follows:

```
# client using localhost:9200 and http requests transport
from elasticsearch.connection import RequestsHttpConnection
es = elasticsearch.Elasticsearch(sniff_on_start=True,
connection_class=RequestsHttpConnection)
```

How it works...

To communicate with an Elasticsearch cluster, a client is required.

The client manages all communication layers from your application to an Elasticsearch server using HTTP REST calls.

The Elasticsearch Python client allows you to use one of the following library implementations:

- `urllib3`: This is the default implementation provided by the Elasticserch Python driver (https://pypi.python.org/pypi/urllib3)
- `requests`: The `requests` library is one of the most used libraries to perform HTTP requests in Python (https://pypi.python.org/pypi/requests)

The Elasticsearch Python client requires a server to connect to. If one is not defined, it tries to use one on the local machine (localhost). If you have more than one node, you can pass a list of servers to connect to.

> The client automatically tries to balance operations on all cluster nodes. This is a very powerful functionality provided by the Elasticsearch client.

To improve the list of available nodes, it is possible to set the client to autodiscover new nodes. I recommend using this feature because you will often find yourself with a cluster with a lot of nodes and will need to shut down some of them for maintenance. The options that can be passed to the client to control discovery are as follows:

- `sniff_on_start`: The default value is `False`, which allows you to obtain the list of nodes from the cluster at startup time

- `sniffer_timeout`: The default value is `None`; it is the number of seconds between the automatic sniffing of the cluster nodes
- `sniff_on_connection_fail`: The default value is `False`, which controls whether a connection failure triggers a sniff of cluster nodes

The default client configuration uses the HTTP protocol via the `urllib3` library. If you want to use other transport protocols, you need to pass the type of the transport class to the `transport_class` variable. The current implemented classes are as follows:

- `Transport`: This is a default value—that is, a wrapper around `Urllib3HttpConnection` that uses HTTP (usually on port `9200`)
- `RequestsHttpConnection`: This is an alternative to `Urllib3HttpConnection` based on the `requests` library

See also

- The official documentation about the Python Elasticsearch client, available at `https://elasticsearch-py.readthedocs.io/en/master/index.html`, provides a more detailed explanation of the several options that are available to initialize the client

Managing indices

In the previous recipe, we saw how to initialize a client to send calls to an Elasticsearch cluster. In this recipe, we will look at how to manage indices via client calls.

Getting ready

You need an up-and-running Elasticsearch installation, as we described in the *Downloading and installing Elasticsearch* recipe in `Chapter 1`, *Getting Started*.

You also need the Python-installed packages from the *Creating a client* recipe in this chapter.

The full code for this recipe can be found in the
ch15/code/indices_management.py file.

How to do it...

In Python, managing the life cycle of your indices is very easy. To do this, we will
perform the following steps:

1. We will initialize a client, as shown in the following code:

```
import elasticsearch

es = elasticsearch.Elasticsearch()

index_name = "my_index"
```

2. We need to check whether the index exists, and if it does, we need to delete
it. We can set this up using the following code:

```
if es.indices.exists(index_name):
    es.indices.delete(index_name)
```

3. All the indices methods are available in the client.indices
namespace. We can create and wait for the creation of an index using the
following code:

```
es.indices.create(index_name)

es.cluster.health(wait_for_status="yellow")
```

4. We can close/open an index using the following code:

```
es.indices.close(index_name)

es.indices.open(index_name)

es.cluster.health(wait_for_status="yellow")
```

5. We can optimize an index by reducing the number of segments via the
following code:

```
es.indices.forcemerge(index_name)
```

6. We can delete an index using the following code:

```
es.indices.delete(index_name)
```

How it works...

The Elasticsearch Python client has two special managers: one for indices (`<client>.indices`) and one for the cluster (`<client>.cluster`).

For every operation that needs to work with indices, the first value is generally the name of the index. If you need to execute an action on several indices in one go, the indices must be concatenated with a comma , (that is, `index1, index2, indexN`). It's possible to also use glob patterns to define multi-indexes, such as `index*`.

To create an index, the call requires `index_name` and other optional parameters, such as index settings and mapping, as shown in the following code. We'll see this advanced feature in the next recipe:

```
es.indices.create(index_name)
```

Index creation can take some time (from a few milliseconds to a few seconds); it is an asynchronous operation and it depends on the complexity of the cluster, the speed of the disk, the network congestion, and so on. To be sure that this action is completed, we need to check that the cluster's health has turned `yellow` or `green`, as follows:

```
es.cluster.health(wait_for_status="yellow")
```

 It's good practice to wait until the cluster status is `yellow` (at least) after operations that involve index creation and opening, because these actions are asynchronous.

The method we use to close an index is `<client>.indices.close`, along with the name of the index to close, as follows:

```
es.indices.close(index_name)
```

The method we use to open an index is `<client>.indices.open`, along with the name of the index to open, as shown in the following code:

```
es.indices.open(index_name)
```

```
es.cluster.health(wait_for_status="yellow")
```

Similar to index creation, after an index is opened, it is good practice to wait until the index is fully opened before executing an operation on the index; otherwise, there will be errors with the execution of commands on the index. This action is done by checking the cluster's health.

To improve the performance of an index, Elasticsearch allows us to optimize it by removing deleted documents (documents are marked as deleted, but are not purged from the segment's index for performance reasons) and reducing the number of segments. To optimize an index, `<client>.indices.forcemerge` must be called on the index, as shown in the following code:

```
es.indices.forcemerge(index_name)
```

Finally, if we want to delete the index, we can call `<client>.indices.delete`, giving the name of the index to remove.

 Remember that deleting an index removes everything related to it, including all the data, and this action cannot be reversed.

There's more...

The Python client wraps the Elasticsearch API in groups such as the following:

- `<client>.indices`: This wraps all the REST APIs related to index management
- `<client>.ingest`: This wraps all the REST APIs related to ingest calls
- `<client>.cluster`: This wraps all the REST APIs related to cluster management
- `<client>.cat`: This wraps the CAT API, a subset of the API that returns a textual representation of traditional JSON calls
- `<client>.nodes`: This wraps all the REST APIs related to nodes management
- `<client>.snapshot`: This allows us to execute a snapshot and restore data from Elasticsearch
- `<client>.tasks`: This wraps all the REST APIs related to task management
- `<client>.remote`: This wraps all the REST APIs related to remote information
- `<client>.xpack`: This wraps all the REST APIs related to `xpack` information and usage

Standard document operations (CRUD) and search operations are available at the top level of the client.

See also

- The *Creating an index* recipe in `Chapter 3`, *Basic Operations*
- The *Deleting an index* recipe in `Chapter 3`, *Basic Operations*
- The *Opening/closing an index* recipe in `Chapter 3`, *Basic Operations*, for more details about the actions that are used to save cluster/node memory

Managing mappings include the mapping

After creating an index, the next step is to add some type mappings to it. We have already seen how to include a mapping via the REST API in `Chapter 3`, *Basic Operations*.

Getting ready

You need an up-and-running Elasticsearch installation, which we described how to get in the *Downloading and installing Elasticsearch* recipe in `Chapter 1`, *Getting Started*.

You also need the Python packages that we installed in the *Creating a client* recipe in this chapter.

The code for this recipe is in the `ch15/code/mapping_management.py` file.

How to do it...

After initializing a client and creating an index, the steps for managing the indices are as follows:

1. Create a mapping
2. Retrieve a mapping

These steps are easily managed by performing the following steps:

1. We initialize the client, as follows:

```
import elasticsearch

es = elasticsearch.Elasticsearch()
```

2. We create an index, as follows:

```
index_name = "my_index"
type_name = "_doc"

if es.indices.exists(index_name):
    es.indices.delete(index_name)

es.indices.create(index_name)
es.cluster.health(wait_for_status="yellow")
```

3. We include the mapping, as follows:

```
es.indices.put_mapping(index=index_name, doc_type=type_name,
body={type_name:{"properties": {
    "uuid": {"type": "keyword"},
    "title": {"type": "text", "term_vector":
"with_positions_offsets"},
    "parsedtext": { "type": "text", "term_vector":
"with_positions_offsets"},
    "nested": {"type": "nested", "properties": {"num":
{"type": "integer"},
                                                "name":
{"type": "keyword"},
                                                "value":
{"type": "keyword"}}},
    "date": {"type": "date"},
    "position": {"type": "integer"},
    "name": {"type": "text", "term_vector":
"with_positions_offsets"}}}})
```

4. We retrieve the mapping, as follows:

```
mappings = es.indices.get_mapping(index_name, type_name)
```

5. We delete the index, as follows:

```
es.indices.delete(index_name)
```

How it works...

We have already seen how to initialize the client and create an index in the previous recipe.

To create a mapping, the method call is `<client>.indices.create_mapping`, giving the index name, the type name, and the mapping, as shown in the following code. The creation of the mapping is fully covered in Chapter 3, *Managing Mapping*. It is easy to convert the standard Python types into JSON and vice versa:

```
es.indices.put_mapping(index_name, type_name, {...})
```

If an error is generated in the mapping process, an exception is raised. The `put_mapping` API has two behaviors: create and update.

 In Elasticsearch, you cannot remove a property from a mapping. The schema manipulation allows us to enter new properties with the `put_mapping` call.

To retrieve a mapping with the `get_mapping` API, use the `<client>.indices.get_mapping` method, providing the index name and type name, as shown in the following code:

```
mappings = es.indices.get_mapping(index_name, type_name)
```

The returned object is obviously the dictionary describing the mapping.

See also

- The *Putting a mapping in an index* recipe in Chapter 3, *Basic Operations*
- The *Getting a mapping* recipe in Chapter 3, *Basic Operations*

Managing documents

The APIs for managing a document (index, update, and delete) are the most important after the search APIs. In this recipe, we will see how to use them in a standard way and use bulk actions to improve performance.

Getting ready

You need an up-and-running Elasticsearch installation, which we described how to get in the *Downloading and installing Elasticsearch* recipe in Chapter 1, *Getting Started*.

You also need the Python packages that we installed in the *Creating a client* recipe in this chapter.

The full code for this recipe can be found in the ch15/code/document_management.py file.

How to do it...

The three main operations to manage the documents are as follows:

- index: This operation stores a document in Elasticsearch. It is mapped on the index API call.
- update: This allows us to update values in a document. This operation is composed internally (via Lucene) by deleting the previous document and reindexing the document with the new values. It is mapped to the update API call.
- delete: This deletes a document from the index. It is mapped to the delete API call.

With the Elasticsearch Python client, these operations can be performed by going through the following steps:

1. We initialize a client and create an index with the mapping, as follows:

```python
import elasticsearch
from datetime import datetime

es = elasticsearch.Elasticsearch()

index_name = "my_index"
type_name = "_doc"

from code.utils import create_and_add_mapping


if es.indices.exists(index_name):
    es.indices.delete(index_name)


create_and_add_mapping(es, index_name)
```

2. Then, we index some documents (we manage the parent/child), as follows:

```
es.index(index=index_name, doc_type="_doc", id=1,
                body={"name": "Joe Tester", "parsedtext":
"Joe Testere nice guy", "uuid": "11111",
                "position": 1,
                "date": datetime(2018, 12, 8),
"join_field": {"name": "book"}})
es.index(index=index_name, doc_type="_doc", id="1.1",
                body={"name": "data1", "value": "value1",
"join_field": {"name": "metadata", "parent": "1"}},
                routing=1)
... truncated ...
```

3. Next, we update a document, as follows:

```
es.update(index=index_name, doc_type=type_name, id=2,
body={"script": 'ctx._source.position += 1'})

document=es.get(index=index_name, doc_type=type_name, id=2)
print(document)
```

4. We then delete a document, as follows:

```
es.delete(index=index_name, doc_type=type_name, id=3)
```

5. Next, we bulk insert some documents, as follows:

```
from elasticsearch.helpers import bulk
bulk(es, [
    {"_index":index_name, "_type":type_name, "_id":"1",
"source":{"name": "Joe Tester", "parsedtext": "Joe Testere
nice guy", "uuid": "11111", "position": 1,
                "date": datetime(2018, 12, 8)}},

    {"_index": index_name, "_type": type_name, "_id": "1",
     "source": {"name": "Bill Baloney", "parsedtext": "Bill
Testere nice guy", "uuid": "22222", "position": 2,
                "date": datetime(2018, 12, 8)}}
])
```

6. Finally, we remove the index, as follows:

```
es.indices.delete(index_name)
```

How it works...

To simplify this example, after instantiating the client, a function of the `utils` package is called, which sets up the index and places the mapping, as follows:

```
from code.utils import create_and_add_mapping
create_and_add_mapping(es, index_name)
```

This function contains the code for creating the mapping of the previous recipe.

The method that's used to index a document is `<client>.index`, and it requires the name of the index, the type of the document, and the body of the document, as shown in the following code (if the ID is not given, it will be autogenerated):

```
es.index(index=index_name, doc_type="_doc", id=1,
                body={"name": "Joe Tester", "parsedtext": "Joe
Testere nice guy", "uuid": "11111",
                    "position": 1,
                    "date": datetime(2018, 12, 8), "join_field":
{"name": "book"}})
```

It also accepts all the parameters that we have seen in the REST index API call in the *Indexing a document* recipe in Chapter 3, *Basic Operations*. The most common parameters that are passed to this function are as follows:

- `id`: This provides an ID that is used to index the document
- `routing`: This provides a shard routing to index the document in the specified shard
- `parent`: This provides a parent ID that is used to put the child document in the correct shard

The method that is used to update a document is `<client>.update`, and it requires the following parameters:

- `index_name`
- `type_name`
- `id` of the document
- `script` or `document` to update the document
- `* lang`, which is optional, and indicates the language to be used, usually `painless`

If we want to increment a position by 1, we will write similar code, as follows:

```
es.update(index=index_name, doc_type=type_name, id=2, body={"script":
'ctx._source.position += 1'})
```

Obviously, the call accepts all the parameters that we discussed in the *Updating a document* recipe in `Chapter 3`, *Basic Operations*.

The method that is used to delete a document is `<client>.delete`, and it requires the following parameters:

- `index_name`
- `type_name`
- `id` of the document

If we want to delete a document with `id=3`, we will write a similar code, as follows:

```
es.delete(index=index_name, doc_type=type_name, id=3)
```

 Remember that all the Elasticsearch actions that work on documents are never seen instantly in the search. If you want to search without having to wait for the automatic refresh (every 1 second), you need to manually call the refresh API on the index.

To execute bulk indexing, the Elasticsearch client provides a `helper` function, which accepts a connection, an iterable list of documents, and the bulk size. The bulk size (the default is 500) defines the number of actions to send via a single bulk call. The parameters that must be passed to correctly control the indexing of the document are put in the document with the `_` prefix. The documents that are to be provided to the bulker must be formatted as a standard search result with the body in the `source` field, as follows:

```
from elasticsearch.helpers import bulk
bulk(es, [
    {"_index":index_name, "_type":type_name, "_id":"1",
"source":{"name": "Joe Tester", "parsedtext": "Joe Testere nice guy",
"uuid": "11111", "position": 1,
            "date": datetime(2018, 12, 8)}},

    {"_index": index_name, "_type": type_name, "_id": "1",
    "source": {"name": "Bill Baloney", "parsedtext": "Bill Testere
nice guy", "uuid": "22222", "position": 2,
            "date": datetime(2018, 12, 8)}}
])
```

See also

- The *Indexing a document* recipe in Chapter 3, *Basic Operations*
- The *Getting a document* recipe in Chapter 3, *Basic Operations*
- The *Deleting a document* recipe in Chapter 3, *Basic Operations*
- The *Updating a document* recipe in Chapter 3, *Basic Operations*
- The *Speeding up atomic operations (Bulk operations)* recipe in Chapter 3, *Basic Operations*

Executing a standard search

Second to document insertion, the most commonly executed action in Elasticsearch is the search. The official Elasticsearch client APIs for searching are similar to the REST API.

Getting ready

You need an up-and-running Elasticsearch installation, which we described how to get in the *Downloading and installing Elasticsearch* recipe in Chapter 1, *Getting Started*.

You also need the Python packages that were installed in the *Creating a client* recipe in this chapter.

The code for this recipe can be found in the ch15/code/searching.py file.

How to do it...

To execute a standard query, the client search method must be called by passing the query parameters, as we saw in Chapter 4, *Exploring Search Capabilities*. The required parameters are index_name, type_name, and the query DSL. In this recipe, we will learn how to call a match_all query, a term query, and a filter query. We will perform the following steps:

1. We initialize the client and populate the index, as follows:

```
import elasticsearch
from pprint import pprint
```

```
es = elasticsearch.Elasticsearch()
index_name = "my_index"
type_name = "_doc"

if es.indices.exists(index_name):
    es.indices.delete(index_name)

from code.utils import create_and_add_mapping, populate

create_and_add_mapping(es, index_name)
populate(es, index_name)
```

2. Then, we execute a search with a `match_all` query and print the results, as follows:

```
results = es.search(index_name, type_name, {"query":
{"match_all": {}}})
pprint(results)
```

3. We then execute a search with a `term` query and print the results, as follows:

```
results = es.search(index_name, type_name, {
    "query": {
        "term": {"name": {"boost": 3.0, "value": "joe"}}}
})
pprint(results)
```

4. Next, we execute a search with a `bool` filter query and print the results, as follows:

```
results = es.search(index_name, type_name, {"query": {
    "bool": {
        "filter": {
            "bool": {
                "should": [
                    {"term": {"position": 1}},
                    {"term": {"position": 2}}]}
        }}}})
pprint(results)
```

5. Finally, we remove the index, as follows:

```
es.indices.delete(index_name)
```

How it works...

The idea behind the Elasticsearch official clients is that they should offer a common API that is more similar to REST calls. In Python, it is very easy to use the query DSL, as it provides an easy mapping from the Python dictionary to JSON objects and vice versa.

In the preceding example, before calling the search, we need to initialize the index and put some data in it; this is done using the two helpers available in the `utils` package, which is available in the `ch_15` directory.

The two methods are as follows:

- `create_and_add_mapping(es, index_name, type_name)`: This initializes the index and inserts the correct mapping to perform the search. The code of this function was taken from the *Managing mappings* recipe in this chapter.
- `populate(es, index_name, type_name)`: This populates the index with data. The code for this function was taken from the previous recipe.

After initializing some data, we can execute queries against it. To execute a search, the method that must be called is `search` on the client. This method accepts all the parameters that were described for REST calls in the *Searching* recipe in Chapter 4, *Exploring Search Capabilities*.

The actual method signature for the `search` method is as follows:

```
@query_params('_source', '_source_exclude', '_source_include',
    'allow_no_indices', 'allow_partial_search_results',
'analyze_wildcard',
    'analyzer', 'batched_reduce_size', 'default_operator', 'df',
    'docvalue_fields', 'expand_wildcards', 'explain', 'from_',
    'ignore_unavailable', 'lenient', 'max_concurrent_shard_requests',
    'pre_filter_shard_size', 'preference', 'q', 'request_cache',
'routing',
    'scroll', 'search_type', 'size', 'sort', 'stats', 'stored_fields',
    'suggest_field', 'suggest_mode', 'suggest_size', 'suggest_text',
    'terminate_after', 'timeout', 'track_scores', 'track_total_hits',
    'typed_keys', 'version')
def search(self, index=None, doc_type=None, body=None, params=None):
```

The `index` value could be one of the following:

- An index name or an alias name
- A list of index (or alias) names as a string separated by commas (that is, `index1,index2,indexN`)
- `_all`, the special keyword that indicates all the indices

The `type` value could be one of the following:

- A `type_name`
- A list of type names as a string separated by a comma (that is, `type1,type2,typeN`)
- `None` to indicate all the types

The body is the search DSL, as we saw in `Chapter 4`, *Exploring Search Capabilities*. In the preceding example we have the following:

- A `match_all` query (see the *Matching all the documents* recipe in `Chapter 4`, *Exploring Search Capabilities*) to match all the index-type documents, as follows:

  ```
  results = es.search(index_name, type_name, {"query":
  {"match_all": {}}})
  ```

- A `term` query that matches a name term, `joe`, with `boost 3.0`, as shown in the following code:

  ```
  results = es.search(index_name, type_name, {
      "query": {
          "term": {"name": {"boost": 3.0, "value": "joe"}}}
  })
  ```

- A filtered query with a query (`match_all`) and an `or` filter with two `term` filters matching `position 1` and 2, as shown in the following code:

  ```
  results = es.search(index_name, type_name, {"query": {
      "bool": {
          "filter": {
              "bool": {
                  "should": [
                      {"term": {"position": 1}},
                      {"term": {"position": 2}}]}
  }}}})
  ```

The returned result is a JSON dictionary, which we discussed in `Chapter 4`, *Exploring Search Capabilities*.

If some hits are matched, they are returned in the hits field. The standard number of results that's returned is `10`. To return more results, you need to paginate the results with the `from` and `start` parameters.

In `Chapter 4`, `Exploring Search Capabilities`, there is a list of definitions for all the parameters that are used in the search.

See also

- The *Executing a search* recipe in `Chapter 4`, *Exploring Search Capabilities*, for a detailed description of some search parameters
- The *Matching all the documents* recipe in `Chapter 4`, *Exploring Search Capabilities*, for a description of the `match_all` query

Executing a search with aggregations

Searching for results is obviously the main activity for a search engine, and therefore aggregations are very important because they often help to augment the results.

Aggregations are executed along with the search by performing analytics on the results of the search.

Getting ready

You need an up-and-running Elasticsearch installation, which we described how to get in the *Downloading and installing Elasticsearch* recipe in `Chapter 1`, *Getting Started*.

You also need the Python packages that we installed in the *Creating a client* recipe of this chapter.

The code for this recipe can be found in the `ch15/code/aggregation.py` file.

How to do it...

To extend a query with aggregations, you need to define an aggregation section, as we saw in Chapter 7, *Aggregations*. In the case of the official Elasticsearch client, you can add the aggregation DSL to the search dictionary to provide aggregations. To set this up, we will go through the following steps:

1. We need to initialize the client and populate the index, as follows:

```
import elasticsearch
from pprint import pprint

es = elasticsearch.Elasticsearch()
index_name = "my_index"
type_name = "_doc"

if es.indices.exists(index_name):
    es.indices.delete(index_name)

from code.utils import create_and_add_mapping, populate

create_and_add_mapping(es, index_name)
populate(es, index_name)
```

2. Then, we can execute a search with a terms aggregation, as follows:

```
results = es.search(index_name, type_name,
                    { "size":0,
                        "aggs": {
                            "pterms": {"terms": {"field":
"name", "size": 10}}
                        }
                    })
pprint(results)
```

3. Next, we execute a search with a date histogram aggregation, as follows:

```
results = es.search(index_name, type_name,
                    { "size":0,
                        "aggs": {
                            "date_histo": {"date_histogram":
{"field": "date", "interval": "month"}}
                        }
                    })
pprint(results)

es.indices.delete(index_name)
```

How it works...

As described in Chapter 7, *Aggregations*, the aggregations are calculated during the search in a distributed way. When you send a query to Elasticsearch with the aggregations defined, it adds an additional step in the query processing, allowing for the computation of aggregations.

In the preceding example, there are two kinds of aggregations: terms aggregation and date histogram aggregation.

The first is used to count terms, and it is often seen in sites that provide facet filtering on term aggregations of results, such as producers, geographic locations, and so on. This is shown in the following code:

```
results = es.search(index_name, type_name,
                    { "size":0,
                        "aggs": {
                            "pterms": {"terms": {"field": "name",
"size": 10}}
                        }
                    })
```

The term aggregation requires a field to count on. The default number of buckets for the field that's returned is 10. This value can be changed by defining the `size` parameter.

The second kind of aggregation that is calculated is the date histogram, which provides hits based on a `datetime` field. This aggregation requires at least two parameters: the `datetime` field, to be used as the source, and the `interval`, to be used for computation, as follows:

```
results = es.search(index_name, type_name,
                    { "size":0,
                        "aggs": {
                            "date_histo": {"date_histogram": {"field":
"date", "interval": "month"}}
                        }
                    })
```

The search results are standard search responses that we saw in Chapter 7, *Aggregations*.

See also

- The *Executing the terms aggregation* recipe in `Chapter 7`, *Aggregations*, on aggregating term values
- The *Executing the date histogram aggregation* recipe in `Chapter 7`, *Aggregations*, on computing the histogram aggregation on date/time fields

Integrating with NumPy and scikit-learn

Elasticsearch can be easily integrated with many Python machine learning libraries. One of the most used libraries for works with datasets is NumPy—a NumPy array is a building block dataset for many Python machine learning libraries. In this recipe will we seen how it's possible to use Elasticsearch as dataset for the `scikit-learn` library (`https://scikit-learn.org/`).

Getting ready

You need an up and running Elasticsearch installation, as we described in the *Downloading and installing Elasticsearch* recipe in `Chapter 1`, *Getting Started*.

The code for this recipe is in the `ch15/code` directory and the file used in the following section is the `kmeans_example.py`.

We will use the `iris` dataset (`https://en.wikipedia.org/wiki/Iris_flower_data_set`) that we have used in `Chapter 13`, *Java Integration*. To prepare your index dataset `iris`, we need to populate it executing the `PopulatingIndex` class available in the source code of `Chapter 13`, *Java Integration*.

How to do it...

We are going to use Elasticsearch as a data source to build our dataset and we will execute a clusterization using the `KMeans` algorithm provided by `scikit-learn`. To do so, we will perform the following steps:

1. We need to add the required machine learning libraries required in the file `requirements.txt` and install them:

   ```
   pandas
   matplotlib
   sklearn
   ```

2. Now we can initialize the Elasticsearch client and fetch our samples:

   ```
   import elasticsearch
   es = elasticsearch.Elasticsearch()
   result = es.search(index="iris", size=100)
   ```

3. Now we can read our dataset iterating on Elasticsearch hit results:

   ```
   x = []
    for hit in result["hits"]["hits"]:
        source = hit["_source"]
        x.append(np.array([source['f1'], source['f2'],
   source['f3'], source['f4']]))
    x = np.array(x)
   ```

4. After having loaded our dataset, we can execute a clusterization using the `KMeans` algorithm:

   ```
   # Finding the optimum number of clusters for k-means
   classification
    from sklearn.cluster import KMeans
    # Applying kmeans to the dataset / Creating the kmeans
   classifier
    kmeans = KMeans(n_clusters=3, init='k-means++', max_iter=300,
   n_init=10, random_state=0)
    y_kmeans = kmeans.fit_predict(x)
   ```

5. Now that the clusters are computed, we need to show them to verify the result. To do this, we use the `matplotlib.pyplot` module:

   ```
   plt.scatter(x[y_kmeans == 0, 0], x[y_kmeans == 0, 1], s=100,
   c='red', label='Iris-setosa')
    plt.scatter(x[y_kmeans == 1, 0], x[y_kmeans == 1, 1], s=100,
   c='blue', label='Iris-versicolour')
   ```

```
plt.scatter(x[y_kmeans == 2, 0], x[y_kmeans == 2, 1], s=100,
c='green', label='Iris-virginica')

# Plotting the centroids of the clusters
plt.scatter(kmeans.cluster_centers_[:, 0],
kmeans.cluster_centers_[:, 1], s=100, c='yellow',
label='Centroids')

plt.legend()
plt.show()
```

The final output will be the following plot:

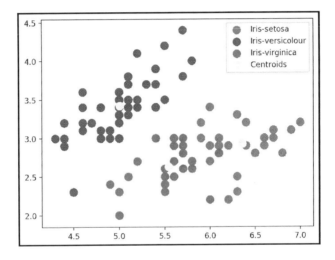

How it works...

Elasticsearch is a very powerful data store for machine learning datasets. It allows using its query capabilities to filter the data and retrieve what is needed to build a dataset used for machine learning activities.

As you can see from the preceding code, to fetch the data from the Elasticsearch with Python we use just a few lines of code—one line to initialize the client and the another one to retrieve the results:

```
import elasticsearch
es = elasticsearch.Elasticsearch()
result = es.search(index="iris", size=100)
```

When you have the results hits, it's easy to iterate on them and extract the NumPy array required for the machine learning libraries.

In the preceding code, we generate a NumPy array for every sample iterating on all the hits:

```
x = []
 for hit in result["hits"]["hits"]:
     source = hit["_source"]
     x.append(np.array([source['f1'], source['f2'], source['f3'],
source['f4']]))
 x = np.array(x)
```

The resulting Numpy array x can be used as input for every statistic or machine learning libraries.

Using Elasticsearch to manage datasets gives more advantages against typical approach to use CSV or data files such as:

- Automatically distribute your datasets to everyone that is able to connect to Elasticsearch
- The samples are already in correct type format (int, double, string): not needed to covert values due to file reading
- You can easily filter the samples without reading all the data in memory using Elasticsearch queries
- You can use Kibana for data exploration before creating your machine models

See also

You can refer to the following URLs for further reference, which are related to this recipe:

- A more detailed description of Iris dataset at `https://en.wikipedia.org/wiki/Iris_flower_data_set`
- The official site of scikit-learn (`https://scikit-learn.org/stable/`) for more example and references about this library.
- The official site of NumPy (`https://www.numpy.org/`) for more details about this library.

16
Plugin Development

Elasticsearch is designed to be extended with plugins to improve its capabilities. In the previous chapters, we installed and used many of them (new queries, REST endpoints, and scripting plugins).

Plugins are application extensions that can add many features to Elasticsearch. They can have several usages, such as the following:

- Adding a new scripting language (that is, Python and JavaScript plugins)
- Adding new aggregation types
- Extending Lucene-supported analyzers and tokenizers
- Using native scripting to speed up computation of scores, filters, and field manipulation
- Extending node capabilities, for example, creating a node plugin that can execute your logic
- Monitoring and administering clusters

In this chapter, the Java language will be used to develop a native plugin, but it is possible to use any JVM language that generates JAR files.

The standard tools to build and test Elasticsearch components are built on top of Gradle (https://gradle.org/). All our custom plugins will use Gradle to build them.

In this chapter, we will cover the following recipes:

- Creating a plugin
- Creating an analyzer plugin
- Creating a REST plugin
- Creating a cluster action
- Creating an ingest plugin

Creating a plugin

Native plugins allow several aspects of the Elasticsearch server to be extended, but they require good knowledge of Java.

In this recipe, we will see how to set up a working environment to develop native plugins.

Getting ready

You need an up and running Elasticsearch installation, as we described in *Downloading and installing Elasticsearch* recipe in `Chapter 1`, *Getting Started*.

Gradle or an **integrated development environment** (**IDE**) that supports Java programming with Gradle, such as Eclipse or IntelliJ IDEA, is required.

The code for this recipe is available in the `ch16/simple_plugin` directory.

How to do it...

Generally, Elasticsearch plugins are developed in Java using the Gradle build tool and deployed as a ZIP file.

To create a simple JAR plugin, we will perform the following steps:

1. To correctly build and serve a plugin, some files must be defined:

    * `build.gradle` and `settings.gradle` are used to define the build configuration for Gradle
    * `LICENSE.txt` defines the plugin license
    * `NOTICE.txt` is a copyright notice

2. A `build.gradle` file is used to create a plugin that contains the following code:

    ```
    buildscript {
      repositories {
        mavenLocal()
        mavenCentral()
        jcenter()
      }
    ```

```
   dependencies {
     classpath "org.elasticsearch.gradle:build-tools:7.0.0-
  alpha2"
   }
}

group = 'org.elasticsearch.plugin.analysis'
version = '0.0.1-SNAPSHOT'

apply plugin: 'java'
apply plugin: 'idea'
apply plugin: 'elasticsearch.esplugin'

// license of this project
licenseFile = rootProject.file('LICENSE.txt')
// copyright notices
noticeFile = rootProject.file('NOTICE.txt')
esplugin {
  name 'simple-plugin'
  description 'A simple plugin for ElasticSearch'
  classname 'org.elasticsearch.plugin.simple.SimplePlugin'
  // license of the plugin, may be different than the above
license
  licenseFile rootProject.file('LICENSE.txt')
  // copyright notices, may be different than the above notice
  noticeFile rootProject.file('NOTICE.txt')
}

dependencies {
 compile 'org.elasticsearch:elasticsearch:7.0.0-alpha2'

 testCompile 'org.elasticsearch.test:framework:7.0.0-alpha2'
}

// Set to false to not use elasticsearch checkstyle rules
checkstyleMain.enabled = true
checkstyleTest.enabled = true

dependencyLicenses.enabled = false

thirdPartyAudit.enabled = false
```

3. The `settings.gradle` file is used for the project name, as follows:

```
rootProject.name = 'simple-plugin'
```

4. The `src/main/java/org/elasticsearch/plugin/simple/SimplePlugin`
`.java` class is an example of the basic (the minimum required) code that
needs to be compiled for executing a plugin, as follows:

```
package org.elasticsearch.plugin.simple;


import org.elasticsearch.plugins.Plugin;

public class SimplePlugin extends Plugin {

}
```

How it works...

Several parts make up the development life cycle of a plugin, such as designing,
coding, building, and deploying. To speed up the build and deployment steps, which
are common to all plugins, we need to create a `build.gradle` file.

The preceding `build.gradle` file is a standard for developing Elasticsearch plugins.
This file is composed of the following:

- A buildscript section that depends on the Gradle building tools for
  Elasticsearch, as follows:

```
buildscript {
  repositories {
    mavenLocal()
    mavenCentral()
    jcenter()
  }

  dependencies {
    classpath "org.elasticsearch.gradle:build-tools:7.0.0-
alpha2"
  }
}
```

- The group and the version of the plugin, as follows:

```
group = 'org.elasticsearch.plugin'
version = '0.0.1-SNAPSHOT'
```

- A list of Gradle plugins that must be activated, as follows:

```
apply plugin: 'java'
apply plugin: 'idea'
apply plugin: 'elasticsearch.esplugin'
```

- The license and notice file definition, as follows:

```
// license of this project
licenseFile = rootProject.file('LICENSE.txt')
// copyright notices
noticeFile = rootProject.file('NOTICE.txt')
```

- The information that's needed to populate the plugin description: that is used to generate the `plugin-descriptor.properties` file that will be available in the final distribution ZIP. The most important parameter is the class name, which is the main entrypoint of the plugin:

```
esplugin {
  name 'simple-plugin'
  description 'A simple plugin for ElasticSearch'
  classname 'org.elasticsearch.plugin.simple.SimplePlugin'
  // license of the plugin, may be different than the above
license
  licenseFile rootProject.file('LICENSE.txt')
  // copyright notices, may be different than the above notice
  noticeFile rootProject.file('NOTICE.txt')
}
```

- For compiling the code, the dependencies are required, as follows:

```
dependencies {
  compile 'org.elasticsearch:elasticsearch:7.0.0-alpha2'

  testCompile 'org.elasticsearch.test:framework:7.0.0-alpha2'
}
```

After configuring Gradle, we can start writing the main plugin class.

Every plugin class must be derived from a `Plugin` one and it must be public, otherwise it cannot be loaded dynamically from the JAR, as follows:

```
package org.elasticsearch.plugin.simple;

import org.elasticsearch.plugins.Plugin;
```

After having defined all the files that are required to generate a ZIP release of our plugin, it is enough to invoke the `gradle clean check` command. This command will compile the code and create a `zip` package in the `build/distributions/` directory of your project: the final ZIP file can be deployed as a plugin on your Elasticsearch cluster.

In this recipe, we configured a working environment to build, deploy, and test plugins. In the following recipes, we will reuse this environment to develop several plugin types.

There's more...

Compiling and packaging a plugin are not enough to define a good life cycle for your plugin: a test phase for testing your plugin functionalities needs to be provided.

Testing the plugin functionalities with test cases reduces the number of bugs that can affect the plugin when it's released.

The order is very important, so make sure to put the following line in your dependencies:

```
testCompile 'org.elasticsearch.test:framework:7.0.0-alpha2'
```

 The extension of Elasticsearch for Gradle has everything to set up test and integration tests.

Creating an analyzer plugin

Elasticsearch provides a large set of analyzers and tokenizers to cover general needs out of the box. Sometimes, we need to extend the capabilities of Elasticsearch by adding new analyzers.

Typically, you can create an analyzer plugin when you need to do the following:

- Add standard Lucene analyzers/tokenizers that are not provided by Elasticsearch
- Integrate third-party analyzers
- Add custom analyzers

In this recipe, we will add a new custom English analyzer, similar to the one provided by Elasticsearch.

Getting ready

You need an up and running Elasticsearch installation, as we described in the *Downloading and installing Elasticsearch* recipe in `Chapter 1`, *Getting Started*.

Gradle or an IDE that supports Java programming with Gradle, such as Eclipse or IntelliJ IDEA, is required. The code for this recipe is available in the `ch16/analysis_plugin` directory.

How to do it...

An analyzer plugin is generally composed of the following two classes:

- A `Plugin` class, which implements the `org.elasticsearch.plugins.AnalysisPlugin` class
- An `AnalyzerProviders` class, which provides an analyzer

To create an analyzer plugin, we will perform the following steps:

1. The `plugin` class is similar to the ones we've seen in previous recipes, but it includes a method that returns the analyzers, as follows:

```
package org.elasticsearch.plugin.analysis;

import org.apache.lucene.analysis.Analyzer;
import org.elasticsearch.index.analysis.AnalyzerProvider;
import
org.elasticsearch.index.analysis.CustomEnglishAnalyzerProvider
;
import org.elasticsearch.indices.analysis.AnalysisModule;
import org.elasticsearch.plugins.Plugin;

import java.util.HashMap;
import java.util.Map;

public class AnalysisPlugin extends Plugin implements
org.elasticsearch.plugins.AnalysisPlugin {
    @Override
    public Map<String,
AnalysisModule.AnalysisProvider<AnalyzerProvider<? extends
```

```
Analyzer>>> getAnalyzers() {
        Map<String,
AnalysisModule.AnalysisProvider<AnalyzerProvider<? extends
Analyzer>>> analyzers = new HashMap<>();
        analyzers.put(CustomEnglishAnalyzerProvider.NAME,
CustomEnglishAnalyzerProvider::getCustomEnglishAnalyzerProvide
r);
        return analyzers;
    }
}
```

2. The `AnalyzerProvider` class provides the initialization of our analyzer, and passes the parameters that are provided by the settings, as follows:

```
package org.elasticsearch.index.analysis;

import org.apache.lucene.analysis.en.EnglishAnalyzer;
import org.apache.lucene.analysis.CharArraySet;
import org.elasticsearch.common.settings.Settings;
import org.elasticsearch.env.Environment;
import org.elasticsearch.index.IndexSettings;

public class CustomEnglishAnalyzerProvider extends
AbstractIndexAnalyzerProvider<EnglishAnalyzer> {
    public static String NAME = "custom_english";

    private final EnglishAnalyzer analyzer;

    public CustomEnglishAnalyzerProvider(IndexSettings
indexSettings, Environment env, String name, Settings
settings,
                                          boolean useSmart) {
        super(indexSettings, name, settings);

        analyzer = new EnglishAnalyzer(
                Analysis.parseStopWords(env, settings,
EnglishAnalyzer.getDefaultStopSet(), true),
                Analysis.parseStemExclusion(settings,
CharArraySet.EMPTY_SET));
    }

    public static CustomEnglishAnalyzerProvider
getCustomEnglishAnalyzerProvider(IndexSettings indexSettings,
Environment env, String name,
Settings settings) {
        return new
CustomEnglishAnalyzerProvider(indexSettings, env, name,
settings, true);
```

```
        }

        @Override
        public EnglishAnalyzer get() {
            return this.analyzer;
        }
    }
```

After building the plugin and installing it on an Elasticsearch server, our analyzer is accessible as any native Elasticsearch analyzer.

How it works...

Creating an analyzer plugin is quite simple. The general workflow is as follows:

- Wrap the analyzer initialization in a provider
- Register the analyzer provider in the plugin

In the preceding example, we registered a CustomEnglishAnalyzerProvider class, which extends the EnglishAnalyzer class:

```
public class CustomEnglishAnalyzerProvider extends
AbstractIndexAnalyzerProvider<EnglishAnalyzer> {
```

We need to provide a name to analyzer, as follows:

```
public static String NAME = "custom_english";
```

We instantiate a private scope Lucene analyzer (in Chapter 2, *Managing Mapping*, we have discussed custom Lucene analyzers usage)r to be provided on request with the get method, as follows:

```
private final EnglishAnalyzer analyzer;
```

The CustomEnglishAnalyzerProvider constructor can be injected via Google Guice, with settings that can be used to provide cluster defaults via index settings or elasticsearch.yml, as follows:

```
public CustomEnglishAnalyzerProvider(IndexSettings indexSettings,
Environment env, String name, Settings settings, boolean ignoreCase) {
```

To make it work correctly, we need to set up the parent constructor via the `super` call, as follows:

```
super(indexSettings, name, settings);
```

Now, we can initialize the internal analyzer, which must be returned by the `get` method, as follows:

```
analyzer = new EnglishAnalyzer(
        Analysis.parseStopWords(env, settings,
EnglishAnalyzer.getDefaultStopSet(), ignoreCase),
        Analysis.parseStemExclusion(settings,
CharArraySet.EMPTY_SET));
```

This analyzer accepts the following:

- A list of stopwords that can be loaded via the settings or set by the default ones
- A list of words that must be excluded by the stemming step

To easily wrap the analyzer, we need to create a `static` method that can be called to create the analyzer. We'll use it in the plugin definition, as follows:

```
public static CustomEnglishAnalyzerProvider
getCustomEnglishAnalyzerProvider(IndexSettings indexSettings,
Environment env, String name, Settings settings) {
  return new CustomEnglishAnalyzerProvider(indexSettings, env, name,
settings, true);
}
```

Finally, we can register our analyzer in the plugin. To do so, our plugin must derive from `AnalysisPlugin` so that we can override the `getAnalyzers` method, as follows:

```
@Override
public Map<String, AnalysisModule.AnalysisProvider<AnalyzerProvider<?
extends Analyzer>>> getAnalyzers() {
    Map<String, AnalysisModule.AnalysisProvider<AnalyzerProvider<?
extends Analyzer>>> analyzers = new HashMap<>();
    analyzers.put(CustomEnglishAnalyzerProvider.NAME,
CustomEnglishAnalyzerProvider::getCustomEnglishAnalyzerProvider);
    return analyzers;
}
```

The `::` operator of Java 8 allows us to provide a function that will be used for the construction of our `AnalyzerProvider`.

There's more...

A plugin extends several Elasticsearch functionalities. To provide them with this requires extending the correct plugin interface. In Elasticsearch 7.x, the following are the main plugin interfaces:

- `ActionPlugin`: This is used for REST and cluster actions
- `AnalysisPlugin`: This is used for extending all the analysis stuff, such as analyzers, tokenizers, tokenFilters, and charFilters
- `ClusterPlugin`: This is used to provide new deciders
- `DiscoveryPlugin`: This is used to provide custom node name resolvers
- `EnginePlugin`: This is used to provide new custom engine for indices
- `IndexStorePlugin`: This is used to provide a custom index store
- `IngestPlugin`: This is used to provide new ingest processors
- `MapperPlugin`: This is used to provide new mappers and metadata mappers
- `ReloadablePlugin`: This allows you to create plugins that reload their state
- `RepositoryPlugin`: This allows the provision of new repositories to be used in backup/restore functionalities
- `ScriptPlugin`: This allows the provision of new scripting languages, scripting contexts, or native scripts (Java based ones)
- `SearchPlugin`: This allows extending all the search functionalities: Highlighter, aggregations, suggesters, and queries

If your plugin needs to extend more than a single functionality, it can extend from several plugin interfaces at once.

Creating a REST plugin

In the previous recipe, we read how to build an analyzer plugin that extends the query capabilities of Elasticsearch. In this recipe, we will see how to create one of the most common Elasticsearch plugins. This kind of plugin allows the standard REST calls to be extended with custom ones to easily improve the capabilities of Elasticsearch.

In this recipe, we will see how to define a REST entrypoint and create its action; in the next one, we'll see how to execute this action distributed in shards.

Getting ready

You need an up and running Elasticsearch installation, as we described in *Downloading and installing Elasticsearch* recipe in `Chapter 1`, *Getting Started*.

Gradle or an IDE that supports Java programming with Gradle, such as Eclipse or IntelliJ IDEA, is required. The code for this recipe is available in the `ch16/rest_plugin` directory.

How to do it...

To create a REST entrypoint, we need to create the action and then register it in the plugin. We will perform the following steps:

1. We create a REST `simple` action (`RestSimpleAction.java`) as follows:

```
public class RestSimpleAction extends BaseRestHandler {
    public RestSimpleAction(Settings settings, RestController
controller) {
        super(settings);
        controller.registerHandler(POST, "/_simple", this);
        controller.registerHandler(POST, "/{index}/_simple",
this);
        controller.registerHandler(POST, "/_simple/{field}",
this);
        controller.registerHandler(GET, "/_simple", this);
        controller.registerHandler(GET, "/{index}/_simple",
this);
        controller.registerHandler(GET, "/_simple/{field}",
this);
    }

    @Override
    public String getName() {
        return "simple_rest";
    }


    @Override
    protected RestChannelConsumer prepareRequest(RestRequest
request, NodeClient client) throws IOException {
        final SimpleRequest simpleRequest = new
SimpleRequest(Strings.splitStringByCommaToArray(request.param(
"index")));
        simpleRequest.setField(request.param("field"));
```

```
                    return channel ->
client.execute(SimpleAction.INSTANCE, simpleRequest, new
RestBuilderListener<SimpleResponse>(channel) {
            @Override
            public RestResponse buildResponse(SimpleResponse
simpleResponse, XContentBuilder builder) throws Exception {
                try {
                    builder.startObject();
                    builder.field("ok", true);
                    builder.array("terms",
simpleResponse.getSimple().toArray());
                    builder.endObject();

                } catch (Exception e) {
                    onFailure(e);
                }
                return new BytesRestResponse(OK, builder);
            }
        });
    }
}
```

2. We need to register it in the plugin with the following lines:

```
public class RestPlugin extends Plugin implements ActionPlugin
{

    @Override
    public List<RestHandler> getRestHandlers(Settings
settings, RestController restController, ClusterSettings
clusterSettings, IndexScopedSettings indexScopedSettings,
SettingsFilter settingsFilter, IndexNameExpressionResolver
indexNameExpressionResolver, Supplier<DiscoveryNodes>
nodesInCluster) {
        return Arrays.asList(new RestSimpleAction(settings,
restController));
    }
    @Override
    public List<ActionHandler<? extends ActionRequest, ?
extends ActionResponse>> getActions() {
        return Arrays.asList(new
ActionHandler<>(SimpleAction.INSTANCE,
TransportSimpleAction.class));
    }
}
```

3. Now, we can build the plugin via the `gradle clean check` and manually install the ZIP. If we restart the Elasticsearch server, we should see the plugin loaded as follows:

> ...truncated...[2019-02-05T21:15:35,250][WARN][o.e.n.Node] [iMacParo.local] version [7.0.0-alpha2] is a pre-release version of Elasticsearch and is not suitable for production
> [2019-02-05T21:15:36,306][INFO][o.e.p.PluginsService] [iMacParo.local] loaded module [aggs-matrix-stats]
> ... *truncated*...
> [2019-02-05T21:15:36,311][INFO][o.e.p.PluginsService] [iMacParo.local] loaded plugin [rest-plugin]
> [2019-02-05T21:15:38,736][INFO][o.e.x.s.a.s.FileRolesStore] [iMacParo.local] parsed [0] roles from file [/Users/alberto/elasticsear

4. We can test out custom REST via `curl` as follows:

```
curl -XPUT http://127.0.0.1:9200/mytest
curl -XPUT http://127.0.0.1:9200/mytest2
curl 'http://127.0.0.1:9200/_simple?field=mytest&pretty'
```

5. The result will be something similar to the following:

```
{
  "ok" : true,
  "terms" : [
  "mytest_[mytest2][0]",
  "mytest_[mytest][0]"
  ]
}
```

How it works...

Adding a REST action is very easy: We need to create a `RestXXXAction` class that handles the calls.

The REST action is derived from the `BaseRestHandler` class and needs to implement the `handleRequest` method.

The constructor is very important. So let's start by writing the following:

```
public RestSimpleAction(Settings settings, RestController controller)
{
```

The public constructor takes the following parameters:

- `Settings`: This can be used to load custom settings for your REST action
- `RestController`: This is used to register the REST action to the controller

In the constructor of the REST action, the list of actions that must be handled is registered in the `RestController` as follows:

```
super(settings);
controller.registerHandler(POST, "/_simple", this);
```

To register an action, the following parameters must be passed to the controller:

- The REST method (GET/POST/PUT/DELETE/HEAD/OPTIONS)
- The URL entrypoint
- The `RestHandler`, usually the same class, which must answer the call

After having defined the constructor, if an action is fired, the class method `prepareRequest` is called as follows:

```
@Override
protected RestChannelConsumer prepareRequest(RestRequest request,
NodeClient client) {
```

This method is the core of the REST action. It processes the request and sends back the result. The following parameters are passed to the method:

- `RestRequest`: This is the REST request that hits the Elasticsearch server
- `RestChannel`: This is the channel used to send back the response
- `NodeClient`: This is the client used to communicate in the cluster

The returned value is a `RestChannelConsumer` that is a `FunctionalInterface` that accepts a `RestChannel`—it's a simple Lambda.

A `prepareRequest` method is usually composed of these phases:

- Process the REST request and build an inner Elasticsearch request object
- Call the client with the Elasticsearch request
- If it is okay, process the Elasticsearch response and build the resulting JSON
- If there are errors, send back the JSON error response

In the following example, we created a `SimpleRequest` processing the request:

```
final SimpleRequest simpleRequest = new
SimpleRequest(Strings.splitStringByCommaToArray(request.param("index")
));
simpleRequest.setField(request.param("field"));
```

As you can see, it accepts a list of indices (we split the classic comma-separated list of indices via the `Strings.splitStringByCommaToArray` helper) and we had the `field` parameter if available.

Now that we have a `SimpleRequest`, we can send it to the cluster and get back `SimpleResponse` via the Lambda closure as follows:

```
return channel -> client.execute(SimpleAction.INSTANCE, simpleRequest,
    new RestBuilderListener<SimpleResponse>(channel) {
```

`client.execute` accepts an action, a request, and a `RestBuilderListener` class that maps a future response. We can now process the response via the definition of a `onResponse` method.

`onResponse` receives a `Response` object that must be converted in a JSON result as follows:

```
@Override
public RestResponse buildResponse(SimpleResponse simpleResponse,
XContentBuilder builder) {
```

The builder is the standard JSON `XContentBuilder` that we have already seen in Chapter 13, *Java Integration,*

After having processed the cluster response and built the JSON, we can send the REST response as follows:

```
@Override
public RestResponse buildResponse(SimpleResponse simpleResponse,
XContentBuilder builder) {
```

Obviously, if something goes wrong during the JSON creation, an exception must be raised such as the following:

```
try {
    //JSON creation
} catch (Exception e) {
    onFailure(e);
}
```

We will discuss `SimpleRequest` in the next recipe.

See also

Google Guice is used for dependency injection. See `https://code.google.com/p/google-guice/` for more information on the dependency injection system used by Elasticsearch

Creating a cluster action

In the previous recipe, we saw how to create a REST entrypoint, but to execute the action at the cluster level, we will need to create a cluster action.

An Elasticsearch action is generally executed and distributed in the cluster and, in this recipe, we will see how to implement this kind of action. The cluster action will be very bare; we send a string with a value to every shard and the shards echo a result string concatenating the string with the shard number.

Getting ready

You need an up and running Elasticsearch installation, as we described in *Downloading and installing Elasticsearch* recipe in `Chapter 1`, *Getting Started*.

Gradle or an IDE that supports Java programming with Gradle, such as Eclipse or IntelliJ IDEA, is required. The code for this recipe is available in the `ch16/rest_plugin` directory.

How to do it...

In this recipe, we will see that a REST call is converted to an internal cluster action. To execute an internal cluster action, the following classes are required:

- A `Request` and `Response` class to communicate with the cluster
- A `RequestBuilder` used to execute a request to the cluster
- An `Action` used to register the action and bound `Request`, `Response`, and `RequestBuilder`

- A `Transport*Action` to bind the request and response to `ShardResponse`: it manages the reduce part of the query

- A `ShardResponse` to manage the shard results

We will perform the following steps:

1. We write a `SimpleRequest` class as follows:

```
public class SimpleRequest extends
BroadcastRequest<SimpleRequest> {

    private String field;

    SimpleRequest() {
    }

    public SimpleRequest(String... indices) {
        super(indices);
    }

    public void setField(String field) {
        this.field = field;
    }

    public String getField() {
        return field;
    }

    @Override
    public void readFrom(StreamInput in) throws IOException {
        super.readFrom(in);
        field = in.readString();
    }

    @Override
    public void writeTo(StreamOutput out) throws IOException {
        super.writeTo(out);
        out.writeString(field);
    }
}
```

2. The `SimpleResponse` class is very similar to the `SimpleRequest`

3. To bind the request and the response, an action (`SimpleAction`) is required as follows:

```
import org.elasticsearch.action.Action;

public class SimpleAction extends Action<SimpleResponse> {

    public static final SimpleAction INSTANCE = new
SimpleAction();
    public static final String NAME = "custom:indices/simple";

    private SimpleAction() {
        super(NAME);
    }

    @Override
    public SimpleResponse newResponse() {
        return new SimpleResponse();
    }

}
```

4. The `Transport` class is the core of the action. It's quite long so we'll present only the main important parts as follows:

```
public class TransportSimpleAction
        extends TransportBroadcastByNodeAction<SimpleRequest,
SimpleResponse, ShardSimpleResponse> {

    private final IndicesService indicesService;

    @Inject
    public TransportSimpleAction(ClusterService
clusterService,
                                    TransportService
transportService, IndicesService indicesService,
                                    ActionFilters actionFilters,
IndexNameExpressionResolver indexNameExpressionResolver) {
        super(SimpleAction.NAME, clusterService,
transportService, actionFilters,
                    indexNameExpressionResolver,
SimpleRequest::new, ThreadPool.Names.SEARCH);
        this.indicesService = indicesService;
    }

    @Override
    protected SimpleResponse newResponse(SimpleRequest
request, int totalShards, int successfulShards, int
```

```
failedShards,
List<ShardSimpleResponse> shardSimpleResponses,
List<DefaultShardOperationFailedException> shardFailures,
                                    ClusterState
clusterState) {
        Set<String> simple = new HashSet<String>();
        for (ShardSimpleResponse shardSimpleResponse :
shardSimpleResponses) {
            simple.addAll(shardSimpleResponse.getTermList());
        }

        return new SimpleResponse(totalShards,
successfulShards, failedShards, shardFailures, simple);
    }


    @Override
    protected ShardSimpleResponse shardOperation(SimpleRequest
request, ShardRouting shardRouting) throws IOException {
        IndexService indexService =
indicesService.indexServiceSafe(shardRouting.shardId().getInde
x());
        IndexShard indexShard =
indexService.getShard(shardRouting.shardId().id());
        indexShard.store().directory();
        Set<String> set = new HashSet<String>();
        set.add(request.getField() + "_" +
shardRouting.shardId());
        return new ShardSimpleResponse(shardRouting, set);
    }


    @Override
    protected ShardSimpleResponse readShardResult(StreamInput
in) throws IOException {
        return ShardSimpleResponse.readShardResult(in);
    }

    @Override
    protected SimpleRequest readRequestFrom(StreamInput in)
throws IOException {
        SimpleRequest request = new SimpleRequest();
        request.readFrom(in);
        return request;
    }

    @Override
    protected ShardsIterator shards(ClusterState clusterState,
```

```
SimpleRequest request, String[] concreteIndices) {
        return
clusterState.routingTable().allShards(concreteIndices);
    }

    @Override
    protected ClusterBlockException
checkGlobalBlock(ClusterState state, SimpleRequest request) {
        return
state.blocks().globalBlockedException(ClusterBlockLevel.METADA
TA_READ);
    }

    @Override
    protected ClusterBlockException
checkRequestBlock(ClusterState state, SimpleRequest request,
String[] concreteIndices) {
        return
state.blocks().indicesBlockedException(ClusterBlockLevel.METAD
ATA_READ, concreteIndices);
    }
}
```

How it works...

In this example, we used an action that is executed in every cluster node and for every shard that is selected on that node.

As you have seen, to execute a cluster action, the following classes are required:

- A couple of `Request`/`Response` to interact with the cluster
- A task action on the cluster level
- A Shard `Response` to interact with the shards
- A `Transport` class to manage the map/reduce shard part that must be invoked by the REST call

These classes must extend one of the supported actions, for example:

- `TrasportBroadcastAction`: For actions that must be spread across the all cluster.
- `TransportClusterInfoAction`: For actions that need to read information at the cluster level.

- `TransportMasterNodeAction`: For actions that must be executed only by the master node.(such as index and mapping configuration). For simple acknowledge on the master, there are also `AcknowledgedRequest` response.

- `TransportNodeAction`: For actions that must be executed on nodes (that is, all the node statistic actions).

- `TransportBroadcastReplicationAction`, `TransportReplicationAction`, `TransportWriteAction`: For actions that must be executed by a particular replica, first on primary and then on secondary ones.

- `TransportInstanceSingleOperationAction`: For actions that must be executed as a singleton in the cluster.

- `TransportSingleShardAction`: For actions that must be executed only in a shard (that is, GET actions). If it fails on a shard, it automatically tries on the shard replicas.

- `TransportTasksAction`: For actions that need to interact with cluster tasks.

In our example, we have defined an action that will be broadcasted to every node and for every node, it collects its shard result and then it aggregates as follows:

```
public class TransportSimpleAction
        extends TransportBroadcastByNodeAction<SimpleRequest,
SimpleResponse, ShardSimpleResponse> {
```

All the request/response classes extend a `Streamable` class, so the following two methods for serializing their content must be provided:

- readFrom, which reads from an `StreamInput`, a class that encapsulates common input stream operations. This method allows the deserialization of the data we transmit on the wire. In the preceding example, we read a string with the following code:

  ```
  @Override
  public void readFrom(StreamInput in) throws IOException {
      super.readFrom(in);
      field = in.readString();
  }
  ```

- `writeTo`, which writes the contents of the class to be sent via the network. The `StreamOutput` provides convenient methods to process the output. In the following example, we serialized the `StreamOutput` string:

```
@Override
public void writeTo(StreamOutput out) throws IOException {
    super.writeTo(out);
    out.writeString(field);
}
```

In both actions, `super` must be called to allow the correct serialization of parent classes.

 Every internal action in Elasticsearch is designed as a request/response pattern.

To complete the request/response action, we must define an action that binds the request with the correct response and a builder to construct it. To do so, we need to define an `Action` class as follows:

```
public class SimpleAction extends Action<SimpleResponse> {
```

This `Action` object is a singleton object: we obtain it by creating a default static instance and private constructors as follows:

```
public static final SimpleAction INSTANCE = new SimpleAction();
public static final String NAME = "custom:indices/simple";

private SimpleAction() {
    super(NAME);
}
```

The static string `NAME` is used to uniquely identify the action at the cluster level.

To complete the `Action` definition, the `newResponse` method must be defined, which is used to create a new empty response as follows:

```
@Override
public SimpleResponse newResponse() {
    return new SimpleResponse();
}
```

When the action is executed, the request and the response are serialized and sent to the cluster. To execute our custom code at the cluster level, a transport action is required.

The transport actions are usually defined as map and reduce jobs. The map part consists of executing the action on several shards, and then reducing parts consisting of collecting all the results from the shards in a response that must be sent back to the requester. To speed up the process in Elasticsearch 5.x or above, all the shard's responses that belong in the same node are reduced in place to optimize the I/O and the network usage.

The transport action is a long class with many methods, but the most important ones are the ShardOperation (map part) and newResponse (reduce part).

The original request is converted in a distributed ShardRequest that is processed by the shardOperation method as follows:

```
@Override
protected ShardSimpleResponse shardOperation(SimpleRequest request,
ShardRouting shardRouting) {
```

To obtain the internal shard, we need to ask at the IndexService to return a shard based on wanted index.

The shard request contains the index and the ID of the shard that must be used to execute the action as follows:

```
IndexService indexService =
indicesService.indexServiceSafe(shardRouting.shardId().getIndex());
IndexShard indexShard =
indexService.getShard(shardRouting.shardId().id());
```

The IndexShard object allows the execution of every possible shard operation (search, get, index, and many others). By this method, we can execute every data shard manipulation that we want.

 Custom shard action can execute the application's business operation in a distributed and fast way.

In the following example, we have created a simple set of values:

```
indexShard.store().directory();
Set<String> set = new HashSet<String>();
set.add(request.getField() + "_" + shardRouting.shardId());
```

The final step of our shard operation is to create a response to send back to the reduce step. In creating `ShardResponse`, we need to return the result plus information about the index and the shard that executed the action as follows:

```
return new ShardSimpleResponse(shardRouting, set);
```

The distributed shard operations are collected in the reduce step (`newResponse` method). This step aggregates all the shard results and sends back the result to the original `Action` as follows:

```
@Override
protected SimpleResponse newResponse(SimpleRequest request, int
totalShards, int successfulShards, int failedShards,
                                 List<ShardSimpleResponse>
shardSimpleResponses,
List<DefaultShardOperationFailedException> shardFailures,
                                 ClusterState clusterState) {
```

Other than the shard's result, the methods receive the status of the shard level operation and they are collected in three values: `successfulShards`, `failedShards`, and `shardFailures`.

The request result is a set of collected strings, so we create an empty set to collect the term's results as follows:

```
Set<String> simple = new HashSet<String>();
```

Then you collect the results that we need to iterate on the shard responses as follows:

```
for (ShardSimpleResponse shardSimpleResponse : shardSimpleResponses) {
    simple.addAll(shardSimpleResponse.getTermList());
}
```

The final step is to create the response collecting the previous result and response status as follows:

```
return new SimpleResponse(totalShards, successfulShards, failedShards,
shardFailures, simple);
```

Creating a cluster action is required when there are low level operations that we want to execute very fast, such as special aggregations, server side join, or a complex manipulation that requires several Elasticsearch calls to be executed. Writing custom Elasticsearch actions is an advanced Elasticsearch feature, but it can create new business use scenarios that can level up the capabilities of Elasticsearch.

See also

Creating a REST plugin in this chapter for how to interface the cluster action with a REST call

Creating an ingest plugin

Elasticsearch 5.x introduces the ingest node that allows the modification, via a pipeline, to the records before ingesting in Elasticsearch. We have already seen in Chapter 12, *Using the Ingest Module,* that a pipeline is composed of one or more processor actions. In this recipe, we will see how to create a custom processor that stores in a field the initial character of another one.

Getting ready

You need an up and running Elasticsearch installation, as we described in *Downloading and installing Elasticsearch* recipe in Chapter 1, *Getting Started*.

Gradle or an IDE that supports Java programming with Gradle, such as Eclipse or IntelliJ IDEA, is required. The code for this recipe is available in the ch16/ingest_plugin directory.

How to do it...

To create an ingest processor plugin, we need to create the processor and then register it in the plugin class. We will perform the following steps:

1. We create the processor and its factory as follows:

```
public final class InitialProcessor extends AbstractProcessor
{
```

```
public static final String TYPE = "initial";

private final String field;
private final String targetField;
private final String defaultValue;
private final boolean ignoreMissing;

public InitialProcessor(String tag, String field, String
targetField, boolean ignoreMissing, String defaultValue) {
    super(tag);
    this.field = field;
    this.targetField = targetField;
    this.ignoreMissing = ignoreMissing;
    this.defaultValue = defaultValue;
}

String getField() { return field; }
String getTargetField() { return targetField; }
String getDefaultField() { return defaultValue; }
boolean isIgnoreMissing() { return ignoreMissing; }

@Override
public IngestDocument execute(IngestDocument document) {
    if (document.hasField(field, true) == false) {
        if (ignoreMissing) { return document;
        } else {
            throw new IllegalArgumentException("field [" +
field + "] not present as part of path [" + field + "]");
        }
    }
    // We fail here if the target field point to an array
slot that is out of range.
    // If we didn't do this then we would fail if we set
the value in the target_field
    // and then on failure processors would not see that
value we tried to rename as we already
    // removed it.
    if (document.hasField(targetField, true)) {
        throw new IllegalArgumentException("field [" +
targetField + "] already exists");
    }

    Object value = document.getFieldValue(field,
Object.class);
    if( value!=null && value instanceof String ) {
        String myValue=value.toString().trim();
        if(myValue.length()>1){
            try {
```

```
                    document.setFieldValue(targetField,
myValue.substring(0,1).toLowerCase(Locale.getDefault()));
                } catch (Exception e) {
                    // setting the value back to the original
field shouldn't as we just fetched it from that field:
                    document.setFieldValue(field, value);
                    throw e;
                }
            }
        }
        return document;
    }

    @Override
    public String getType() { return TYPE;}

    public static final class Factory implements
Processor.Factory {
        @Override
        public InitialProcessor create(Map<String,
Processor.Factory> registry, String processorTag,
                                       Map<String, Object>
config) throws Exception {
            String field =
ConfigurationUtils.readStringProperty(TYPE, processorTag,
config, "field");
            String targetField =
ConfigurationUtils.readStringProperty(TYPE, processorTag,
                    config, "target_field");
            String defaultValue =
ConfigurationUtils.readOptionalStringProperty(TYPE,
processorTag,
                    config, "defaultValue");
            boolean ignoreMissing =
ConfigurationUtils.readBooleanProperty(TYPE, processorTag,
                    config, "ignore_missing", false);
            return new InitialProcessor(processorTag, field,
targetField, ignoreMissing, defaultValue);
        }
    }
}
```

2. We need to register it in the `Plugin` class with the following lines:

```
public class InitialIngestPlugin extends Plugin implements
IngestPlugin {
    @Override
    public Map<String, Processor.Factory>
```

```
getProcessors(Processor.Parameters parameters) {
        return Collections.singletonMap(InitialProcessor.TYPE,
                (factories, tag, config) -> new
InitialProcessor.Factory().create(factories, tag, config));
    }
}
```

3. Now we can build the plugin via `mvn package` and manually install the ZIP. If we restart the Elasticsearch server, we should see the plugin loaded as follows:

> **[2019-02-09T11:47:53,126][WARN][o.e.n.Node] [iMacParo.local] version [7.0.0-alpha2] is a pre-release version of Elasticsearch and is not suitable for production [2019-02-09T11:47:54,797][INFO][o.e.p.PluginsService] [iMacParo.local] loaded module [aggs-matrix-stats]**
> `... truncated ...`
> **[2019-02-09T11:47:54,802][INFO][o.e.p.PluginsService] [iMacParo.local] loaded plugin [initial-processor]**
> **[2019-02-09T11:47:54,802][INFO][o.e.p.PluginsService] [iMacParo.local] loaded plugin [rest-plugin]**

4. We can test our custom ingest plugin via Simulate Ingest API with a `curl` as follows:

```
curl -XPOST -H "Content-Type: application/json"
'http://127.0.0.1:9200/_ingest/pipeline/_simulate?verbose&pret
ty' -d '{
"pipeline": {
    "description": "Test my custom plugin",
    "processors": [
      {
        "initial": {
          "field": "user",
          "target_field": "user_initial"
        }
      }
    ],
    "version": 1
  },
"docs": [
    {
      "_source": {
        "user": "john"
      }
    },
    {
      "_source": {
        "user": "Nancy"
```

```
                }
              }
            ]
          }'
```

5. The result will be something similar to the following:

```
{
  "docs" : [
    {
      "processor_results" : [
        {
          "doc" : {
            "_index" : "_index",
            "_type" : "_type",
            "_id" : "_id",
            "_source" : {
              "user_initial" : "j",
              "user" : "john"
            },
            "_ingest" : {
              "timestamp" : "2019-02-09T10:50:16.011932Z"
            }
          }
        }
      ]
    },
    {
      "processor_results" : [
        {
          "doc" : {
            "_index" : "_index",
            "_type" : "_type",
            "_id" : "_id",
            "_source" : {
              "user_initial" : "n",
              "user" : "Nancy"
            },
            "_ingest" : {
              "timestamp" : "2019-02-09T10:50:16.011973Z"
            }
          }
        }
      ]
    }
  ]
}
```

How it works...

First, you need to define the class that will manage your custom processor, which extends an `AbstractProcessor`:

```
public final class InitialProcessor extends AbstractProcessor {

    public final class InitialProcessor extends AbstractProcessor {
```

The `processor` needs to know the fields on which it operates. They are kept in the internal state of the processor as follows:

```
public static final String TYPE = "initial";

private final String field;
private final String targetField;
private final String defaultValue;
private final boolean ignoreMissing;

public InitialProcessor(String tag, String field, String targetField,
boolean ignoreMissing, String defaultValue) {
    super(tag);
    this.field = field;
    this.targetField = targetField;
    this.ignoreMissing = ignoreMissing;
    this.defaultValue = defaultValue;
}
```

The core of the processor is the `execute` function, which contains our processor login as follows:

```
@Override
public IngestDocument execute(IngestDocument document) {
```

The `execute` function is composed of the following steps:

1. Check if the `source` field exits as follows:

   ```
   if (document.hasField(field, true) == false) {
       if (ignoreMissing) {
           return document;
       } else {
           throw new IllegalArgumentException("field [" + field +
   "] not present as part of path [" + field + "]");
       }
   }
   ```

2. Check if the `target` field does not exist as follows:

```
if (document.hasField(targetField, true)) {
    throw new IllegalArgumentException("field [" + targetField
+ "] already exists");
}
```

3. We extract the value from document and check if it's valid as follows:

```
Object value = document.getFieldValue(field, Object.class);
if( value!=null && value instanceof String ) {
```

4. Now, we can process the value and set in the `target` field as follows:

```
String myValue=value.toString().trim();
if(myValue.length()>1){
    try {
        document.setFieldValue(targetField,
myValue.substring(0,1).toLowerCase(Locale.getDefault()));
    } catch (Exception e) {
        // setting the value back to the original field
shouldn't as we just fetched it from that field:
        document.setFieldValue(field, value);
        throw e;
    }
}
```

To be able to initialize the processor for its definition, we need to define a `Factory` object as follows:

```
public static final class Factory implements Processor.Factory {
```

The `Factory` object contains the `create` method that receives the registered processors, the `processorTag`, and its configuration that must be read as follows:

```
@Override
public InitialProcessor create(Map<String, Processor.Factory>
registry, String processorTag,
                               Map<String, Object> config) throws
Exception {
    String field = ConfigurationUtils.readStringProperty(TYPE,
processorTag, config, "field");
    String targetField = ConfigurationUtils.readStringProperty(TYPE,
processorTag,
            config, "target_field");
    String defaultValue =
ConfigurationUtils.readOptionalStringProperty(TYPE, processorTag,
            config, "defaultValue");
```

```
        boolean ignoreMissing =
ConfigurationUtils.readBooleanProperty(TYPE, processorTag,
            config, "ignore_missing", false);
```

After having recovered, we can initialize the processor parameters as follows:

```
        return new InitialProcessor(processorTag, field, targetField,
ignoreMissing, defaultValue);
    }
```

To be used as a custom processor, it needs to be registered in the plugin. This is done by extending the plugin as `IngestPlugin` as follows:

```
public class InitialIngestPlugin extends Plugin implements
IngestPlugin {
```

Now, we can register the `Factory` plugin in the `getProcessors` method as follows:

```
@Override
public Map<String, Processor.Factory>
getProcessors(Processor.Parameters parameters) {
    return Collections.singletonMap(InitialProcessor.TYPE,
            (factories, tag, config) -> new
InitialProcessor.Factory().create(factories, tag, config));
    }
```

Implementing an ingestion processor via a plugin is quite simple, and it's an incredibly powerful feature. With this approach, a user can create custom enrichment pipelines.

17
Big Data Integration

Elasticsearch has become a common component in big data architectures, because it provides several of the following features:

- It allows you to search on massive amounts of data in a very fast way
- For common aggregation operations, it provides real-time analytics on big data
- It's more easy to use an Elasticsearch aggregation than a Spark one
- If you need to move on to a fast data solution, starting from a subset of documents after a query is faster than doing a full rescan of all your data

The most common big data software that's used for processing data is now Apache Spark (`http://spark.apache.org/`), which is considered the evolution of the obsolete Hadoop MapReduce for moving the processing from disk to memory.

In this chapter, we will see how to integrate Elasticsearch in Spark, both for write and read data. In the end, we will see how to use Apache Pig to write data in Elasticsearch in a simple way.

In this chapter, we will cover the following recipes:

- Installing Apache Spark
- Indexing data using Apache Spark
- Indexing data with meta using Apache Spark
- Reading data with Apache Spark
- Reading data using Spark SQL
- Indexing data with Apache Pig

Installing Apache Spark

To use Apache Spark, we need to install it. The process is very easy, because its requirements are not the traditional Hadoop ones that require Apache Zookeeper and Hadoop HDFS.

Apache Spark is able to work in a standalone node installation that is similar to that of Elasticsearch.

Getting ready

You need a Java Virtual Machine installed. Generally, version 8.x or above is used.

How to do it...

To install Apache Spark, we will perform the following steps:

1. Download a binary distribution from `https://spark.apache.org/downloads.html`. For a generic usage, I would suggest that you download a standard version using the following request:

   ```
   wget
   https://www.apache.org/dyn/closer.lua/spark/spark-2.4.0/spark-
   2.4.0-bin-hadoop2.7.tgz
   ```

2. Now, we can extract the Spark distribution using `tar`, as follows:

   ```
   tar xfvz spark-2.4.0-bin-hadoop2.7.tgz
   ```

3. Now, we can test if Apache Spark is working by executing a test, as follows:

   ```
   2019-02-09 13:56:11 WARN NativeCodeLoader:62 - Unable to load
   native-hadoop library for your platform... using builtin-java
   classes where applicable
    2019-02-09 13:56:12 INFO SparkContext:54 - Running Spark
   version 2.4.0
    2019-02-09 13:56:12 INFO SparkContext:54 - Submitted
   application: Spark Pi
    ... truncated...
    2019-02-09 13:56:13 INFO DAGScheduler:54 - ResultStage 0
   (reduce at SparkPi.scala:38) finished in 0.408 s
    2019-02-09 13:56:13 INFO DAGScheduler:54 - Job 0 finished:
   ```

```
reduce at SparkPi.scala:38, took 0.445820 s
 Pi is roughly 3.139915699578498
 2019-02-09 13:56:13 INFO AbstractConnector:318 - Stopped
Spark@788ba63e{HTTP/1.1,[http/1.1]}{0.0.0.0:4040}
 2019-02-09 13:56:13 INFO SparkUI:54 - Stopped Spark web UI at
http://192.168.1.121:4040
 2019-02-09 13:56:13 INFO MapOutputTrackerMasterEndpoint:54 -
MapOutputTrackerMasterEndpoint stopped!
 2019-02-09 13:56:13 INFO MemoryStore:54 - MemoryStore cleared
 ... truncated...
 2019-02-09 13:56:13 INFO ShutdownHookManager:54 - Deleting
directory
/private/var/folders/0h/fkvg8wz54d30g1_9b9k3_7zr0000gn/T/spark
-fac6580a-7cb6-48ae-8739-3675365dbcd4
 2019-02-09 13:56:13 INFO ShutdownHookManager:54 - Deleting
directory
/private/var/folders/0h/fkvg8wz54d30g1_9b9k3_7zr0000gn/T/spark
-8fc0bf8e-0d30-440e-9965-72b77ba22c1d
```

How it works...

Apache Spark as a standalone node is very easy to install. Similar to Elasticsearch, it requires only a Java Virtual Machine installed in the system. The installation process is very easy—you only need to unpack the archive and there will be a complete working installation.

In the preceding steps, we also tested whether the Spark installation was working. Spark is written in Scala and the default binaries are targeting version 2.11.x. Major Scala versions are not compatible, so you need to pay attention to make sure that both Spark and Elasticsearch Hadoop are using the same version.

When executing a Spark job, the simplified steps are as follows:

1. The Spark environment is initialized
2. Spark `MemoryStore` and `BlockManager` masters are initialized
3. A `SparkContext` for the execution is initialized
4. `SparkUI` is activated at `http://0.0.0.0:4040`
5. The job is taken
6. An execution graph, a **Direct Acyclic Graph (DAG)**, is created for the job
7. Every vertex in the DAG is a stage, and a stage is split into tasks that are executed in parallel
8. After executing the stages and tasks, the processing ends

9. The result is returned

10. The `SparkContext` is stopped

11. The Spark system is shut down

There's more...

One of the most powerful tools of Spark is the shell (Spark shell). It allows you to enter commands and execute directly on the Spark cluster. To access the Spark shell, you need to invoke it using `./bin/spark-shell`.

When invoked, the output will be something like this:

```
2019-02-09 14:00:02 WARN NativeCodeLoader:62 - Unable to load native-
hadoop library for your platform... using builtin-java classes where
applicable

Setting default log level to "WARN".
 To adjust logging level use sc.setLogLevel(newLevel). For SparkR, use
setLogLevel(newLevel).
 Spark context Web UI available at http://192.168.1.121:4040
 Spark context available as 'sc' (master = local[*], app id =
local-1549717207051).
 Spark session available as 'spark'.
 Welcome to
      ____              __
     / __/__  ___ _____/ /__
    _\ \/ _ \/ _ `/ __/  '_/
   /___/ .__/\_,_/_/ /_/\_\   version 2.4.0
      /_/

Using Scala version 2.11.12 (Java HotSpot(TM) 64-Bit Server VM, Java
11.0.2)
 Type in expressions to have them evaluated.
 Type :help for more information.

scala>
```

Now, it's possible to insert the command-line commands that are to be executed in the cluster.

Indexing data using Apache Spark

Now that we have installed Apache Spark, we can configure it to work with Elasticsearch and write some data in it.

Getting ready

You need an up and running Elasticsearch installation, as we described in the *Downloading and installing Elasticsearch* recipe in `Chapter 1`, *Getting Started*.

You also need a working installation of Apache Spark.

How to do it...

To configure Apache Spark to communicate with Elasticsearch, we will perform the following steps:

1. We need to download the ElasticSearch Spark JAR, as follows:

   ```
   wget -c
   https://artifacts.elastic.co/downloads/elasticsearch-hadoop/el
   asticsearch-hadoop-7.0.0-alpha2.zip
   unzip elasticsearch-hadoop-7.0.0-alpha2.zip
   ```

2. A quick way to access the Spark shell in Elasticsearch is to copy the Elasticsearch Hadoop file that's required in Spark's `.jar` directory. The file that must be copied is `elasticsearch-spark-20_2.11-7.0.0.jar`.

The versions of Scala that are used by both Apache Spark and Elasticsearch Spark must match!

To store data in Elasticsearch using Apache Spark, we will perform the following steps:

1. Start the Spark shell by running the following command:

   ```
   ./bin/spark-shell
   ```

2. Apply the Elasticsearch configuration, as follows:

   ```
   val conf = sc.getConf
   conf.setAppName("ESImport")
   conf.set("es.index.auto.create", "true")
   ```

3. We will import Elasticsearch Spark implicits, as follows:

```
import org.elasticsearch.spark._
```

4. We will create two documents to be indexed, as follows:

```
val numbers = Map("one" -> 1, "two" -> 2, "three" -> 3)
val airports = Map("arrival" -> "Otopeni", "SFO" -> "San
Fran")
```

5. Now, we can create a **Resilient Distributed Datasets (RDD)** and save the document in Elasticsearch, as follows:

```
sc.makeRDD(Seq(numbers, airports)).saveToEs("spark/docs")
```

How it works...

Storing documents in Elasticsearch via Spark is quite simple. After having started a Spark shell in the shell context, an `sc` variable is available that contains the SparkContext. If we need to pass values to the underlying Elasticsearch configuration, we need to set them in the Spark configuration.

There are several configurations that can be set; the following are the most commonly used ones:

- `es.index.auto.create`: This is used to create indices if they do not exist
- `es.nodes`: This is used to define a list of nodes to connect with (default `localhost`)
- `es.port`: This is used to define the HTTP Elasticsearch port to connect with (default `9200`)
- `es.ingest.pipeline`: This is used to define an ingest pipeline to be used (default `none`)
- `es.mapping.id`: This is used to define a field to extract the ID value (default `none`)
- `es.mapping.parent`: This is used to define a field to extract the parent value (default `none`)

Simple documents can be defined as `Map[String, AnyRef]`, and they can be indexed via **Resilient Distributed Dataset (RDD)**, a special Spark abstraction on a collection.

Via the implicits that are available in `org.elasticsearch.spark`, the RDD has a new method called `saveToEs` that allows you to define the pair index or document to be used for indexing.

See also

You can refer to the following for further reference related to this recipe:

- To download the latest version of Elasticsearch Hadoop, go to the official page, at `https://www.elastic.co/downloads/hadoop`.
- The official documentation for installing Elasticsearch Hadoop can be found at `https://www.elastic.co/guide/en/elasticsearch/hadoop/current/install.html`. This page also provides some `border` cases.
- For a quickstart on using Spark, I suggest the Spark documentation at `http://spark.apache.org/docs/latest/quick-start.html`.
- For a detailed list of configuration parameters that can be set in Spark config, look at `https://www.elastic.co/guide/en/elasticsearch/hadoop/7.x/configuration.html`.

Indexing data with meta using Apache Spark

Using a simple map for ingesting data is not good for simple jobs. The best practice in Spark is to use the `case` class so that you have fast serialization and can manage complex type checking. During indexing, providing custom IDs can be very handy. In this recipe, we will see how to cover these issues.

Getting ready

You need an up and running Elasticsearch installation, as we described in the *Downloading and installing Elasticsearch* recipe in `Chapter 1`, *Getting Started*.

You also need a working installation of Apache Spark.

How to do it...

To store data in Elasticsearch using Apache Spark, we will perform the following steps:

1. Start the Spark shell by running the following command:

```
./bin/spark-shell
```

2. We will import the required classes, as follows:

```
import org.apache.spark.SparkContext
import org.elasticsearch.spark.rdd.EsSpark
```

3. We will create a `case class Person`, as follows:

```
case class Person(username:String, name:String, age:Int)
```

4. We will create two documents that are to be indexed, as follows:

```
val persons = Seq(Person("bob", "Bob",19),
Person("susan","Susan",21))
```

5. Now, we can create a RDD, as follows:

```
val rdd=sc.makeRDD(persons)
```

6. We can index them using `EsSpark`, as follows:

```
EsSpark.saveToEs(rdd, "spark2/persons", Map("es.mapping.id" ->
"username"))
```

7. In Elasticsearch, the indexed data will be as follows:

```
{
  ... truncated ...
  "hits" : {
    "total" : {
      "value" : 2,
      "relation" : "eq"
    },
    "max_score" : 1.0,
    "hits" : [
      {
        "_index" : "spark2",
        "_type" : "persons",
        "_id" : "bob",
        "_score" : 1.0,
```

```
        "_source" : {
          "username" : "bob",
          "name" : "Bob",
          "age" : 19
        }
      },
      {
        "_index" : "spark2",
        "_type" : "persons",
        "_id" : "susan",
        "_score" : 1.0,
        "_source" : {
          "username" : "susan",
          "name" : "Susan",
          "age" : 21
        }
      }
    ]
  }
}
```

How it works...

To speed up computation in Apache Spark, the `case` class is used to better describe the domain object we used during job processing. It has fast serializators and deserializators that allow easy conversion of the `case` class to JSON and vice verrsa. By using `case` class, the data is strongly typed and modeled.

In the preceding example, we created a `Person` class that designs a standard person. (Nested `case` classses are automatically managed.) Now that we've instantiated some `Person` objects, we need to create a Spark RDD that will be saved in Elasticsearch.

In this example, we have used a special class called `EsSpark`, which provides helpers to pass metadata that's used for indexing. In our case, we have provided information on how to extract the ID from the document using `Map("es.mapping.id" -> "username")`.

There's more...

Often, the ID is not a field of your object—it's a complex value that's computed on the document. In this case, you can manage to create an RDD with a tuple (ID, document) to be indexed.

For the following example, we can define the function that does the ID computation on the `Person` class:

```
import org.elasticsearch.spark._
case class Person(username:String, name:String, age:Int) {
  def id=this.username+this.age
}
```

Then, we can use it to compute our new RDD, as follows:

```
val persons = Seq(Person("bob", "Bob",19),Person("susan", "Susan",21))
val personIds=persons.map(p => p.id -> p)
val rdd=sc.makeRDD(personIds)
```

Now, we can index them, as follows:

```
rdd.saveToEsWithMeta("spark3/person_id")
```

In this case, the stored documents will be as follows:

```
{
  ... truncated ...
    "hits" : [
      {
        "_index" : "spark3",
        "_type" : "person_id",
        "_id" : "susan21",
        "_score" : 1.0,
        "_source" : {
          "username" : "susan",
          "name" : "Susan",
          "age" : 21
        }
      },
      {
        "_index" : "spark3",
        "_type" : "person_id",
        "_id" : "bob19",
        "_score" : 1.0,
        "_source" : {
          "username" : "bob",
          "name" : "Bob",
          "age" : 19
        }
      }
    ]
  }
}
```

Reading data with Apache Spark

In Spark, you can read data from a lot of sources but, in general, with NoSQL datastores such as HBase, Accumulo, and Cassandra, you have a limited query subset, and you often need to scan all the data to read only the required data. Using Elasticsearch, you can retrieve a subset of documents that matches your Elasticsearch query.

Getting ready

You need an up and running Elasticsearch installation, as we described in the *Downloading and installing Elasticsearch* recipe in `Chapter 1`, *Getting Started*.

You also need a working installation of Apache Spark and the data that we indexed in the previous example.

How to do it...

To read data in Elasticsearch via Apache Spark, we will perform the following steps:

1. Start the Spark Shell by running the following command:

   ```
   ./bin/spark-shell
   ```

2. Import the required classes, as follows:

   ```
   import org.elasticsearch.spark._
   ```

3. Now, we can create a RDD by reading data from Elasticsearch, as follows:

   ```
   val rdd=sc.esRDD("spark2/persons")
   ```

4. We can watch the fetched values using the following command:

   ```
   rdd.collect.foreach(println)
   ```

5. The result will be as follows:

   ```
   (bob,Map(username -> bob, name -> Bob, age -> 19))
   (susan,Map(username -> susan, name -> Susan, age -> 21))
   ```

How it works...

The Elastic team has done a good job in allowing the use of a simple API to read data from Elasticsearch.

You only need to import the implicit that extends the standard RDD with the `esRDD` method to allow data retrieval from Elasticsearch.

The `esRDD` method accepts the following parameters:

- `resource`: This is generally an index or type tuple.
- `query`: This is a query that is used to filter the results. It's in the query args format (an optional string).
- `config`: This contains extra configurations to be provided to Elasticsearch (an optional `Map[String, String]`).

The returned value is a collection of tuples in the form of the ID and `Map` objects.

Reading data using Spark SQL

Spark SQL is a Spark module for structured data processing. It provides a programming abstraction called DataFrames and can also act as a distributed SQL query engine. Elasticsearch Spark integration allows us to read data using SQL queries.

 Spark SQL works with structured data; in other words, all entries are expected to have the same structure (the same number of fields, of the same type and name). Using unstructured data (documents with different structures) is not supported and will cause problems.

Getting ready

You need an up and running Elasticsearch installation, as we described in the *Downloading and installing Elasticsearch* recipe in Chapter 1, *Getting Started*.

You also need a working installation of Apache Spark and the data that we indexed in the *Indexing data using Apache Spark* recipe of this chapter.

How to do it...

To read data in Elasticsearch using Apache Spark SQL and DataFrame, we will perform the following steps:

1. Start the Spark shell by running the following command:

   ```
   ./bin/spark-shell
   ```

2. We will create a DataFrame in the format `org.elasticsearch.spark.sql` and load data from `spark3/person_id`, as follows:

   ```
   val df =
   spark.read.format("org.elasticsearch.spark.sql").load("spark3/
   person_id")
   ```

3. If we want to check the schema, we are able to inspect it using `printSchema`, as follows:

   ```
   df.printSchema
   root
    |-- age: long (nullable = true)
    |-- name: string (nullable = true)
    |-- username: string (nullable = true)
   ```

4. We can watch fetched values as follows:

   ```
   df.filter(df("age").gt(20)).collect.foreach(println)
   ```
   [21,Susan,susan]

To read data in Elasticsearch using Apache Spark SQL through SQL queries, we will perform the following steps:

1. Start the Spark shell by running the following command:

   ```
   ./bin/spark-shell
   ```

2. We will create a view for reading data from `spark3/person_id`, as follows:

   ```
   spark.sql("CREATE TEMPORARY VIEW persons USING
   org.elasticsearch.spark.sql OPTIONS (resource
   'spark3/person_id', scroll_size '2000')" )
   ```

3. We can now execute a SQL query against the previously created view, as follows:

```
val over20 = spark.sql("SELECT * FROM persons WHERE age >=
20")
```

4. We can watch fetched values as follows:

```
over20.collect.foreach(println)
[21,Susan,susan]
```

How it works...

The core of data management in Spark is the DataFrame that allows you to fetch values from different datastores.

You can use SQL query capabilities at the top of DataFrames and, depending of the driver used (`org.elasticsearch.spark.sql`, in our case), the query can be pushed down at the driver level (a native query in Elasticsearch). For example, in our preceding example, the query is converted into a Boolean filter with a range that is executed natively by Elasticsearch.

The Elasticsearch Spark driver is able to do inference reading information from the mappings and to manage the datastore as a standard SQL datastore. The SQL approach is very powerful and allows you to reuse SQL expertise that is very common.

A good approach in using Elasticsearch with Spark is to use the Spark Notebooks: interactive web-based interfaces that speed up the testing phases of application prototypes. The most famous ones are Spark Notebook, available at `http://spark-notebook.io`, and Apache Zeppelin, available at `https://zeppelin.apache.org`.

Indexing data with Apache Pig

Apache Pig (`https://pig.apache.org/`) is a tool that's frequently used to store and manipulate data in datastores. It can be very handy if you need to import some **comma-separated values** (CSV) in Elasticsearch in a very fast way.

Getting ready

You need an up and running Elasticsearch installation, as we described in the *Downloading and installing Elasticsearch* recipe in `Chapter 1`, *Getting Started*.

You need a working Pig installation. Depending on your operating system, you should follow the instructions at `http://pig.apache.org/docs/r0.17.0/start.html`.

If you are using macOS X with Homebrew, you can install it with `brew install pig`.

How to do it...

We want to read a CSV file and write the data in Elasticsearch. We will perform the following steps to do so:

1. We will download a CSV dataset from the GeoNames site to get all the GeoName locations of Great Britain. We can fast download them and unzip them as follows:

   ```
   wget http://download.geonames.org/export/dump/GB.zip
   unzip GB.zip
   ```

2. We can write `es.pig`, which contains the Pig commands to be executed, as follows:

   ```
   REGISTER /Users/alberto/elasticsearch/elasticsearch-
   hadoop-7.0.0/dist/elasticsearch-hadoop-pig-7.0.0.jar;


   SET pig.noSplitCombination TRUE;


   DEFINE EsStorage org.elasticsearch.hadoop.pig.EsStorage();


   -- launch the Map/Reduce job with 5 reducers

   SET default_parallel 5;


   --load the GB.txt file

   geonames= LOAD 'GB.txt' using PigStorage('\t') AS
   (geonameid:int,name:chararray,asciiname:chararray,
   ```

```
alternatenames:chararray,latitude:double,longitude:double,
feature_class:chararray,feature_code:chararray,
country_code:chararray,cc2:chararray,admin1_code:chararray,
admin2_code:chararray,admin3_code:chararray,
admin4_code:chararray,population:int,elevation:int,
dem:chararray,timezone:chararray,modification_date:chararray);


STORE geonames INTO 'geoname/gb' USING EsStorage();
```

3. Now, execute the `pig` command, as follows:

```
pig -x local es.pig
```

The output will be similar to the following:

> 2019-02-10 14:51:12,258 INFO [main] pig.ExecTypeProvider
> (ExecTypeProvider.java:selectExecType(41)) - Trying ExecType : LOCAL
> 2019-02-10 14:51:12,259 INFO [main] pig.ExecTypeProvider
> (ExecTypeProvider.java:selectExecType(43)) - Picked LOCAL as the ExecType
> 2019-02-10 14:51:12,283 [main] INFO org.apache.pig.Main - Apache Pig version
> 0.17.0 (r1797386) compiled Jun 02 2017, 15:41:58
> *... truncated ...*
> 2019-02-10 14:51:13,693 [LocalJobRunner Map Task Executor #0] INFO
> org.apache.pig.builtin.PigStorage - Using PigTextInputFormat
> 2019-02-10 14:51:13,696 [LocalJobRunner Map Task Executor #0] INFO
> org.apache.pig.backend.hadoop.executionengine.mapReduceLayer.PigRecordRea
> der - Current split being processed file:/Users/alberto/Projects/elasticsearch-7.x-
> cookbook/ch17/GB.txt:0+7793280
> *... truncated ...*
> 2019-02-10 14:51:18,586 [main] INFO
> org.apache.pig.tools.pigstats.mapreduce.SimplePigStats - Script Statistics:
>
> HadoopVersion PigVersion UserId StartedAt FinishedAt Features
> 2.7.3 0.17.0 alberto 2019-02-10 14:51:13 2019-02-10 14:51:18 UNKNOWN
>
> Success!
>
> Job Stats (time in seconds):
> JobId Maps Reduces MaxMapTime MinMapTime AvgMapTime
> MedianMapTime MaxReduceTime MinReduceTime AvgReduceTime
> MedianReducetime Alias Feature Outputs
> job_local1289431064_0001 1 0 n/a n/a n/a n/a 0 0 0 0 geonames MAP_ONLY
> geoname/gb,
>
> Input(s):
> Successfully read 63131 records from:
> "file:///Users/alberto/Projects/elasticsearch-7.x-cookbook/ch17/GB.txt"

```
Output(s):
Successfully stored 63131 records in: "geoname/gb"

Counters:
Total records written : 63131
Total bytes written : 0
Spillable Memory Manager spill count : 0
Total bags proactively spilled: 0
Total records proactively spilled: 0

Job DAG:
job_local1289431064_0001


2019-02-10 14:51:18,587 [main] INFO org.apache.hadoop.metrics.jvm.JvmMetrics -
Cannot initialize JVM Metrics with processName=JobTracker, sessionId= -
already initialized
2019-02-10 14:51:18,588 [main] INFO org.apache.hadoop.metrics.jvm.JvmMetrics -
Cannot initialize JVM Metrics with processName=JobTracker, sessionId= -
already initialized
2019-02-10 14:51:18,588 [main] INFO org.apache.hadoop.metrics.jvm.JvmMetrics -
Cannot initialize JVM Metrics with processName=JobTracker, sessionId= -
already initialized
2019-02-10 14:51:18,591 [main] WARN
org.apache.pig.backend.hadoop.executionengine.mapReduceLayer.MapReduceLa
uncher - Encountered Warning TOO_LARGE_FOR_INT 1 time(s).
2019-02-10 14:51:18,591 [main] INFO
org.apache.pig.backend.hadoop.executionengine.mapReduceLayer.MapReduceLa
uncher - Success!
2019-02-10 14:51:18,604 [main] INFO org.apache.pig.Main - Pig script completed in
6 seconds and 565 milliseconds (6565 ms)
```

After a few seconds, all the CSV data is indexed in Elasticsearch.

How it works...

Apache Pig is a very handy tool. With a small number of code lines, it's able to read, transform, and store data in different datastores. It has a shell, but it's very common to write a Pig script with all the commands to be executed.

To use Elasticsearch in Apache Pig, you need to register the library that contains `EsStorage`. This is done using the register script: the JAR position depends on your installation, as follows:

```
REGISTER /Users/alberto/elasticsearch/elasticsearch-
    hadoop-7.0.0/dist/elasticsearch-hadoop-pig-7.0.0.jar;
```

By default, Pig splits the data into blocks and then combines them before sending the data to Elasticsearch. To maintain maximum parallelism, you need to disable this behavior using `SET pig.noSplitCombination TRUE`.

To prevent typing the full path for the `EsStorage`, we must define the following shortcut:

```
DEFINE EsStorage org.elasticsearch.hadoop.pig.EsStorage();
```

By default, the Pig parallelism is set to 1. If we want to speed up the process, we need to increase this value, as follows:

```
-- launch the Map/Reduce job with 5 reducers

SET default_parallel 5;
```

Reading a CSV in Pig is very simple; we define a file, the `PigStorage` with the field separator, and the format of the fields, as follows:

```
--load the GB.txt file

geonames= LOAD 'GB.txt' using PigStorage('\t') AS
(geonameid:int,name:chararray,asciiname:chararray,
alternatenames:chararray,latitude:double,longitude:double,
feature_class:chararray,feature_code:chararray,
country_code:chararray,cc2:chararray,admin1_code:chararray,
admin2_code:chararray,admin3_code:chararray,
admin4_code:chararray,population:int,elevation:int,
dem:chararray,timezone:chararray,modification_date:chararray);
```

After reading the CSV file, the lines are indexed as objects in Elasticsearch, as follows:

```
STORE geonames INTO 'geoname/gb' USING EsStorage();
```

 As you can see, all the complexity in using Pig is to manage the format of input and output. The key advantage of Apache Pig is the ability to load different datasets, join them, and store them in a few lines of code.

Using Elasticsearch with Alpakka

Alpakka project (`https://doc.akka.io/docs/alpakka/current/index.html`) is a reactive enterprise integration library for Java and Scala, based on Reactive Streams and Akka (`https://akka.io/`).

Reactive streams are based on components—the most important ones are **Source** (that are used to read data from different sources) and **Sink** (that are used to write data in storages).

Alpakka supports Source and Sink for many data stores and Elasticsearch is one of them.

In this recipe, we will go through a common scenario—read a CSV file and ingest it in Elasticsearch.

Getting ready

You need an up-and-running Elasticsearch installation as we described in the *Downloading and installing Elasticsearch* recipe in Chapter 1, *Getting Started*.

An IDE that supports Scala programming, such as IntelliJ IDEA, with the Scala plugin should be installed globally.

The code for this recipe can be found in the ch17/alpakka directory and the referred class is CSVToES.

How to do it...

We are going to create a simple pipeline that reads a CSV and write the record in Elasticsearch. To do so, we will perform the following steps:

1. Add the alpakka dependencies to build.sbt:

    ```
    "com.github.pathikrit" %% "better-files" % "3.7.1",
    "com.lightbend.akka" %% "akka-stream-alpakka-csv" % "1.0.0",
    "com.lightbend.akka" %% "akka-stream-alpakka-elasticsearch" %
    "1.0.0",
    ```

2. Then, initialize the Akka system:

    ```
    implicit val actorSystem = ActorSystem()
    implicit val actorMaterializer = ActorMaterializer()
    implicit val executor = actorSystem.dispatcher
    ```

3. Now we can initialize the Elasticsearch client, in this case we use the default Rest client:

```
import org.elasticsearch.client.RestClient
implicit val client: RestClient = RestClient.builder(new
HttpHost("0.0.0.0", 9200)).build()
```

4. The data will be stored in the `Iris` class and we will also create a Scala `implicit` to allow encoding and decoding in JSON. All this stuff is done using a few lines of code:

```
final case class Iris(label: String, f1: Double, f2: Double,
f3: Double, f4: Double)
import spray.json._
import DefaultJsonProtocol._
implicit val format: JsonFormat[Iris] = jsonFormat5(Iris)
```

5. Before initializing the `sink`, we define some policies to manage back pressure and retry logic:

```
val sinkSettings =
   ElasticsearchWriteSettings()
      .withBufferSize(1000)
      .withVersionType("internal")
      .withRetryLogic(RetryAtFixedRate(maxRetries = 5,
retryInterval = 1.second))
```

6. Now we can create a pipeline, the source will be read by a CSV, for every line, we will create a Iris Index message and will ingest in an index `iris-alpakka` using the Elasticsearch Sink:

```
val graph
=Source.single(ByteString(Resource.getAsString("com/packtpub/i
ris.csv")))
   .via(CsvParsing.lineScanner())
   .drop(1)
   .map(values => WriteMessage.createIndexMessage[Iris](
   Iris(
     values(4).utf8String,
     values.head.utf8String.toDouble,
   values(1).utf8String.toDouble,
 values(2).utf8String.toDouble,
   values(3).utf8String.toDouble)))
   .via(
     ElasticsearchFlow.create[Iris](
       "iris-alpakka",
       "_doc",
```

```
        settings = sinkSettings
      ))
    .runWith(Sink.ignore)
```

7. The preceding pipeline is executed asynchronously, we need to wait for it to finish, to process the items and then we need to close all the used resources:

```
val finish=Await.result(graph, Duration.Inf)
 client.close()
 actorSystem.terminate()
 Await.result(actorSystem.whenTerminated, Duration.Inf)
```

How it works...

Alpakka is one of the most used tools to build modern **ETL (Extract, Transform, Load)** with a lot of convenient features:

- **Back pressure**: If a data store is under high load, it automatically reduces the throughput.
- **Modular approach**: A user can replace Source and Sink to read and write to other different data stores without massive code refactoring.
- **Numerous operators**:A plethora of operators (map, flatMap, filter, groupBy, mapAsync, and so on) to build complex pipelines.
- **Low memory footprint**: It doesn't load all the data in memory as Apache Spark, but it streams data from the Source to the Sink. It can be easily dockerized and deployed on a Kubernetes cluster for large scaling of your ETL.

The Elasticsearch Source and Sink uses the official Rest client of Elasticsearch. As you can see from the preceding code it can be initialized with a single line of code:

```
implicit val client: RestClient = RestClient.builder(new
HttpHost("0.0.0.0", 9200)).build()
```

The client variable must be implicit so that is automatically passed to the Elasticsearch Source and Sink or Flow constructors.

By default, it supports serialize and deserialize case classes in JSON using spray.json using the Scala macro jsonFormatN (with *N* being the number of fields):

```
implicit val format: JsonFormat[Iris] = jsonFormat5(Iris)
```

Also in this case, the variable should be implicit so that it can be automatically passed to the required methods.

We can customize the parameters used to write in Elasticsearch using an `ElasticsearchWriteSettings`:

```
ElasticsearchWriteSettings()
    .withBufferSize(1000)
    .withVersionType("internal")
    .withRetryLogic(RetryAtFixedRate(maxRetries = 5, retryInterval =
1.second))
```

The most common methods of this class are:

- `withBufferSize(size:Int)` : The number of items to be used for a single bulk.
- `withVersionType(vType:String)`: It sets the type of record versioning in Elasticsearch.
- `withRetryLogic(logic:RetryLogic)`: It sets the retry policies. `RetryLogic` is a Scala trait class that can be extended to provide different implementations. You can implement your RetryLogic policy extending the trait class; the following ones are already available be default:
    - `RetryNever`: To never retry.
    - `RetryAtFixedRate(maxRetries: Int, retryInterval: scala.concurrent.duration.FiniteDuration)`: It allows `maxRetries` at a fixed interval (`retryInterval`).

Elasticsearch Sink or Flow accepts only `WriteMessage[T,PT]`, where *T* is the type of the message and *PT* is a possible `PassThrough` type (used, for example, in case you want pass a Kafka offset and commit it after the Elasticsearch write response).

`WriteMessage` has helpers to create the most common used messages, that are:

- `createIndexMessage[T](source: T)`: This is used to create an index action
- `createIndexMessage[T](id: String, source: T)`: This is used to create an index action with provided id
- `createCreateMessage[T](id: String, source: T)`: This is used to build a create action
- `createUpdateMessage[T](id: String, source: T)`: This is used to create an update action

- `createUpsertMessage[T](id: String, source: T)`: This is used to create an upsert action (it tries to update the document, if the document doesn't exist it create a new one)
- `createDeleteMessage[T](id: String)`: This is used to create a delete action

To create these messages, the most common practice it to use a map function to do the transformation from a value to the required `WriteMessage` type.

After having created the `WriteMessages`, we can create a Sink that will write the records in Elasticsearch. The required parameters for this Sink are:

- `indexName:String` the index to be used
- `typeName:String` the mapping name (usually _doc in Elasticsearch 7.x). Probably it will be removed in future release of Alpakka Elasticsearch.
- `settings: ElasticsearchWriteSettings` (optional) the setting parameters for write, that we have discussed previously.

In this short introduction, we have only scratched the surface of Akka or Alpakka, but it is easy to understand how powerful this system is for orchestrating simple and complex ingestion jobs.

See also

You can refer to the following URLs for further reference, which are related to this recipe:

- The official website of Akka at `https://akka.io/` and Alpakka at `https://doc.akka.io/docs/alpakka/current/index.html`
- Alpakka documentation about Elasticsearch at `https://doc.akka.io/docs/alpakka/current/elasticsearch.html` which provides more example of using Sources and Sinks.

Using Elasticsearch with MongoDB

MongoDB (`https://www.mongodb.com/`) is one of the most popular documented data stores, due to its simplicity of installation and the large community that is using it.

It's very common to use Elasticsearch as search or query layer and MongoDB as more secure data-stage in many architectures. In this recipe we'll see how simple it is to write in MongoDB reading from an Elasticsearch query stream using Alpakka.

Getting ready

You need an up-and-running Elasticsearch installation as we described in *Downloading and installing Elasticsearch* recipe in `Chapter 1`, *Getting Started*.

An IDE that supports Scala programming, such as IntelliJ IDEA, with the Scala plugin should be installed globally.

A local installation of MongoDB is required to run the example.

The code for this recipe can be found in the `ch17/alpakka` directory and the referred class is `ESToMongoDB`. We will read the index created in the previous recipe.

How to do it...

We are going to create a simple pipeline that reads a CSV and write the record in Elasticsearch. To do so, we will perform the following steps:

1. We need to add the `alpakka-mongodb` dependencies to `build.sbt`:

```
"org.mongodb.scala" %% "mongo-scala-bson" % "2.4.2",
"com.lightbend.akka" %% "akka-stream-alpakka-mongodb" %
"1.0.0",
```

2. The first step is to initialize the Akka system:

```
implicit val actorSystem = ActorSystem()
implicit val actorMaterializer = ActorMaterializer()
implicit val executor = actorSystem.dispatcher
```

3. Now we can initialize the Elasticsearch client, in this case we use the default `RestClient`:

```
import org.elasticsearch.client.RestClient
implicit val client: RestClient = RestClient.builder(new
HttpHost("0.0.0.0", 9200)).build()
```

4. The data will be stored in a `Iris` class—we also create a Scala `implicit` to allow encode and decode in JSON and a codec for mongoDB. All this stuff is done using a few lines of code:

```scala
final case class Iris(label: String, f1: Double, f2: Double,
f3: Double, f4: Double)
 import spray.json._
 import DefaultJsonProtocol._
 implicit val format: JsonFormat[Iris] = jsonFormat5(Iris)

 val codecRegistry =
 fromRegistries(fromProviders(classOf[Iris]),
 DEFAULT_CODEC_REGISTRY)
```

5. Now we can create a `irisCollection` that will store our data in MongoDB:

```scala
private val mongo =
MongoClients.create("mongodb://localhost:27017")
 private val db = mongo.getDatabase("es-to-mongo")
 val irisCollection = db
   .getCollection("iris", classOf[Iris])
   .withCodecRegistry(codecRegistry)
```

6. Finally, we can create a pipeline, the source will be an `ElasticsearchSource`, and all the records will be ingested in MongoDB using its `MongoSink`:

```scala
val graph =
   ElasticsearchSource
     .typed[Iris](
     indexName = "iris-alpakka",
     typeName = "_doc",
     query = """{"match_all": {}}"""
   )
     .map(_.source) // we want only the source
     .grouped(100) // bulk insert of 100
     .runWith(MongoSink.insertMany[Iris](irisCollection))
```

7. The preceding pipeline is executed asynchronously, an we need to wait for it finish to process the items and then close all the used resources:

```scala
val finish=Await.result(graph, Duration.Inf)
 client.close()
 actorSystem.terminate()
 Await.result(actorSystem.whenTerminated, Duration.Inf)
```

How it works...

Using MongoDB Source and Sink in a pipeline is very easy. In the preceding code we have used an `ElasticsearchSource`, that, given an index or `typeName` and a query, is able to generate a typed stream of items:

```
ElasticsearchSource
    .typed[Iris](
    indexName = "iris-alpakka",
    typeName = "_doc",
    query = """{"match_all": {}}"""
)
```

The returned type is a `Source[ReadResult[T], NotUsed]` where *T* is our type (that is `Iris` in the example).

A `ReadResult[T]` is a wrapper object that contains:

- `id:String`: This is the Elasticsearch ID
- `source:T`: This is the source part of the document converted to object T
- `version:Option[Long]`: This is an optional version number

To write in MongoDB, we need to create a connection, select a database, and get a collection:

```
private val mongo = MongoClients.create("mongodb://localhost:27017")
 private val db = mongo.getDatabase("es-to-mongo")
 val irisCollection = db
   .getCollection("iris", classOf[Iris])
   .withCodecRegistry(codecRegistry)
```

In this case, we have defined that the `irisCollection` is of type `Iris` and we have provided a codec to do data marshaling (conversion).

The `codecRegistry` is built using Scala Macro:

```
import org.bson.codecs.configuration.CodecRegistries.{fromProviders,
fromRegistries}
 import org.mongodb.scala.bson.codecs.DEFAULT_CODEC_REGISTRY
 import org.mongodb.scala.bson.codecs.Macros._
val codecRegistry = fromRegistries(fromProviders(classOf[Iris]),
DEFAULT_CODEC_REGISTRY)
```

To speed up the writing we have chosen to execute a bulk write in MongoDB of 100 elements, so we first convert the stream in a group of 100 elements using:

```
.grouped(100) // bulk insert of 100
```

And the results are written in the collection using the MongoSink:

```
.runWith(MongoSink.insertMany[Iris](irisCollection))
```

In case of streaming, I suggest to always write in bulk both in Elasticsearch and MongoDB.

In the preceding examples, we have seen how to use Elasticsearch Source and Sink and MongoDB Sink and it's very easy to understand how you can combine different Sources or Sinks to build you own pipelines.

See also

Alpakka documentation about MongoDB at `https://doc.akka.io/docs/alpakka/current/mongodb.html` which provides more example of using Sources and Sinks for MongoDB.

Another Book You May Enjoy

If you enjoyed this book, you may be interested in these other books by Packt:

Machine Learning with the Elastic Stack
Rich Collier, Bahaaldine Azarmi

ISBN: 9781788477543

- Install the Elastic Stack to use machine learning features
- Understand how Elastic machine learning is used to detect a variety of anomaly types
- Apply effective anomaly detection to IT operations and security analytics
- Leverage the output of Elastic machine learning in custom views, dashboards, and proactive alerting
- Combine your created jobs to correlate anomalies of different layers of infrastructure
- Learn various tips and tricks to get the most out of Elastic machine learning

Leave a review - let other readers know what you think

Please share your thoughts on this book with others by leaving a review on the site that you bought it from. If you purchased the book from Amazon, please leave us an honest review on this book's Amazon page. This is vital so that other potential readers can see and use your unbiased opinion to make purchasing decisions, we can understand what our customers think about our products, and our authors can see your feedback on the title that they have worked with Packt to create. It will only take a few minutes of your time, but is valuable to other potential customers, our authors, and Packt. Thank you!

Index

A

aggregation
  about 287
  executing 288, 290, 292
  scripting, using 378, 382
  used, for executing search 558, 563
aggregators
  bucketing aggregators 293
  matrix aggregators 293
  metric aggregators 293
  pipeline aggregators 293
alias field
  mapping 77, 78, 79
Alpakka
  features 679
  reference link 681
  using, with Elasticsearch 676, 681
analyzer plugin
  creating 630, 634
analyzers
  ICU analysis plugin, reference link 88
  Japanese (kuromoji) analysis plugin,
    reference link 88
  phonetic analysis plugin, reference link 88
  smart chinese analysis plugin, reference link
    88
  specifying 86, 87, 88
Apache Pig
  reference link 672
  used, for indexing data 672, 676
Apache Spark
  installing 660, 662
  used, for indexing data 663, 665
  used, for indexing data with meta 665
  used, for reading data 669
API
  node statistics, obtaining via 409, 414
  used, for controlling cluster health 392, 396
  used, for controlling cluster state 396, 400,
    402
  used, for obtaining cluster node information
    403, 408, 409
Application Performance Monitoring (APM) 474
arc
  reference link 330
arrays
  mapping 54, 55, 56
atomic operations (bulk operations)
  speeding up 145, 146, 147, 148
Azure Cloud
  reference link 435

B

base types
  mapping 50, 51, 53
Boolean query
  filter 202
  query 202
  using 201, 204
bulk actions
  managing 547, 551

C

cache 428
Cerebro
  installing 450, 453, 456, 458
  reference link 451
  using 450, 452, 457, 458
child document
  managing, with join field 65, 68, 69
children aggregations
  executing 331, 332, 334
circuit breaker 23

client
  creating 600, 602
cluster action
  creating 641, 645, 650
cluster health
  controlling, API used 392, 396
cluster level
  issues 391
cluster node information
  obtaining, API used 403, 406, 409
cluster state
  controlling, API used 396, 400, 402
comma-separated values (CSV) 672
common terms query
  using 252, 254
completion field
  mapping 88, 90
coordinator node
  setting up 22, 23
correct query
  suggesting 183, 184, 185
create-read-update-delete (CRUD) 91
curl
  reference link 46

D

data
  indexing, Apache Spark used 663, 665
  indexing, with Apache Pig 672
  reading, Spark SQL used 670
  reading, with Apache Spark 669
  script plugins 371
  sorting, scripts used 366
date histogram aggregations
  executing 315, 317, 319
  reference link 319
DeepLearning.scala
  integrating with 593, 596
DeepLearning4J (DL4J)
  integrating with 566, 571
delete_by_query function
  about 192
  executing 193, 194, 195
Docker
  node, setting up via 33, 36

reference link 34, 36
document mapping
  dynamic templates, using 60, 61
document
  deleting 138, 140, 193, 194
  indexing 130, 132
  managing 541, 545, 546, 583, 587, 609, 613
  mapping 58, 59
  obtaining 135, 137
  updating 141, 143
  updating, with scripts 382
Domain Script Language (DSL) 579
Domain Syntax Language (DSL) 577
dynamic templates
  used, in document mapping 60, 61, 62

E

Elastic Beats
  reference link 44
elastic4s 573
Elasticsearch Cloud Enterprise (ECE)
  deploying 36, 40, 43, 44
  reference link 44
Elasticsearch Cloud
  reference link 36
Elasticsearch HQ
  installing 459, 461, 464, 468
  reference link 459
  using 459, 461, 464, 467, 468
Elasticsearch plugin
  removing 30, 31
Elasticsearch, Logstash, and Kibana (ELK)
  reference link 36
Elasticsearch
  about 9
  documentation link 54
  download link 8
  downloading 8
  index 130
  index tuning, options 123
  installing 8, 10, 12
  plugins, installing 26, 28, 30
  reference link 185
  required services 12

search 130
  using, with Alpakka 677, 679
  using, with MongoDB 682, 685
ETL (Extract, Transform, Load) 679
exists query
  exists field 264
  missing field 264
  using 264, 266
explicit mapping creation
  using 46, 47, 48, 49

F

Fast Vector Highlighter (FVH) 171
feature field
  mapping 82, 84
feature vector fields
  mapping 82, 84
field
  adding, with multiple mappings 69, 71
filter aggregations
  executing 319, 322
filters aggregations
  executing 322, 325
fine-tuning mapping
  advantages 50
finite state transducer (FST)
  reference link 89
ForceMerge operation
  performing, on index 113, 114, 115
function score query
  using 258, 261, 263

G

geo bounds aggregations
  executing 343
geo centroid aggregations
  executing 345, 347
geo distance aggregations
  executing 327
geo_bounding_box query
  using 278, 279
geo_distance query
  using 283, 285
geo_polygon query
  using 280, 282

GeoPoint field
  mapping 72, 74
GeoShape field
  mapping 74, 75
GET operations (multi GET)
  speeding up 148, 149
GET operations
  speeding up 150
glob pattern
  reference link 62
global aggregations
  executing 325
Google Cloud
  reference link 435
grok processor
  using 507, 509

H

has_child query
  using 268, 269, 271
has_parent query
  using 272, 275, 277
HDFS
  reference link 435
High Availability (HA) cluster 22
high frequency terms 254
high-level REST client
  creating 530, 532
histogram aggregations
  executing 310, 314
Homebrew
  reference link 9
hot threads API
  using 420
HTTP Elasticsearch client
  creating 525, 527, 530

I

IDs query
  using 256, 258
index aliases
  using 124, 127
index settings
  managing 121, 123
index

closing 98, 100
creating 92, 94, 96
deleting 96, 98
existence, checking 120, 121
flushing 111, 112
ForceMerge operation, performing 113, 114, 115
mapping, building 100, 102
opening 98, 100
refreshing 109, 110
reindexing 105, 107, 108
shrinking 115, 116, 117, 118, 119
indexing 45
indices
managing 533, 536, 577, 580, 603, 606
ingest attachment plugin
using 511, 514
ingest GeoIP plugin
using 514, 516
ingest pipeline
built-in processors 503, 506
deleting 496
obtaining 495
putting 493, 494
simulating 498, 500, 502
ingest plugin
creating 650, 655
ingestion node
setting up 24, 26
inner hits
returning, in results 180, 183
integrated development environment (IDE) 626
IP field
mapping 76, 77

J

Java Virtual Machine (JVM)
about 9, 571
reference link 8
join field
used, for managing child document 65, 68, 69

K

Kibana Dev tool
Dev-Console 486
Grok Debugger 486
Search Profiler 486
using 486, 488
Kibana
discovery, managing 474, 477, 479
installing 468, 473
reference link 76, 287, 449
used, for data visualization 479, 483, 485

L

Linux systems
file descriptors, reference link 19
setting up 18, 19, 20
log4j library
reference link 33
logging settings
modifying 32, 33
Logstash
reference link 76, 125
low frequency terms 254
Lucene
documentation, reference link 53

M

machine learning (ML) 24
mapping fields
reference link 54
mappings
building, by indexing documents 100, 102
including, via REST API 607, 609
managing 537, 540, 541, 580, 583
metadata, adding 85, 86
obtaining 103, 104
match query
using 238, 241, 242
match_all operator
using 199, 201
matched results
counting 185, 187, 188
matrix stats aggregation
executing 341, 343

metadata
  adding, to mapping 85, 86
MongoDB
  reference link 681
  using, with Elasticsearch 681, 685
mustache
  reference link 208

N

Natural Language Processing (NLP) 24
near real-time (NRT) 110
nested aggregations
  executing 334, 337
nested objects
  managing 63, 65
nested queries
  using 275
Network File System (NFS) 431
networking
  setting up 13, 14, 16
NFS share
  setting up, for backups 443, 446
node statistics
  obtaining, via API 409, 414
node
  setting up 16, 17, 18
  setting up, via Docker 34, 36
  types, setting up 20, 21, 22
NumPy
  integrating with 621, 624

O

object relational mapping (ORM) 86
object
  mapping 56, 57
operating system (OS) 407
optimistic concurrency control
  reference link 134

P

PAAS
  reference link 44
Painless language 143
painless scripting 354, 356, 358
Percolator field

mapping 79, 80, 81
pipeline aggregations
  executing 347, 351
pipeline definition process 490, 492
plugin
  creating 626, 628, 630
  installing, in Elasticsearch 26, 28, 30
  reference link 30
postman
  reference link 46
prefix query
  using 221, 223, 225
public key infrastruture (PKI) 450

Q

query parameters 156
query string query
  using 242, 246
query
  building 551, 554
  explaining 188, 190
  profiling 190, 192

R

range aggregations
  executing 305, 307, 310
range query
  using 249, 252
re-index module 193
regexp query
  using 228, 230
remote cluster
  reindexing from 446
repositories
  executing 439
  managing 432, 434
required services, for node startup
  aggregation services 12
  cluster services 12
  indexing service 12
  ingesting services 12
  language scripting services 12
  mapping service 12
  network services 12
  plugin service 12

Resilient Distributed Dataset (RDD) 664
REST plugin
  creating 635, 639
results
  highlighting 168, 170, 171
  sorting 162, 164, 166, 167
return fields
  computing, with scripting 372, 374
rolling index
  enabling 128, 130

S

S3 repository
  reference link 435
Scala
  client, creating 574, 577
scikit-learn
  integrating with 621, 624
script plugins
  installing 359, 362
scripting
  used, for computing return fields 372, 375
  used, for filtering search 375
  using, in aggregations 378, 382
scripts
  managing 362, 365, 366
  used, for reindexing 390
  used, for sorting data 371
  used, for updating documents 382
scroll search
  executing 563, 566
scrolling query
  executing 172, 174, 175, 176
search template
  using 205, 208
search
  executing 152, 153, 154, 155, 156, 157,
    158, 159, 160, 161
  executing, with aggregations 558, 563, 590,
    593, 618, 621
search_after functionality
  using 177, 179
searching 45
segments
  monitoring, with segment API 425, 428

shard allocation
  managing 422, 425
significant terms aggregation
  executing 301, 304
simple query string query
  using 246, 249
Single Page Application (SPA) 451
snapshot
  executing 436, 441
  restoring 441, 442
span queries
  using 230, 234, 236
Spark SQL
  used, for reading data 670
split brain
  reference link 22
standard Java HTTP client
  creating 520, 522, 525
standard search
  executing 554, 558, 588, 590, 614, 617
stats aggregations
  executing 294, 297, 300, 301
  reference link 297

T

task management API
  using 417, 420
term query
  using 212, 215
terms aggregation
  executing 297
terms query
  using 217, 218, 219
top hit aggregations
  executing 338, 340
transmission control protocol (TCP) 415

U

Unified Modeling Language (UML) 268
update_by_query API 196, 198, 199

V

vega
  reference link 483
virtual index 128

W

wildcard query
using 225, 227

Made in the USA
San Bernardino, CA
04 November 2019

59404068R00403